A STREET IN MARRAKECH

Books by Elizabeth Warnock Fernea

GUESTS OF THE SHEIK

A VIEW OF THE NILE

A STREET IN MARRAKECH

A Street in Marrakech

Elizabeth Warnock Fernea

ANCHOR BOOKS
ANCHOR PRESS/DOUBLEDAY
GARDEN CITY, NEW YORK
1980

Detail of Koutoubia mosque, courtesy of William E. Berry
All other photos, courtesy of Robert A. Fernea

This book was originally published in
hardcover edition by Doubleday & Company, Inc.

First Anchor Books Edition: 1976
Second Anchor Books Edition: 1980

Library of Congress Cataloging in Publication Data

Fernea, Elizabeth Warnock.
A street in Marrakech.

1. Marrakesh, Morocco—Description. 2. Fernea,
Elizabeth Warnock. I. Title.
DT329.M3F47   916.4'6
ISBN 0-385-12045-1

FOR AISHA

CONTENTS

8 Contents

PART IV

FOREWORD

From August 1971 to August 1972, my husband and I and our three children lived on Rue Trésor, a small street in the medina or traditional city of Marrakech, Morocco. Rue Trésor is a real street and all of the people and incidents in the book are real, but I have changed names of both streets and people so that no one may be embarrassed.

I would like to thank Laura Ann Fernea for allowing me to use one of her letters as the prologue; David, for the sketch map of Rue Trésor; and Laila, for reading and proofing the entire manuscript.

My appreciation also goes to Abdul Aziz Abbassi, Adele Fath, James Malarkey, and Dagmar Hamilton, who read the manuscript and made many valuable suggestions.

Finally, I would like to thank my husband, Bob, for taking me to Marrakech in the first place, and for helping me to think through the narrative of the book that follows.

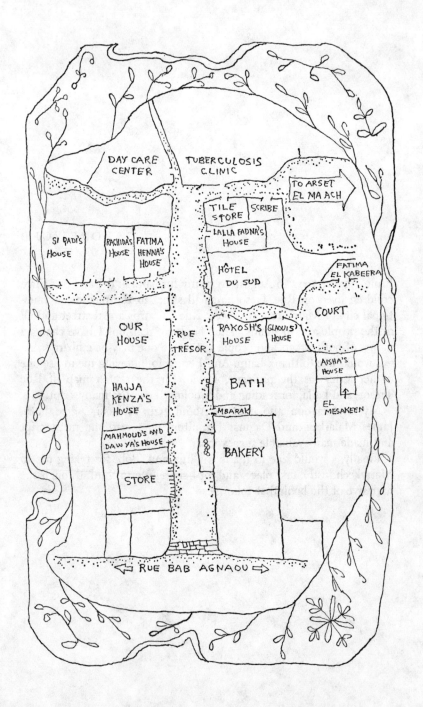

CAST OF CHARACTERS

Hajja Kenza, a rich widow
Naima, her daughter

Khaddour, a porter
Aisha, his wife
Najiya, their daughter
Youssef
Abdul Krim } their sons
Saleh

Boushta, a railroad employee
Lalla Fadna, his wife
Hamid, their married son

Abdul Kabeer, proprietor of a grocery store
Moussa, his brother, a baker

Hassan Glaoui, a metalworker
Glaoui, his wife
Brika, their daughter

Hussain, a bus driver
Fatima, his wife
Fatima Henna, his oldest daughter
Jameela, a younger daughter

Brahim
Benasser } their sons
Mina, daughter of Fatima Henna
Rakiya, sister of Fatima
Hind
Salima } her daughters

Omar, a djellaba merchant
Abdullah, his father
Nezha, his mother
Malika, his sister
Mohammed, his brother
Faneeda, his baby sister

Si Qadi, judge of the district court
Lalla Fawzia, his wife

Lalla Yezza, a cook in the day care center
Amal
Farida } teachers in the center

Rakosh, widow, head of the extended household, Ait Rakosh
Hassan, her oldest son, a waiter
Khadooj
Zahia } wives of Hassan
Rabia, daughter of Khadooj and Hassan
Shadeeya, Ali, and Kamal, children of Zahia and Hassan
Abdeslam, younger son of Rakosh, a repairman
Fadhila, his wife
Samia and Fatima, their daughters
Lateefa, grandniece of Rakosh
Khadija, great-grandniece of Rakosh

Sadiq, a hospital administrator
Rachida, his wife, a schoolteacher
Laila, their daughter
Fuad, their son

Mahmoud, a vendor of nuts
Dawya, his wife

Marzook, doorman at the Hôtel du Sud

Mbarak, attendant at the public bath
Thami, attendant at the public bath

Fatima el Kabeera, an elderly invalid widow
Abdul Moumin, her blind son

Moulay Mustapha, teacher in a Koranic school
Abdul Lateef, his friend, a bicycle mechanic

M. Abdul Aziz, a teacher of French
Zainab, his wife

El Mesakeen, an elderly pair of beggars (man and wife)

Ernest Harris, an American scientist
Bettye, his wife
Tanya, their daughter
Greg, their son

Jean-Yves, a teacher in the French lycée

Mark, Sheryl, Alan, and Lena, young Americans

August 25, 1971
Casablanca, Morocco

Laura Ann Fernea (11) to Emily Williams (4)

Dear Emily,

I'm sorry I haven't written lately. When I heard about your baby sister I was very excited . . . I wish I was there in Austin to see her. We got a house but I haven't seen it, we're still at La Residence in Casablanca. Tomorrow we are moving to the house. My father and mother and David have seen the house. Because David went with my father a few days ago with a load. They told us that it's a Moroccan house with a courtyard in the middle and a fountain. It has colored tile all over it. There are four big rooms and a kitchen and a bathroom. There are two storys. Also, in the room downstairs there are colored lights. David says he doesn't like it very much because it's in the slums in the Medina. But it's quiet because it's in a street off the main street. You'd think it would be noisey but it isn't. One of the reasons my mother got it was because some foreign people once lived in it and it has a bathtub and a toilet and running water which you can't usually find in the Medina. It was unfurnished when we got it but we got Monsieur Bonn (the manager of La Residence) to help us get a lot of beds and chairs, desks, a refrigerator, closets, tables for a cheap price. Also, my mother went down this morning with Monsieur Bonn to get a dining room table and a stove. Most

everything is in Marrakech now so all we have to do is pack our remaining clothes and move tomorrow morning. O Joy at last! Also
there is this maid who is going to work for us, she lives right across
the street. The landlady is a very Moroccan widow (veil and all)
with a daughter about my age (shows some prospect). What is
especially lucky for Laila, David, and I is that we're not going to
school until October instead of September (Yahoo!) but of course
they end school here June 21 but we won't be here then (Yeah).
Are all of you in Boston yet? How is the town and the people in
your house? Is Hilary a good baby or does she cry a whole bunch?
Are you all going to visit us next summer? I hope you have as good
a year in Boston as we hope we're going to have in Morocco.

                                              Love,
                                              Laura Ann

A STREET IN MARRAKECH

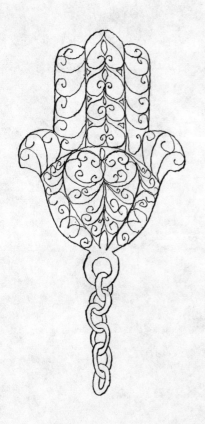

Part I

Chapter 1

The House on Rue Trésor

We had left the white roofs and minarets of Casablanca behind us, driving away from the bright blue Atlantic, heading south into the heart of Morocco. We thought we knew what we were doing. We were going to spend a year in Marrakech—"Marrakech *la rouge*," as the French had titled it—the rose-red city of poem and legend. Marrakech, oasis city at the foot of the High Atlas Mountains; Marrakech, far-out place of modern nomads; Marrakech, stop on the old Sahara caravan routes from Timbuktu to the Barbary coast.

Bob had a year's leave from the University of Texas to accept a research grant in anthropology. We would be together as a family. The three children would go to Moroccan schools, we would all learn the dialect of Moroccan Arabic, so different from the Egyptian and Iraqi dialects we had spoken a long time ago. Hopefully we would learn something about Morocco and North Africa, a part of the Middle East we had not lived in before, a very different area, everyone told us, from Egypt and Iraq.

"Will it be sort of like Cairo? Will I remember anything?" Eleven-year-old Laura Ann, born in Cairo, had been six when we had come home to the United States.

"How could it?" David was ten. He had been born in Cairo too. "We were just little kids then and Laila was only three."

"But I remember I had my birthday party on the desert," Laila offered.

Davy scoffed. "That's just because you've seen pictures of it in your baby book. Besides, this place is different. It's gonna be a new thing, Laila."

A new thing. We were all excited and hopeful as we drove into the green valley, past the junction to the airport road, where the signposts said Oued Zem, Kasba Tadla, Fez, Meknes.

"Remember Meknes, Baba?" David was leaning over the seat to talk into his father's ear. "That was fun."

The children had already had an introduction to Morocco, in the three-month overseas program in Middle Eastern Studies that Bob had organized for the University of Texas. With fifty-five American students, they, too, had lived in Casablanca and taken side trips to the desert, to Fez, to Meknes.

"How long till we reach Marrakech?" Alta, Bob's mother, had spent the summer with us in Casablanca and was coming to Marrakech to stay a few weeks.

Bob looked at his watch. "By dark, I hope," he said. "The truck with all our stuff is supposed to be there by seven."

"It's hot," volunteered Laura Ann.

The late summer sun pressed down on our new Peugeot station wagon, heating the faint breeze stirred by our movement, whitening the brown stubble and the loaf-shaped mounds of hay in the harvested fields around us.

"Why do we have to live in the medina?" asked Laila, the most reluctant of our carful of would-be adventurers. "Those tiny little streets are scary, and people stare at you!" As the fairest of the three children, she had earned a great number of stares during the past summer, which had upset her. When I had suggested that people might be staring because they found her pretty, she had sniffed in disdain.

"Me? They think I'm pretty? Oh, Mama, look at all the Moroccans with their black hair and their black eyes and their sun-tanned skin. Beside them, I look like a white peeled onion! And who likes onions?"

"Well, I, for one; I've always liked them," Bob said, but Laila refused to be comforted. Being different was an experience she did not enjoy.

Bob was saying, patiently and perhaps for the fortieth time, that we had chosen to live in the medina because it was the most typical area of Marrakech, the place where most Moroccans lived. Why live in Gueliz, he argued, the new part of the city that the French had built during the colonial administration? Gueliz was like what we already knew, full of Western-style houses with gardens.

"What's wrong with that?" Laila wanted to know.

"Nothing's wrong with that," Bob went on, still in his patient tone, "but if that's what we'd wanted, we might as well have stayed home in Austin."

Laila opened her mouth to speak, but I caught her eye and shook my head.

"We'll be close to the snake charmers, anyway, Laila," said Davy. He felt a bit superior, since he had driven down to Marrakech with his father a few days before to take a load of baggage and check to see that the landlady was having a hot-water heater installed, as promised. Thus he had seen our house in the medina. The girls had not.

"You mean Djemaa el Fna, the big square with dancers and acrobats, just in front of the *suq*?" Alta asked. "Is it really close to there?"

"Well, not far," temporized Bob. "A ten-minute walk maybe."

"Are there lots of children?" Laura Ann asked. "On the street where our house is?"

"Yeah, tons."

"So you'll have plenty of people to play with," said Alta.

The children took that in.

"But how can we? How can we talk to them?" Laila asked. "They can't speak English. We can't speak Arabic."

"Oh, you can learn," responded Alta stoutly. "Children learn languages faster then grownups, they say. Why, I bet you'll be speaking Arabic before you know it!"

"How about some water?" asked Bob, rather quickly.

"Me, too," said Laura Ann. "The jug is nearly empty," she added.

We rounded an abrupt turn. "Hey! Look!" David shouted.

Ahead of us on the road to Marrakech was the flatbed truck we had hired from the CTM Company to transport our belongings, its dark tarpaulin flapping from side to side in the hot wind, displaying corners of trunks, a mattress, a bedstead, the goods we had bought in Casablanca to furnish our tiled, empty house. The truck navigated a corner badly, and the pile of chairs teetered dangerously.

"Well, Bob, I certainly hope they tied everything up securely, or you're going to have a pile of kindling on your hands instead of furniture," Alta said crisply.

"Oh, Mother, don't be a pessimist."

But Alta's words had stirred a flicker of worry in my mind. Surely they had tied up the chairs. But what if they hadn't? What about the refrigerator? And which trunk had I packed the sheets in? The landlady, Hajja Kenza, was to have found someone to work for us. How was I going to speak to her? It must be the heat, I told myself sharply, and tried resolutely to think of something else.

"Where are we?" I asked, looking around at a desolate, flat plain. The fields and loaves of harvested hay had long since disappeared, and the heat shimmered now over dark piles of pebbles, stretches of dun-colored sand, prickly clumps of foliage growing so close to the ground they could hardly be called bushes.

Laura Ann picked up the guidebook.

"This is the Rehamna Plain," she read. "It is mostly desert."

"I guess," said David.

It seemed much longer than three hours since we had left the sea breezes of Casablanca.

"I'll be glad when we get there," sighed Laura Ann. "Will it be cooler, Mama?"

"Oh yes," I responded immediately. "Our house has tiles. That makes it cooler."

I hope, I added to myself. I realized I had only seen the house once. After a week of house-hunting in the broiling sun, looking at one dull villa after another, a four-story palace with no plumbing, two tiny apartments with shared toilets, Bob and I had been enchanted by the traditional Moroccan house we had finally been shown: the brilliant color of the tiles, the arrangement of the rooms around an open courtyard with its own small fountain and garden, the view of the city from the roof. But the city of Marrakech remained relatively unknown. Now, with the desolate, dark hills around us, bare of vegetation, animals, or people, we might have been on our way to some undetermined place, never to be reached, the truckload of furniture ahead the only indication that we were bound for a real house in a real city. I told myself that I had never had any illusions that it was going to be easy for us, and especially the children, to adjust to living in the Marrakech medina. It had seemed like such a great idea, back in Austin, Texas. A year with the family to learn and grow together. Now, faced with setting up a household in a strange city where few spoke English, with finding schools that would take our children (who spoke nothing but English, having forgotten their Egyptian Arabic long ago), I was not at all sure. Friends had pointed out that the Moroccan schools were so overcrowded that they would not take kindly to accepting foreign children. Other friends had reminded us that the French schools accepted only a few "outsiders," usually diplomats' children who already knew French. Whom did we know in Marrakech who could or would help us with such problems? No one.

"Where are we going to eat dinner tonight?" Laura Ann's practical question ended my gloomy reverie.

"Why not one of those French restaurants in the new town?" I suggested.

"Oh, B.J., you're not going to go colonialist right off."

"But Baba," interrupted David, "we don't want to eat couscous again. It's too hot."

Alta took our side. "And besides, Bob, we can't cook at home, the stove isn't connected, and we haven't any groceries."

"Can we have Coca-Cola too?"

"Oh, Laila," Bob sounded impatient.

From a rocky pass, between the barren hills, we had come down onto another plain, "the Haouz," according to the guidebook, bounded on east and west by the bluish shapes of distant mountains and cut by a winding riverbed, dry and cracked from a long summer of sun. We passed over it on a narrow bridge, hand-cut of worn stone.

"There!" cried Bob. "There it is! Doesn't it look like a storybook oasis? That's Marrakech! Home for a year!"

The dots on the horizon ahead resolved themselves into palm trees, roofs, minarets. Beside us on the road two men in djellabas were shepherding flocks of goats and sheep aside with sticks so our car could pass. Closer, among the green trees, the walls and flat roofs of the houses glowed red, with the river clay that is mixed into all Marrakech plaster and gives the city its distinctive coloration. We passed boys on donkeys, veiled women in djellabas riding motorcycles, a gas station, and from a rocky promontory on our right we turned onto a wide, paved boulevard centered and bounded with palms, orange trees, and thickly spreading oleanders. The sun had set and the street lights were flashing on ahead of us illuminating suddenly, at the end of the boulevard, the majestic square-based minaret of the Koutoubia mosque.

"Oh, that's beautiful, Bob!" breathed Alta. "What is it?"

"The Koutoubia, oldest and most famous of all the buildings in this city."

"How old?" asked David.

"Built when the city was built, in the twelfth century."

"Eight hundred years! Wow!" exclaimed Laila.

"Be careful, Bob!" cried Alta.

Her voice had risen as Bob swerved to avoid a child running pell-mell across the street directly in front of our Peugeot. A policeman on a raised red-and-white stand blew a whistle, but the child had disappeared into the crowds that filled the sidewalks ahead and on both sides of us. The air resounded with voices and horns. We passed a park. Bob turned into a street around another policeman's circle and crossed a square where boys were playing soccer with a piece of tire tied up into the shape of a ball. Davy followed them with his eyes.

At the far end of the square our truck was maneuvering itself into the best position for unloading down the narrow street, and already a crowd of children had assembled to watch. They quickly gathered around our Peugeot, tapping on the doors, shouting and gesturing, pressing their faces against the windows to stare at the children. Laura Ann, David, and Laila stared back.

"Come on, B.J., let's go."

We got out of the car before a growing audience of children and adults who eyed us from the tops of our heads down to our bare legs. I felt very uncomfortable under their scrutiny. They followed us into the narrow passage that was Rue Trésor, "our street," a strip of pale asphalt flung down between the shadowy dark walls of houses, which stretched high above on either side of us, blocking the sky.

"Which is our house, Mama? They all look the same," whispered Laila, clutching tightly to my hand and trying not to notice the children who pushed and sidled around us.

She was right. The walls merged together in the dimness, their rosy clay gray in the twilight, the massive dark wooden doors glimmering only where metal bindings and brass studs reinforced their impregnability.

It must be . . . yes, "It's the door with the silver hand," I said, recognizing the gleam of a door knocker halfway down the narrow street, a knocker in the shape of the hand of Fatima, the Prophet's daughter, traditional Islamic protective symbol against the Evil Eye.

A strange child at my elbow said something, and when I did not

reply, he reached up and banged the silver door knocker with a venge-
ance, then in a hysterical titter at his own bravery, he turned and
ran down the street, calling, calling. What was he calling? Our
children, wooden-faced, did not ask.

The door opened to Hajja Kenza, our landlady, a large woman in a
faded caftan, her hair covered and bound up in a flowered scarf, her
gold teeth flashing in a smile.

"Come in! Come in!" The gesture was unmistakable, and we
crossed the threshold. The door shut for a moment. I felt a great
sense of relief and security. We were inside, the street was outside.

"Open! Open up! They're bringing the things!"

And I stood there for a moment, between the inside and the outside, until I came to my senses and began to direct the unloading.

A single small bulb shone in the courtyard, which was larger than I
remembered, its bright tiles hidden in the shadows. The fountain was
still, the plants drooped. The doors to the rooms on each end of the
courtyard had been thrown open, revealing further shadows. Hajja
Kenza had obviously not splurged on light bulbs to celebrate our arrival.

"Here! Up here!" Bob had mounted the stairway to the balcony
and stood in front of the second-floor room. He leaned over the
wrought-iron railing and gestured to the first pair of porters, who had
our double-bed mattress on their heads and were trying to deposit
it against the downstairs wall. "No! No!" Bob brought ropes and
prepared to hoist the mattress up over the balcony.

Naima, the landlady's daughter, had been stationed by the front
door, and her mother ran back and forth, shouting alternately at Bob
and the porters. Near her stood another woman, smaller and thinner,
a woman in shabby clothes, twisting her hands in the folds of her
dress, wrinkling her forehead and squinting.

Who was this woman? Hajja Kenza propelled her toward me, and
indicated, with elaborate gestures, that this was the woman she had
found to work for us.

"Aisha."

Aisha tried to smile politely, but the worry lines on her forehead
got in the way. The hand she gave me was rough and hard. I wondered whether this was a good idea, simply accepting the landlady's
arrangements.

"Good. Good worker." Hajja Kenza wiped her finger along the

tiles to indicate to me that no dust was to be found. She made another gesture. Money. Something about money. Oh dear, how would I ever be able to communicate? The Moroccan Arabic was incomprehensible.

"Betty . . ." Alta stood against a wall, looking as bewildered as I felt. The children were rushing around, exploring the two rooms downstairs, the kitchen and the bathroom off the court, the two rooms upstairs, the balcony, the toilet.

"Is this where we're going to sleep?"

"Or here?"

"I'd rather sleep outside on the balcony, in my sleeping bag."

"Where's the toilet?"

"How do you flush it?"

The porters were shouting at each other. Bob, sweating, was trying to ease the desk into our bedroom. Hajja Kenza continued to talk to me urgently. Aisha watched me, her forehead wrinkled, her hands twisting in her dress. I could not understand a word Hajja Kenza was saying and felt incomprehension must surely be visible, a mask of idiocy on my sweaty, dusty face.

At that moment, the fountain spurted up in a great silvery jet toward the sky and splashed down merrily and crazily all over the newly washed yellow-and-blue tiles. David had found the water tap.

"Stop that!" shouted Bob from the balcony, angrily, like any irritated father. "Turn it off!"

Aisha smiled. The lines were erased from her forehead, her eyes crinkled up in amusement, the hands stopped twisting. She moved forward and showed David how to turn the tap off and on, lightly, so as not to splatter the green and dusty leaves of the red canna lilies, the lemon tree, the paling tiles.

"Thank you," I said in Arabic, and tried out a phrase of my Egyptian dialect. "This is Davy, Laura Ann, Laila, he is ten, she is eleven, Laila is nine."

"Madame speaks Arabic?"

"Only Egyptian Arabic. I don't know the Moroccan dialect."

The face cleared and that smile appeared again. "Ah, Madame, that is fine. I understand Egyptian Arabic very well. I used to work for an Egyptian lady."

I could have hugged her.

"Betty . . ." In all the confusion I had forgotten to present Alta.

They shook hands. Aisha smiled again and said, "Your husband's mother lives with you?"

"No, she is just visiting."

"Ahh."

The children hovered, ran off, came back. "Can you understand her, Mama?"

I nodded.

"Mama can understand her, Baba," shouted David. "Isn't that great?"

"That's lucky," said Alta. "Then your father will be able to understand her too."

"Ask Aisha where we can get something to drink," called Bob.

I did. Aisha took me to our open door, where the crowds of children and adults seemed to have doubled in size to watch the moving operation; she pointed down Rue Trésor to a small blue wooden shutter. "The store," she said.

"Good. Thank you, Aisha. Okay, when we're finished unloading we can have some Coca-Cola. Now let's everybody help get the beds made up."

The men had unloaded one of the trunks upside down. We turned it over, with Bob's help. We found the sheets. We made the beds. The sky above us in the courtyard was dark and they were still unloading.

"If you ever need me, Madame, I live just across the street. Come, I will show you."

Aisha took my hand, and, with Laura Ann behind me, we crossed Rue Trésor quickly and headed directly into an even narrower, completely dark passageway.

"Mama, I can't see a thing," said Laura Ann.

"Take my hand."

Aisha was guiding me. The passage, so narrow I could touch the rough stone or plaster on each side, turned and sloped downward into a courtyard, where two separate cooking fires were burning. The women bent over the low flames turned to look at us briefly, but Aisha said nothing, and I said nothing. She opened the door of a narrow, neat room. Beds lined three walls, and a long mat had been affixed to the fourth. Above the mat were arranged a faded photograph of King Mohammed V, father of the present ruler, who symbolized Moroccan independence from the French; a small Mo-

roccan flag, an Arabic calender, and an overexposed picture of a staring man in skullcap and djellaba.

"My father," said Aisha proudly, and then showed me another
photo, a full-length wedding picture. A younger Aisha wore a long,
flowered dress, her hair was bound up in a scarf, she clasped her
hands behind her back and smiled at her husband, taller than she,
with a new haircut and a suit that did not fit well.

"My wedding." She used the Egyptian word. The floor of the room
was covered with cracked linoleum, imprinted in a faded pattern of
tiles.

We went back out into the courtyard. Here the walls had been
whitewashed, but a long time ago. The women cooking over open
fires seemed to be older than Aisha; they both wore head scarves, and
their caftans were tucked up around their waists in folds; one wore a
chin scarf like a wimple. They did not look at us, but tended their
pots; the steam rose up into the hot night to the top of a high wall
where a bird perched in a tuft of grass growing between the tiles. The
floor was dirt, swept carefully. Laura Ann and I stood awkwardly for
a moment, while Aisha showed us another room, "for sleeping." It
was a cave, really, without windows. She shut the door again.

"We have two rooms, because of the four children."

I smiled, not knowing what else to do. Laura Ann fidgeted. The
two silent women stirred their pots. What now?

"Shall I make you some tea?" said Aisha politely. It was the ritual
remark, and it sounded like the same words I had heard long ago,
first in the village in Iraq, and then in Egypt and in Nubia. This I understood. Hospitality. The code of hospitality.

"Oh, no, thank you," I answered just as politely. "You're too
kind," while Laura Ann murmured that she didn't want any tea, it
was too hot.

"Only a moment. I will light a fire," said Aisha.

"No, no. I must get back to the house. Thank you, but my husband and children will be wondering where I am."

"Well," she gave in gracefully, "another time."

"Another time," I repeated. "Thank you."

We had been through the familiar statements and responses. I
began to feel better.

Returning through the dark passage was not so difficult, for the
street lights and the noise of the porters gave us direction.

"Where have you been?" shouted Bob.

I explained.

"Now, for heaven's sake?"

I explained again.

"Well . . ." he temporized, "ask Aisha what the landlady wants. She is full of advice about something, but frankly I don't know what she's saying." He wiped his hand across his forehead wearily. "Do you think we could find some beer?"

"Madame . . ." A long, incomprehensible sentence from Hajja Kenza followed.

I turned to Aisha. "What is she saying?"

Aisha smiled. "She says that all porters are thieves, you have to watch them every minute and that it is your turn to stay here, all this time you were gone her daughter Naima has been standing by the door, to make sure porters didn't steal anything."

I opened my mouth to reply, but Hajja Kenza was off again, shouting first up to Bob, then repeating the long sentences to me. I turned to Aisha for the second time. She looked embarrassed and dropped her eyes.

"She is saying that I refused to work for what you offered me, and that it's terrible what people demand these days, but honestly," she said looking up, "I work hard and I will do my best."

I had already decided to pay her more than the minute sum Hajja Kenza had indicated, and I said this to her. But Hajja Kenza was repeating it all again to Bob. The same set of words, punctuated with gestures toward Aisha and her ragged clothes. I was suddenly annoyed with our overweening landlady and wished she would leave. The men had gone and been paid off. Why *didn't* she leave? Her loud, twanging voice was irritating.

"Can we have Coca-Cola now, Mama?" Laila looked weary, too, and she hung on my skirt as she had done when she was very small.

"Yes," I said, interrupting Hajja Kenza's tirade to ask Aisha if the store down the street had beer.

She looked embarrassed. "No beer," she said, "Abdul Kabeer is a good Muslim. But they have Coke and Fanta."

Hajja Kenza was staring at me, open-mouthed, for I had interrupted her very rudely, and suddenly I was sorry I had shown irritation. After all, she had found a hot-water heater for us, she had helped us with the porters, she had found me Aisha (with whom I could communicate, thanks be!). The long, trying day was having its effects.

"Would you have a Coca-Cola, too, Madame?" I asked.

She stared and wrinkled her brow. "What's she saying?" she asked Aisha, and when Aisha had translated, her face broke up into a gold-toothed grin of pleasure.

"Yes, yes, thank you."

David and I set off for the little store, with Alta.

The three of us were followed by a band of children, the last of the observers, who formed a tight circle around us as we stopped at the window. The proprietor, a large man with a receding hairline, and a hairlip imperfectly concealed by a thin mustache, nodded at me, at Alta, at David. He said, "*Bon soir, Madame*," and began indicating the wares in his shop: sugar (he took a scoop from a sack to show me it was clean); plastic bags of rice; macaroni in a jar; tomato sauce in red cans; milk and yogurt in the refrigerator; eggs in a wire basket suspended above our heads (very tiny eggs); pastries, looking rather gray and worn, in a covered plastic display case on the counter; and . . .

"Bubble gum," cried Davy. The proprietor smiled. We bought bubble gum from a covered glass jar.

"And Vim and Tide and brooms and soap," the proprietor continued in imperfect French.

The street children were pressing closer to us as the cold Coca-Colas were opened with a flourish. David seemed remarkably self-possessed to me, but he whispered, "Let's go back, Mama, please. Somebody is pulling on my shirt all the time."

We went back. We sat on a bed in the downstairs room nearest the door (designated as Alta's room) and sipped our bottles of icy Coca-Cola. The door of the room was open, and the weak courtyard light shone on the plants, the colored panes of glass in the windows that opened on the court, the fountain that bubbled gently into its octagonal blue-and-yellow-tiled basin.

"Well, we're home," said Bob.

"A beautiful house, a beautiful house," Hajja Kenza was murmuring over and over. "The hot-water heater is excellent. And the bathroom works fine." She had shown me three times. She had not, as promised, painted the kitchen walls, but I was too tired to point this out tonight.

"Let's go eat, Baba, I'm starved," said Laura Ann.

Aisha shook our hands and said good night and that she would be back in the morning, and Naima rose to leave, but Hajja Kenza sat still and carefully drank the last drops of her Coca-Cola. Bob finally stood up and we all made it out of the house. Two or three children followed us up the street to the car.

In ten minutes we were sitting in a restaurant in the French section of the city, eating roast lamb and green beans almondine and drinking French wine, followed by *crème caramel*. Ten minutes. Two miles. Yet the distance from Aisha's narrow room and the courtyard where the two silent women cooked seemed far greater.

"I think the house is pretty, but the children didn't seem very friendly." Laura Ann was obviously making an effort to be pleasant.

"Well, it's too early to tell," said Alta.

"At least Mama can talk to Aisha," said Davy.

"She has worked for an Egyptian woman," I said to Bob. "That is a real piece of luck."

"You're right," Bob agreed.

We had cognac with our coffee. We might have been a continent away from our new house, sitting there in the European-style restaurant. Life in Marrakech was going to be complicated.

An insistent twittering and the sound of rushing wings brought me to the edge of wakefulness. I opened my eyes and looked up to a white ceiling, nearly fifteen feet above, noting, sleepily, a carved plaster cornice that followed the ceiling all around the high, rectangular room. A flower merged into a leaf, the leaf twined about a braided stem that extended forward into the calyx of another flower. Stem, calyx, flower, leaf, stem. Was that the sequence? I had never seen a cornice like this one before. It stopped at the light brackets, openwork constructions of carved plaster into which bits of colored glass had been inserted. Presumably the electric light glowed through the openwork, flashing green, rose, and blue stars and circles onto the ceiling and the tiled floor. Then the cornice ran straight again with the same molded flower, the same sinuous leaf, the same twining stem. A more complicated version of the pattern decorated the center of the ceiling. I closed my eyes. We were in Marrakech. All of us. We had arrived last night at sunset, in the fabled, fierce, and barbaric city of the Almohades. Or was it the Almoravides? I had the sleepy impression that it was both. This high, spacious room seemed anything but fierce and barbaric; it was elaborately decorated, but restful.

Perhaps the old chroniclers had exaggerated. I had a confused impression of noise all night long. Birds? No, I told myself, the twittering must have been part of a dream.

But at that moment I opened my eyes again in time to see a small brown bird fly into the room, through the double doors opening onto the balcony and the central courtyard below. I remembered getting up and opening the doors wider in the middle of the night, hoping for a slight breeze to stir the hot stillness of the bedroom. Now the sun poured through those wooden doors, dulling their aubergine and green paint, laying a wide path of light onto the green-and-white tiles of the floor. The bird paused in the path of light, hopped a few steps, and hovered near our bed for a moment while I hurriedly pulled up the sheet in some vague motion of defense. Then it rose, chirping, to fly the length of the room, past our trunk to the only other pieces of furniture, the desk and chair beneath built-in shelves. Here the bird fluttered, pecking at the cornice, rose to the light bracket, and disappeared. I raised my head to look but could see nothing. Did the bird have a nest in the bracket of colored lights? Good heavens! Something would have to be done about that.

In a whoosh of wings the bird flew out again, and the sound of chirping in the court was now overwhelmed by a mother scolding a child somewhere nearby. Martial music blared on a radio and was replaced by the cracked voice of a news commentator; a motorcycle roared past, and I heard the thump of a cane on cement and the high, clear voice of a beggar in the street below. Even in the Moroccan dialect of Arabic, which was unfamiliar to us, the classic appeal "Alms! Alms for the love of Allah!" was unmistakable.

The night had been hot and close. No breath of breeze had drifted through the doors and windows, not even in the early-morning hours. How had we slept? I considered breakfast for a moment, but discarded the idea and lay still instead, contemplating that design of leaves and flowers. For the same pattern banded the walls, it seemed; midway from the floor, between the colored tiles below and the stark white expanse above, ran a delicate ribbon of carved plaster: stem, calyx, flower, leaf, stem.

Bob snored beside me. The children, sleeping in the upstairs room on the other side of the balcony, made no sound. Alta, in the downstairs bedroom, was not awake.

How could they sleep through the shrill voices, the birds gathering by the fountain, more motorcycles gunning in the street? The noise grew, but here above the street, in this high-ceilinged, multicolored Marrakech room, shielded by Spanish wrought-iron screens and wooden window shutters, enclosed by thick-rose-red walls, where the sun cast its wide pale swath through the open door and washed the rest of the room in color, I felt suddenly quite protected, alone, and at peace. Was it the Almoravides or the Almohades that had laid the foundations for the design of such a lovely room?

Someone was banging on the door. I put on a robe and ran across the sunny balcony to the narrow stairway that led directly to the foyer and the iron-studded double front door with its silver hand.

"Aisha?"

"Ah!" She stepped inside, shut the door quietly, pulled down her face veil, smiled at me, and produced from the wide sleeve of her djellaba a great round loaf of brown Marrakech bread. Breakfast had appeared!

"Thank you!" It was still warm from the oven and smelled wonderful.

Would we like mint tea? Aisha was whispering conspiratorially so as not to wake the rest of the family. I wondered idly why she had donned her full outside regalia, including the veil, just to walk down the street a few feet to the bakery. How would we make mint tea, since we had no way to cook and nothing to cook or serve in? The refrigerator had been plugged in the night before, but as yet we had no tank of butagaz, and the stove stood a foot away from the badly peeling walls of faded green, waiting to be hooked up.

"We have a fire in our court. I'll make the tea in my house." She pulled up her veil again and was gone.

Half an hour later we were all sitting around the table in the "dining room," so selected because it was closest to the kitchen, sleepily sipping mint tea from thin glasses and devouring the good brown bread.

"It's all mint and no tea," said Laila.

"So don't complain," said her father.

There was no butter for the bread, since, Aisha said, the local shop did not carry such luxuries, but I had unearthed a half bottle of strawberry jam from our picnic basket.

"Baba," said Laila, "now show us on the map where we are."

Bob unfolded our new tourist map of Marrakech, and we gathered close to look. We found the medina, a great irregular rectangle marked with the old city gates: Bab el Robb, Bab Taghzout, Bab el Doukkala, Bab el Khamis.

"Do they still shut them at night?" asked Laura Ann.

"No, not any more, but they used to, to keep pirates and bandits out."

The children exchanged furtive glances. "Now, Bob," said Alta, "don't scare the children."

"I'm not," said Bob. "I'm just trying to give them a sense of history."

"But where is Rue Trésor?"

We stared at the map. Bob twisted it this way and that. We found Djemaa el Fna, the entertainment center of town, an oversized triangle marking the entrance to the great bazaars.

"That's where the snake charmers are, Laila," Davy said softly.

We found Boulevard Mohammed Cinq, the lighted tree-lined avenue down which we had driven the night before. We found the Koutoubia mosque. We even found Rue Bab Agnaou, a long, straight street leading from the old city gate of Bab Agnaou to the square of Djemaa el Fna. But we could not find Rue Trésor.

"Well, it must be here, somewhere off Rue Bab Agnaou. It's there, because here we are!" said Bob in annoyance.

"Maybe it's one of these," said Davy, pointing to the scores of tiny winding lines, stretching like the traceries of broken spiderwebs across the irregular rectangle that was the medina.

"It's awfully tiny," said Laura Ann. "Rue Trésor."

"Maybe Aisha knows," suggested Alta. "Let Betty ask her."

Aisha peered at the great piece of colored paper unfolded on the dining-room table, among the tea glasses still filled with the green leaves of fresh mint, the crumbs of bread for which hungry birds were already waiting. She narrowed her eyes at the curious squares and triangles and stylized arches symbolizing, for the tourists, the monuments of interest in the medina: Medersa Ben Youssef, Dar Si Said Museum, the Bahia Palace.

"Where is Sharia Trésor?" I asked.

She shook her head. "It won't be on there, because it isn't a street." (She, too, used the Arabic word *sharia*).

"Not a street?" I echoed.

"No, it's not a *sharia*, it's a *zanka*."

Bob and I looked at each other, puzzled.

Laura Ann wrinkled her forehead. "But how can it *not* be a street, when we live on it?"

Aisha was trying to explain. "Sh," I said, translating, "she's saying that *sharia* means a big street like Bab Agnaou; *zanka* is like an alley, sort of."

That made sense to the children, who had already decided that Rue Trésor was so narrow it couldn't be a real street.

"So Aisha says it wouldn't be on the map," I finished triumphantly.

"And so I'll be lost all the time." Laila's eyes filled with tears.

"Come now, Laila," said Alta briskly, putting her arm around Laila, "no need to cry. You just have to look for landmarks, like when you're hiking in the woods at home."

"Yes," said Bob. "The landmark in the back is the big hospital where the truck unloaded our stuff last night, and the landmark in the front is that movie theater, whatever it's called."

"The Cinema Marhaba!" said Aisha, when I asked.

Laila looked troubled again. "What does *that* mean?"

I laughed. "In Arabic it means 'hello theater.'"

Laila smiled finally. "The hello theater! The hello theater! Will they have movies in English and can we go?"

"Maybe, who knows?"

"Let's go up to the roof and look down!" suggested Davy. The three children were off and running, across the sunny court where the birds twittered and sipped from our blue-and-yellow fountain, up the first stairway to the roomy balcony rimmed by wrought iron, and up another stairway past a heavy door to the roof of the house.

"Is it safe for them there, Bob?" from Alta. "It's awfully high," looking up, up, to where three small heads peered at us, giggling, from the top of the wall, forty feet above.

"I think so, but I'll go check." Bob sipped the last of the oversweet mint tea and grimaced. "It was nice of Aisha, but really I can't stand mint tea in the morning. Please, B.J., buy some coffee! I'll get the gas tank and connect the stove today."

I had already decided that since I was able to communicate with Aisha in Egyptian Arabic, I would ask her to take me shopping. Maybe she would lead me to the meat market, introduce me to fruit and vegetable merchants, explain the going rates and prices. But when I proposed this, her face changed and became strangely inexpressive. She shook her head.

What had I done? Broken some unwritten law of Moroccan ladies' relationships? Surely it was not an unusual request; other Middle Eastern friends, even in Casablanca during the summer, had seemed pleased to lead me to their merchant, their café. Why this sudden refusal on Aisha's part?

"But . . ." I started and stopped.

Aisha was silent. We gathered the mint tea glasses onto a tray for her to take home. I folded up the map. She began to explain. She told me how good the bread was on Rue Trésor. Wasn't it good? Yes, I answered. Homemade bread was better, of course, she said. I agreed again. She bought Tide and tomato paste and salt and sugar and milk from our tiny shop. Didn't Abdul Kabeer, the proprietor, seem nice? I agreed, once more. Meat. Well, pause. Vegetables. Well, there was a peddler who came sometimes. She picked up my jar of strawberry jam and looked at it and shook her head. "We don't eat things like this," she said.

I began to understand. Aisha did not go far afield to make her meager purchases. Vegetables from the peddler. Meat seldom. And her husband probably bought it, as men did much of the shopping here. Everything she needed was available in the little cubbyhole with the blue shutter, just a few feet down the street. I realized that she did not know where to purchase the special cuts of meat, the luxuries like coffee and butter and jam that she assumed that I, as a foreigner, would want.

"In the big market in Gueliz they have everything the foreigners want," Aisha was saying. She used the word *Nasrani* (Christian) as a generic term for foreigner.

"Go to Gueliz," she urged. "Ask the bus driver where the market is. Everybody knows."

This was not at all what I had had in mind. It was going to be hard enough, I thought, to make friends on Rue Trésor, to get to know anyone who lived behind the high, thick, rose-red walls, so private and shut off from each other, to get to know the women behind their face veils and all-enveloping djellabas. But marketing was one thing that everyone had to do, every day, and presumably one could strike up acquaintances, even with veils, over the marketing: picking through the eggplants, arguing about the best pieces of lamb. To go to Gueliz and shop with other foreigners would only cut me off further from the traditional city, in which we had chosen to live. My

face must have shown my disappointment, for Aisha assured me
again that Gueliz had everything.

"Prices are marked," she went on eagerly. "Policemen are there to
make sure they don't overcharge you."

I understood that Aisha did not know the prices of items I might
want and did not want to be placed in a position where she was
responsible for my bargaining and purchasing. Well, perhaps today
and for the first few days, we would have to shop in Gueliz until we
understood the medina a bit more. After all, we had to eat.

Laila and David wanted to stay to explore the house and watch
from the window what went on among the children on the street.
Bob would wait for the gas man. Laura Ann and Alta volunteered to
go shopping with me.

Out on Rue Trésor, our *zanka* that we could not find on any map,
the sun and the heat hit us like a blast. A crowd of curious children
immediately appeared and followed us, running and giggling and
pointing to the end of the street. Here at a dry-cleaning shop I asked
the way in Arabic and got fishy stares and heads shaken in noncomprehension until I switched to French. In a moment directions
were forthcoming, and we picked our way slowly across Rue Bab Agnaou, among a pair of motorcycles, a horse-drawn carriage that came
to an abrupt stop, hoping to lure us into it, and a staggered row of pe-
destrians who spilled over from the crowded sidewalks. It was mid-
morning. The main business of the day seemed to be under way, and
everyone was shouting: the shopkeeper at his patrons; the cart driver
at his donkey; the taxi drivers at us. We had been directed to a narrow street between the Cinema Marhaba and what looked like an
auto repair shop; two kebab stands and several office fronts later, we
emerged on Parc Foucauld (that was on the map). Several rows of
red buses were drawn up beneath signs in French and Arabic; we
boarded the bus marked Mohammed Cinq, only to be put off politely and told to go to the rear door and pay our fare. The bus was
nearly full of men in heavy djellabas despite the heat, women veiled
to the eyes carrying babies in slings on their backs, many children, a
few young Europeans with beards. Starting jerkily around the park,
the bus soon passed the Koutoubia mosque and headed down
Boulevard Mohammed Cinq. We were crowded against the back
wall, and the combined scent of incense, perfume, sweat, and exhaust
fumes was overpowering. Alta got out a handkerchief to cover her

nose, sensibly enough, and I noticed two Moroccan ladies doing the same.

"*Marché! Marché!*" The bus driver was calling our stop, and we quickly dismounted before a long, enclosed market. Everything was of rosy-red clay against a bright, blue, cloudless sky.

The large kiosk at the entrance to the market sold Nestlé chocolate bars, French and American cigarettes, razor blades, the Paris edition of the *Herald Tribune*, and newspapers from all of the major cities in the world. And there stood the policeman in a white uniform, as Aisha had promised.

After the blinding sun and the odiferous bus ride, the covered market was cool and filled with the marvelous odors of fresh produce. It was everything Aisha had promised and more. Laura Ann ran from one fruit stall to the next, calling, to the alternate perplexity and amusement of the customers and the proprietors, "Look, Mama, peaches! Look, Mama, pears! Oh, do buy some grapes. And maybe a watermelon?"

Here in these dim, cool stalls had been gathered the rich fruits of the Moroccan farmland: milk, cream, double cream, butter, eggs, couscous, rice; vegetables in piles of green and yellow squash, purple eggplants, fat red tomatoes. The meat markets looked immaculate, and legs of lamb and quarters of beef hung on hooks or were displayed as chops and steaks, in refrigerated cases. Plucked chickens also sat there pristinely, ready for roasting. In the grocery shops, the products of the French countryside had been bottled and tinned and shipped out to the colonies for the native sons to enjoy: jams, jellies, snails, asparagus, chestnuts, Dijon mustard, cheeses from every province: Brie, Roquefort, Port Salut. Specialty delicatessens advertised homemade patés, sausages, country-cured hams.

We bought colorful hand-woven market baskets and filled them with the fruits of two continents. We bought dishes. We bought a teapot. We bought flowers.

"Did you realize there were so many Europeans in Marrakech?" Alta asked.

I hadn't. One expected to find them in the port city of Casablanca, but in provincial Marrakech, fifteen years after Independence? This market was full of French people, a few Englishmen, some young Americans. Even as I loaded my baskets, I wondered how I was ever going to manage shopping in *our* part of the city.

"I didn't see a single foreigner on Rue Trésor," said Alta.

"Nor did I." They all live here, I thought, clustering together, building their own city in defiance of the labyrinthian medina, those narrow alleys that my own daughter Laila found so frightening.

We sat down at an umbrella-shaded table in an outdoor café and ordered lemonade while we waited for Bob to pick us up.

"Well, this certainly isn't like the medina at all," said Laura Ann, setting into her iced lemonade enthusiastically.

It wasn't. Had we come all the way to the heart of Morocco to find this oasis of Western culture? Rue Trésor was another world. How could one possibly join the two parts of the city, live in both, and learn anything? I knew that I would be tempted to shop here frequently, if the produce tasted as good as it looked. We had even found a French bakery with superb croissants—we had nibbled one—and fresh napoleons.

I sipped my lemonade and looked out at the rosy-red walls of the city buildings, watched the embroidered hooded djellabas and the French miniskirts and the long, ragged blue jeans of the people strolling by under the nodding leaves of the orange and jacaranda trees. Laura Ann was reading the comics in the *Herald Tribune*. The sun was still hot, but the scalloped blue umbrella offered us shade. I took another sip of lemonade and decided not to face any more problems right now. This was far too pleasant.

Chapter 2

Djemaa el Fna: Myth and Magic

The afternoon sun beat down upon the open courtyard, reducing the colored tiles to a pale wash of glare. All was quiet, in the house and in the street, for it was siesta hour. Drip, bubble, splash, drip, bubble, bubble, splash, the fountain played quietly in the silence. The broad green leaves of the canna lilies stood up stiffly in their tile-rimmed plots of earth, under the burgeoning orange and lemon trees. But a fine film of dust lay on the upper leaves of the lemon tree. Hajja Kenza, our landlady, had not been in for four days, since Bob had asked her to relinquish her key to our house. This confrontation had taken place after she had arrived one morning just as Bob strode out of the bedroom in his underwear. Hajja Kenza had laughed. Bob had not.

"What right does that woman have to come in here, any time of the day or night, whenever it pleases her? At the rent we pay . . ."

Hajja Kenza had gone about her business, oblivious to this tirade in English, which of course she could not possibly understand. She was weeding and digging and watering the four octagonal plots. I had found some fresh dill in the Gueliz market and had planted it. I noticed she was digging it out. This, too, was annoying.

Clothed, Bob descended the stairway from the balcony in a suitably majestic manner and approached Hajja Kenza, bent over in the garden. He stood beside her.

"Ahem!" he said, loudly and clearly.

Hajja Kenza straightened up and grinned her golden-toothed grin at him. He did not respond. In his most icy tone he asked for the key. Hajja Kenza pounded him playfully on the arm with her earth-crusted trowel and pretended not to understand. Bob told Aisha, in no uncertain terms, to translate his request. Alta and the children had gathered in the courtyard to watch. Life was not so full of drama and activity these days that a scene like this could be ignored. Aisha looked at the ground, after communicating Bob's request. Hajja Kenza went on weeding.

Finally, Aisha looked up and laughed and said again that Bob needed the key.

Bob followed suit and laughed a bit, though not very enthusiastically.

Hajja Kenza then decided to take the whole thing as a joke, and after two or three minutes of banter, announced she would give us the key when she had finished gardening.

Deciding that a peace gesture might be in order, I sent Davy to buy a bottle of grenadine syrup, one of our recent discoveries. With ice water and sugar, it was "even better than Kool-Aid," the children had announced.

But when we sat down to drink, Aisha, Alta, Hajja Kenza, the children, and myself, Bob decided to leave, begging a previous business appointment. David sidled away with his father.

"Business!" said Hajja Kenza mockingly. "And just what *is* his business?" rolling her eyes at Aisha, Alta, and finally me.

"He is a teacher," I said, "a professor in America."

"Then why doesn't he teach here?"

"He has a *bourse*, a scholarship, to study and read and think and learn about Morocco."

Aisha translated this in a very flowery way, it seemed to me, putting her finger to her head to indicate the profundity and difficulty of Bob's activity.

Hajja Kenza snorted, "I bet! All day long he thinks! Men!" She laughed derisively and launched into a long diatribe about the uselessness of the male species. "My lemon tree is no good. It gives me no lemons. Why? Because it's a *male* tree! If I had known that, I would never have planted it."

I did not translate this for Alta, but let it pass, aware that Hajja Kenza realized she had lost the battle of the key and had to let off steam somehow. Since then, she had not been back to see us. No one dug in the garden plots or washed the upper leaves of the lemon tree. We were all too hot and tired. Even Naima, Hajja Kenza's daughter, who had come over two or three times to play with the children, had not returned. The initial forays with Naima had been mildly success-ful, even with no language between the children but gesture. They had drunk grenadine, Naima had been shown the children's rooms, she had felt the thickness of the mattresses, had peered out every one of our second-floor windows and shouted to her friends in the street below. Laura Ann had in the end suggested drawing; I got out the felt-tipped pens and pads of paper, and everybody drew something. Davy drew a horse, Laura Ann a tree, Laila a house, and Naima? Naima drew a picture of the Koutoubia mosque. Everybody seemed delighted until Naima had pointed to Laila's square Western house with its gabled roof and two windows. Where was the court?

"No court," assured Laila. "Much better."

Naima, Laura Ann reported, had shrugged and made it clear that no house could possibly be worth living in that did not have a court-yard.

I knew that Bob's general irritability these days was partly due to the fact that he was having difficulty sleeping through the barrage of familiar and unfamiliar noises that seemed to continue all night long on Rue Trésor. Alta had moved her bed out into the court and said she couldn't hear a thing, and the children, though they had two win-dows overlooking the street, seemed to sleep heavily despite it. But Bob was beside himself and I was having trouble, too.

"We should have thought about the fact that Rue Trésor was in a commercial section of the medina. Why didn't we take a house far-ther inside?"

When I mentioned this to Aisha, she looked shocked.

"Oh, no, Rue Trésor is not a commercial area. It is a residential street. We are a *quarter*. This is a very nice place to live. Close to ev-erything, but a little bit out of it."

"Not far enough out of it," grumbled Bob, who started searching methodically and unsuccessfully through the pharmacies of Marrakech for ear plugs.

It was true that everyone seemed awake at night, both in the houses and in the street. Except for the brief siesta time in midaf-ternoon, the noise went on all the time. By midnight, the bustle of people passing by below our window had receded, but the radios went on and on, as did the shouting and quarreling and the crying of babies in houses near us.

Order, classify, sort out, and identify the various noises, I told myself, keep our minds clear or we will all go mad. I had identified the radios easily enough, the boys playing and shouting on the street, the rustle of djellabas, the crying of children, the braying of donkeys, the bicycle bells, the motorcycles.

What I could not identify was a new incessant nighttime pounding, scraping, sweeping, and grinding. "Whang, rumble, rumble, rumble, *whang, whang*, rumble, rumble, rumble." From my window I could see nothing. Two A.M., 3 A.M., 4 A.M., "Whang, rumble, rumble, rumble, *whang, whang*"; it was infuriating.

In the morning I asked Aisha about the noise, and she thought a moment and said it must be the workmen building an annex to the public bath. David and Laura Ann ran up to the roof to look and reported that Aisha was right. The grinding and scraping involved the mixing of cement, and the sweeping and the scraping noise that set my teeth on edge was a smoothing process before the final coat of plaster was applied on the roof. The plaster was pounded methodically and rhythmically by five men bearing what looked like wooden mallets mounted on broom handles. Scrape, sweep, pound, pound. One man scraped, two men swept, two men pounded. All this twenty feet from our bedroom windows!

"And when it is finished, there will be a bath for men and a bath specially for women, each with its own door," said Aisha. "It will be wonderful. We won't have to wait for ladies' time like we do now."

"But do they have to work at night?" I grumbled.

"It's cooler," Aisha pointed out.

Building a roof to the public bath; that went into the list of noises that were slowly forming some kind of pattern in the night: radios, babies crying, bicycles on the run through the zanka, and the clapping, the incessant clapping.

"They do it for fun," Aisha explained, when the children asked me why the teen-age boys, the girls, the children, clapped off and on, loudly, in different rhythms. Human percussion. My own children began to try it out, clapping off and on in response to the clapping outside.

"Stop that noise!" hollered Bob from the bedroom where he lay reading.

After the mixing of gravel and the scraping and pounding on the bath roof, an hour or two of relative quiet ensued before a reassuring swoosh and sweep sounded about 5 A.M. These were the city garbage men, methodically sweeping the street of the night's refuse. Then came the delicious scent of fresh bread from the bakery ovens across the street, next door to the public bath, and only fifty feet from our window. As in medina streets and quarters of old, the bath and the bakery were located next to each other, so that one fire could heat the ovens and the water at the same time. I pointed this out to the children.

"Conserving energy," said Laura Ann, whose sixth-grade class in Austin had been studying ecology before we left.

"They've been doing it for a long time," said Bob. "It costs less."

After the brooms had ceased, the bicycle bells sounded; the delivery boys were setting out with their baskets filled with long flutes of French bread and dark, round loaves of Moroccan bread, fresh from the ovens, to be delivered to small neighborhood shops in the quarter. The day was beginning again.

Of course, by the time I really had all the noises classified, I no longer even noticed them. Nor did Bob ever use the ear plugs he eventually found. The noises were still there, but we were not bothered by them, sleep being more compelling or our adjustive faculties better than we had guessed.

I was learning bits and pieces about life on Rue Trésor, but I felt no more a part of it than I did when we arrived. Further, we had pressing problems to solve. The children *had* to go to school. But the situation was more complicated than we realized. Not only were the Moroccan schools overcrowded; classes, it seemed, were conducted in a combination of Arabic and French. Since our children knew neither language, it seemed foolish to expect them to sit for a year trying to make sense out of such a mixture. The two French convent schools in Marrakech had turned us down. All that remained was the Lycée Victor Hugo, the school run by the French cultural mission in Morocco; we had received no reply to our application.

Kenza predicted that our children would never be admitted to the Lycée.

"Never, Madame, never!" She had wagged a finger at me. "Nobody is admitted unless they speak French, and know somebody rich and influential. Who do you know?"

Nobody, obviously, except Aisha and Hajja Kenza.

"The French run things, especially the schools. They won't let Americans in the Lycée."

"But Morocco is independent," I protested.

Our landlady laughed.

Aisha laughed.

"Oh, yes, we are independent," said Aisha, "but the French still run everything."

Four weeks had passed on Rue Trésor. And it seemed to get hotter every day. That was because the tiles held and stored the heat, Bob explained. They did indeed. I wandered aimlessly back and forth from sink to drainboard, making potato salad for supper.

What were we going to do in this beautiful, alien house for a solid year? The children were very quiet, lying on their beds, rereading the paperbacks we had carefully brought from home (English books were unavailable in Marrakech, except for a small shelf of old thrillers in French bookstores near the market). The paperbacks would not last much longer. I could teach with correspondence or home instruction courses, I thought, but the children deserved something better than being immured in the house all year, meeting no one, seeing no one, teased and twitted whenever they went out on the street where we were to have learned so much, firsthand, about the people of Morocco, North Africa, Marrakech. They all had romantic ideas and pleasant associations with their childhood in the Middle East, in Egypt; would these turn sour now? I sighed, realizing it could very well happen. But what to do?

The children had been resourceful in combating boredom, making up games to be played in the house, including one that consisted of lying out flat on the roof with crumbs scattered over their arms and legs, hoping the birds would stop and eat the crumbs. No bird had alighted, and after some time, the children had risen stiffly and given that game up. Alta bought knitting needles and was teaching them to knit. We played pinochle, and they pretended to camp out on the inside balcony. Was it for this we had come to Morocco?

Bob was definitely in retreat, spending more time in our beautiful tiled and plastered bedroom, reading, than he did outside. Worrying about eighty American students and professors all summer in Casablanca seemed to have sated his taste for people of any description. "I want to be *alone*," he would shout, glaring down at us over the balcony.

We were becoming bogged down, discouraged. We went each day
to the French quarter to eat ice cream and to shop, partly as an escape from the giggling, pointing children on Rue Trésor, the men
who accidentally bumped into Laura Ann, the ladies who pulled
blond hairs from Laila's head for use as charms. Laura Ann and I
had had a cruel blow on our bus trip to the French quarter two days
before. We sat opposite a mother and a fat, rosy-cheeked toddler,
who kept staring at us. Laura Ann would smile and I would smile.
The child did not smile back. He began to jump up and down, whining and complaining. His mother, to quiet him, kept pointing to us
and saying something. Suddenly I realized that she was threatening
him with *us*. We, Laura Ann and I, were witches who would kidnap
and eat him if he didn't behave! Nice baby-loving people like us! I
felt close to tears and could not bring myself to explain this to my
daughter.

Had Hajja Kenza somehow turned the whole street against us after
her fit of pique over the key? It would be easy to have a scapegoat,
but somehow I did not think that was the answer.

We were called in the street *Nasrani*, i.e., Christian, which was
synonymous with foreigner, and foreigner mostly meant the colonialist French, who had been ousted only fifteen years ago. It was ridiculous to expect to be embraced for our unknown selves, our good
intentions, when our appearance, our presence in the medina, and
our seemingly idle but expensive life (even Hajja Kenza had remarked on this) signaled qualities about foreigners that Moroccan
adults had come to envy and hate.

I chopped an onion into the potato salad, wiped the onion tears
from my eyes, and decided we could not sit here and vegetate.

"Let's go to the café by Djemaa el Fna today," I said brightly over
cold lemonade in the dining room (the court was still hot at 5 P.M.).
"There's supposed to be a terrific view of the performers from the
roof of that café."

Grunts from the children. "I'd rather stay in and read," said Laila.

"Oh, come on," urged Bob, temporarily tired of his solitude.
"We'll look at the snake charmers and then have Coca-Cola at the
café."

Some enthusiasm for the Coke helped, and we marshaled everyone
out. That split second before the front door slammed and the
children stood there, was the hardest, for them, for me, for all of us;
for at that moment, or so it seemed, all activity of hopscotch and

marbles stopped. The neighbor children stood up to watch us all walk down the street, and shutters of windows above us banged open and people peered out. This is ridiculous, I told myself, we are all getting paranoid, especially me. Surely they are not only staring at *us* (but who else?). We marched forward over the broken pavement of Rue Trésor, Laila clutching tightly to my hand and keeping to the rough, rosy walls of the houses, the least-visible position. Even so, we had to go single file to allow a small Renault to pass and then a motorcycle driven by a veiled lady in a djellaba.

People, donkeys, and cars combined to fill the afternoon air with sound and movement. Rue Bab Agnaou was opening up after the siesta; shutters of shops were flung open, and the metal door of the Bata shoe store clanged upward. The odor of fresh coffee drifted toward us from the shop next to Bata.

"Why don't you buy your coffee here, B.J.?" said Bob, lingering by the rough gunny sacks marked Colombia, Yemen, Yucatan.

"I don't know how to explain how I want it ground. They grind everything fine for Turkish coffee."

Bob looked exasperated and stopped as though *he* could make them understand, but the clerk disappeared at this moment, and we walked on.

"You have just shut your mind to the whole area of shopping possibilities that lies right under your nose," he said sharply. "Going to the European section every day. What kind of picture of Morocco are you getting? Besides, this is just around the corner, and Gueliz is more than a mile away."

I had heard this before. He was right, of course, but I had tried twice with this coffee merchant, and he had laughed and ground the coffee too fine for our percolator, and there was nothing left but to pay the very expensive price for that Arab coffee I didn't want. Revenge for colonialism. I shook myself. I really was getting silly.

"Now, Bob, don't be hard on Betty, you've been here only a month, you can't learn everything right away," said Alta.

"No, but you can start by not shutting yourself off from such possibilities," answered Bob, rather primly.

I wanted to shout back, what are *you* doing sitting up in the beautiful bedroom, meditating on the plaster flowers and leaves, other than shutting yourself off from possibilities? The moment, punctuated as it was by the bells of horses and buggies, the cries of beggars and the sudden wailing of a police siren, did not seem appropriate.

David walked along with his father, occasionally staring into a shop window; Alta and Laura Ann followed, and Laila and I brought up the rear, straggling as usual, since Laila shrank from the brushing against people that was necessary to get through the crowds thronging the streets and the sidewalks.

We passed the "Fruit Shake," filled with young Americans and young Moroccans, drinking mild mixtures of yogurt, fruit juice, and "ice cream" amid ear-splitting rock music. The pirate turbans of the young Moroccan men set them apart from the Americans with their multicolored locks, patched jeans, backpacks, and boots. But they were all stoned together in the postsiesta heat, under a large, languid ceiling fan. I stared at them. They seemed content. And they don't worry, I thought to myself. Why should I? Why worry about learning about Marrakech and getting acquainted with my neighbors? What is the point of it all?

"Come on, B.J.," Bob turned and shouted, but no one turned around to stare at us as they did in Rue Trésor. On Rue Bab Agnaou, bound for Djemaa el Fna, we were just one more group of European tourists looking for the exoticism that far-out Marrakech was supposed to offer.

"*Baksheesh!*" A beggar boy with a twisted arm stuck his dirty hand, extending from a ragged piece of sleeve, under Laila's elbow. She recoiled as if struck. Pressing his advantage, the boy followed on. We were tourists; he was shameless. "*Baksheesh,*" he hissed. I stopped and took a coin out of my purse while Laila avoided looking at the boy's eyes as though her own might be burned on contact. I dropped the money into his dirty palm. The eyes stared at me, at Laila, went blank. He was gone.

"Mama, why did you do that?" Laila looked sick, and I reflected, after consoling her and pointing out that the child was hungry, that she was, after all, only experiencing what many well-brought-up Westerners, not so young as Laila, experience the first time they have personal contact with poverty, disease, the horror of destitution, of deformity. Most Western cities manage very neatly to bundle up all of those troublesome sights and put them into institutions called old people's homes and prisons, orphanages and correctional centers, or into sections of town and country not frequented by our middle classes. The law-abiding, affluent citizen does not need to be bothered by such sights, to constantly be reminded of the impermanence of health, affluence, the shortness of life, the uncertainty of good fortune. In Marrakech, rich and poor, healthy and sick were not so neatly separated.

"B.J.!" Bob was waiting at the big square, with Alta, Laura Ann, and David, looking hot and impatient. "What took you so long?"

I explained about the beggar, and waited with Bob to cross the street into the square against the stream of six-o'clock traffic. The dancers, the snake charmers, the magicians, and the storytellers were out and performing. This was the time to visit Djemaa el Fna, but whether it was the heat, the noise and crowds, which I ordinarily liked and enjoyed, or Laila's cringing into the side of my dress to avoid seeing the cluster of boys who thronged around us, we all stood there a moment longer than necessary, and the next surge of traffic moved in front of us.

"Bob," said Alta unexpectedly, "let's go up to the roof of the café and have our drink first, and then maybe it won't be so crowded."

Without a word, we turned and headed up the three flights of stairs to the Café des Glaciers; Alta and Laila sank down in chairs that Bob had pulled up to the wall of the roof, from which one got a superb view of the square below.

Djemaa el Fna. A tourist agent's dream.

A great open triangular space in the shadow of one of the oldest and most distinguished mosques in Islamic history. The Koutoubia. Sister of the Giralda in Spain. Descendant of Tinmel in the Atlas Mountains. Worn rosy stone and broken green and white tiles only added to the structure's basic majesty, where every noon and sunset the flags flew from the top of the minaret, indicating that the imam has just arrived and the prayers have begun. We could see the flags from our own roof, as we could see the roofs of the post office and police station, and the trees of the Parc Foucauld, which bounded the square of Djemaa el Fna.

Alta had gotten up to walk with Bob around the roof of the café along with the guides and their group of German tourists, French tourists, and elderly English ladies in red-tasseled sunhats from Tangier. They all sipped Coca-Cola judiciously, holding down their straw hats in case a breeze might whip them away, peering tentatively over the wall, edged with iron railings (too many people have tried to jump from the Glaciers) at the medieval fair, the folk and fairy tale below.

"What's that, Mama?" Laila stood beside me, still clutching me with one hand and holding a bottle of Judor, the Moroccan bottled lemon drink, in the other.

"Where?" I peered over the edge, too, wondering what specific detail she had picked out of the mass of people walking, bicycling, driving, pushing carts, scooting along below us on wheeled boards specially made for beggars who could not walk.

"Look! The black box and the lady sitting on top of it with a black sheet over her!"

"Ah, yes!" From the myriads of performers moving in the hundreds of people milling in the square, Laila had indeed picked a new one.

"A magician? Makes the lady disappear into the black box?" I suggested.

"Yes, look, look!" She let go of my hand excitedly and pointed. The lady seemed to be lying down on the black box, and the gentleman magician or whoever he was, seemed to be instructing her. Laila leaned closer and I looked at her, seeing that, away from the pressures and personal touches of Rue Trésor and the market crowd, here, removed from the contact, she was enjoying it, could enjoy, as I had hoped all the children would enjoy, the marvelous fairy-tale quality of the living, sounding scene below us.

For what was Djemaa el Fna but one of the open squares of peddlers and performers and hustlers and vagabonds that had been the economic, recreational, and religious centers of European medieval life, in villages as well as towns and cities? The great squares of Europe have become more sophisticated pleasure places in modern times. The cafés in San Marco in Venice, Saint Germain des Prés in Paris, St. Peter's in Rome, are tidy, refined, catering to a different clientele. Here in Marrakech still survived, marvelously, the lusty quality and flavor of the squares as they figure in medieval chronicles, in histories and in fairy tales and in the adventures of the Arabian nights.

"Mama, look, he's covering her up. She's dropping into the black box!"

The crowd around the new performer was growing, and it was difficult to see the next step in the performance.

From here, through the haze, one could see and feel the past projected before one. My child's imagination said, aloud, beside me, "Oh, I can't see it. How did she do it? How did he make her disappear?"

"Let's go down. Then maybe he'll do it again."

Laila hesitated. For a moment she was tempted, I could tell. He might do it again, and she might learn the secret. But then, too, she might see and hear and feel all the things that upset her, that closed the distance between the fairy tale and the reality that passed our door every day.

"No. I don't want to, Mama, I always think of those heads up there, those dead heads the square is supposed to be named after."

Some guidebooks do call it the square of the dead, though the exact meaning of Djemaa el Fna is doubtful; it is so named, some say, because in some former, more violent times in the history of Marrakech, the heads of those decapitated for unnamed crimes against the sultan were hung up in the square as a hideous warning to other would-be rebels and transgressors. A hundred years ago such squares, it is said, were to be found throughout Morocco, but in the new modernization, in the advent of the French colonialist regimes, they have been abolished, as natural centers of crime and traffic in drugs and human beings.

Why did Djemaa el Fna survive? Legend credits Eleanor Roosevelt. During the Casablanca conference in the Second World War, Mrs. Roosevelt is supposed to have confided to her host, King Mohammed V, that she looked forward to visiting Winston Churchill in Marrakech because there, as a child, many years ago, she had been taken to Djemaa el Fna and found it one of the most wonderful places in the world. The King, it is said, thus arranged that Djemaa el Fna should be saved, and tourist interest has kept it alive ever since. Who knows? It is a charming story, and perhaps true.

"What are you looking at, Betty?" Alta came and stood with us.

"Just admiring the view, isn't it glorious?"

Above us, the sky was turning golden and red. The peaks of the Atlas were no longer visible. But below, the square was punctuated with lights, flicking on in the scores of narrow shops, winking on the barrows of vendors, as they hawked smoking kebab, roasted almonds, sugar-covered peanuts, iced bottles of Judor. And beyond the lights loomed the dark shapes of the houses and shops and the narrow streets of the great medina.

"We can see the outlines so well from up here," Alta pointed out. "Down there you're just lost in the crowd, and can't see anything."

"Maybe that's why it bothers the children so," I said.

"Oh, B.J., they love Djemaa el Fna, don't put thoughts in their heads," said Bob, with irritation.

"Well, they liked it at first, it's a great novelty, the snake charmers and the pigeon men and those children who do leaps and pyramids and the black men who dance with bells and castanets, or whatever they're called! But they don't like to go much any more."

"They don't like the beggars, Bob, and they're on us all the time," said Alta.

I felt, but did not say, that the first few times the square had perhaps retained the fairy-tale quality that Laila had experienced again just a moment ago, watching the lady being packed into the magician's black box. The square remains in one's mind the same way that a dream, forgotten for hours after waking, will suddenly return vividly to consciousness. And surely the children had recognized here fragments of old illustrations from their fairy-tale books, images from the stories and fantasies they had always loved: the flying carpet whereon sits the turbaned prince in embroidered vest, and his dream maiden with flying hair and almond-shaped eyes; the gnarled, misshapen dwarf; the lost children crying; acrobats and jesters in costumes tipped with bells; snake charmers with magic pipes to soothe evil serpents.

They are all there, in Djemaa el Fna, I thought, and now, in twilight, in the dreamlike haze of dusk, the square looked indeed enchanted.

But the children had seen these sights every day for a month now, and at close quarters fairy-tale characters tend to lose their evanescence. The gnarled, misshapen dwarf is real and he is blind and he stands with a little band of misshapen and maimed men like himself, each day, with a tin bowl in his hand, singing, "O God, the most merciful, the most compassionate, hear our prayer! Alms."

The jesters and acrobats are pale children, and the cheap, shiny silk of their costumes clings to their bony bodies. The lost children are there, too, the brave child who cares for her baby sister, but the child has sores around her mouth and the thin baby carried in a sling on her back has infected eyes. Even the prince on the magic carpet sits there, but his carpet is frayed a little; he sells coconuts and ivory trinkets from his faraway country; his princess wears a marvelous spotted turban wrapped about her proud black head, but she looks unhappy.

"Mama, look!" Laura Ann pointed to three young Moroccan men who had two young English girls engaged in conversation, one in jeans and a shirt tied up under her bosom, the other in a new caftan, the cheap kind made for tourists, of ribbed white cotton embroidered around the sleeves and neck in a machine pattern of red swirls and circles.

One of the boys, in a leather hat, was gesturing. "The beeyootiful High Atlas Mountains . . . my village . . . Ourika . . ." reached us.

Now Laura Ann was giggling. "Mama, they're braless," she said, bringing my musings back to sharp reality.

"Let's go home, Bob, we're all tired," said Alta.

The Koutoubia suddenly came alight, glowed, dominating the whole view. Several of the tourists gasped with surprise and delight.

The sun had not quite set.

"Let's take a horse and buggy," Laila begged when we had reached the street. "Instead of Djemaa el Fna. Please, Baba!"

Bob and I looked at each other.

"Why not?" he said. "That's supposed to be one of the treats of Marrakech. They tell all the tourists, Mother, to take a horse-and-buggy trip around the walls at sunset."

We found one large buggy along the ranks that was willing to take all six of us, for an extra fee, of course. Davy elected to sit up with the driver, and in a flash we were bounding along the medieval turreted walls toward Gueliz.

"No, no!" shouted Bob. "Stop!"

The driver pulled his horse up. "What?"

"We don't want to go to Gueliz, we want to go through the medina!"

"Walls, palaces, very beautiful!" insisted the driver.

"Walls, then medina," Bob insisted.

The driver turned around to look at Bob, shrugged, adjusted his skullcap, wiped his nose with a hand, and turned around in the middle of the boulevard.

"Why not the palaces, Bob?" asked Alta.

"We can see the palaces later," said Bob. "We need to get a general idea of the whole medina so we can see Rue Trésor in some perspective."

"At-lass!" the driver pointed with his whip toward the mountain peaks, and we all nodded.

Along the fortified city walls, their crenelated ramparts still intact, families were walking or simply sitting in little knots, eating a picnic supper. To the right stretched fields, gardens, the palm groves edging the oasis. There was no doubt where the city of Marrakech began and ended; the walls told us clearly.

Informal evening markets were in progress outside the walls: chicken, fodder, cloth. A crowd of boys and young men watched a soccer game near the gate where our carriage rattled over the stones and turned across the gardens lying close to the King's royal palace in Marrakech. The gates were locked; King Hassan, son of Mohammed Cinq, was away.

"He's afraid to come to Marrakech!" cackled the mustached driver, turning to see our reaction. We did not reply.

We rattled under a stone archway and in a moment were in the enclosed medina again, the charcoal market, the blacksmiths' quarter, each shop with a distinctive hole above its door, darkened by smoke from the forges.

Between the ironmongers, the charcoal merchants, and the machine shops, one saw occasional houses, with an entrance open, displaying a tiled step or no entrance at all but a dirt floor and a staircase ascending straight up off the street to a half level above. I looked carefully, for I had not seen inside any house on Rue Trésor but my own and, briefly, Aisha's.

We passed the tiled sign of a public bath, a sidewalk restaurant. Then the narrow street widened and we were in a larger square, where, from a large public fountain in the side of a long wall, women and children were drawing jugs of water for their evening needs.

"Bab Doukkala!" shouted the driver. A community laundry was in progress at the far end of the fountain; lines of sheets and djellabas stretched over the square. Farther down, in a small canal made by the runoff from the fountain, two men were washing horses, the animals' wet skins glistening in the last light from the sun.

Our driver sped through the gate at Bab Doukkala and headed, by a circuitous route that we were never able to duplicate, through an old residential quarter where the streets seemed even narrower than Rue Trésor. We could have reached out and touched the doors of the houses on either side. The heavy doors were studded with nails and marked with brass and silver knockers like ours, in the shape of the hand of Fatima. But in a moment, we were in a suq or market again, the shops reopened with the sunset. A caftan of red velvet was being embroidered on a special sewing machine. Four little boys, each holding a different gold thread, moved as the man working the embroidery pattern called first for one thread, then the other. The children moved in a stylized way, one finger, a hand, a half step forward as the complicated machine stitched the pattern, line by line and whorl by whorl onto the red velvet.

"They're probably apprentices to the caftanmaker," Bob explained to his mother.

Then we stopped. We were in a traffic jam, cars blowing their horns ahead of us in the narrow, dark streets. Quickly a group of children gathered around our carriage, to stare at Laila with her long blond hair, Davy up on the driver's seat, Laura Ann in her sleeveless striped dress. The street children were saying things I did not want to understand, and making unpleasant gestures; Laura Ann, David, and Laila stared straight ahead. Why didn't we move? Someone threw a big clod of dirt that hit the side of the carriage and broke. The driver stood up, snapping his whip, and the children scattered. Why couldn't we move?

Still another clod of dirt hit the carriage. Another. The driver shouted and cracked his whip again. But now it was a stone. A small one, I hoped. Not seriously intended, but the ominous clink made me shiver.

The children were absolutely quiet. David, next to the coachman in the most vulnerable position, scrunched down on the seat. What else could he do? Would the next rock hit him?

The cars ahead of us moved along a few inches. Another, larger rock hit the carriage wheel. The driver whipped his old horse and in a few moments we were hurtling down winding zankas in a part of the medina we did not know. Faster we went, and the girls clung to each other and Davy held on to the high seat in front of us with both hands, rocking back and forth with the motion of the carriage.

These zankas were darker than ours and badly lit. Night had come by the time the driver deposited us near the Cinema Marhaba, and we got out while Bob paid him silently.

"Tourists don't usually want to go in the medina," said the driver unexpectedly. "They're riffraff, those children, no decent family." He spat in the street, looked at the money Bob had given him, touched his forehead in a kind of salute, and clop-clopped away.

The dimness of Rue Trésor closed around us. No one spoke as we hurried down the empty street to our door—and safety. We were almost there when two boys emerged without warning from around the corner.

"Madame, baksheesh!" shouted one, and tweaked Laila's hair.

Bob raised his hand above his head and the boys cowered back. I was astonished. So were the children.

"Enough!" Bob thundered in English, and the two boys ran away without another sound.

Inside the house Bob turned on the light. We had bought larger globes so the tiles and the little pool now gleamed brightly under the dark sky above the courtyard, outshining the stars high above us.

Alta said, "I'm sorry the children had to go through that, Bob. It could have been dangerous."

"Why did they throw those stones at us, Baba?"

"Well, you know I've told you about foreigners and what they did to Morocco and how Moroccans feel about foreigners. We are foreigners, that's all. Kids do what grown-ups think sometimes."

I could see he was too tired to continue the cheery lecture.

"But what can we do?" asked Laura Ann, "to show them we're *not* like that, that we're friendly, I mean."

What, indeed? The tiles gleamed brightly, the pond glimmered in the artificial light, the door was shut on the narrow, forbidding street. This was no fairy tale, I told myself. We were alone, strange and alien, in a strange and alien world.

Chapter 3

A Moroccan Education

After the shattering end to our enchanted evening on Djemaa el Fna, the children refused to go outside the house unaccompanied, even the few feet to the little window store to buy bubble gum.

"We knew it would be difficult, B.J., damn it," said Bob. "We just have to give it time. A city is different from the country, in the Middle East as well as in America. Would we know our neighbors in New York after one month? Hardly!"

"But would they be panhandling the children, and insulting us?"

Bob shrugged. "Don't make the situation worse than it is. No one complains about mugging, do they?"

"How could it be worse? We don't even have the school problem settled. What will we do if the Lycée turns down the children?"

"Don't anticipate problems before they arise. After all, surely the French, in the interests of Franco-American relations . . ." Bob smiled wearily, "well, it's a hope."

A thin hope, I wanted to say, but didn't. We tried to explain it once more to ourselves. After all, what had we expected on Rue Trésor? Instant friendship and neighborliness—people rushing in with hot couscous as signs of welcome, inviting our children to play? Probably—even though an instant's reflection would have told us this was sheer nonsense. In the Middle East, where the family is still the dominant and most important social institution, one's relations are with one's relations, literally, and not with people who are strangers, and particularly not with foreigners.

"The hippies think you're in the CIA," I said. "Some boy told Davy so on the street."

"What?" Bob looked really irritated. "Now I'm an espionage agent too? How about the drug traffic, and we can use mother and the children as cover."

We smiled at each other, rather weakly. It was not a particularly amusing situation. After all, when Bob had done anthropological research in Iraq and in Nubia, and in Afghanistan, we had lived in villages, and had been the guest or under the patronage of someone already living in the village, someone respected who was, presumably, responsible for us. Here we knew no one. We had landed cold on Rue Trésor, a family of strangers in a city filled with strangers: French, American, English, Polish, Berbers from the mountains, *harateen* from the Sahara. We were just one tiny unit in the crowds of nomadic strangers who had wandered through Marrakech during the past seven or eight hundred years. Some had stayed. We would not. We, too, were vagabonds, seeking something, then passing on. The outlaws from the mountains looked for anonymity in the crowds, in the maze of tiny alleys that were not on any city map and where Laila was certain she would get lost. The traders came from the desert to exchange their goods for the wares of the city. The beggars sought food, for they were hungry. We, too, were looking for baksheesh, seeking to learn and to discover the secret springs of life in Marrakech. What arrogance! And we expected it to be given to us, as one gives the beggar a small coin in the palm of his hand? No wonder people threw stones at us!

"No, no, B.J., you're exaggerating!"

"Am I?"

In a city that is literally divided, physically as well as emotionally, between the medina, or "native quarter," and the new city, built by the colonialist foreigners for themselves, our choice to live in the old city rather than in the new among our own "kind" must have seemed a bit strange.

"Why *did* we choose to live here rather than in that nice villa where the Harrises live?" Laila had asked.

Before we could reply, David had supplied the best and simplest answer. "Well, Mr. Harris is here to find out about fruit flies for the American Government, but Baba is here to find out about the life of the city. Mr. Harris doesn't have to live in the medina to find out about fruit flies, but we do, to find out about the people."

The Harrises themselves, an American family with two children (nine and eleven) who had also applied to the French school, had politely questioned our choice of housing arrangements.

Bettye Harris said she would have found the medina interesting, but the American aid mission had indicated in no uncertain terms where they were to live, in a villa owned by the Governor of Marrakech, an edifice suitable for an employee of the American Government.

If our fellow Americans found it strange that we should choose to live in the medina, why had we not expected that our neighbors in the medina might also find it strange?

"They think of us as rich and foreign," said Bob, "and identify us with the French. I guess I didn't expect quite this degree of hostility or indifference. They either hassle you or cut you dead."

"The children . . ."

Bob shook his head wearily. "Don't talk to me about the children. You'll be putting ideas in their heads next."

I was suddenly angry. "I'm not the one who pulls Laila's blond hairs out of her head. I didn't throw those stones at the carriage yesterday. What do you mean, put ideas in their heads? They won't even sit in the window sills, talking to the children outside any more. What are they supposed to do, lie on the ground of Rue Trésor and let the kids trample on them?"

"Oh, B.J.," Bob shook his head. "Shhh. Mother will hear. I don't want to upset her. At least they've met the Harrises. That's something. Children to play with. Speak English with. Thank God."

"True. But I can't invite myself to the Harrises every day. Something has to be done *here*."

"What?"

The knocker sounded and a bell rang at the same time, indicating the arrival of our postman, a pleasant, middle-aged man in khaki government uniform who came by on his bicycle every morning. An official-looking letter from the Lycée Victor Hugo. The children had not been admitted to the French school. We sat around the table and passed the letter back and forth. It was brief but final. An hour later the knocker sounded again. It was the Harrises. They had received the same letter.

"Well," said Bettye Harris tentatively. "I was a substitute teacher

A Street in Marrakech

64

in Hawaii, I suppose we could tutor the kids ourselves, get books from home. . . ."

"Yes," I said. "I suppose so." I subsided in a fit of coughing. My cold was worse. The old bronchitis had come upon me in the heat of Marrakech.

"We could go see the French consul," Bob suggested, "and plead on our knees that our children be allowed to drink at the fountain of French civilization and culture."

"Bob!" said his mother in shocked surprise.

"Wine instead of Coca-Cola?" suggested Ernest in an ironic tone.

"What's going on?" All the children stood there, Tanya Harris (almost as tall as Laura Ann), Greg Harris, David, and Laila. "The French school doesn't want us, right, so we don't need to go to school, right?"

Bettye Harris and I exchanged glances, amused in a desperate sort of way. "Your dear mothers are going to teach you all," she said.

"Oh, no!"

"Gross-o!"

"Please change your tone of voice!" said Bob.

"Okay, okay, but it would be so great not to have to go to school."

"Yes, for a few days it would, but what would you *do* all year?"

Greg grinned. All the children nudged each other and laughed and were off, up to the roof, to look down on us. It was the one place where they still had the advantage over the children on Rue Trésor.

"Well," said Bettye. "When we got that letter, I was all ready to rush up there and shout, racial discrimination, racial discrimination, but then Ernest said let's see what the Ferneas have heard, and now, what are we going to shout?"

"It's not racial discrimination, it's anti-Americanism!" cried Bob. "Join the party!"

We tried to laugh. It was not a success.

Alta looked from one to the other of us. "Can you and Bettye Harris really teach them?" she asked.

"You can't conduct classes if you cough all the time, B.J.," said Bob. "Better get some of those strong French codeine medicines!"

"Let's try once more," said Ernest finally, after a cup of coffee. "I'll go see the French consul and talk about friendly international relations."

"Okay," laughed Bob, "and I'll go see the school director and talk educator to educator!"

Meanwhile, I thought, something must be done here. Even if the children were admitted to the French school, which seemed unlikely now, we still had to live on Rue Trésor. It was Laura Ann's refusal to go to the suq with me that afternoon that finally jogged me into action.

"But why, dear? You've always liked to go before."

She looked down, and looked up, as though she had suddenly decided to say something difficult. "I can't stand it anymore, Mama. They pinch me and they poke me here" (she indicated her young breasts), "and that's okay, I poke them back, but last time somebody reached out and stuck his hand up my dress. It was awful. I didn't want to say anything then because of Grandma Tanny."

I stared at Laura Ann. The expression on her face made me wince. She loved the Semmarine market filled with the silks and brocades and jewels of a dozen countries. Was this, too, to be ruined for her?

"Okay, let's not go today. I don't feel very well anyway, my cold is getting bad. Why don't you ask Naima to come over?"

Laura Ann shook her head. "She has her own friends. And besides, it's so hard. We can't talk to each other. She dresses differently. She probably thinks we're all weirdo's."

"Maybe we could buy you a djellaba like Naima's. Would you like that? That might help with the pinching and the poking." Why hadn't I thought of *this* before?

Her eyes lighted up. "Oh, that would be great, Mama."

Fool, I told myself, and looked for Kleenex. I could not seem to stop coughing. Why had I not profited by my own experience in Iraq and Egypt? Here, where the majority of women I had seen in the medina went around more covered up than in Egypt, Nubia, or parts of Iraq, why had I assumed standards were different?

Well, I thought, I really don't want to wear a djellaba, but in the interests of possible greater accommodation with my neighbors, why couldn't I? And why shouldn't Laura Ann wear one if she would feel more like one of the girls her own age on Rue Trésor, and hence be more comfortable?

"I'll ask Aisha about it," I said to Laura Ann, and she ran off to confide my latest idea to Alta and to Davy and Laila.

What would Aisha say? Aisha was always pleasant and friendly, but our relationship had not developed beyond the discussion of chores in the house. She had not asked us back to her house, and she still did not speak about her family or encourage me to discuss mine.

But she lived in the medina; she lived on our street; she was a neighbor, and she worked for us. She had been noncommittal in her answers when I had asked specific questions about Rue Trésor. How would she react to my asking her for help? What would I do if she refused? I put that thought out of my mind.

"Aisha," I began the next morning, as we shelled fresh peas for lunch, "does your daughter wear the djellaba?"

"Of course!"

"Do you think Laura Ann should wear one?"

She looked at me, a bit startled, I thought, and her eyes narrowed —brown, dark, intelligent eyes—and she looked away and resumed her shelling. She shelled rapidly and efficiently, without mess, not like me.

"Laura Ann is not a Moroccan. She is an American, a Nasrani. They don't wear djellabas."

In the short pause that followed we both continued shelling peas. Inwardly I took a breath and started again, recounting our trip to the bazaar and the incident with Laura Ann, and how I didn't want to have it happen again. And how, I rushed on, having lived in Egypt, and in Iraq, and in other parts of the Middle East, I realized their customs were different from ours in America, and that since we had chosen to live in the medina, I wanted to have Laura Ann learn to understand those customs and like Morocco, and behave like the girls here. Aisha said nothing. She drew in a deep breath. I waited.

"You would like to buy a djellaba for Laura Ann?"

"If you think it is a good idea so people on the street don't say bad things to her."

Aisha snorted. It was her first emotional reaction, and I was delighted.

"People on the street, outside your house, always say bad things. They say bad things to everyone. One must pay no attention. Ignore them."

Pause. I returned to the subject. "Do you think a djellaba would be a good idea?"

Aisha considered. "It would be nice for her to take back a souvenir of Morocco," she allowed.

Okay, I thought. "Yes," I said. "It would."

Aisha finished the peas, swept the pods into the garbage can, rinsed the peas, covered them, and put them on the stove. She scrubbed the tile drainboard with hard, strong strokes of her arms.

"Hajja Kenza," she pronounced, "will know an honest merchant who makes djellabas of good quality, and will not cheat you."

"Would she take me and Laura Ann?"

"I'll ask her," said Aisha.

Hajja Kenza, Aisha reported next morning at breakfast, would be happy to take us to a djellaba merchant. Today, in fact, about six.

"Six? So late?"

"It's so crowded then, Betty," said Alta. "Ask her if she can't go earlier." Alta and Laila were united in their distaste for the pushing, milling crowds that jammed the markets after sunset.

But when I told Aisha this, she said, surprised, "Of course it's crowded. That's when everyone goes to the market. The merchants only open their shops when there is a crowd. So . . ."

"I guess we'll have to go when Hajja Kenza wants to."

"Not me," said Laila. "I'll stay here with Baba."

Alta was wavering, but I think she was interested in watching Hajja Kenza bargain. So was I.

At six o'clock promptly Hajja Kenza herself knocked ceremoniously at our door.

"You see, I have no key, Elizabetha," she said, slyly, and gave me her golden grin. Her daughter Naima slipped in behind her, and she and Laura Ann examined the cloth of Naima's new blue djellaba.

"Would you like to drink some tea, Madame?"

Hajja Kenza held up her hand. "Later, later, when our business is done. So Laura Ann wants a djellaba." She nodded her head in approval. "Girls her age need one," she said to me in a loud conspiratorial tone, making her meaning clear by pressing her hand upon her ample, if dropped, bosom.

"Alta wants one, too, and so do I."

Hajja Kenza furrowed her brow, and the eyebrows contracted around the tiny tattoo between them. She nodded her head again. "Three djellabas." Her eyes grew round. "We must be very careful. These days everyone is out to cheat you!"

"Tell her I like the material of her djellaba, and if we can find one like that it would be fine . . . ," said Alta.

We all fingered the material of Hajja Kenza's djellaba, peach-colored sharkskin with faint pin stripes of brown. Very effective and cool-looking. With her white veil adjusted over her face and her enormous tortoise-shell-framed sunglasses, she looked very chic.

I was glad Aisha was coming, for although my understanding of local Arabic was improving, I was not sure I would be able to grasp the complicated bargaining sessions I felt lay ahead of us.

"*Yallah!*" Hajja Kenza led the way, like a marshal of her troops, and we followed obediently behind, Naima in her blue djellaba, Laura Ann and I in sleeveless dresses, Alta in a flowered shift, Aisha in her old brown djellaba, which was all she had.

The children of Rue Trésor, so ready for action when we went out alone, scattered before Hajja Kenza as she marched magnificently forward, deigning to speak only to the bath boy lounging before the pit where the fires were built to heat the water, to tell *him* to get out of the way. Two women with their bundles of clean clothes were going into the public bath and spoke to Aisha. The children at the little store did not say a word. We emerged onto Rue Bab Agnaou, clogged now with the after-siesta traffic, and tried to keep pace with Hajja Kenza, who tunneled ever forward, off the pavement, on the pavement, not bothering to dodge the trucks and taxis and donkeys. They seemed to be dodging *her!*

I was seized with a sudden strange sense of exhilaration. Was it the effect of a decision and some action at last? I did not know. But I found it cheering to be taken into the market by a guide as formidable as Hajja Kenza. Who knew what she might lead us into? The air was filled with a fine haze of dust that set me to coughing again. Aisha pounded me on the back. Our leader, in her chic djellaba, still showing the perfect creases on each side where it had been ritually folded, was an easy figure to follow, peach-colored against the grays of the donkeys, the browns of the other djellabas, the red walls, the faded blues of the young men's Tuareg cotton summer robes.

Hajja Kenza charged into the street from the Café des Glaciers toward Djemaa el Fna, and we followed her blindly, not even pausing for the carriages and cars that normally blocked our way for several minutes. Laura Ann turned around when we had gotten to the other side and shouted gleefully, "She doesn't stop for anybody, does she?" Then she hurried to catch up, for Hajja Kenza was going on, not pausing before the snake charmer or the storyteller or the pigeon man, nor before the dancers or the *oud* players or the man walking on broken glass. The child beggars and the young men yearning to be your "guide through marvelous market of Marrakech" fell away before her advance, and she did not even favor the beggars' chorus with a glance. We were eased suddenly and together into the large alley that gives onto the spice market: henna, pepper, dates, nuts, pickled lemons, olives, chick-peas, split peas, beans, rice. The aroma, pungent and marvelous, cut through the hundreds of other odors—

the combination of sweat, perfume, wood, garbage, varnish, urine, and the faint, musty odor of carpets kept for long periods in chests and closed cupboards.

We could not walk together in the mobs that were pouring now through the narrow arched gate into the Semmarine, so we walked in a ragged single file, though Laura Ann kept close to me. Hajja Kenza was our vanguard, and she pushed on steadily, peach-colored shark-skin breasting the crowd, not casting a backward look at all the shirts, embroideries, golden stuffs, brass, sequined slippers, and hubbly-bubblies that had been strung up to attract, and were attracting, our eyes. We went on and on, passing through another bottleneck. The cobblestones became more uneven and the passage far more narrow. Where were we? Barefooted, ragged men with heavy burdens on their backs and men with pushcarts and a man with a donkey shouted "*balak, balak*" (watch out, watch out) and charged, apparently without glancing or hesitating, straight into the crowd. We flattened ourselves against the wall of a shop upon which rows of embroidered blue shirts hung, and by the time the mountain of wooden boxes, painted yellow with blue corners, had passed, we had lost sight of our mentor and guide.

"Betty, I don't see Hajja Kenza," said Alta, tentatively stepping out from our flattened position against the wall. "What do we do now?"

"Where are we, Mama?" said Laura Ann, leaning forward toward me and nearly getting clopped on the head by the second load of yellow-and-blue chests heading past us down the narrow passage.

I hated to confess that I didn't know, and wasn't, in fact, exactly certain which turn would take us to the Semmarine and eventually to Djemaa el Fna. I played for time by saying brightly, "Why don't we just stay here a moment? Surely Aisha will notice we've gone, and come back."

Which is what we did, fortunately, for another load of boxes threatened us with extinction. (Where were all these chests going?) When they had passed and we had nodded and smiled at the shirt merchant against whose display we had pressed ourselves for the third time, we felt we had to pretend that we really wanted a blue shirt for Laura Ann, who looked mutinously at me as the merchant, young and obviously delighted, held up the shirt over her front to see "whether it might do."

"Ha, Elizabetha!" sounded above the noise. Aisha came out of a tiny cubicle perhaps three doors ahead of the shirt shop and opposite it, and indicated that we were to follow.

We did as we were told. "Aren't you glad to see Aisha, Mama?" said Laura Ann, jumping forward. I was more than glad. Alta breathed an audible sigh of relief.

The shop to which our valiant mentor had brought us was tiny, narrow, and contained perhaps twenty djellabas in various conservative colors: brown, blue, wine, hung up three or four rows to the ceiling. A young man, slim, dark, mustached, was arguing with Hajja Kenza; she had stationed herself at the one point in the shop that prevented him from leaving his place behind the counter. He was trapped. This young man, we were told in a subwhisper by Aisha, was "a very good merchant" whom "Kenza knew and was friendly with."

I translated this for Alta and Laura Ann, and Alta said, "Well, Betty, if that is a demonstration of friendliness, what, might I ask, is unfriendliness?"

For it was true that Hajja Kenza seemed on the verge of physically attacking the young man, whose alternate sitting and rising seemed simply another form of pacing nervously within a cage. She had caught him and would not let him go until she had said her piece.

While the haranguing was going on, two lady customers (heavily veiled) had silently melted away, followed by the young man's mournful eyes, and we were alone in the narrow shop, Alta, Laura Ann, Aisha, Naima, Hajja Kenza, and myself. This had been Hajja Kenza's aim, for now she came out and introduced us, with a grand gesture. We all shook hands. The young man smiled tentatively at us, one eye still on our leader.

A boy with a shaved head materialized from the street; small stools were brought forward and we were urged to sit down. We sat down.

But after half an hour's discussion, during which we sat unnoticed on our hard stools, I began to wonder whether Hajja Kenza had come on her own business or on ours.

I decided to take bold, firm action. I stood up. The young man looked gratefully at me.

"My daughter," I said in French, "needs a djellaba. Also my mother-in-law. Also, perhaps me."

Hajja Kenza interrupted loudly. We were off. The young man, using a long pole with a hook on the end of it, brought down several djellabas for us to try, but our leader had rejected them all before we had time to open our mouths.

Laura Ann said crossly, "I'm the one who wants a djellaba, not her. I want a blue one like Naima's."

Naima picked that up and signaled to her mother that Laura Ann wanted a blue one like hers. Hajja Kenza shook her head. "No blue ones! Can't you see for yourselves?"

"Isn't it possible to have one made?" I said.

The young man (Omar) said of course, Hajja Kenza said only if the price was right, and Omar signaled to the boy, who returned with a tape measure. Everyone began to smile, but Hajja Kenza held up her peach-covered arm imperiously. The young man held the tape, suspended. Through Aisha, I learned that we should not begin measuring and ordering until the price had been set.

Omar sat down. He was by now perspiring. So were we all. The real business had begun.

In between floods of unrecognizable Arabic, I caught flashes.

"Much too high for such poor material."

"It is not poor material, it is excellent material."

"I bring you all this business—three djellabas—three—and you cannot even given me a decent price. . . ."

Naima and Laura Ann gestured together, Alta looked worried, I was getting exceedingly hot and tired, but Aisha seemed pleased and not at all upset.

"Kenza is a very good bargainer," she said to me. "She is working hard for you."

Ah, yes. I was beginning to have new respect for Hajja Kenza's powers of survival and over-all energy. Who had said that in the Middle East all women are passive and submissive?

"Your friend is very difficult," said Omar in French, turning to me in appeal.

That prompted a veritable flood of what sounded like abuse from Hajja Kenza, and Aisha looked positively delighted.

Finally, after an hour, we seemed to be at a stalemate.

"Betty, I think we should go," said Alta, and rose.

"Sit down," thundered our leader.

We sat down.

She sniffed, adjusted her sunglasses, and turned as if to leave.

"Get up," thundered Hajja Kenza.

We got up.

Omar passed his hand over his eyes and capitulated.

Hajja Kenza was triumphant. "Sixty dirhams," she hissed.

"For all three?" muttered Alta. I knew this was wrong but could not resist repeating it to Kenza.

She looked scandalized. She took off her sunglasses. "For *each!*" she said scathingly. "Look at the material, the sewing, the braid, the zipper fastener. Doesn't shrink. What do you think, he'd give them to us free?" She sounded like Omar. "It is excellent material!"

We agreed. Laura Ann was measured. Alta was measured. I was measured. Mine was to be sea green, Laura Ann's and Alta's blue, the same blue Laura Ann had indicated at least a full hour ago. With black braid trim. And a zipper. And two hoods. Yes. Yes.

Kenza pulled her veil back up, preparatory to leaving. Omar shook hands with all of us, and smiled, but at Hajja Kenza he did not smile; his glance, however, was admiring, I thought. "She is very hard," said he to me in French. The djellabas were to be ready in a week.

We went home, Kenza leading the way once more, faster, like a girl let out of school. She was obviously pleased with herself. And she sat in our courtyard, drinking Coca-Cola from the store, and regaled us for some time about how one had to know the right people (i.e., herself) to get along in Marrakech, where everyone was out to make money and you could be cheated any day of the week if you weren't careful. According to Kenza the streets were full of trash, vagabonds, people who had no respect and no family.

With Aisha's help we managed to get across to her our inexpressible thanks for her help.

"Yes," she said, "it is always better to have someone go with you to the market, because you look like tourists and anyone will overcharge a tourist. Why not? They're rich, they can afford it. You, my dear, of course, with the children . . ." As she and I understood, children are a great expense and allowances were obviously being made for our being rich because presumably we would spend our large supplies of dollars on our children's upbringing and education—as well as the rent!

We thanked her again. When we picked up the djellabas a week later, they were beautifully made, they fit, and everyone was pleased. We paid what we'd been told to pay, and on the way home we bought face veils worked in cross-stitch with a Berber geometric design. In the courtyard we tried everything on, and Kenza and Aisha showed Laura Ann how to pin the veil in the back and adjust the hood around it.

"Now," Kenza said, "you look proper. You'll be all right. But don't go to Djemaa el Fna alone. It's not safe. Not safe. Full of riffraff."

And wagging her finger in my face as a last admonishment, she put on her sunglasses and left.

We felt quite set up. Djellabas, veils, and perhaps the beginning of a new relationship with Hajja Kenza? Who knew what might happen next on Rue Trésor?

The next morning our landlady arrived at the door early. I offered her coffee, which she took absent-mindedly, after sitting down in one of our new canvas lawn chairs—for courtyard sitting, I explained.

"Ah, yes. How much?" The ultimate compliment, I knew.

She settled back and sipped her coffee noisily. I coughed and sneezed and sputtered over mine. Alta came out and joined us. Kenza had something on her mind.

"Well." She set down her empty coffee cup on the tile floor. (We had no coffee table yet, but were looking for one of the round wooden tables common in Moroccan households.)

"There is one more school that might admit your children."

The Moroccan schools had been in session for a week, and although the French Lycée had not yet begun, I was certain she had heard, via Aisha, the news that our children were not considered worthy.

"What school is that?"

"The Hebrew School."

"The Hebrew School?"

"Yes, the Hebrew School," Kenza replied pettishly. I was being dense again. "It's a good school, near the Kasbah gate. Naima will take you there, now. Put on your djellaba and go with her."

I turned to Naima, standing against the wall, waiting.

"They speak in French or in Arabic or in Hebrew?" For some reason (native intelligence, I thought, and perhaps more experience with listening occasionally), Naima did not have as much difficulty understanding my Egyptian Arabic as her mother.

"All three, Madame," answered Naima. "My mother thought maybe the children could speak Hebrew. It's easier than French."

I could not think what to reply. "No," I said sadly. "I'm afraid my children only speak English," certain again that one foreign language would be difficult enough for them; three would be impossible.

"Take them! Take them!" Kenza was urging me on like a cheerleader, patting me on the shoulder, pounding me on the knee.

"They *must* go to school. Don't children go to school in America, or do they all run on the streets like those . . . (she groped for a word) those dirty *heepees* next door?"

I coughed to gain time.

"We will try to teach them at home, Mrs. Harris, the other American lady, and me."

"What? Are you a teacher?" She whacked me on the arm, playfully. "If so, why not teach me, too?" She laughed uproariously at the absurdity of such a possibility. "Do you think I could learn from you, Elizabetha? Hahahahaha! Tell Madame, your husband's mother" (leaning close and whispering as though Alta, sitting right with us, might overhear), "that I will learn English from you. Hahahahaha! She won't believe you for a minute."

Alta smiled politely. Aisha tried to translate. I tried to explain about home tutoring and books sent from America, but it was too difficult to get across. Even Aisha shook her head. I was obviously a hopeless case, and there was nothing more to be done with me. Kenza stood up, slapped her sides in a gesture of despair, and bade me farewell. A fit of coughing prevented my replying.

The next day I discovered I had a fever, and I stayed in bed in the tiled room, meditating on the plaster flowers and vines that twined about our ceiling. Bob and Ernest Harris had found me some strong cough syrup, and it helped, but I felt weak from fever, heat, and codeine. The future seemed more bleak than ever, and I dreamed of streets lined with iron doors and high, forbidding walls where I heard people whispering from barred windows and felt unseen eyes staring into my head. But when, in my dream, I looked up, the windows in the walls had disappeared and the whispering had stopped and I stood in a narrow, empty street, alone.

Bob had taken the children out, and Alta was helping Aisha make lunch. It never ceased to amaze me how Aisha and Alta talked together in different languages and seemed to understand each other perfectly. Obviously I was trying too hard to learn Moroccan Arabic. What was the use anyway? Their murmuring voices and the soft splash of water in our little fountain reached me where I lay, high up in the bright tiled room. The fever must be rising, I thought, for I dozed and dreamed again that the flowers on the tiles had bloomed before my eyes and died and now were blossoming again in different, iridescent colors.

"They're in! They're in!" Bob's voice penetrated the half dream and I sat up, suddenly awake.

"We're in, Mama!" The children came rushing up the stairs. "The French school says we can start on Monday, only two days late. . . ."

". . . if we're good and don't misbehave . . ."

". . . and if Baba gets us a tutor to help us with our French . . ."

". . . and if we eat lunch there."

"What do they eat for lunch, do you think?" Laila was suddenly anxious again.

". . . and if we go to French classes at night, too. Why do we have to go at night if we go in the daytime?"

"What's that, Bob? The French school said yes?" cried Alta. "I don't understand. Why did they change their minds?"

"I don't know and I didn't ask," said Bob. "I paid the tuition and so did Ernest and they start on Monday, thank God!"

"The Harris kids, too! Oh, great!" The children rushed around the courtyard, telling Aisha, telling Grandma Tanny, and then rushing up the stairs to tell me the good news all over again.

Laura Ann brought my lunch on a tray. "Isn't it wonderful, Mama?" Her face darkened. "But how will we understand what the teachers are saying?"

I patted her hand. "It'll be hard at first, but you'll do it. That's why they want you to have a tutor and go to French classes at night, so you'll understand quicker."

"What does *merde* mean?" asked David, laughing in the doorway.

"Oh, David!"

"How do you ask to go to the bathroom in French?" It was Laila.

"Come down and leave your mother in peace," shouted Bob. "She's sick."

Someone was pounding on the door. In a moment the court was full of hullabaloo and that well-known throaty laugh. What did Kenza want *now*?

"It's Hajja Kenza, Betty, she wants to see you," called Alta. "Shall I send her up?"

Oh, no, I thought, I feel so awful, and this room is such a mess. Bob had begun to unpack his books and papers and office supplies, and they were strewn across the floor and lay in piles over half the room. But then, in my fever, I had an inspiration.

"Yes, yes," I cried. "Send her up."

She was wearing her peach djellaba, and she sat down beside the bed and pulled down her veil and cleared her throat and looked at the bottle of medicine lying on the floor, squinting to read the letters, although I knew she could not read.

I told her the news about the French school, but my triumph was somewhat dimmed by the fact that she had already heard from Aisha. After a cozy little chat (no problem with the Arabic today, I noticed, maybe I should have bronchitis all the time) about how we managed that and who did we know in the French community and how much did it cost, I said shyly, casting my eyes down, "Please excuse the mess of the room, Hajja Kenza. But you see this is where my husband works all day and all night."

And I indicated, with a lofty gesture, the papers and books and file folders and pamphlets that covered the other end of the room.

Kenza turned and looked. She looked again. She stood up. She walked over and stood before the bookcases, filled with multicolored volumes. "Arabic," she breathed.

She touched the two typewriters, one still in its case, one open and with a half-typed letter inserted in the roller. She walked around the desk, peered at the letters from America with their strange stamps, picked up a sheet of crumpled carbon paper, a typewriter eraser, and examined a box of oversized paper clips.

"Ah!" she said. "Ah! He typewrites. Two machines. This is how he works. A real scholar. Ah!"

I tried to suppress a smile at the success of my inspiration, which was not difficult, as a spasm of coughing seized me.

"Ha!" Kenza was all business again. "You sound sick. Try some *aspro*."

I indicated the brown bottle of medicine.

"Hm," she said, picking it up. "Maybe I could use some of this. You give me some and I'll send you to the person who does my cutting."

"Cutting?" I was dumbfounded and tried to make some sense of the quick switch the conversation had taken. Surely my fever was playing tricks on me. She had not said "cutting," had she?

But while I pondered, Kenza had pulled her veil all the way down her neck and lifted her head so that I could see a row of tiny knife cuts, like dark lines, under her tattooed chin. Bits of dried blood still clung to one of the cuts.

"It helped my headache. It might help your cough. Let me know when you decide, and I'll make you an appointment."

I nodded weakly. A cupful of cough syrup in exchange for the name of a person who would let my blood with . . . what? Knives? It looked like knives, but could it be leeches? I had no idea. I shivered and felt hot at the same time.

At the aubergine and green door Kenza paused. "I'm going to buy a television, Elizabetha," she announced.

Tit for tat, I thought wildly. One could never best Hajja Kenza for more than five minutes.

At the time we wondered what made the French school director change his mind. Was it Ernest, black American scientist, representative of the U. S. Government, speaking gently to the consul about French-American co-operation in the field? Was it Bob, white American professor, telling the French schoolmaster about the great benefits that our American children might gain from a taste of French education? Or both? We later discovered that a kind diplomat we had met in the American Embassy had mentioned our plight to an equally kind counterpart in the French Embassy. But at the time we simply accepted the decision with thankfulness. Bettye came over and we embraced in celebration: We would not have to tutor our dear children all year, after all. Aisha was jubilant. She told me how happy she was for me. By virtue of our children's admission into Marrakech's most elitist school, we had attained a degree of respectability in spite of ourselves. Further, Hajja Kenza had decided Bob really did work. I thanked Aisha, turned over, and slept, deeply, and had gorgeous wide-screen technicolored dreams.

The children began classes. Now that we were firmly on the road to respectability, Hajja Kenza had ceased her daily counseling visits about the school problem. I was rather relieved, for I was spared the decision about whether to consult her personal bloodletter. I lay in bed, coughing, with my brown bottle of codeine syrup beside me. Bob and Alta took the children down to the bookstores in Gueliz and invested in dollars' and dollars' worth of books, special pens for penmanship, map pencils, protractors, notebooks, compasses, and bags in which to carry all this paraphernalia back and forth: a black briefcase for Laura Ann, a backpack for David, a yellow-and-white plastic satchel for Laila. They had picked them out themselves, Alta said.

"How can Moroccans afford to send their children to school?" asked Bob. "I must have laid out thirty or forty dollars per child, just for materials."

"Maybe books are free in the government schools," I suggested. "I'll ask Aisha."

"Oh, no," she said. "We have to buy our own, just like you. It's not so bad for Youssef, he's in elementary, but for Najiya and Abdul Karim and Saleh, it becomes more expensive each year.

"There is the book co-operative," she added, explaining that at the end of each school year, parents exchanged books at certain percentage of loss for each year the book had been used. "That helps some."

My bronchitis gradually improved. Ernest Harris and Bob enrolled the children in evening French lessons at the Mission Culturelle Française, as per instructions from the school. We decided to join our children and improve our own French by enrolling in the adult conversation class. We clubbed together, four adult and five child Americans in the crowds of hundreds of Moroccans of all ages and socio-economic groups who flocked to the evening classes to learn French. For although Morocco had been an independent nation since the end of colonial rule in 1956, and Arabic was the official language, many government and business offices still conducted their affairs in French. The tourist trade formed a sizable portion of the Moroccan national income, and hotels and shops and restaurants paid more to employees who could speak French. Parents sent their children to improve their French so that they might pass the baccalaureate examinations at a high enough level to be eligible for the free government universities.

In the beginning Ernest and Bettye, Bob and I entertained notions of making some Moroccan acquaintances in the class where we were, after all, engaged in the endeavor of learning to converse in a mutually foreign language. Our fellow pupils, most in traditional djellabas (though the women wore head scarves rather than veils), nodded politely at the beginning and end of each two-hour session, but otherwise left us strictly alone. Was it the language barrier, traditional reserve, suspicion of foreigners, or a combination of all three? We could not tell.

With the children, the situation at the evening classes was not ambivalent at all. David, Greg, Laila, Laura Ann, and Tanya complained that they were jostled and teased constantly, both in and out of class. They were chased, they said, on their way back to our house, where they waited until our two-hour class was finished. At first we did not take these reports too seriously.

"You're new," Ernest pointed out. "You know how new kids get treated at school."

But one night we came home to find Laila in tears, her bloody knee being washed by Laura Ann and Tanya.

"A whole lotta kids knocked her down, and I helped her up," Greg told us.

"We tried to fight back," said Laura Ann, "and David and Tanya took off after the worst guys, but everybody ran away."

The four adults exchanged glances.

"We've got to put a stop to this sort of thing," said Ernest briskly.

"Why did they knock me down? I didn't do anything to them," Laila sniffled. The cut was only a surface laceration, but it was painful.

"They're jealous," suggested Bettye. "You kids all have new clothes and good shoes and they don't. You have to try to understand how they feel."

"Look," said Bob. "You're foreign, odd-looking, and rich. You can't talk to them, and they don't know how nice you are. Give it some time. Of course they're jealous."

"I don't like them, I don't like them, I don't like them," sobbed Laila.

"But I guess they're sort of mixed up, too," said Laura Ann.

"Yeah, Laila," put in Tanya. "Remember, one of the guys who knocked you down helped us pick you up."

Ernest smiled. "You see, Laila, maybe he doesn't like you as a foreigner, but as a person he does. It's hard to live with, though, I do agree."

"Can't you do something, Baba?" Laura Ann appealed to her father.

"Maybe Aisha would pick them up," he suggested.

Aisha agreed.

"Those boys who tease them have no manners," she said. "They are not polite. Tell your children to ignore them."

I passed this advice on to the children. But with Aisha present, they reported no one bothered them any longer, at least not after class. They also announced that Aisha often brought along one of her own sons, who seemed about Laura Ann's age. This was interesting, since I had never even seen any of Aisha's children. I told her to thank her son. She smiled, and said she would, but did not volunteer any more information about him.

The five American children drew together, as the four adults drew together. Bettye and Ernest and Bob and I were having our problems, too, for it seemed that though all of us in class knew certain amounts of French, our accents were far worse than the Moroccans'. In fact, our accents were abominable. We struggled to sound our *r*'s properly, stammering through seemingly witless phrases about Madame and Monsieur Thibault, a French middle-class family who lived on the fourth floor of an apartment house on Place d'Italie,

Paris! What did it matter that we had studied French for years in
college and had actually visited Place d'Italie, Paris? The men and
women who sat at desks near us in the grubby schoolroom, who had
never been outside Morocco and many of whom had never finished
elementary school, could roll their r's gloriously. They could converse
about the Thibault family quite glibly. Yet we could not say the simplest two-phrase sentence in a way that pleased our teacher, an intense and extremely intelligent young Moroccan whose goal was per-
fection! How humiliating!

While my French seemed to languish, despite the hours I spent on
it, my Arabic was improving. Bettye Harris had introduced me to a
butcher and a vegetable merchant, to whom *she* had been introduced
by a Moroccan colleague of Ernest's. These shops were in a small
market off Djemaa el Fna, a convenient walk from our house. The
personal introduction made a difference. The butcher, Haj Mahmoud, had previously shaken his head in noncomprehension when I
tried to describe in Arabic the cut of beefsteak I wanted. Now he
shook hands warmly whenever I appeared, and he produced not only
beefsteak but also lamb chops and even a plucked chicken when
before it seemed he was insisting he had no chickens at all! As the
days passed, my marketing Arabic improved in regular contacts with
the dozen merchants in that small suq, and my ties with the Western
city weakened.

"You have lived in Egypt?" said the young vegetable merchant. He
cut away the ragged tops of onions as he talked.

"Yes."

"And what did your husband do there?"

"He was a professor at the university."

"Which is more beautiful, Egypt or Morocco?"

"Oh," said I, diplomatically, "they are both beautiful, but
different. Egypt is on the river Nile, Morocco has the mountains and
the sea."

"Which are nicer, Moroccans or Egyptians?"

"Both are nice," I answered dutifully, but added mutinously,
"Egyptians are friendlier."

Then, as I was turning to go, my market basket filled with green
peppers and cucumbers, tomatoes and bananas, the vegetable
merchant said, "Is it true that you are really an Egyptian and only
your husband is American?"

I opened and shut my mouth in amazement. "Who says that?"

"Haj Mahmoud the butcher thinks that's the reason you can speak Arabic."

"No, I am an American, too."

"Then why do you speak Arabic?" asked the merchant.

"Arabic is a beautiful language," I answered, and moved on to the Berber grocer on the corner, who stood behind his display case full of jam, raisins, rice, packaged puddings from France, cheese, cornstarch.

"*Lebas, Alalla?*" (How are you, Madame?) he greeted me warmly in Arabic.

Whatever my reputed nationality, he had me figured out, and he was right. He knew if he spoke Arabic, I made regular purchases at his shop. Why not? He was closer to home, I could practice Arabic, and I was learning to bargain. But the vegetable merchant's question had startled me. Why had I learned Arabic in the first place? For the same reason most people learn a second language—because I had need of it. In the village of Iraq, no other language was understood. But in a colonially dominated city, it was obviously the natives who had to learn their masters' language; I was odder here than I had realized.

On November 1, Alta sailed for America and we drove to Casablanca to put her on board the boat. By the time we returned to Marrakech, the weather had changed. The hot summer was over, and keeping warm became a real problem. Those beautiful tiles that stored the heat so neatly during the summer now seemed to hold the cold equally well. We invested in two small portable kerosene heaters and bought long underwear for everyone, heating the person, not the rooms, as Bob pointed out. There was no heat in the schoolrooms either, the children reported. At night, we wore our coats and scarves in the French classes, and went to bed early.

Rue Trésor seemed quieter than in the summer. Perhaps everyone else went to bed earlier, too. Aisha reported that Hajja Kenza was ailing.

"Should I go to visit her?"

"Why?" asked Aisha, surprised.

"It is our custom in America to visit a sick person."

"She is not that sick," said Aisha. And that was that.

Naima and Laura Ann's friendship had promised well in the beginning. They had gone to the suq together in their blue djellabas, and Laura Ann reported no one even looked at them. The djellaba made a difference, then, if one were in the traditional city. But the friendship was dying through lack of contact. Our children were in the French school and Naima was in the Moroccan school all day long.

Laura Ann and Naima still greeted each other on the street, I noticed, or Naima would call down to Laura Ann from the second-floor window sill, where a single white geranium, Hajja Kenza's pride, bloomed in its pot. On Wednesdays, when the French school had a holiday, Laura Ann went to her tutor, a pleasant and intelligent young Frenchwoman who was working on a doctorate in English from Bordeaux University. Her help was invaluable to Laura Ann, who was now expected to write essays and record scientific experiments in proper French.

"She must attempt them," her teacher had written, and we agreed. Laura Ann was generally cheerful. She reported friendliness from her classmates, especially Eve, daughter of a Polish engineer working for the Moroccan Government, who had come to the Lycée three years before, not knowing a single word of French. That experience had probably given her the sympathy to understand Laura Ann's similar plight. I began to hear about Denise, whose father was a "rose farmer," and Simy, whose father was a master jeweler in the gold market. We went to visit his shop in the enclosed square near the Bahia Palace and looked at the Berber silver, the jade earrings, the pearls, the gold bracelets and the charms—tiny worked hands of Fatima. Laura Ann was invited to a birthday party.

Laila and David were not so lucky at first, but they had Tanya and Greg for company in the lower school, "L'École Renoir," and did not have to make the same gestures of friendship as Laura Ann. All four talked about how good the lunches were and how complicated the "rules" of the school were. Lunchroom etiquette seemed nonexistent; one was allowed to overturn one's plate if the food was not good, and no one scolded. But the seating in the lunchroom seemed fixed. "I finally figured it out," said Davy. "The Moroccans sit by themselves and the French sit by themselves; they're at one long table, but not together."

"Where do you sit?"

"In between," he answered.

Schoolroom etiquette was strict. First rule: Stand up automatically whenever an adult enters the room. After David had been castigated twice for remaining seated when the director marched in unannounced, David leaped to his feet one morning when an unknown gentleman entered. David was perplexed to find himself the only person standing, while all the children tittered and even the teacher and the gentleman who had entered smiled.

"I don't understand," I had said.

"I didn't either, but they told me later the guy was the custodian and you don't stand up for custodians."

Breaking the classroom rules brought immediate punishments such as slapping, being sent to stand in a corner, or whacking with a ruler. Since the children could not always understand the reason for the punishment witnessed, the pattern at first seemed sinister and threatening. Laila later told me that for the first weeks she sat, hands clasped, with a permanent lump in her throat. Why?

"Well, I didn't know exactly what anybody was saying and I was scared I'd do the wrong thing and then they'd punish me for something I didn't even know I'd done!"

I chided myself for complaining about the lack of neighborliness on Rue Trésor. That was a problem I could cope with or not, as I wished. The children had no such option.

David's school problems were somewhat complicated. He had to establish himself in this particular male society, and as on schoolyards everywhere, this involved fighting. The first week he came home with a suspicious-looking eye; surely it was black, I thought.

"It's nothing," he said.

He refused to talk about it until two weeks later, when we were all sitting together at the Harris's house, around their lovely enormous space heater, newly arrived from the capital in Rabat.

"You should've seen Davy, he beat up the meanest boy in school yesterday," said Greg admiringly.

Davy looked offhand or tried to, but the story gradually emerged.

Each day on entering the schoolground, he had been waylaid by three French boys. Hence the black eye. Each day he had fought back. Stalemate. These were short skirmishes, apparently, because adult surveillance of the schoolyard was intense and all-encompassing, and once the boys were caught and punished by the teachers. Finally the time came for the match between Davy and Jean-Pierre, "the meanest," said Laila.

"What happened?"

"Well, I was sort of scared," Davy confessed, "because I really didn't think I could beat him. Besides, the French boys don't fight like us. They hit below the belt, they pinch, scratch, bite, anything goes. This day I put on all the clothes I could find, to protect me, and when I came in the gates, everybody was standing around waiting. Boy, was I scared!"

"Why didn't you say something about it?"

Davy looked at me scathingly.

"So?"

"So," said Davy, "Jean-Pierre came up to me, and everybody was looking on and I was getting ready to put my schoolbag down, and he dismissed the fellas and said, come over here. And we went behind a tree and I thought oh, boy, now we get something new, but what? And then . . ."

"Yes?" Even his older sister and Bettye Harris were hanging on every word.

"Well, when we got behind a tree, Jean-Pierre raised his hand and I put up my schoolbag to counter that one, and then he held out his hand and said, 'Let's not fight, okay? Let's finish.'"

"Boy, was I surprised! I said okay, but even though he had his hand out, I thought it might be a trick, those guys are *mean*, and so I gave him the Longhorn salute and he said, 'What's that?'"

"I said, 'Texas. Friends.' He turned white and said, 'You're from *Texas?*'"

"Yes."

"Can you ride horses?"

"Yes!"

"And your father has guns that go pow pow?"

"I said 'Yeah,' and he believed me. Boy, was he dumb. He shook my hand over and over again and then he went back and told everybody I was from Texas and, guess what, no trouble since. They figure I have a secret weapon."

"What?" we asked.

Davy laughed. "Baba's a cowboy!"

We all laughed, a bit hollowly, perhaps. Bob groaned.

"And so everything is okay now?"

"Yeah. Let's go play soccer, you-all."

Tanya and Greg and Davy and Laura Ann and Laila went outside to play in the palm grove beside the Harris house, with Mohammed, the son of the Harris's cook. They relaxed together. What would they have done without each other?

The weather turned colder, rain poured into our courtyard, we bought rubber boots for the children from the BATA store on Rue

Bab Agnaou, and were glad of our down sleeping bags, which we used as quilts. Who would have believed that sunny, rosy Marrakech could be so cold, damp, and gray? The basin of our fountain overflowed, the goldfish swam crazily around, and the days were punctuated by the surging sound of water, water pouring into the courtyard drains, into the manhole outside on Rue Trésor, where Aisha regularly emptied the pails of water she mopped up from the bright-tiled floors. I wondered about my neighbors, but reflected that I probably would never find out whether they were damp and cold or not, since I still knew no one except Aisha, Abdul Kabeer the shopkeeper, Moussa the baker, and Hajja Kenza, who hollered at me from her upstairs window, elbows propped on the sill beside a fern, which had replaced the geranium since the rains had begun.

"Oh, I'm poorly, Elizabetha. This weather is bad for my stomach!"

"I hope you feel better soon," I would shout back politely, as I picked my way down Rue Trésor, its broken asphalt somewhat muddy and treacherous in the rainy weather.

She would laugh and shout back, "What? What? I can't understand you," before she closed her window. One or two veiled ladies passing by would turn and look, then look away.

Our life on Rue Trésor gradually assumed a kind of pattern. Very early, the rhythmic swish of the garbage man's broom would be heard, cleaning up the night's litter and sweeping the standing rainwater into the central drain. Then came the crying of newly wakened babies and a mother shouting, "Quick, quick, get some milk from the store," and an obedient child's feet splashing down the street. The bakery truck roared and bicycles pealed their bells as they set off with the morning supply of fresh bread, its tantalizing scent cutting through the rain and damp to reach as high as our bedroom. The bakery's bicycle bells were my signal to get out of my warm bed, dress in all my clothes as quickly as possible, and run down to the freezing courtyard, to light the oven in the kitchen and the heater in the dining room, and put on the kettle for tea. Aisha's key would sound in the lock.

"*Lebas*, Aisha?" (How are you?)

"*Lebas. Intii lebas?*"

"*Lebas, el hamdillaa.*"

After we had comforted each other by repeating several times that yes, we were well, indeed, thanks be to God, the children would be downstairs, fully dressed, warming their hands over the kerosene heater before eating their eggs and bread, drinking up mugs of tea and hot chocolate. The books and notebooks and special pens would be packed into the schoolbags, their heavy coats would be buttoned, they would bid Aisha and me good-by and run along Rue Trésor with all the other children on their way to school. David always whammed the wall of the kitchen when he went by, a final kind of farewell, imitating the boys who knocked on all the doors of the houses as they passed through the zanka. The children would board the seven-thirty bus in front of the Parc Foucauld; the bus reached the other end of the line just in time for them to walk the last three blocks to the entrance of the Lycée Victor Hugo and L'École Renoir before the 8 A.M. closing of the school's massive iron gates.

I would eat a solitary breakfast and plan the meals for the day. Aisha would put the laundry to soak and then go home to have breakfast. Her own children would be off to school, and I could hear her shouting farewell, "Bslama Najiya! Bslama Youssef!" Bob would come down and, after a second cup of coffee, tell me his plans. By this time, he had emerged from his book-littered refuge and was exploring Marrakech. He had decided to focus his research on the markets and he spent his days visiting the scores of markets within the city and on its outskirts, markets in animals, vegetables, leather, grain, gold. Marrakech was still a clearinghouse for all the surrounding countryside, for goods from Mauritania and the Sahara to the south, for the manufactured articles from the new northern factories in Casablanca, for the imports from Europe. He had looked up Abdul Lateef, a Moroccan friend of a friend who lived near us in the medina, and with Abdul Lateef's help, was setting up tours and regular interviews at our house, over tea, in the evenings.

"It's an amazing system of markets," he explained to me. "All originally pre-industrial; some of the goods have changed, but the system seems to be the same as it was years ago, and the marvelous thing is that it is still working very efficiently."

A clanking of harness and a squeaking of wheels outside would interrupt our discussion.

"Whoa! Whoa!" The horse-drawn wagon had arrived at the bakery. One day the wagon brought flour, the next day it appeared with wood, cut into lengths to keep the fires burning in the public bath, to keep the ovens going in the bakery. From the window I could see the bath attendant, a teen-aged boy, opening up the long, dark passage where he slept at night on a pile of sacks and cardboard, with his djellaba for a blanket.

"He has the warmest bed on the street," sniffed Aisha, when I expressed sympathy for the boy. "He's right next to the fires."

The boy, Mbarak, his dark head wrapped turban fashion in a towel, and the old cart driver, in a patched coat and a fringed turban of faded orange silk, unloaded the wood, throwing the logs down and piling them in the passage, while the horses flicked their tails and jingled their harness, nosing at the bits of straw on the street.

The wagon was finally emptied, and the driver took the reins and began the complicated task of backing his horses out of Rue Trésor (the end of the street where the clinic was located was too narrow for the wagon to navigate the turn). Mbarak held the horses' halters and pushed, the old man in the frayed orange turban screamed and cursed and flicked his whip. It was not easy to back into the rush of traffic on Rue Bab Agnaou.

Eventually they were gone, and another, more modest clatter was heard, the clatter of coins in a metal bowl.

"Allah! Allah! Alms for the love of Allah!"

Down the street stumped a beggar, a tall man in immaculate skull-cap and patched olive-drab djellaba, a somewhat distinguished-looking personage despite his sightless half-shut eyes and the shabbiness of his attire. Aisha explained that this was "our beggar," Rue Trésor being his territory, that he was very worthy and clean and had a good wife. He knocked on the doors of those houses known to be attentive to the duties of the fourth pillar of Islam, tithing a certain percentage of one's income and giving alms to the poor. He did not stop at Kenza's, I noted, nor at our house, though occasionally I opened the door when I heard his step and dropped a coin into the chipped white enamel bowl chained to his wrist (How did he get it off at night—did his good clean wife have a key?).

Scarcely had the beggar's resonant cry receded than the cries of the peddlers were upon us.

"*Matishah! Matishah!*" (Tomatoes!)

"*Khizzu! Khizzu zween!*" (Good carrots!)

The mailman appeared on his bicycle, bringing letters and English newspapers for us. Down the street, the delivery boys had returned to the bakery from their morning rounds, and the hiccuping, hyenalike laugh of one of them sounded a note of hysteria up and down Rue Trésor.

"He's not crazy," Aisha had told me. "He's deaf and dumb, and this is the only sound he makes. But he is a good worker."

The vegetable peddler, the orange peddler, and the flower seller had come and gone. On Aisha's recommendation, I had begun to purchase eggs from the egg peddler, a man with a dry, seamed face, his djellaba patched, his fingers that handled the eggs in his basket so gently, knobbed and swollen with arthritis.

By ten Bob was off on his rounds and I left for the market, to buy meat and vegetables and fruits for lunch and dinner. Although the children ate a full meal at school, they were starving again when they got home, and I found that a cake would disappear at one meal, a batch of cookies lasted fifteen minutes, and a pot roast that would have fed us twice at home in Austin was gobbled up at one sitting. No one gained an ounce, but we seemed to be relatively healthy. Heaven knows, we had lots of fresh air!

"This is a much more reasonable way to live," Bob said to the children. "We adjust to the weather by dressing warmly, and keep our insides warm and our energy up by eating well."

"Yeah," David sounded unconvinced, but like me, he suffered more from the cold than his father.

"In America, we heat the whole house. Here," went on Bob, "they are much more economical. They heat the person rather than the house, to conserve energy."

"You've said that before, Baba," pointed out David.

"It's worth repeating," Bob answered.

After lunch, I would read, write letters, write in my notebook, then force myself out for a solitary visit to some as yet unknown part of the city of the Almohade, the Saadian, and the Almoravide dynasties. Following those colorful symbols on the tourist map, I found the Badi Palace (ruined abode of the Saadian rulers), the Saadian tombs, the old Koranic school (Medersa Bin Youssef), the museum of Dar Si Said. I glanced wistfully into the entrances of historic mosques and the saints' tombs found throughout the medina. The saints' tombs were always marked by a row of shoes beside the door, removed out of reverence by the faithful who were inside, paying their respects to the saints' memory. But my shoes never found a place there, since entrance to mosques and holy shrines was forbidden to non-Muslims.

"Visiting monuments doesn't tell you much about the people who live in the city," said Bob.

I knew this, but feeling stymied on Rue Trésor, I believed I had to make some effort to get out of my beautiful alien cage of a house and try at least to learn something about the history of the city we were living in.

Almost every day I passed through Djemaa el Fna, to do my shopping for food and other household errands. No longer did the would-be guides hassle me; I had learned to put them off with the one unanswerable retort: "I live in Marrakech." I gave coins to the beggars and the entertainers, and realized that I now recognized and was recognized in turn by many of the regulars who frequented the square. With the coming of winter, the population had thinned, but there were always a few Saharan dancers, the Gnaoua, to be found; even on the coldest days, they would be there in their white cotton robes and black hats embroidered with cowrie shells, jingling their *chkacheck* cymbals and moving their bare feet in rhythm on the damp ground. Every day at least one storyteller and one evangelist appeared, a snake charmer, an oud player, and perhaps the pigeon man with his birds. The carts and barrows sold mint tea, soup, and hot boiled potatoes with salt, and a man who drank boiling water had replaced the man who walked barefoot over broken glass, an apt adaption of the miracle to the season. But the beggars' chorus never failed to appear, dwindled or augmented depending on whether it was sunny or rainy, but always in the same place, the entrance to the Semmarine market.

"Allah! The most merciful, the most compassionate! Allah! Alms!"

Their call, discordant but insistent, cut through the roaring of the buses that loaded and unloaded near Haj Mahmoud's meat market, the grinding of cement for the new minaret rising, block by block, beside the small mosque that stood on the edge of the great square.

But though it was satisfying to be greeted and recognized occasionally, if only for the coins I contributed, I thought that the performers and beggars were probably somewhat marginal to the lives of the average Marrakshi. I could give a thousand coins to the pigeon man or the storyteller without ever learning anything about them or about the hooded and veiled men and women who comprised the audiences for the pigeon acts, the stories, the miracle of drinking of boiling water. What did these people think, feel, want? Where did they live? What did they do all day when they weren't in Djemaa el Fna? Just as Rue Trésor seemed as walled and secret as it had the first day we had arrived, so the city of Marrakech seemed to conduct its life in secret.

By four I was home again, in time to hear the calls of the knife

sharpener, the old man who bought and sold small amounts of grain
from housewives in need of instant cash, the tinker, the fortune teller
("*Shu-wa-fa!*"), the woman who bought old clothes ("*Mulat el
bali!*"), and the long thin sound of what sounded like a child's tin
birthday party horn. "Wheet! Wheet!" went the horn. The housewives gathered up the scraps of paper, and dust sweepings, the
peelings that could not be fed even to animals. They dropped these
bits into the frayed straw basket borne by the two afternoon garbage
collectors, an old man with a white beard, a younger man with a gray
beard. Even our garbage filled less than a gallon can each day—a
small fraction of our Stateside quota. The two old men dumped the
day's refuse into a larger basket, carried by a donkey patiently waiting
at the end of the street, where the tuberculosis clinic stood. Ulti-
mately this refuse would again be sorted and fed to cows—or to less
discriminating goats.

While the door was open for the garbage men, I sometimes saw
groups of djellabaed and veiled women going into the public bath,
bundles of towels and clean clothes carried in baskets over their arms.
I would hear them laughing together and be struck by a pang of envy
at the sound of that camaraderie, which seemed forever unavailable
to me. Taking a bath was a real social event, particularly in a bath
like our renovated Rue Trésor edifice. Bob had visited the bath, pro-
nouncing it adequate but unexceptional. I wondered whether I
should go, but I shrank from going alone, and Laura Ann had refused
to accompany me.

Before dark the children banged the silver knocker, unloaded their
schoolbags by the front door, and sat down to an early supper. The
winter night came down quickly and we would turn on the courtyard
lights, which illumined and reflected in the fountain, where Bob's
five new goldfish swam around and around in the cold water, orange
against the blue-and-yellow-tiled basin. Soon we were off to French
class, notebooks in hand, Bob and I, Laura Ann, David, and Laila,
down Rue Trésor to the tuberculosis clinic, a right turn across the
square where the boys were playing soccer, past the "pink hotel," as
Laila called it, the bicycle repair shop, and the cubbyhole where the
scribe still waited for customers. He sat beside his typewriter, hands
hidden in his wool djellaba for warmth, under the sign that pro-
claimed that here, for a modest fee, letters of all kinds could be
written in both French and Arabic.

We went through a narrow alley, held our breath as we passed the men's *pissoir,* and emerged onto Rue Mellah, where a man and a boy sat on the corner before a tiny charcoal fire, offering roasted field corn for sale. We crossed together the stream of winter evening traffic, dodging the brown-and-yellow taxis, the bicycles, motorcycles, and donkey carts, all traveling at different speeds, and finally made it to the secondary school of Arset el Ma'ach, which was rented at night by the Mission Culturelle Française. We sat at desks covered with revolutionary slogans carved there day after day by rebellious students: "Death to traitors!" "Down with the King!" And we struggled with French sentences describing further dull events in the lives of Monsieur and Madame Thibault; we talked about their dining room and their summer vacation, repeating again and again for our perfectionist teacher, "*Madame Thibault est dans la cuisine. Elle prepare le dîner. Monsieur Thibault est dans son bureau.*" Our teacher, Monsieur Abdul Aziz, was patient and pleasant, but he was never satisfied.

One evening he turned over the conversation to the pupils and, one after the other, we recited, "*Mon nom est—; ma profession est —; j'habite—.*" From this we discovered that almost all of our fellow pupils lived in the medina, and were tailors, policemen, post office employees, students, a watch repairman, and a judge. At the end of this exercise we all smiled foolishly at each other. But after a moment of rest, Monsieur Abdul Aziz rapped on the desk.

"*S'il vous plaît. . . .*" We were back again to the Thibaults and their two boring children, Paul and Catherine, who were now rummaging in their grandparents' attic. An attic! What is that? Monsieur Abdul Aziz took ten minutes to explain that in France the roofs are peaked, not flat, and the peak formed a storehouse for grain in past times. Surely we could find more interesting topics than the Thibaults just in the streets around us!

By eight-thirty we were home again, the Harrises had set off for their villa in Gueliz, and we sat down to help the children with their homework. Laura Ann had her tutor once a week, but every day Bob worked with David and I with Laila, reading and helping them translate the daily French lesson, checking the spelling dictation, and hearing them stumble over the poems that they were expected to memorize each week. Their tongues were more nimble than their parents', for already their accents were better than ours. A great day came in November, when Laila received her first commendation for a recitation, and I suppose the entire family can still quote that poem:

> Des oiseaux gris viennent de passer
> Vol! Vol! Bel oiseau, vol! . . .

By nine-thirty the children were in bed, and Bob's interviews were about to begin. Abdul Lateef would come with a merchant or artisan to talk about the markets of the city. They sat in the room where Alta had slept, the room that had become a "salon" with the addition of our canvas lawn chairs, a round wooden coffee table, and a red Moroccan rug from Chichaoua. I would take in a tray of cookies and tea for the interview sessions, and then I would go upstairs, grateful for a warm bed on a freezing winter night. When I turned out the bedroom lamp, the courtyard lights gleamed through the windows, shut against the cold, casting magnificent multicolored shadows— rose, green, blue—on the ceiling and the plaster walls, magnifying parts of the carved plaster cornices I had not noticed before. Was that the wing of a bird, abstracted, beneath the calyx of a flower? Downstairs in the court, the fountain dripped into the basin. I would fall asleep, listening to the last sounds of Rue Trésor, Mbarak shutting down his dark cubicle for the night, the bakery employees arriving for work, to mix and shape the morning bread, the hoarse voices of two men cutting through our street on their way home, deeper into the labyrinth of the medina.

One wet morning as I stood uncertainly in the kitchen with market basket in hand, the vegetable man banged on my door.

There he stood, in the pouring rain, a djellaba folded over his head, his donkey standing patiently in the lane, while he held up, in a gnarled hand, three or four small new carrots, still with the earth clinging to them, scraping it off as he stood there, smiling, the rain dripping from the sodden hood of his djellaba onto his cheeks, and down onto the frayed neck of his old djellaba.

"*Khizzu zween!*" (Good carrots!) He smiled. I peered over his shoulder and saw the glistening oranges and the green tops of new onions protruding from the straw baskets. Why trudge all the way to Djemaa el Fna in the mud and wet?

Aisha appeared, and the jostling, friendly ritual of bargaining began.

"How much for carrots?"

The peddler named a figure, and Aisha laughed loudly.

"For these?" She plucked a few new carrots from the basket and shook them close to the peddler's face. "Twenty francs the kilo."

"No," said the peddler. He backed into the shelter of the covered passage leading to Aisha's house to get out of the rain. This was going to take time.

"Little carrots," I said. "I only want little carrots."

The peddler rummaged in his basket until he had a handful of little new carrots loaded onto his brass scale. Out of her door came Hajja Kenza, dressed and veiled for marketing.

"*Lebas*, Elizabetha," she said, nodding.

"*Lebas*, Hajja Kenza."

"What on earth do you want these silly little carrots for?" she said. "They're too hard to peel, and they're only a bite each. Don't let him cheat you." She glanced at the peddler.

"I want little carrots," I insisted.

A woman looked out of an iron-grilled window above the street and giggled. Kenza muttered darkly about the carrots and my foolishness and began to root among the oranges.

"How much?"

"Thirty-five francs."

"Thirty-five francs! They're old and dry!"

"No! No! They're fresh this morning at Bab el Doukkala!"

"You bought them this morning! But where have they been lying around waiting to be bought?"

"Thirty-five francs."

"Ridiculous!" Kenza walked off, but the peddler did not call her back. He knew he could sell them.

Aisha was buying carrots, too, and a kilo of potatoes. Kenza hollered from the end of the street.

"Thirty-francs for the oranges!"

"Thirty-five," returned the peddler, and laughed loudly as Kenza disappeared around the corner. The rain rolled down the deep lines in his face as down a series of small rivulets in the earth; he adjusted his hood, prodded his donkey forward, and moved on, calling to the next house, "*Khizzu! Khizzu!*"

Down the street the small store was serving impromptu stand-up lunches to the garage men from Rue Bab Agnaou, the presser in the dry-cleaning shop, the students passing by on their way to or from school; half a loaf of bread spread with cheese, jam, butter, or a combination of same, sardines, olives, milk . . .

The rain still poured into the courtyard. Aisha and I stood at the door of the kitchen and stared at it disconsolately. There was no point in mopping up the water, no point at all. I had to remember to ask Bob to get planks from the roof to put in front of the children's bedroom door, the one place in the house where the tiles slanted backward enough for the water to form a large puddle, just the thing for the children to step into on first arising!

"Well," said Aisha, "at least we got the carrots for a good price," and smiled reflectively. She had enjoyed her bargaining morning.

It was not a routine I would have predicted, but then, I asked myself, what would I have predicted? We had come to Marrakech so Bob could do research in a traditional Muslim city of North Africa. I knew nothing of North Africa, and there was no reason to assume that it shared all the characteristics of Egypt and Iraq. The children's interest had shifted from Rue Trésor to school and their friends the Harrises; Bob was absorbed in the market system of the city. It was I who was left with Rue Trésor, who had expected more from people, from my neighbors, from my classmates at the Mission Française. Bob, too, admitted that although the merchants he met were pleasant enough, they seemed closed and wary. Was the political situation, uncertain and explosive after the attempted coup of the previous summer, to blame? Were Moroccans that different from other Middle Eastern peoples? Or were we changing, becoming more ingrown, less tolerant, and less willing to make the first move? Perhaps some cultures have more affinity for one than others, I suggested, and we were wrong for Morocco.

"You're overstating it, B.J.," said Bob. "Wait awhile."

We sat at Sunday lunch with the children, once more trying to talk together and hopefully ease everybody's situation somewhat.

"Why does everybody hide in their houses here?" Laura Ann wanted to know. "You can't tell whether people are poor or rich from the outside."

Bob nodded.

"It's a private matter," he said. "They don't want to show off whatever wealth they have. They don't want everyone to know."

"Why not?"

"Well, their taxes might go up, or people might envy them, and that's supposed to be bad."

Laura Ann shook her head. "I don't understand."

"The split between public and private life and behavior seems greater here than in Egypt and Iraq," Bob went on.

"What does that mean?" Laila wanted to know—Laila, who still seemed to suffer the most, at least outwardly. It did no good to keep telling her that people pulled blond hairs out of her head to bring themselves good fortune; it hurts to have hair pulled out of your head, and it's frightening when it happens unexpectedly on the street.

"It means, Laila dear, that people have one way of behaving with each other, in the privacy of their homes, where they have some responsibility for behaving, and that they behave differently outside, on the street, where people are strangers and they don't feel they owe anybody anything."

"We're not like that," Laila persisted, scraping up the last of her bowl of custard and holding it out for more.

"No," agreed Bob. "We're the opposite. You children fight and are rude in the house, but are polite outside."

After a moment's silence, Laura Ann said, rather meekly, "We don't *always* fight in the house."

"And not everybody is mean to you on the street!" returned Bob triumphantly.

"Oh, Baba, you started that argument on purpose!" said Davy.

Bob laughed. "Of course. We have to try to understand why people act the way they do, that's what I've been telling you all along. Even in the French school, where you say the teachers hit all the time, you have to ask yourself why they do it. They don't hit you, do they?"

This was a sore point. The initial interest and novelty of the school situation had worn off; after two months the teachers no longer made allowances for the fact that our children did not speak French. The children were expected to work, and they did so. But the stories that came home every night, especially from Laila, were less about the work than about the old-fashioned methods of discipline.

"My teacher isn't fair," insisted Laila. "There's one girl she never, never hits and one girl she hits all the time. But then, sometimes my teacher is nice, too."

"What about Austin?"

"They never hit us there. They just sent us to the principal's office."

"Did you ever go to the principal's office in Austin? Where you could get paddled?" he added.

"No."

"Then why worry about being hit here in Marrakech? It hasn't happened and probably won't."

Laila's eyes filled. "It's because I'm not sure, I don't *know*."

"Yes, yes," I broke in and tried to explain how I felt when I went out on Rue Trésor and people said rude things, and how the veiled and djellabaed women seem to glare at me and never even nod in a friendly way.

"But how do you know they don't like you, Mama?"

"I don't, but because I'm not sure, I expect the worst."

"You're just like Laila," said Bob. "What about the Lycée, Laura Ann?"

"Oh, they don't hit in the Lycée," she answered. "They just give you more homework or bad grades, that's supposed to be worse, and they say it's all for your own good."

David laughed. "Teachers are all the same. In Austin, they make you stay after school and write out your spelling a hundred times and they say, with that sicky smile, 'I'm not doing this to punish you, Davy, I'm doing it for your own good.' Here, the teacher whops you and says, with the same sicky smile, 'I'm doing it for your own good.' "

"But here it hurts more," Laila complained.

I agreed with Laila, but Bob thought it was healthier for the teachers to get their irritation out and be more open. Laura Ann said that was wrong, teachers were grown-ups and should learn to control their tempers, otherwise how did they expect children to do it?

"And so," Bob brought the argument back where we started, "we have to look at the public aspects of society, since that's all we are witnessing. The private side of Morocco is not for strangers such as us!"

We all went to the movies at the Cinema Marhaba and watched a spaghetti Western, made in Italy with a fake Texas locale. The children found this screamingly funny, and so did we.

We invited Laura Ann's teacher to lunch. "Why not? He was born and brought up in Marrakech, maybe he can help us understand this city," said Bob.

Jean-Yves accepted the invitation, and we decided to make an occasion of our first Marrakech lunch guest. I made a special trip to

Gueliz to buy pork chops, which were available only at the French butcher's (pork being forbidden to Muslims) and found lovely, pebbly-looking wild mushrooms from the mountains. Bob bought wine, and I made lemon sponge with cream.

I had told Aisha, and she seemed much impressed.

"Laura Ann's teacher from the Lycée is coming here?"

"Yes."

"What time?"

"One o'clock."

"And what are you going to serve him?"

I told her, and at the look of surprise on her face, explained hurriedly that in Europe and America pork was a delicacy and eaten like lamb or beef. It was not forbidden by our religion.

Aisha ducked her head so I could not see whatever expression might be on her face.

The day of the luncheon party was dark and wet, but Jean-Yves arrived promptly, a big black umbrella shielding him from the pelting, driving rain. Bob helped him pick his way through the puddles in the courtyard to the salon, where we had laid out preluncheon drinks. All was ready in the kitchen; the children had eaten, greeted Jean-Yves in proper French, and retired to our room, where they had settled down with a new batch of English paperback books, fortuitously arrived by mail the day before. We chatted over drinks, using our "new" French accents, which, we noted happily, did not seem quite as ridiculous to Jean-Yves, a good-looking, polite young Frenchman, as they did to our Moroccan classmates at night school. We talked about the advantages and disadvantages of living in the medina, and I was just rising to serve lunch when the doorknocker sounded.

"Now who can that be?" Bob said, surprised. Sometimes the children on the street banged the knocker to try to get us to come to the door, so they could giggle and run away, but I did not think this was likely weather for such games.

When I opened the salon door, Aisha stood there, holding in both hands a dish as big as our coffee table, with a cover like a straw hat; it was neatly set within its own table. She set this down before Jean-Yves and raised the straw cover with a flourish.

"Hajja Kenza has sent lunch!" she announced grandly.

The three of us stared at an enormous steaming platter of yellow couscous, topped with carrots, turnips, and pieces of chicken.

"Wh-what?" stammered Bob.

"For your honored guest," explained Aisha, gesturing toward Jean-Yves to make her meaning clear.

"*C'est magnifique!*" he muttered politely.

"Thank you, Aisha," I said quickly, and she replaced the cover and smiled benignly on us all. Had we been in Kenza's house, all we would have had to do now was sit down on our red Chichaoua rug, remove the straw-hat cover, and eat Kenza's offering, rolling the couscous into balls with our hands and popping into our mouths first a carrot or a bit of chicken for flavor and then the steamed semolina itself. Instant lunch was within our reach.

"Shall I bring napkins and spoons?" asked Aisha, and now I was perplexed. She knew perfectly well that the table was set in the dining room with flowers and wine, and that in the kitchen oven reposed lovely pork chops baked with herbs, a dish of rice with mushrooms, salad, lemon sponge cream.

"No, thank you," I answered, and made a split-second decision.

"I'm sure you've eaten couscous all your life, Jean-Yves," I rushed on in bad French, "but I have made pork chops for you, so I think I will forgo Hajja Kenza's kindness and insist instead that you try my American cooking!"

"*Bien! Comme vous voulez, Madame!*"

"But, B.J.," cautioned Bob in English, "we don't want to hurt Kenza's feelings. This is the first time she's ever done something like this for us and . . ."

True. I did not want to bruise Kenza's feelings either or make a great error in Moroccan etiquette, but I was proud of my lunch and wanted selfishly to serve it to Jean-Yves!

How to do it? Swear Aisha to secrecy, obviously. I made up an elaborate story about how Jean-Yves, being French, loved pork chops and I had cooked them especially for him, and how the children loved couscous, so we'd eat it for dinner, but she must promise me not to tell Kenza.

Aisha looked doubtful. "She asked me to come back and tell her. . . ."

"I'll go," I said, and went out in the pouring rain, Jean-Yves' umbrella over my head. I knocked on Kenza's door and when she flung open the shutter and leaned over the window sill (narrowly missing the fern), I called up effusive and grateful thanks.

She seemed pleased, and nodded her head over and over again.

"Well, it's not every day you have a teacher to lunch!" She

shouted over the sound of the rain. "And no foreigner can make decent couscous. I think mine is very good, if I do say so myself." And she waved three fingers in my direction, grinned her golden grin, and closed the shutter.

We ate the pork chops and the mushrooms and drank the wine and had a pleasant afternoon with Jean-Yves, which finished with an invitation from his mother to all of our family for next week!

"And I promise no couscous!" he shouted gaily as he went down Rue Trésor. The rain had stopped and we had stepped outside to bid him good-by. Was Hajja Kenza's shutter open a fraction? Thank heavens she spoke no French!

In the evening, two of Bob's students who had stayed over from the summer program in Casablanca arrived unexpectedly, and we were glad of the couscous, which lived up to its maker's boast. But what were we to make of Hajja Kenza's sudden gesture? Was it a Marrakech custom to present a meal to one's tenant? We had been living in the house for more than two months, so it was a bit late for that. Had she misunderstood the nationality of our guest and sent the couscous along to prevent us from making a ghastly social gaffe by serving pork to a Muslim?

I decided that I knew even less about the conventions of life on Rue Trésor than I had thought; the people, the street, the city around me had their own pace, their own sets of rules. Kenza's kindly gesture, after the months of general indifference, was more confusing than some token hostility, which, I had to admit, I was prepared to receive. What next? The only certainty was that I didn't have the faintest idea.

Chapter 5

Rooftops and Zankas

One morning in late November I lingered too long over shopping and, hurrying, cut through a side entrance to the Semmarine to avoid the crowds on Djemaa el Fna. The narrow street between the police station and the post office was half empty, and I congratulated myself at successfully negotiating the shortcut (I won't be late after all, I thought, and lunch will be served on time).

"*Balak! Balak!*" (Take care!) The well-known cry sounded behind me, and I stepped aside to let a cart pass, heavily loaded with gunny sacks of grain. I looked to my right, and there on the ground, under an empty cart, lay a man.

It was difficult to tell whether he was alive or dead, for his face was smeared with blood, and his ragged clothes and broken shoes were smudged with dirt and mud. I stood there a moment, clutching my shopping basket. What should I do? Call the police? But surely the police would find him, for he lay only a block from the station. He groaned and turned over, away from me, and a man's voice said from behind, in French, "Go on, please, Madame, it is not your business."

I started to move on, thinking that this kind person would do something, but when I looked back, the man with the bloody face still lay there, untouched, uncared for. A hundred people must have passed him in the last hour, but no one had lifted a finger.

The sun shone brightly. People were hurrying home for lunch, the kebab stands on the corner were cooking skewers of meat, the marquee of the Cinema Marhaba advertised *The Guns of Navarone*, and a baby lolled its head before me in the towel sling where it slept on its mother's back. Everyone was going about his business. But the man under the cart—whose business was he?

At lunch Bob pointed out that the man who had spoken in French had obviously thought it inappropriate for a foreigner, and particularly a woman, to get involved in the situation.

"As we've said before, it's easy to misinterpret the public aspect of this society, which is all we see! Maybe he's a convicted murderer or got in a fight with his brother or is just a drunkard. . . ."

I shook my head.

"Go up on the roof after lunch," said Bob kindly, putting his hand over mine. "The sun is warm. It will make you feel better."

I did as I was told, wrapping myself in my heavy coat against the chill. When I sat down in the chair Bob had brought earlier, the half wall of the roof protected me from the wind, and I could still see the glorious view across the rooftops: the weathered stone of the Koutoubia minaret on my right, its chipped green-and-white tiles gleaming in the sun; the green-tiled roofs of the Saadian monarchs' tombs on my left, across several lines of laundry (djellabas, long baggy trousers, and sheets). In the center, the row of mountain peaks, the High Atlas, stood out clearly, blanketed in new snow against the blue sky. Yes, it was a lovely view.

But the man with the bloody face stayed in my mind, and a host of other pictures came, unbidden: the vagabond children who slept in doorways around Djemaa el Fna; the babies, crying unnoticed in the slings in which their mothers carried them on their backs; the fighting in the streets, the teasing and the insults that seemed to be general, for Bob and I had both realized that the Moroccans were as hard on each other as they were on us, the foreigners! What kind of people were these, to let a man lie half dead for hours on a public thoroughfare? I remembered stories about big cities where supposedly no one cared about anyone else and everyone lived in independent anonymity. But Marrakech was a medium-sized city in the Middle East, where the extended family allowed everyone to feel responsible for his neighbor, or at least for his cousin. But what about people who had no cousins to turn to?

I must have dozed briefly, for the sound of laughter and conversation woke me. Aisha was standing nearby, hanging up the laundry and talking to someone. I stood up to see who, and my sudden appearance was greeted with muffled exclamations of surprise by a group sitting on the opposite rooftop: a half-grown girl with a school-book open on her lap, a small boy clambering over some broken baskets, and two women. One of the women lay on her back in the sun with her eyes closed; the other, who was young and sturdy, sat cross-legged, picking over a golden pile of grain. None of the women wore djellabas or veils, and their several layers of skirts were tucked up in folds into their waistbands as Aisha tucked hers when she was washing the floors in our house.

Aisha laughed loudly, and the sleeping woman rolled over, sat up, and looked across at me, adjusting and retying her red-flowered head scarf as she did so.

"I told them not to worry," said Aisha. "It was only you, and you'd just come up to the roof to get warm, like all of us. Say something to them," she added kindly.

"*Lebas!*" I offered, calling out in as friendly a manner as I could.

They all responded with "*Lebas!*" except for the half-grown girl, who simply screwed up her eyes as though to see me more clearly. Had I passed this girl on the street? Had I seen her at the entrance to the narrow passage where Aisha lived? I did not think so, but of course I told myself I could have passed all these women a hundred times, covered in veils and hoods, and never have recognized them now, in their at-home attire.

While the girl continued to eye me, Aisha kept up a running con-versation with the others. They seemed to be teasing the reclining woman, who had turned over on her stomach, propped herself up on her elbows, and was talking in a whining way.

"Is she sick?" I asked Aisha.

Aisha laughed again. "Zahia, are you sick? Madame wants to know."

"Sick? She's not sick," chided the younger woman, who was pains-takingly picking through the wheat and spreading the grains on a length of sacking near her, in the sun. "Zahia's just lazy."

"Ohhh!" howled Zahia, giving forth with a great mock groan. Aisha translated the next sentence, to the effect that this was the first day of Zahia's period and she felt awful, and since we were all women and got our period regularly, why didn't we sympathize with her more?

"The sun is good for that," I called across the roof.

No one replied. The half-grown girl turned back to her books, the little boy was rolling a pebble over the top of the basket to hear how it sounded when it struck the roof, Zahia lay down again, and the young, sturdy woman went on picking through the grain, tossing bits of dirt in all directions as she worked.

"Where do they get the grain?" I asked Aisha. With such an auspicious beginning, I did not want the conversation to stop.

The wheat had been brought from the family's ancestral village near Ourika, in the foothills of the Atlas Mountains. The best grain, according to Aisha, was brought directly from the country like this, from some farmer you knew or were related to. But it needed to be picked over and dried well in the sun before it was taken to the mill to be ground into flour.

"Do you buy your grain in the market or do you get it from a village, too?"

"Oh, from our village, Sidi ben Slimane," said Aisha. She hesitated. "Could I please bring my grain to dry here? We have no roof."

"Of course."

The women opposite were watching us, I noticed. Was Aisha repeating what I had said? While I looked back and forth, trying to make it all out, another head appeared at the top of a ladder that led to the roof.

"Ya Zahia! Rakosh wants you!"

"Ohhhh!" Zahia groaned again, but she sat up quickly and stretched, leaping to her feet suddenly to grab the small boy, who stood dangerously close to the edge of the roof, dropping his small pebbles into the street below. The forty-foot fall would obviously have been fatal. "Kamal!" She snatched him away from the roof edge and he began to howl, but she held on and proceeded to hand him down the ladder to the half-grown girl. Zahia turned back to us and waved.

The other woman went on cleaning the grain, and Aisha continued to hang up the clothes. I sat back in my chair, leaning forward every few minutes to see whether the other young woman was still there. She finally finished, straightened the sacking on which she had spread the grain, and nodding to Aisha, she, too, disappeared down the ladder.

"Who is that?" I asked.

"That's Rabia. She wants to get married, but Rakosh won't agree, because there's too much work around the house."

"Who is Rakosh?" Who would have the power to prevent a marriage, to make Zahia leave the roof so quickly?

"Rakosh is Zahia's mother-in-law, and Rabia's grandmother."

"Ah. Is she old?"

"Oh, yes, very old, and nearly blind."

"So her children and grandchildren take care of her."

Aisha set down the empty clothes basket and snorted.

"Rakosh! Ha! She may be old and nearly blind. But it's she who takes care of *them*. She runs the house, Rakosh. She manages the money. Her two sons give her their wages, they are good sons, and she takes care of everything."

"Do they all live together?"

"Oh, yes." Aisha began to enumerate the members of Rakosh's household; it came to fourteen.

"I thought *you* lived over there," I said, indicating the general area of the house that did seem to be off the passage down which Aisha had led us that first night in Marrakech.

"Oh, I do, but . . ." she stopped and eyed me. "Why do you want to know all this?"

"Because I live here, too, and aren't I their neighbor? The only people I have even met are you and Kenza."

Aisha regarded me doubtfully. I rushed ahead. "I mean, who lives there? The Ourika family in front and you in the back?"

"Not exactly." Aisha pointed to the irregular pattern of roofs and walls across from us. "Rakosh lives in front there where the roof is, the Glaoui live in that square beyond, and farther on, where the open court is, see, that's where I live."

Surely the area at which I was looking, where three families lived, was no larger than the area covered by our house. "All the houses we see have that many people living in them?"

"No, no," said Aisha. "Some houses are big and have only one family, like yours. Some houses are small and have more people in them, like mine."

Aisha had been watching me all the time she was talking, as if searching for something. Her face changed. Had she found what she was looking for?

"Have you always lived there?" I asked. Surely that was a harmless question.

"No, but I have always lived on this *darb*." Aisha drew herself up rather proudly, I thought.

"*Darb?*"

"The whole street is the darb," said Aisha. "The *zanka* here," she indicated first Rue Trésor stretching roughly two blocks in a straight line below us, from the clinic to Rue Bab Agnaou. "The zanka there," and she pointed to the small street giving on Rue Trésor, which seemed to meander off in the opposite direction and dead-end in a small covered passage a block away from where we stood. "The two zankas that form a T—with the *sibhas*, the small covered passages—all together they're called the darb, and I've always lived here. I was born here, and so was Kenza."

I looked down over the wall into the streets and passages that formed Aisha's darb, and ours, too. Rue Trésor formed the length of the T, the smaller zankas formed the top of the T; the sibha to Aisha's house and the sibha at the dead end of the smaller zanka were curliques or flourishes on the basic T formation. Our house was on the join, where the two zankas converged: half of our windows faced Rue Trésor, the other windows faced the smaller zanka.

"So you and Kenza are the oldest residents of the darb."

"Yes," she said proudly again. "Kenza and I and the *qadi*."

"The *qadi*?" I was surprised. Qadis, I knew, were judges of the Muslim religious courts, and somehow I had not expected to find that one of my neighbors on Rue Trésor was a qadi.

Aisha nodded. Her face had brightened as she told me about Si Qadi, who lived at the dead end of the smaller zanka, where the dark passage disappeared.

"And Mahmoud, of course."

"Mahmoud?"

"Mahmoud, who lives with his wife in the house next to Kenza. He sells nuts in front of the Cinema Marhaba. You've seen him."

Yes, I had seen him, a shambling, middle-aged man with a high, piping voice, calling "*Loz! Loz!*" and holding out paper twists of roasted almonds to the patrons passing into the cinema. "Only ten *riyals*."

The sun was warm, the washing was hung up, and Aisha seemed in no hurry to run downstairs.

"I was born in the sibha where the qadi lives now," said Aisha, "and then I married and moved onto this zanka."

We stood together on the roof in the sunshine, while Aisha began to talk about "her" darb. From that day, her manner toward me changed. Why? I will never know. Perhaps she enjoyed talking about her darb, her family, her neighbors, even to me, a stranger, although since we had been there almost four months by this time, presumably I was no longer a complete stranger. Perhaps she sensed a way to make me happier.

Kenza and Aisha had played together as children on this darb, running to the store for milk as their daughters did now. They remembered the boy Mahmoud, whose father had died, and who had begun
to sell nuts on the street corner in front of the Cinema Marhaba to
help support himself and his mother and baby brother. He had gone
no further. But the boy Mumtaz was different. He played in the
darb, too, but he did not have to sell nuts in front of a cinema.

"He went to school," said Aisha. "His father was a qadi, and rich,
so we knew he would probably become a qadi like his father."

Thirty years ago, in 1941. The French protectorate governed
Morocco then, directing all of the affairs of the country, except the
religious sphere, where the qadis and *shaykhs*, who supervised the
mosques and saints' shrines, still held some measure of responsibility
for the personal life of the Moroccans, who were all Muslims. And
Glaoui Pasha, leader of a tribe from the Ouarzazate Valley, was dep-
uty dictator of the Marrakech area then under an agreement with the
French. Thami Glaoui Pasha, "lord of the Atlas," the legendary
tyrant who was a *succès fou* with the ladies of the European court circles, and at home in Marrakech, watched his enemies beheaded in
the morning before breakfast, with a jester in attendance to improve
his moods. Glaoui Pasha had walked the street where I now lived.

"The Glaoui who lives next door to me gives herself airs," said
Aisha, "just because she's a member of the pasha's tribe. But we
don't pay much attention. After all, she's from the country, not from
Marrakech. And the pasha doesn't run Marrakech anymore."

"And Rakosh? And Zahia?"

Aisha sniffed scornfully, and gestured to the rooftop, where the
grain had been spread out in the sun. "They are newcomers, too.
Can't you tell they're from the country by the mess on the roof?" It
was true that broken baskets and discarded kitchen utensils and
pieces of plastic sheets formed a rather untidy blot on the landscape,
which was otherwise filled with clean, well-swept roofs as far as I
could see.

"Ah," said Aisha. "The zanka is changing. All of Marrakech is
changing."

"For the better or the worse?"

Aisha considered. "Well, some things are better," she allowed.
"When I was a little girl, everybody had to salute the foreigners."

"*Salute* them?"

"Yes, it was the law."

No wonder they and their children felt some hostility toward us, obvious foreigners.

"But now Morocco is independent," I said.

"Yes," said Aisha.

"So it will get better."

"If God wills it so," she answered, and went down the stairs to the balcony, locking the door behind us.

I began to spend my afternoons on the roof. The sun was a good excuse, warming my chilled bones; I could read and write on the roof as well as in the "salon," and note who came up and went down from one roof to another. When Aisha was on the roof, too, and waved at somebody, I would follow suit. Gradually I found myself waving to and recognizing several of my neighbors across rooftops, whose names I eventually learned from Aisha.

Zahia, Rabia, and Rakosh lived across from us. Khadooj was the first wife's name; she was fat and pudding-faced, with enormous legs. The half-grown girl was Khadija, not to be confused with Najiya, Aisha's own daughter, a pitifully hunchbacked girl with a beautiful face. The corner house, occupied on the second floor by the young Americans to whom Davy had talked through the window, was occupied on the main floor by a bus driver with a large family; the mother of this family was Fatima, a tall, bright-eyed woman who had more laundry on the roof every day than anyone on the street.

If I stood on tiptoe at the far end of my roof, I could see over the wall onto Kenza's roof, where she stored various items in a wooden shelter, locked and bolted. Here I often found her hanging up washing, and one morning she, too, was spreading her grain on a clean expanse of white sheeting, picking it over to dry in the sun.

"Ha! Elizabetha! You find the sun is warm on the roof, too. Thank God for the sun!"

"Thank God!" I repeated fervently. "How is your stomach?"

"Better, better. I had some more cutting done, and it helped."

She stood up and came over to show me the new set of knife cuts farther under her chin from the old. "Draws the pain away from the stomach," she explained.

Yes, I thought, the cuts on the chin must hurt so much you forget your stomach-ache, but I did not say it.

"Come drink coffee with me, Kenza," I suggested.

"Ha!" she replied. "Thank you, but you see," gesturing at the grain, "I have much more work to do than *you*." *Touché* to Kenza, I thought. If I had more manual work, obviously I wouldn't spend my time thinking and worrying and inviting people to drink coffee. On impulse I said, "Let me help you, then."

Hajja Kenza looked up from the pile of grain and laughed at me uproariously. "You? Oh, thank you, Elizabetha, no! You have to know how to pick this through *correctly*, some of the seeds are hard, like this, see, and must be thrown away. Some hard seeds should be kept. It takes experience."

"Yes, lots of work, too," I added.

Another gleeful laugh followed. "But you get better flour when you clean it yourself. No chaff."

The conversation seemed at an end. I tried once more. I gestured dramatically in the direction of the mountains and exclaimed, "Look how beautiful they are today!"

Kenza, puzzled, stood up, patting all her various skirts into place, to see what I wanted her to look at.

"The mountains? That's all?" She sat down again.

"But they're beautiful," I insisted.

"Beautiful?" She sounded incredulous. "They're freezing cold. You must be crazy. Life is much better here in the city."

I had to agree to that. "Well," I finished lamely, "you must come another day to drink coffee."

"*Enshallah* (If God wills it)," she nodded, and as I turned away, she said, "I understand you let Aisha dry her grain on your roof."

"Why not?" I returned.

"Hmm. Why not, she says?" Kenza was obviously talking to herself. "Well, why not?"

I had been dismissed, and I went downstairs to prepare supper.

Each day, from the rooftops, I was adding a little more to my picture of Rue Trésor, though Aisha had recently informed me that the real name of the street was not Rue Trésor at all.

"That's a French name," she pointed out, as if I were not quite bright.

True. But this, too, was odd, because since Independence, all the Marrakech street names had been changed from French to Arabic. Boulevard de Rennes was now Boulevard Mohammed Cinq, for example, after the late King. Why was our zanka still called Rue Trésor? The obvious answer seemed to be that Rue Trésor was so small and insignificant that no one remembered it was there; in the zeal to change street names, tiny Rue Trésor had been forgotten. After all, as we had found out long ago, it was not even on the map.

On our way home from one of our early forays into the old market with Aisha, Laura Ann and I had both been concerned about finding our street again. Aisha had pointed up to the wall at the round arched entrance to Rue Trésor. Yes, I agreed. I could see the sign, a small rectangular blue-metal plate, painted in white with the letters Rue Trésor in the same kind of type one finds all over France, and throughout North Africa where the French have lived.

"No, no, there," she said, and pointed slightly to the right above the shiny blue-and-white sign, where a second street sign, of some older, more faded material, chipped black Arabic letters on a brick ground, had been set in the wall.

"Sharia Sanduq el Bali," I sounded out the Arabic.

Aisha's eyes opened wide. She leaned closer and said to me, "I did not know you could read Arabic!"

"Not well," I said.

"I cannot even read the Koran," confessed Aisha.

"But I can't either," I insisted.

Aisha shook her head in disbelief. Even when we were back in the house and she had doffed her veil and djellaba and was busy in the kitchen, and I tried to explain that I could not really read the Koran at all but only a bit of newspaper Arabic, she just nodded and smiled.

"You are too modest," she said.

As long as we lived on Rue Trésor, I could not convince her of the meagerness of my Arabic, though Bob reminded me that to one who could not read at all, any ability seemed great.

"We have always called it Sharia Sanduq el Bali, the Street of the Old Post Office," said Aisha.

Street of the Old Post Office. Rue Trésor.

I thought about that. "And all the time the French called it something else," I said to Bob. "But since they never spoke to each other, at least about street names, it obviously didn't matter."

Encouraged by my mild social success on the rooftops, I suggested to Aisha that we might one day invite some of the ladies to tea. Perhaps the women of Rakosh's house, including the young girl Khadija to talk with Laura Ann?

Aisha shook her head. "They are too busy for that."

"Does Hajja Kenza drink tea with them?"

"No."

Was there, then, no informal visiting back and forth from one house to another?

"No," said Aisha. "Everyone is busy," she repeated.

"But I've seen women go into Fatima's house."

"That's her sister, who lives on Riad el Zeitoon. But she is a relative."

Relatives. Cousins. Not friends.

"How can you know about people," Aisha added unexpectedly, "if they are strangers and not of your family?"

Christmas was approaching. Traditionally a time of family gatherings in the West, the Christmas vacation loomed ahead as a lonely time. How could we celebrate our own feast in such an alien place? We decided to treat ourselves to a holiday and meet our friends Ira and Barbara Buchler in Spain. We told ourselves we wanted to visit the monuments of Western Muslim civilization in Granada, where the Moors had ruled, some of them ancestors of our Marrakshi neighbors. It would be a pleasant interlude for all of us.

Bob told us well beforehand that he wanted only one thing from Santa Claus: a burnoose of really good black wool, one of the majestic hooded capes that all the young, semi-Westernized Moroccan men wore over their suits with the coming of the cold. Accordingly, Laura Ann and I revisited Omar, the djellaba merchant to whom Kenza had led us in September. In that time I had brought Omar several customers, friends passing through Marrakech who wanted authentic djellabas of good-quality cloth rather than the shoddy goods often passed off on the tourists. Omar was happy to have the business, naturally, and there had been no need to indulge, as Kenza had done, in hour-long fencing sessions over prices. After some comparative shopping, I had decided that Omar's prices were fair and honest, his merchandise was of good quality, and he was a pleasant person with whom to deal.

But the Christmas present took some time, for it was hard to find a burnoose to fit Bob, who is six feet tall, larger than the average Moroccan. Omar's and my discussions about the wool and the trim and the size of the hood had been going on for nearly two weeks, and in the meanwhile, he had recommended a silver merchant, a slipper merchant.

"One must know whom to approach in Marrakech, Madame," he explained to me in a gentle voice, "or one can be cheated badly." The sentiment was the same as Kenza's, but the style was pleasanter, so Laura Ann and I made it a point to visit the merchants he had suggested. Laura Ann was bargaining for a bracelet for herself and one for Laila's Christmas present. She was learning fast.

Just before Christmas I finally bought the burnoose.

"If it is not his size, bring your husband," said Omar. "I will be glad to make an exchange, and I would like to meet him."

The children were busy, buying and wrapping small presents for each other, for Greg and Tanya, for our friends the Buchlers. The shops in Gueliz were bright with tinsel, ribbons, and toys from France. We hung our strings of Christmas lights on the lemon tree in the courtyard, and they looked so festive against the yellow-and-blue tiles, the bubbling blue-and-yellow fountain, that we were inspired to make Christmas cookies and invite the Harrises to sing carols. Laura Ann took plates of cookies to Kenza and Naima and to Aisha, explaining that this was in honor of our feast.

A giant Christmas party at the Lycée had lightened the children's mood, and they were excited at the possibility of seeing Barbara and Ira Buchler and their new baby.

"Will there be a Christmas tree in the hotel in Spain?" asked Laura Ann.

"Why not?" I answered.

"But how could Santa Claus find us—in a hotel?" said Laila.

"Oh, I think he might," Bob answered. "Santa Claus is very smart."

The children exchanged glances.

We locked our metal door marked with the silver hand of Fatima and set out for Tangier and the ferry to Malaga, escaping temporarily our responsibilities and our life on Rue Trésor, the veiled alien street that was our home.

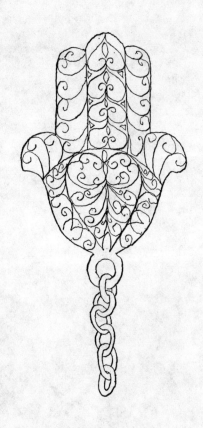

Part II

Chapter 6

Return to Rue Trésor

Winter storms had roughened the Mediterranean, and the ferry crossing from Malaga to Tangier was unpleasant enough to dissipate the glow of holiday cheer generated by our week in Granada. We drove south on the tail end of the storms, along a swelling pewter-colored sea where the waves still peaked so high and white they might have been frosted. In a curious way, I found I was looking forward to returning home to Rue Trésor. But what would greet us when we got there?

"Marrakech is nice," Laura Ann said to Barbara and Ira, who had driven back to spend New Year's with us in Morocco. "It's nicer than Tangier or Rabat."

"But don't be surprised by the street we live on," warned David. "It looks like a slum, but it isn't really."

Laila was holding the Buchler baby. "Our house has a fountain," she added. "And you'll like Aisha, Barbara."

The children seemed to be looking forward to showing off to our friends everything they had learned during their five months in a strange land. As guides, they would no longer qualify as strangers themselves.

Sodden donkeys ambled slowly along the road beside us. Intermittent flashes of sunlight glinted off the puddles lying on the rain-soaked highways, on the plastic bags covering, very practically and simply, the heads of shepherd boys sitting by the road with their flocks of huddled, wet sheep. As the hours passed and night approached, Bob slowed down, not knowing how many carts without reflectors might be stopped on the shadowy, unlit route. We could not see the barren plain I knew must be around us, and we drove quietly in a thick darkness until the lights of Marrakech winked ahead and we rounded the corner past the rocky promontory onto Boulevard Mohammed Cinq. Beyond, the old city walls had been illuminated for the tourists of the Christmas season.

"What's that?" cried Barbara. "It's beautiful!" at the sight of the looming Koutoubia, symbol of the imperial city of Marrakech.

"It's a real old mosque," explained David. "Eight hundred years!"

"Great! I've never been inside a mosque before."

"Oh, but you can't go inside, Barbara," said Laila primly, giving up the baby reluctantly to Laura Ann. "Christians aren't allowed."

"Well, the lights are pretty anyway," said Barbara.

Bob, with a little more flourishing and maneuvering than might be considered absolutely necessary, was picking his way through the evening traffic, past the Koutoubia and the Parc Foucauld, around the red-and-white circle where the policeman in winter black uniform stood on his stand, to the square where the nightly soccer game was in progress.

"God, how can you drive at all in a place like this?" asked Ira.

We parked the car at the end of Rue Trésor and wearily unwound ourselves from our cramped, crowded positions, to find the children of the street surrounding the Peugeot, as they had on our first arrival, giggling, shouting, and pointing.

"My, what a welcoming committee!" laughed Barbara.

I felt suddenly flustered, fumbling to put the key in the lock on our familiar door with its silver hand of Fatima, opening it finally inward on our refuge of carved plaster and tiles, while the children brought in the small bags and baskets, and Ira and Bob carried the baby in, in her carbed.

"*Lebas! Lebas!*"

"*Lebas*, Aisha! *Intii lebas?*"

Aisha and I embraced, and she embraced the children as well, except for David, who ducked out in embarrassment, ostensibly to help his father with the big suitcases. The baby, Neilyn, was admired profusely, her name was repeated by Aisha until she felt she had pronounced it properly, and then Barbara wrapped Neilyn in her own fur coat, for the house, though as beautiful as we remembered, was freezing. I ran to turn on the heater in the salon where our guests were to sleep.

"Look, Barbara!" Laila turned on the fountain, which splashed up and dropped back into its basin, onto the surprised goldfish, who, after a week of peace, were startled into motion, darting back and forth around the blue-and-yellow-tiled basin.

"Yes, it's pretty, Laila, but it's awfully cold," said Barbara, hugging the baby to her.

Aisha had put on a kettle for tea, and Bob and Ira were hauling baggage upstairs when the banging on the door began. The children stared at the door, looking away. The banging continued. Tonight I told myself I was going to ignore this particularly annoying children's street game.

Bang! Bang! Bang! The knocker sounded, over and over.

"Aren't you going to answer it?" Ira called down.

I hesitated. We could not listen to this noise forever. I opened the door abruptly and a teen-aged boy, in a brown wool djellaba fuzzy from the rain, stood there. I glared at him, but he merely smiled and pointed to the outside of the door. There was our key ring, still in the lock, the ring bearing our house keys, our suitcase keys, our car keys. I had been so flustered by the mob of children I did not even remember leaving them there! The boy took out the key ring, handed it to me, and smiled before he turned away.

"Thank you!" I said. "Thank you very much."

"My goodness, what nice neighbors you have!" said Barbara when I explained what had happened.

Bob and I exchanged glances.

"No, I mean it," she insisted. "In New York or Paris somebody would just have taken your keys and then waited for a day when you were gone to come and rob you."

She was right. The boy's friendly gesture, like Hajja Kenza's gift of couscous, did not fit. Or did it? Perhaps it was a good omen for the new year.

"Aisha," I said, two mornings later. "Do you know anyone who can apply henna?"

"Henna? Why?"

"My friend from Paris saw a lady in the suq today with her hands all painted, and she wondered if someone around Rue Trésor could do it. She'll pay, if that's the custom. And she'd like to have her hair done, too. She says," I added, laughing, "that everyone in Paris is using henna on their hair these days."

Aisha nodded. "Naturally. Henna is good for nearly everybody's hair and skin. Well," she said, "I could do her hair, but we'll have to ask Fatima about the hand painting."

"Fatima across the street in the house with the black-and-white-tiled doorstep? The one who has ten children?"

"No, her daughter, who is also called Fatima."

Fatima agreed to do Barbara's hands for fifteen dirhams if we bought the henna, and we went with Aisha—Barbara, Laura Ann, and I—to the spice market near the entrance to the Semmarine. From the big straw baskets full of what looked like dried chopped parsley or mint leaves, Aisha selected a few ounces of henna. Back at our house she brought over her own brass mortar and pestle, and, with Laura Ann's help, pounded the chopped henna into a fine green powder. The powder was sifted like flour, and warm water was added slowly, Aisha mixing it and kneading it like a tiny bit of bread dough.

"Oh, ugh!" exclaimed Laura Ann. "It looks like green slime!"

"And smells like alfalfa," I added.

Aisha, looking from one to the other of us, and seeing Barbara's dubious expression as the gucky mixture was prepared, must have guessed our feelings, for she asked me to reassure the "lady from Paris" that henna was marvelous, superb, the greatest beautifier offered by nature, and cheap besides. I dutifully repeated these sentiments to Barbara, who continued to look doubtful as the green slime was slopped onto her head, rubbed strand by strand into her hair, and finally applied to her scalp. Aisha divided Barbara's long, dark, slime-covered hair into two loose braids, wound them around her head, and wrapped it all up in an old dish towel, which she fastened like a turban.

Bob and Ira grimaced at the sight of Barbara in her fat turban and were moved to rude remarks in the morning when she removed the turban to disclose a head caked with ugly dung-colored mud.

"So this is gorgeous?" inquired Ira.

"Now what happens?" asked Bob.

"Shampoo," Aisha had instructed.

Three shampoos later, Barbara's hair, drying in the sun, disclosed shining auburn highlights.

"Oh, Aisha," sighed Laura Ann. "Can't you do me?"

Aisha eyed Laura Ann's strawberry blond hair. She shook her head.

"It wouldn't work. Your hair's too light. Henna is not for blondes. It would be awful. Fatima," she said, turning to me, "will be over to do the hands as soon as Mr. Bob and Barbara's husband have left. She can't come as long as the men are in the house. But first we make the paste."

Bob and Ira, having been declared *personae non gratae*, departed with David, making jokes about "woman's place," to which Barbara responded, with some asperity, about "man's place."

The moment the door shut behind the men, Fatima knocked, and I let her in, a tall, buxom young woman in a wine-colored djellaba. She pulled down her black veil and shook hands with me perfunctorily; her eyes were too small for her plump, rather discontented face. Before I had a chance to say anything, she was in the kitchen with Aisha, testing the consistency of the henna paste we had made and mixing up a combination of onions, garlic, lemon juice, and black pepper, which would be used, she explained, "to fix" the color. In five minutes she had disappeared, "to get her stylo for the drawing," Aisha told us.

By one o'clock we had all assembled on the roof, so chosen because the sun would help to dry the liquid henna as it was applied. Fatima, Barbara, and five spectators were there: Laura Ann, Laila, Aisha, myself, and Suad, one of Fatima's friends. I had never seen Suad before; she was tall like Fatima, but slimmer, with a high color and straight black eyebrows and a bubbling, gleeful laugh. Her djellaba was navy blue, with a trim of navy and white braid, very natty with her scarlet veil. She did not live on Rue Trésor, she told me, but near Sharia Bahoshy, off Djemaa el Fna. I noticed that although Fatima had doffed her djellaba on the roof, Suad had not, only dropping her hood and veil.

The ritual of the henna began. With a fine stylo of wood, somewhat like an eyebrow pencil minus lead, Fatima proceeded to decorate Barbara's hands with an intricate pattern of abstract geometrics. This was very different from the simple dots and lines we had seen on the women's hands in the suq, different from the palms smeared with rusty red henna, which I had observed in Nubia and Iraq. Elements of traditional Berber design seemed to be present, and details that might have been related to the hand of Fatima, but basically the whole design was unique, created especially for the shape of this particular human hand. Fatima dipped the narrow stick into the viscous green henna paste and deftly drew it along Barbara's palm, and around her fingers, outlining the knuckles, framing the nails. Fatima was careful, for if she once strayed from the line or smudged it, the henna dye spread into the skin, ruining the effect, and that particular piece of skin had to be erased and done over again.

"Where did she ever learn to do this?" Barbara asked. "Does she follow a pattern?"

Aisha relayed this to Fatima, who replied in such a low voice we could hardly hear. "The pattern is in her head, and her hands, and she learned it by herself."

"Oh, I can't believe that," responded Barbara.

Further questioning, via Aisha, revealed that Fatima had enrolled in both embroidery and sewing classes which had been offered free, along with reading and writing, at the women's centers established in Marrakech since Moroccan independence. Fatima had been a prize pupil at embroidery, but she explained that embroidery was too expensive and not many could pay the price. Henna leaves were cheaper than cloth and embroidery thread, and there were always brides who wanted to have their hands and feet decorated in the traditional fashion. With henna, she said, she was asking money only for her skill, and she had simply adapted the cloth designs to skin!

"Isn't it pretty, Mama?" commented Laura Ann. "Do you think she could do me and Laila?"

"Maybe," I temporized, "but not today. It's too late."

We had been on the roof nearly four hours, and only one of Barbara's hands and the second palm were finished. "You can have it done anytime," I comforted Laura Ann. "Barbara's only going to be in Marrakech a few more days."

Barbara was tiring from holding her hands rigid so the henna would dry without smudging, and I suggested we adjourn to the salon, where the heater would supply the drying agent. "And we'll have tea!" I added.

Suad clapped her hands and laughed her gleeful laugh at this announcement. Then her face fell. "But your husband, will he come back? I can't stay if he does."

"If the men come back," Barbara retorted when this had been translated, "we'll just send them out again."

The ritual was finally completed. We all admired the reverse closing Fatima had created (the palm of one of Barbara's hands was like the pattern on the back of the other, and vice versa). Suad laughingly begged for a ring to be painted on her own finger, and a bracelet on her wrist. "You see, I have no real jewelry," she joked. "So I need some fakes. Please!"

Fatima obliged with a ring, but balked at the bracelet; the banter between the two women, which I could not understand completely, had a breathless, edgy quality.

"How about me?" Laura Ann stuck out her hand, a bit shyly, and Fatima good-naturedly penciled an elaborate ring on Laura Ann's index finger.

Fixative was applied with cotton, and with instructions to Barbara to wrap up her hands like she had done her hair and then peel off the paste, dried to black, in the morning, Fatima and Suad shook hands with us all, pulled up their veils scarlet and black, and hoods navy and wine, and departed.

When Bob and Ira returned, Barbara displayed her bundled hands. "Ah ha!" she cried gaily. "Guess what, Ira, I can't use my hands until tomorrow morning. Looks like you'll have to change Neilyn and feed her supper and breakfast."

Ira grumbled mildly. He and Bob made further pointed ironic remarks about "woman's place."

Barbara laughed. "Moroccan ladies are smarter than I realized," she remarked, sitting at leisure in the salon with her decorated hands wrapped up in pieces of old toweling, while Ira mixed the baby's food and warmed the bottle.

Next morning we helped peel off the dry paste, and the pattern created by Fatima Henna, as Laura Ann had renamed her, emerged, a pale red, like rosy lace gloves on Barbara's white skin.

In the week following the henna party, David guided Ira around the miracles and wonders on Djemaa el Fna, Laura Ann and I took Barbara to admire the glittering, hand-worked jewelry in the gold market, and we all drove to Essaouira and picnicked beside the Atlantic Ocean. On the way back, I heard Laila giving advice about beggars. Laila had noticed that they bothered Barbara, too.

"Don't be afraid, Barbara," she was saying. "Just give them a little coin, and they go away. Here they do it because there aren't enough jobs for them."

I let the moment pass, and later repeated the incident to Bob, who remarked that Laila seemed to be adjusting to life on Rue Trésor, despite her determined efforts not to!

New Year's Eve was marked by Aisha's dramatic announcement

that Rabia, Rakosh's granddaughter who had done such a good job of cleaning grain on the roof not so long ago, was getting married.

"Really! Rakosh agreed?" I remembered the long-standing argument over Rabia's marriage, and Rakosh's insistence that Rabia could not possibly marry now, since her willing hands were needed in that large household of fourteen men, women, and children.

"Well, she wasn't too happy about it, Rakosh," admitted Aisha. "But this was such a good marriage offer she couldn't refuse."

"Who is the groom?"

"A friend of her brother's. He doesn't live at home any more, so you haven't seen him. The man who has asked for Rabia is well off, too, richer than her own father. *His* father has a very good kitchenware business right on Djemaa el Fna."

Before I had taken in all this information, Aisha made an even more dramatic announcement. "You're invited to the wedding."

"Me? Are you sure, Aisha?"

"Of course I'm sure. The *aradda*, the lady who does the inviting, came by while you were away. She said I was to tell you. The groom's party is first. Bob and Davy and the man from Paris can go to that; the next day is the bride's party. You and the girls are invited, and your friend from Paris, too. It'll be in Fatima and Hussain's house because Rakosh's house is too small for all the guests."

I was not entirely convinced. "You're *sure* I'm invited?"

Aisha frowned at me. Obviously I was being difficult. "Yes, yes," she said in a rather irritated way. "Why do you ask?"

"Then why doesn't one of the ladies of the family ask me?" I burst out.

Aisha opened her eyes wide, then narrowed them. "Is that the custom in America?"

"Oh, yes," I answered, "but in America the men and women attend the wedding together."

Aisha looked a bit shocked. "Together? How strange! Here the bride doesn't even see the groom till he's ready to sleep with her, and by that time the ladies' party and the men's party are over. We women celebrate by ourselves, in our own way. The men do, too."

"Yes, I understand." Why was I being so stubborn about the invitation? Why hadn't I been willing to take Aisha's word? After so many rebuffs, I suppose I did not want to risk appearing where I might not be wanted.

When we returned from Gueliz that afternoon, having bought

napoleons for New Year's Eve dinner, Bob reported that a veiled lady he did not know had knocked at the door several times, asking for me. Who could it be?

We did not have long to wait, for just as we sat down to supper, Aisha's key could be heard in the lock.

"Can you come, Elizabetha?" she called softly.

I rose from the table, opened the dining room door, and there in the courtyard, standing awkwardly around the little bubbling fountain, stood not one but three veiled ladies!

"*Lebas!*"

"*Lebas!*" they chorused in reply, and after they had pulled down their veils, I recognized two of the three faces, looking somewhat different framed formally in the folded hoods of their djellabas than they did in their head scarves, which they wore on the rooftops; but yes, it was Zahia and Khadooj, the two wives of Hassan, Rakosh's oldest son. I did not know the third, a small woman with a pretty face below the hood of an attractive brown-and-black-striped djellaba.

"Lateefa," Aisha introduced me to her. "Rakosh's child."

My perplexity was obvious, and the ladies giggled a little, while Lateefa, acting as the spokeswoman, delivered the message.

"They have come," intoned Aisha, enjoying this particular confrontation hugely, it appeared, "from the house of Rakosh and Hassan, her son, to invite you to the wedding of Rabia, daughter of Hassan, and Khadooj here. Just like in America!" Then she laughed.

"I accept with pleasure," I replied in as flowery an Arabic phrase as I could muster on the spur of the moment.

Zahia hid a giggle behind the wide sleeve of her blue djellaba. "Is that how they answer in America?" she inquired.

Aisha looked disgusted. "Zahia, stupid, she's speaking Arabic!"

But Zahia was not to be put down. "Well, it doesn't sound like Arabic," she returned.

"It's classical Arabic," declared Aisha, in a tone so scathing even Zahia stopped giggling for a second and batted her eyes at Aisha.

I opened my mouth to speak, but the ladies were already scuttling across the courtyard to the door. I followed them, mouthing those old phrases that sounded somewhat ridiculous as I knew they were leaving and they knew they were leaving because I already had company and so couldn't actually offer them tea at this particular moment. Yet the illusion had to be maintained, I felt.

"No, thank you," they answered, pulling up their veils.

"Another time, *enshallah*," I replied, giving in gracefully, as I was expected to do.

"*Enshallah!*" they echoed. "*Bslama!*"

I shut the door and rushed back jubilantly to the dining room. "They came from Rakosh's house and invited us all," I announced to the New Year's Eve dinner crowd: Bob, Ira, David, Laila, Laura Ann, Barbara, and the baby, Neilyn.

"Even us?" asked Ira.

"Yes, the groom's party is tomorrow night for you and Bob and Davy. The ladies go the day afterward . . . which means . . ."

"I know," said Barbara, "which means we'll be gone by the time of the ladies' party. Oh, well, it was nice of them to invite us anyway."

Early on the New Year's morning Hajja Kenza arrived at the door, the first time we had seen her, except in passing, since our return. She handed me a covered plate, and I raised the towel to find a heap of what looked like buckwheat pancakes piled on the same yellow plate we had sent to Kenza, full of Christmas cookies, the day before our departure for Granada.

"No, no, I can't come in." She waved aside my thanks and invitation with an impatient hand. "They are *baghreer*, special food for the new year. In honor of your guests. Just who are they, anyway?"

I began to explain. "They're friends from America who are living in Paris this year. Come in, Kenza, and meet them."

Hajja Kenza shook her head back and forth several times to indicate the confusion of the statement. "They're friends from America but they live in Paris. How could that be? What do they speak? French? English? How would I know how to speak to them? No, no, thank you anyway, but it's too much for me. I don't want to see them. . . ."

I thanked her for the plate of baghreer. She nodded at that. "But I *will* step in for a moment." She looked about her furtively on Rue Trésor, at the toddlers in Aisha's *sibha*, the bath boy, lounging in his cubicle, the wagonload of wood that had just pulled up at the bakery. "I have something to discuss with you *privately*.

"Look, Elizabetha," she laid a heavy hand on my arm, "I want you to know that I have decided to accompany you to Rabia's wedding."

"Why, thank you, Kenza, but it's not necessary . . . that is . . ."

Kenza had not even heard me. She was now drumming fitfully on my arm with her index finger, punctuating her words as though she wanted to be sure they penetrated my feeble brain. "Look, I'll pick you up early. I know they've invited you for four or five o'clock" (with a glance at Aisha, who had come forward from the kitchen to see what was going on). "But if we want to get a good place near the musicians, we have to get there by three at least."

"Yes, all right," I answered, not sure I wanted to be managed in quite this way by Hajja Kenza. But it seemed I had no choice.

"Wear something attractive," she was going on, "and whatever good jewelry you may have, especially *gold*." (Her tone seemed to imply I couldn't possibly have much.) "Everybody will be dressed to kill. You don't want to look foolish."

"No, I . . ." but Kenza had not yet finished.

"You must wear something warm, though, or at least lots of underwear," she counseled, "because it will be cold . . . oh, dear, here comes your friend. I can't speak to her . . ." and in a second the door had clicked shut behind her.

I turned to Barbara to explain what I was holding in my hand on our yellow plate and why Kenza had disappeared so rudely, when the knocker sounded again. There stood Kenza once more!

"No, no, I won't come in, but I forgot to ask what you're planning to give as a wedding present."

"Wedding present?" I echoed. "I don't know. What would you suggest?"

"Money," returned Kenza crisply, without hesitation. "That's best. No folderol about money. Everybody likes money. They can buy what they want with it."

"Yes, I . . ."

"I'm giving ten dirhams. You give ten dirhams. Ten, you understand?" (with a whack on my arm). "You mustn't give more than me."

"Yes, Kenza, okay."

"And don't be *late*. Three o'clock tomorrow afternoon." She wagged a finger in my face, flashed her golden grin, and was gone.

"Are you going that early, Aisha?" I asked.

"I doubt that I'll make it by *three*," Aisha answered, rather sarcastically.

"I'll save you a place," I offered.

"You promise?"

"Yes, I promise," I answered fervently. I certainly would prefer to sit next to Aisha at the wedding—Aisha, with whom I could communicate quite easily now, and on whom I could depend to tell me who was who and what was what and help me not to make any serious *faux pas*. After all, this was my first foray into local ladies' society, and I found I was rather nervous. Aisha, I knew, would be more helpful if any problem should arrive, more helpful than Hajja Kenza, who would no doubt decide to understand my Arabic only if and when it suited her whim.

"*Enshallah*," Aisha responded, and she smiled at me quizzically; was she amused to see Kenza managing me?

That evening Bob and Ira made an appearance at the groom's party and reported that there had been food and tea and dancing girls, and everyone had been very cordial, especially Hassan, the bride's father, and Hussain, the bus driver in whose house the wedding festivities were being held.

While the men were partying in one house, the sound of drumming and laughter also drifted across the street from Rakosh's windows. Aisha had told me that relatives had been arriving all morning from the village near Ourika; presumably an impromptu family celebration was in progress.

"Why don't you go over?" Bob asked, when he and Ira had returned and the women's gathering, to judge by the noise, was just reaching its peak.

"Nobody invited me."

"Oh, B.J., you're not very adventurous. I doubt they'd send you away if you appeared."

"Probably not, but I don't want to put a damper on what's already going on."

I felt that Aisha or some member of the bride's family would have invited me if I were really welcome. My resolve faltered, however, when I saw, through the iron grill of our balcony window, the figures of Hajja Kenza and Naima slipping across Rue Trésor into the sibha, from which came the clink of tea glasses, the laughter of women, and the measured beat of the drums.

"Too bad you can't go, B.J.," said Barbara. "It sounds like fun."

"Yes," I answered. But I had made my decision to wait for the formal bridal party tomorrow, to meet my neighbors for the first time on their own terms.

Rabia's copious dowry had gone through the streets to her new home, in procession, the day of the groom's party. Traffic on Rue Trésor had been held up for nearly five hours while three large, horse-drawn carts were loaded with mattresses, bedsteads, a dresser, a three-paneled mirror, a chest of drawers, four end tables, and a large round coffee table of pale wood (the *arbor vitae* of Essaouira), inlaid and polished to a high gloss.

"Gee, Mama, they must be really rich," Laura Ann said, after counting the number of cut velvet pillows, embroidered sheets, fringed towels, couscous baskets, and blankets stacked onto the carts.

"No, not so rich," answered her father. "This is Rabia's hope chest and trousseau all in one, everything for her new house. Her fiancé paid her father a certain amount, and since he is a good father, he has spent all of it on his daughter."

Folded on top of the last carts was a red-and-ochre rug, like ours, from Chichaoua, the original home of the groom's grandfather.

The carts stood, roped and ready, for nearly an hour, while Moussa, the baker, made two trips down to inquire when the street might be clear so that he could schedule the afternoon bakery deliveries.

"They're waiting for the *haj* who made the beautiful coffee table," said Aisha. "He's a master craftsman."

A small old man in a gray djellaba finally arrived, to much effusive greeting from the men gathered around the entrance to the sibha. He had come to be paid, said Aisha, and for the customary visit in which he would be congratulated for his work and offered a cup of tea by the satisfied client, in this case the bride's father, Hassan. As the old man emerged, smiling, a joyous noise could be heard from the passage, a loud happy *tzaghreet* or ululation to mark the beginning of the wedding festivities.

Laura Ann, who had been watching the entire morning's affairs with great interest, said, "Is that the way the Moroccans sing 'Here Comes the Bride' or something? I thought that part was tomorrow."

"I don't know," I answered truthfully, so we simply waited by our open door until three women, shepherded by a much older woman, appeared and stationed themselves behind the first cart.

"Relatives from Ourika," whispered Aisha, who had crossed the street to talk to us. "The house is full of them, and the stove doesn't sit idle one minute from cooking and making tea."

"And the old woman?"

"Why, that's Rakosh!" said Aisha, obviously surprised that I had not recognized her, but I had never seen this matriarch before, grandmother of the bride, a frail figure in a dove-colored djellaba and thick rose-tinted glasses. A pattern of tattooing followed her chinline, like a strip of lace along the jawbone, and the three women standing now behind the first cart, but unveiled since they were from the country, bore the same chin tattoos. Was this a design special to Ourika? Rakosh's apparent frailness was only appearance, however; it was she who arranged the women in their proper places behind the cart and called one of the cart drivers to check on the knots. She was worried about the cart with the mirror and the beautiful inlaid table.

"Ah . . . oooooooh!" The woman closest to us started the tzaghreet, that high, ululating women's wail that can be joyful or sad, depending on the occasion, but that now came forth like a cry of triumph from Rue Trésor. It was taken up by other women, in the house, at the windows above the street, and from the sibha, where a crowd of relatives stood to get a last glimpse of the dowry, Rabia's household goods, making its formal way from her natal house to her nuptial house, to establish a new family unit. Ululations sounded from the rooftops along the street and from Hajja Kenza, elbows propped on the window sill beside her pot of fern. Children appeared from every doorway and from Rue Bab Agnaou to watch the cart wheels creaking forward, headed down Rue Trésor, past the bath, the bakery, the store with its blue shutter. Heralded by the three

women of the bride's family, the moving carts announced to the
world at large that the marriage of Rabia, daughter of Hassan; and
Brahim, son of Abdulla, was about to be celebrated. A Berber girl
was marrying into an Arab family, still a relatively new occurrence
in modern Morocco.

Laura Ann and I had watched until the procession turned right
onto Rue Bab Agnaou and the ululating cries of gaiety were taken up
and repeated by the passersby.

The morning of the bride's party dawned dull and cloudy.

"Oh, dear, I hope we have sun today," said Aisha. "Some sun, anyway. Rabia's a good girl and she deserves a lucky beginning to her
marriage. It won't be that easy."

Aisha's comment surprised me. "But I thought you said it was such
a good marriage Rakosh couldn't refuse."

"That's right," Aisha affirmed. "It *is* a good marriage. Brahim's father has a good kitchenware business on Djemaa el Fna. But Brahim
has been married before. His wife died and left two small children.
So Rabia will have a handful to begin with. Let's hope for a good,
happy wedding at least."

During the morning, intermittently sunny and cloudy, the zankas
were full of women going back and forth between the bride's house
and Fatima and Hussain's house, where the party was to be held. By
nine o'clock, djellabaed and hooded ladies were already carrying trays
of cups across the street, tea kettles, primus stoves, bags of onions,
and platters of meat; by noon the protocol had slackened and the
women were rushing back and forth in their house caftans, towels
thrown hastily over their heads, a mere gesture toward decorum.

"They think at least a hundred people are coming," said Aisha excitedly. "Can they borrow your tea kettle?"

"Oh, yes, of course. A hundred people? Where will they all come
from?"

"Oh, the bride's relatives, the groom's relatives, the neighbors,
friends, some from the Kasbah, even a few from Daoudiate. It'll be a
big party," said Aisha. "Lots of fun."

We were still eating lunch when Kenza appeared at the door.

"Elizabetha!" she shouted. "Be ready, you and the girls, in fifteen
minutes!"

"But it's not even two o'clock," I protested.

"I know, I know," she said rather breathlessly, "but I saw the musicians pass by, so they must be already there. We might as well go now and be sure!"

I hesitated.

"You mean you don't want Laura Ann and Laila to get a good view of the bride? Believe me, Elizabetha, this is going to be a big affair, and unless we get good places, you won't see a thing, in fact, you might as well not go at all."

That was that. We rushed upstairs to get into our best and warmest clothes, and our collection of gold jewelry, such as it was. I smiled at our rather dull respectable demeanor, as we lined up for Bob and Davy's inspection before going off to appear for the first time in local society, a prospect that somewhat excited me, but also left me with a rather nervous feeling in the pit of my stomach. What gaffes might I commit in my ignorance, gaffes that would condemn me forever to isolated social disgrace?

"Don't worry," Bob said. "It's the bride who's being presented, not you. Just keep your ten-dirham wedding present ready."

"Yes, it's in my pocket."

"There's Kenza, Mama," cried Laura Ann. "Let's go! Put on your gold chain, Laila! That's all the gold we've got!" And, with a meaningful glance at her father, she rushed downstairs.

"Yallah, Elizabetha!" Kenza was calling. "We've got to hurry!"

Naima was wearing a short gray skirt and a pink turtleneck sweater with a butterfly appliquéd upon the chest, the newest French rage, available in all the Gueliz shops. But Kenza was in more traditional garb, a new dark brown wool djellaba trimmed with braid. And, surprising to me, she wore no hood nor veil, but only a glorious green silk head scarf, patterned with all the monuments of Paris: the Eiffel Tower, Les Invalides, the Arc de Triomphe. What, were not the side slits of the djellaba, from which one could glimpse the two light-colored harmonizing caftans beneath, much higher cut than Kenza's ordinary garments? I had little time to compliment her on the new outfit, for she took my arm in a grip of iron and, chattering all the way, propelled me out of my front door, around the corner, and across the black-and-white-tiled doorstep of Hussain's house.

Here we were. We had arrived.

"Where are all the people, Mama?" Laura Ann asked.

I felt a sudden sense of anticlimax, for the large courtyard was empty. We were the first guests, thanks to Kenza's superanxiety. Lateefa and Zahia, in their everyday caftans, with their skirts tucked up about their waists, were rushing about, smoothing the covers and adjusting the pillows on the banquettes. They looked up briefly and gave us a barely perceptible nod, just as I might have done had dinner guests arrived two and a half hours early while I was still sweeping the floor! Oh, dear, I thought, what an inauspicious beginning!

Kenza, however, seemed not one whit abashed, for she charged forward, between the rows of extra banquettes and pillows set up in the spacious courtyard to accommodate the crowds of expected guests, past the table where musicians (six women and a man) were heating their drums over small pots of glowing charcoal. Then she paused, obviously calculating which bench covered with clean white sheets, which pillows encased in embroidered pillow shams or cretonne covers, would be the most comfortable and offer the best view of the coming proceedings.

"Ha! Zahia!" she called out, and Zahia, bent over to tuck in a stray end of sheeting, straightened up and frowned.

"Where's the bride going to come from?"

Zahia indicated the procession route, and in fifteen seconds Kenza had us sitting down on pillows against the far wall. The bride's reception room was behind us, but we had an excellent view across the court of the front door (we could see who came in and went out); the kitchen (its doors were on our left); and the musicians' table, ten feet ahead. I pretended not to notice the glances being cast in our direction by the orchestra. The oud player, a young man in sunglasses despite the cloudy skies above the courtyard, sported tight black trousers and a black turtleneck sweater; the six women with their drums and tambourines wore sweaters under their flowered dresses, bright head scarves, and armloads of jewelry. It wasn't until the next day that I realized that the presence of a single male in the midst of all the women was somewhat unusual.

Kenza pushed Naima toward a small, low bench between our banquette and the musicians' table. Laura Ann and Laila and Naima's friend Hind followed. Kenza spread out comfortably on the banquette and urged me to do the same, "so there'll be plenty of room for Aisha."

I looked about me curiously at this, the first house I had entered during my five months on Rue Trésor, except for my own house and for the five minutes in Aisha's rooms on the night of our arrival. It was a large, rather shabby court, the tiles cracked with age and wear, the plaster walls above the tiles showing the marks of recent scrubbing. The balcony, which in our house was fenced with ornamental wrought iron and topped with carved plaster pillars, here had been bricked solidly to the ceiling with rough, uneven bricks, much newer than the rest of the house. To keep the family life below private from the renters' activities above? I did not know, but it seemed a reasonable supposition.

"Now what happens, Mama?" asked Laura Ann, turning around from her place on the bench. "All that rush. What do we do? No one else is here."

Naima, too, was talking to her mother, and Kenza nodded and stood up, grumbling, and pulled me to my feet.

"Leave your sweater there, Elizabetha, so no one will take our places," she urged, and I did as I was told, although privately thinking it a ridiculous precaution, since we were the only guests!

She led me up two steps behind us and hissed in my ear, "The bride! The bride!" We were to pay our respects to the bride, it appeared, but before I had time to warn the girls, we stood on the threshold of a long, narrow, freshly whitewashed room, and from a row of black-and-golden velvet pillows arranged around a strip of faded Persian carpet, half a dozen splendidly attired ladies turned to watch us enter.

"Oh, Mama!" breathed Laila.

There, at the end of the room, in the place of honor, sat Rabia in all the finery of her wedding day.

Laura Ann echoed Laila's sigh, and I realized that although I had seen Middle Eastern brides before, elaborately prepared for their nuptials somewhat in this fashion, for my daughters it was their first sight of a fairy-tale bride: not the pristine ladies in white veils and chaste satin gowns, as seen in the women's magazines and the June display windows of Western department stores, but a bride of legend and myth, wrapped in silks and precious brocade, loaded with the jewels of her family and the gifts of her husband, her hands and feet hennaed and painted, her veiled hair crowned with a glittering tiara: a princess!

"Ha, Rabia! *Yom el Baraka!*" Hajja Kenza, not at all impressed by the sight of the bride in all her glory, proffered the ritual greeting, "Truly this is a day of grace," and bestowed a perfunctory kiss on Rabia's rosy cheek, rosy still after all her years in the city. When she tweaked Rabia's green-brocade sleeve to feel the quality of the wedding stuff, Rabia grinned broadly, displaying her rather widely spaced front teeth. In that instant, she was human again, the hard-working, jolly girl I had seen on the rooftops sorting grain.

"Not bad!" Kenza allowed. "Not bad!" and the girls took a step forward, too, for the magic spell of the moment had been broken.

"Shake hands with Rabia! It's the custom! Be polite!" I urged, and Laila, smiling, Laura Ann, her eyes shining, did so. Before their frank admiration, Rabia giggled, a little self-consciously, and shifted in her seat against the velvet pillows. This set all of her jewelry to clinking, and the women on each side of her, taking their cue from my daughters' unmistakable interest, began to point to the individual pieces, telling us the name of each in words we did not understand but that gave us a moment to stare at the bracelets, carved gold against the rosy henna patterns of Rabia's hands; the heavy necklaces of gold chains and medallions draped in a formal way over the high neckline of the green-and-silver dress, which was fastened from hem to collar with scores of tiny silver buttons.

"À la mode!" said one of the women in a pink lace caftan, and her companion, in purple velvet, laughed and nudged her friend.

"She's speaking French, did you hear?" Kenza hissed to me, and this comment started Laura Ann to giggling, and we all, laughing, bent forward to admire Rabia's earrings, held out to us on the finger of the lady in pink: earrings of gold filigree crescents, from which hung delicate individual strings of jade beads and seed pearls.

Laura Ann turned to me. "Wow! I'd like some earrings like that, wouldn't you, Mama?"

Now it was the ladies' turn to laugh at us. Were we speaking English? I nodded. What a funny sound English made, Naima translated, not at all like French.

"À la mode!" repeated the lady in the pink caftan, which set her friends off again.

"Come on! Come on!" Kenza was lobbying to leave, but Laura Ann and Laila had moved closer for a better look at the glittering tiara that held Rabia's bridal veil in place.

"It's just rented for the occasion," announced Kenza, a rather rude remark, I thought, but it did not faze Rabia at all.

"People will be coming in soon, someone will take our seats," Kenza said, and she backed us out, willy-nilly.

I arranged myself as comfortably as I could on our choice banquette and looked at my watch. Three-fifteen. Obviously everyone else had taken the four-o'clock invitation seriously.

The à la mode lady in the pink caftan and her friend in purple wandered out of the bride's room and nodded to us as they headed toward seats on the opposite side of the court. The musicians were warming up, rather halfheartedly, smoking and experimenting with different beats. Laura Ann, Naima, and Hind seemed to be trying to communicate, a hopeful sign, I thought, for I felt now that a very long afternoon lay ahead of us. But Laila sat alone at the end of the bench, fidgeting, jumping up every few minutes to ask me unanswerable questions:

"When will the music start, Mama?"

"Does the bride come at the first or the last?"

"Will we have mint tea soon?" (Laila loved mint tea.)

"What about the food? What will it be?"

Since I knew the answers to none of these questions, I suggested that we should just wait and see what happened, so we could tell Baba and Davy all about it. Laila sighed deeply and went back to her place. Three forty-five. After the initial outlay of energy involved in our slapdash arrival, Kenza had lapsed into brooding silence, occasionally handing me a roasted almond from a cache secreted somewhere inside the folds of her voluminous garments. I stifled a yawn. We had been here almost two hours and were still practically the only guests. Even the members of the bride's family, Rakosh, Zahia, Khadooj, Lateefa, and the tattooed relatives from Ourika, were visible only in glimpses as they ran back and forth between the two kitchens to our left, preparing enough food to serve a hundred people. Outside the farthest kitchen, primus stoves had been lighted and half a dozen kettles were boiling (including my own), but no one seemed to notice. Next to the stoves stood a row of trays of glasses, beaten silver teapots, and sugar bowls, each tray covered with a crocheted white lace tea cloth, presumably to keep out the flies. But nobody made tea and nobody came near the trays. Had someone forgotten to buy the fresh mint?

Four o'clock.

"Mama, what is there to do?" cried Laila despairingly. Obviously fairy-tale weddings were supposed to move along at a faster clip than this.

I said I didn't know. I told myself that if something didn't happen soon, we would all go home, no matter what Kenza said, but fortunately I did not express this possibility aloud, for the scene around us began to change. The guests were arriving.

At four-thirty, ladies were crowding at the door, filling the foyer, and Laila jumped up to watch them come in. It was quite a performance. Across the black-and-white-tiled doorsteps, the ladies poured into the courtyard, wearing their conservative outer garments: djellabas and all-enveloping hoods of sober cut and color, their faces, except for the eyes, hidden beneath voluminous veils.

But once across the threshold, everything changed. The public mien was cast aside. One was at home, and one assumed a different personality. Off came the veils, hoods, and djellabas, to be folded quickly and efficiently into narrow rectangular packages (compact, kept the creases in, and useful to sit on as well if the pillows were all taken). The ladies emerged in their caftans, those garments designed for private life, relaxation, pleasure: flattering, feminine, colorful!

Why, I wondered, why had I ever worried about what to wear to the wedding? My dark plaid dress was noticeable only as a drab sparrow shows off to greater advantage the flock of tropical birds around it. Here, in the spacious courtyard, cut into segments of light and shade by the oblique winter afternoon sun, a fantastic display of fashion, fabric, and color was unfolding before me. How many months had I spent wondering what lay behind the high, thick walls of Rue Trésor, the barred windows of the houses, the heavy-hooded djellabas of the people? Here it was before me at last: color! light! sound! action! I realized I could have seen all of these women at one time or another, traversing Rue Trésor or Rue Bab Agnaou, bargaining for tomatoes or watching the pigeon man on Djemaa el Fna, but I would not have recognized a single one of them as they were dressed at this moment, a group of glittering, animated ladies now filing into the wedding party, looking for seats on the banquettes, greeting neighbors and friends, discussing babies. The babies were shifted from slings on their mothers' backs to apparently more satisfying positions cradled in their mothers' arms or on shoulders. The babies themselves wore their best: lace bonnets, embroidered wool hoods and capes, froths of dresses.

Suddenly inspired, the musicians burst into a loud, heavily accented popular song. One of the drummers stood up, holding high her multicolored pottery drum from the sardine town of Safi. Two more drummers began to sing.

"Mama! Just look at the caftans!" Laura Ann called.

I nodded and smiled. Velvets, brocades, embroideries, lace: The glittering wares of the Semmarine market had been cut and sewed into garments designed to set off each lady's particular charms, to show off her best jewelry. Green velvet with gold; blue with silver; scarlet with black; plum velvet with silver; purple with gold; white brocade; rose brocade; mauve lace over pink; purple over white; dark-brown velvet with a scattering of gold stars embroidered across the floating panels of the skirt.

"Elizabetha! Wake up!" Kenza, in an irritated voice, interrupted my fascinated perusal of the Moroccan fashion show passing before my eyes. She handed me another roasted almond. I commented on the lovely caftans. She nodded absently, obviously having seen such displays hundreds of times before and thus not the least bit impressed by the show today.

I munched the almond and turned back to watch the rainbow colors whizzing past me, the feet in lacy tights and embroidered Moroccan slippers, gold sandals, pink knee socks, black suede pumps with silver piping.

The sun poured out its last brilliance on the gold at the throats, wrists, ears, fingers, and teeth of the scores of women milling about the room; on rhinestones, jade and pearls, coral, smoky yellow amber, little chokers of sequins; necklaces of paste stones; belts of heavy chased silver and gold, which girdled the glittering caftans.

Aisha had told me that one was supposed to wear one's best jewelry to a wedding, and all of it if one wanted. It seemed that most of the women had taken the last alternative, for many wore combinations of paste and real stone, gold and plastic; the overall textural effect seemed to be the important thing, and the effect was dazzling.

"There's Aisha," Laila stood beside me, a little flushed and confused by all the excitement and the growing crowds.

I looked toward the door and for a split second did not recognize my friend Aisha, in her magnificent new caftan of gold brocade. She had already folded her shabby djellaba into a thin package, and she waved to us across the room, the sky-blue satin scarf around her head visible against all the colors she passed. Aisha, too, was transformed.

"Well, well!" Hajja Kenza remarked, fingering the material of Aisha's caftan. "Not bad!" and her eye passed over Aisha as ours had done, noting how the gold of the brocade brought out the tawny color of Aisha's skin, the darkness of her brown eyes. Out of her drab work clothes, Aisha too was someone else.

Laila stared at her, wondering, I suppose, if this could be the same person she saw every day, and Aisha laughed and pulled Laila down beside her. We had stood up, then, to make a place on the crowded banquette, and for a second Kenza had hesitated. Then she, too, was moved to shed her djellaba, displaying an apricot velvet confection beneath, bound with dark gold braid, the side slits revealing a froth of yellow and orange nylon print beneath.

At Kenza's insistence Aisha's daughter Najiya had sat down with the girls. Her blue-and-silver caftan was obviously more flattering to her pathetic hunchbacked figure than any other garment would have been, and yet it marked her out from the four other girls on the bench, in their Western clothes: Laura Ann and Laila in plaid jumpers and blouses, Naima in her short gray skirt and pink turtleneck sweater, Hind in a checked pants suit.

The beat of the music was faster, the drums were louder, and two of the drummers were dancing, performing for the wedding guests, who occasionally slipped small notes of money under the dancers' belts. A great deal of giggling and suggestive comment accompanied this activity, which both dancers and spectators seemed to enjoy hugely.

"*Lebas* Kenza! Aisha!"

"*Lebas intii*, Fatima!"

"*Lebas* Madame!" Fatima, mother of the house where we sat in state, had come over to greet me, apologizing for her everyday clothes. Tall, handsome, she had an arrow tattooed on her chin, an arrow that pointed up toward her smiling eyes.

"My name is Elizabetha," I said. I did not like being referred to as "Madame" when everyone else was called by their own names—this seemed as good a time to correct the situation as any.

"What's that?" Fatima displayed the usual confusion at the first sound of my strange Egyptian Arabic.

"She's saying her name is not Madame, but Elizabetha," translated Aisha, and she smiled at me.

"Ah! Welcome!"

More women came over. I was being introduced to my neighbors so fast that I could barely keep track of who was who.

Rachida, a plump figure in a royal-blue velvet caftan and steel-rimmed spectacles was the schoolteacher who lived next door to Fatima. With gestures and a friendly smile, Rachida indicated to me that her daughter was also named Laila and was enrolled in the French classes at Arset el Ma'ach. I looked at Laila, daughter of Rachida, in a print wool dress; was she the mean one who teased *my* Laila after class? The girl smiled at me, plump and cheerful, like her mother; perhaps it was not she, after all.

Glaoui, descendant of the Pasha of Marrakech, wore green and gold and had an incipient mustache. Her daughter wore a pink nylon party dress, with much lace and many frills, that was either too tight or too scratchy, for the child held out her arms stiffly and glowered when anyone spoke to her.

There was Lalla Fadna, a massive old woman in black velvet, weighted down with gold necklaces and bracelets. A single large black pearl was set in a ring worn on her index finger. Curls of gray hair were just visible at the sides of her tight black-satin head scarf.

"She lives next to the empty house. Her husband works for the railway," Aisha whispered to me, and Kenza and Lalla Fadna launched into some kind of heated discussion. Lalla Fadna's daughter-in-law did not join in the discussion but stared at me fixedly instead, out of dark lazy eyes heavily outlined with kohl; she wore a shiny red-silk head scarf dripping with carefully braided fringe. Hajja Kenza complimented her on this scarf, one of a half dozen like it to be seen throughout the room.

"It's a new fad," Aisha was telling me. "It has mosques printed on it."

Rakiya, a tall woman, well along in pregnancy, with a prominent goiter on one side of her neck, was Fatima's sister. Hind, Naima's friend, who was sitting with Laura Ann and Laila, was her older daughter. Rakiya wore pink and white and silver, cinched in by an enormous silver belt studded with turquoise. Another tiny daughter, sporting newly hennaed bright red hair, sat beside her mother, pulling on the pink-and-silver skirt, whining and whining, but earning nothing from such tactics except a sharp rebuke from her mother, who plopped her down firmly between us and told her to be quiet.

And there was a tall, stately woman in a black caftan shot with silver whom I had noticed passing through the room. When she stopped to shake hands, the other women would inevitably rise to greet her. This was Lalla Fawzia, Aisha whispered, the qadi's wife, a good-looking woman in her late forties who wore no head scarf over her hair, which was fashionably puffed around her face and fastened in a neat dark chignon at the back of her head, a chignon crowned with silver combs to match her gown. She spoke to us briefly, shaking hands with Aisha, Kenza (who did not rise), and me, at whom she stared rather as though I were a creature from another planet. She left a small contribution at the musicians' table, went into the kitchen (to leave a wedding present, said Aisha), and then she passed out the front door. Rerobing herself in a djellaba, hood, and veil took her exactly a minute and a half!

The clinking of glasses was the welcome signal for tea, being served to all the guests by members of the family. Trays of teapots and glasses balanced above their heads, Zahia and Lateefa and Khadooj stepped among the crowds of women who now occupied all the banquette spaces, and even the floor. The tea was poured from a great height into the thin glasses, on the theory that the stronger the force with which the hot water struck the fresh mint, the better the flavor! Laila stood by Lateefa, waiting for a glass. Perhaps now, I thought, she will settle down and enjoy herself and stop fidgeting.

"Mama! Mama! Can you hear what the music is doing?" Laura Ann, as she turned to me, looked as though she were blushing.

Over the laughter and conversation and cries of more than a hundred women and children, I recognized the familiar strains of "Ya Mustapha," that long-popular Egyptian song, belted out by the seven-piece orchestra in front of me. Yet the words, somehow, had a strange ring. Was it . . . could it . . . yes, it was: "Ya Mustapha" had become "Ya Elizabetha" for our special benefit! The oud player was giving me his crooked smile, and the lady drummers looked coy. I smiled and nodded at them, but I was puzzled. How did they know we had lived a long time in Egypt?

"They asked me was it true I was born in Cairo," reported Laura Ann, "and when I said 'Yes,' they asked me what your name was."

Kenza was pounding on my knee and hissing "money" in my ear. Obviously I was not responding to the musical gesture in the accepted fashion, but I had nothing in my pocket except the ten-dirham note prescribed for the wedding present.

"Laila," I whispered, "run home and get five dirhams from your father."

When she returned and had placed the mony on the table beside the pots of charcoal, the oud player brought the last chorus to an end with a trill and a flourish. He bowed in our direction. Kenza decided to bow back. Apparently the tale of my Egyptian origins had traveled far beyond the confines of Haj Mahmoud's meat market. Had Kenza told them? Told everybody? One never knew about Hajja Kenza.

Dancing had spread to the guests and was in progress all around the courtyard. The sun had set, the electricity had been turned on; caftans glowed and jewelry flashed in the artificial light, as the women moved, singly and in pairs, around the room, in time to the throbbing beat of the drums. I recognized two of the more accomplished amateur dancers: Fatima, who had done the henna for Barbara Buchler, in pale blue, and her friend Suad in a beautiful black moire caftan bound in gold matt braid.

They were very good, Fatima and Suad, graceful and rhythmic, their dark hair swinging long and loose in contrast to the tightly bound heads of the other women in the room.

"Fatima's married!" whispered Kenza to Aisha. "She should be covering her head." (I noted privately that they had not criticized the qadi's elegant wife for a similar breach of custom.)

The girls' dance had a certain tension, a drama, that was absent from the more light-hearted gyrations of the other dancers. The musicians accelerated their beat and conversation died in the crowded room, as more and more people focused their attention on the tall girl in black moire, the buxom one in pale blue gauze, circling, bending, turning, dancing for each other in the crowded room. The professionals, judging, rightly, the mood of the crowd, had already sat down, deciding to rest until this free entertainment was finished.

Suad and Fatima moved closer to each other, locked elbows, circled together, then broke away. Kenza stared at them, as fascinated as I was. The music rose a half tone, the luminous notes of the oud vibrating higher and higher above the counterpoint of the drums. Suddenly Najiya, Aisha's daughter, spat out a phrase that sounded in the relatively quiet room like a pistol shot. Suad and Fatima stopped dancing in the middle of a movement. I did not understand what Najiya had said, but judging by the expressions on Suad's and Fatima's faces and the sharp intake of breath all around me, it could hardly have been pleasant. The intense, vibrating music continued a moment until the oud player, seeing that something was happening, switched quickly to another, lighter tune.

Aisha had risen and stood with her hand on Najiya's shoulder; the little hunchback pushed her mother away. Bitter, angry words poured out of Fatima's mouth, and Najiya returned them, word for word;

Suad began to cry, and Rakiya, my friend with the goiter, quickly stood up and went to her. Rakosh and Fatima's own mother stepped out of the kitchen, and the older women guided Fatima and Suad out of the room.

The laughing and gossiping and tea drinking resumed. The professional dancer stood up, pushed back the sleeves of her caftan, raised her arms, and arched her back in the preparatory movements of the belly dance. Aisha continued talking to Najiya in a low, urgent voice.

"She insulted them," Kenza said to me quietly. "I don't know what has come over Najiya. She is not herself today."

I wondered whether the gaiety and magnificence of the occasion might not have been a bit much for poor Najiya, who was no fool and who must have realized that no such celebration would be organized for her wedding, if she were ever to find a husband at all, that is; a hunchback did not have much appeal in a society where health was a prime factor in the choice of a marriage partner. (Later I was to discover that Najiya's deformity could also be viewed as an asset, a touch of God's inscrutable hand, which might work wonders provided the personality of the afflicted was pleasant as well.)

"Mama, I want to go home!" Laila stood beside me, looking pale.

"But we haven't even seen the bride's procession."

Rakiya interrupted to ask what was the matter. "Ah yes," she nodded, "mint tea makes all children sick."

"Oh, Laila," I urged, "stay a minute. Don't you want to see the bride?"

"I'm going to throw up!"

I rose quickly. It was seven o'clock. I hated to leave now, after waiting for five solid hours to see the bridal procession, but Laila looked miserable. Kenza grabbed my hand and pulled me down.

"Where are you going? The fun is just beginning!"

"Laila is sick!"

"Children are always sick," returned Kenza hardheartedly. "Go home to your father, Laila," she said peremptorily, waving my daughter away as the sounds of the bridal procession were heard. Laila bolted without a word. "Her father can take care of her!" insisted Kenza. "Surely he can manage that. You stay here!" And in case I might be tempted to run away, she took my arm once more in that grip of iron.

"The bride! The bride! Here she comes, Rabia, daughter of Hassan, here she comes!"

It was Fatima and Suad, chanting together the formal processional verses, introducing the bride to the wedding guests. The altercation of a moment ago was forgotten as they escorted Rabia, decked out in her green-and-silver-brocade wedding dress, her jewels, her silver sandals, her rented tiara holding her white bridal veil in place. But the face of the bride under the rented tiara was hidden, covered completely by a second veil, this one green.

"The bride! The bride! See, sisters, here is Rabia, *bint* Hassan, the bride!"

Still with her face covered completely by the green veil, Rabia was hoisted high upon a throne of pillows, set up against the courtyard wall. Her escorts semisupported her as they sang—luckily, I thought, for the pillow throne looked rather wobbly to me.

"See her beauty, sisters!" chanted Suad and Fatima. "See her beauty, like milk and honey!"

And they whisked off the green veil, revealing the broad, rosy face of Rabia, who kept her eyes cast down modestly, her hands decorated with traditional designs in henna, folded in her lap. Her two long, dark, thick braids had been tucked over her breasts into the heavy belt of silver (a present from her husband, Aisha said), which cinched in the bridal caftan.

"The bride, Rabia!"

With a rattle of drums, the chant and procession ended, and all of the women and children exclaimed and ululated with pleasure over the marvelous, wondrous appearance of Rabia, the bride of the day. The principal lady drummer stood up beside the bride, and raising her arm loaded with gold bracelets, she asked for silence and in a loud, clear voice began to announce the wedding gifts.

"One beautiful white nightgown from Hadha, daughter of Abdul Kader, may she sleep well in it, *enshallah!*"

The assembly giggled.

"One pitcher and twelve fine glasses from Zainab, daughter of Mohammed!"

On went the announcer, present after present, nightgowns, slips, a blue-wool caftan, several lengths of material, beaten silver teapots and sugar bowls, a bread container, more glasses, an embroidered tablecloth and napkins, a bouquet of plastic flowers and a painted glass vase to contain them, and then money, a good deal of money in small denominations.

"*Meetayn riyal* (two dollars) from Kenza, daughter of

Mohammed!" Kenza did not look down modestly at all as her name was called, but held her head up high and smiled grandly.

"*Meetayn riyal* from Elizabetha, daughter of . . . who?" There was a pause, as the lady announcer, momentarily stymied, whispered to ask my father's name. For here, as in all Muslim societies, women were identified, not by the names of their husbands, but by the names of their fathers.

"Who the hell is she?" someone called out.

Before I had time to say anything, Kenza had shouted, at the top of her voice, "This is her!" pointing to me. "This is Elizabetha! She lives in my house."

Everyone looked at me, curiously, but in a moment they had turned away again to the far more interesting process of watching the wedding gifts accumulate. Khadooj, the bride's mother, stood next to the lady announcer, carefully recording in a little notebook each gift and the name of the person who had offered it.

"This lady is the best wedding announcer," Aisha said to me. "People like her because she calls the names out very loudly and clearly so everyone can understand."

"Does she get paid for this?"

Kenza looked at me. "Does she get paid? Does she do it for love? She's probably richer than all of us."

"And she has five good sons," Aisha put in, "and they're worth more than gold."

Kenza was silent. I knew Aisha had touched a weak point in her old friend. For all her wealth of houses and djellabas and television sets and white geraniums and ferns in her window sill, Kenza had no sons, and at this moment her only daughter did not seem to be behaving too well. She was dancing the twist with Hind, to the amusement of several older ladies.

"Children should not dance at weddings!" shouted Kenza, and Naima, looking mutinous, sat down. "Look at Laura Ann! Is she behaving in such a foolish way? No, she is being quiet and proper!"

That kind of talk, I thought, will hardly improve friendly relations between Laura Ann and Naima, but in a moment I noticed that Naima had tiptoed out of her mother's vision and was dancing the twist in another part of the room.

Food was being served. At the tantalizing aroma of tajeen, that flavorful Moroccan stew, my stomach contracted and I realized I had eaten nothing since a sandwich at one o'clock. It was now eight. La-teefa, in a cream-colored silky caftan, a beige scarf tied around her head so that a few dark curls showed becomingly at her ears, set a tray down near us, bread cut into eighths and a platter of chicken tajeen.

"Come join us, Elizabetha!" Aisha called, settling around the table with Suad, Fatima, Rakiya, and Rakiya's tiny red-headed daughter.

I rose eagerly, but Kenza pushed me down, jabbing her elbow hard into my knee.

"Ow!" The shriek was involuntary, for Kenza's elbow was very hard.

"Shhhh!" Kenza admonished me, for Aisha was smiling and Fa-tima and Suad had turned to look. "Sorry, Elizabetha, but we mustn't start yet. I have made other arrangements. We'll eat later, privately, with Laura Ann and Naima."

I frowned, watching Aisha and Suad and Fatima, after washing their hands ritually, set into the fragrant chicken. I was very hungry. Laura Ann turned around and looked mournful and Aisha sent her a piece of chicken in a quarter of bread. Then Suad, perhaps in an attempt at reconciliation, offered a similar sandwich to hunchbacked Najiya, with the beautiful face, who twisted her shoulders sulkily and refused. Her mother spoke sharply to her, and she finally accepted, not very graciously, Suad's peace offering of meat and bread.

Some people were eating, a few were dancing to the now subdued music, but people were also leaving, greeting the bride for a final time, shaking hands with friends, expressing their thanks to Khadooj, mother of the bride, to Rakosh, her grandmother, to Fatima, the lady of the house. They stood by the door, unfolding their djellabas, slipping them over their heads, fastening hoods and veils, tying their babies once more into slings on their backs. The velvets and silks and cloths of gold, the glittering earrings and the red and gold mosque-printed fringed scarves disappeared under the sober browns and blues and grays. The tropical birds assumed their public mien and became sparrows once more. The party was nearly over.

But not for us. We sat on and, as my stomach rumbled with hunger and my head began to ache and my cramped legs developed needles and pins and finally went to sleep, my irritation with Kenza grew. Would we ever eat? Or was I destined to sit here until every single lady was gone and the court empty as when we had first arrived?

Kenza leaned over to a tray near us, pulled a succulent piece of chicken off the breast, and thrust it at me. I wolfed it down. Were the good ladies of the house waiting to see how long greedy Kenza could hold out? I did not know, but I wished mightily that something would happen. Maybe I could just get up and leave and go home and have a cheese sandwich? Anything, anything.

At 9:25 P.M. by my watch, Lateefa ushered us into a back room, opposite the bride's reception hall. The ewer and basin were brought, we washed our hands, and then a table was set down before us. A whole chicken, all to ourselves! I marveled once more at Kenza's canniness: She had used me, oh, how she had used me, to get her own private meal! It was not that she wanted to eat in snobbish isolation, as I had first thought. She just wanted to eat *more*.

"Oh, this is good," Laura Ann was saying enthusiastically, and we nibbled and chewed, trying to keep ahead of Hajja Kenza and Naima, while a pair of women, one old, one young, with a large healthy baby balanced between them on the banquette opposite, watched us light into the tajeen.

"Mmm! Mm!" The large serious baby held his hand out and asked for food. His mother and grandmother smiled at him proudly, and Kenza, in her pleasure at the triumph of her dinner strategy, handed him a bit of bread. He refused, scornfully, and gestured, "Mm, Mm," toward the meat. Laura Ann picked out a sliver of chicken and passed it across to him; he ingested it slowly and carefully and held out his hands for more.

The mother and grandmother pretended to be distressed, but I could see how pleased they were at the aggressive, unfrightened manner of this healthy, determined baby, who had obviously already learned how to survive. Laura Ann handed him another piece of meat, and I heard the grandmother ask Lateefa, standing by politely to make sure all was well, about us.

"Oh," she said, "yes, they speak Arabic."

The older woman's face changed and she consulted quickly with her daughter and then Lateefa.

"They want you to know, Elizabetha," she said, "that they've heard about you. Aren't you the Nasrani who speaks Arabic?"

I nodded. Everyone smiled and exclaimed. The atmosphere, filled with aromas of tajeen and bread, and lightened by Laura Ann's delight in the sober baby, was definitely pleasant. Perhaps, I thought, as I sopped up a bit of the delicious sauce of the second tajeen (this

one with prunes), a Nasrani who spoke Arabic was a cut more respectable than a plain old Nasrani who only spoke French or English.
I hoped so.

Kenza stood up and stretched. "Let's go," she said, "*Yallah!*"

But this time I was not to be hurried, and I smiled, but said I
wanted to finish the lovely tajeen before us. Lateefa laughed and said
she was sorry there wasn't more, and I insisted there had been more
than enough. Thanks to me, Kenza had been served with two tajeens,
and I was going to sit until I finished mine!

Aisha came in, and Kenza confided that I was being stubborn, I
just loved to eat, more than anything, look at me. Lateefa and Aisha
exchanged amused glances. I mopped up the last of the tajeen juice,
and, emboldened by the pleasant atmosphere and the delicious food,
I looked up and said, "*Yallah*, Kenza! Let's go!"

Kenza clapped me on the shoulder with a hefty hand. "Listen to
her!" she cried. "She's telling *me* to go!"

"*Baraka-llahufik*" (Thank you) I murmured to Lateefa, to the
lady with the sober baby, the nodding grandmother. "*Yom el baraka*"
(Truly this is a day of grace) I murmured to the bride; to Lateefa; to
Khadooj, the bride's mother; and to Hassan, the bride's father, who
stood outside the door, shaking hands and thanking the guests for
their presents. I noted that we were, indeed, almost the last to leave,
but Hassan politely urged us to stay. Aisha had said she would watch
the end of the dancing.

"*Bslama! Bslama!*" Kenza and I called to each other, and when we
got inside our own door, Laura Ann exploded with the details of our
great experience.

"Boy, was it ever fun, Baba! And the dresses were just beautiful,
and there was dancing, and boy, did the bride ever get a lot of
presents and money and she had a beautiful crown and a dress and
we had tajeen with prunes. Boy, weddings in Morocco are sure more
fun than in America!"

I sat, exhausted from my eight-hour marathon debut into local society, and finally crawled upstairs to my tiled and plastered room.

But I did not sleep long. Aisha had told me that the bride would
go in procession to her groom about midnight, when the marriage
would be consummated in the groom's house. A loud drumming and
ululation erupted onto Rue Trésor as the last guests spilled out of
Hassan's house, and I caught glimpses of the procession from my
window. At four-thirty another, smaller procession passed back; the

news was being conveyed to the bride's parents that all was well, Rabia was a virgin. At breakfasttime a third procession brought the bride's blood-stained bloomers back to be washed ceremonially by the bride's mother. No one undressed for the consummation of the marriage; it was considered indecorous to make love while nude.

At four in the afternoon we were to join the women from Rakosh's house who, accompanied by friends and neighbors, would take to the bride a sumptuous dinner, the last meal offered by the father to his daughter, the first meal offered by the bride to her groom. But when I saw the cart loaded with presents and the djellabaed and veiled ladies beside it, I somehow did not want to follow along in my colonial-type winter coat with brass buttons, so I put on my djellaba, as did Laura Ann. Laura Ann, Laila, Aisha, Kenza, and I straggled along at the end of the crowd, following the cart. The presents offered the bride the day before had been packed carefully to show off discreet details of the most splendid items, and the display was crowned with four large tajeen baskets filled with food, their straw-hat covers laced with red, keeping the dinner warm for its journey. Ululating, crying, and shouting we went, across Djemaa el Fna (the pigeon man paused to look, the line of Gnaoua dancers turned as we passed); we turned right off the square past the beggars' chorus to Sharia Bahoshy, picking up scores of excited children in our train as we went. Two doors down from a small mosque at the end of Sharia Bahoshy, the cart stopped.

"Ah, it's near a mosque, a good Arab house," pronounced Kenza. Abdul Lateef had commented approvingly about this marriage. "Only in such a way," Abdul Lateef had told us, "will we Moroccans join together as one people and erase the divisions that the French colonialists created between us, Arabs and Berbers."

We passed into the good Arab house with the other ladies from Rue Trésor, after being greeted formally by the groom's oldest brother, a tall, good-looking man in a djellaba and skullcap, a neat mustache set in an angular face. The ladies stood in line while he ritually pecked everyone on the cheek. But when it came to Kenza's turn and he met that cold stare of hers through her tortoise-shell sunglasses, his buss died in his mouth, so to speak. No stranger, however proper and Arab he might be, was going to be given the opportunity to peck the cheek of Hajja Kenza, *bint* Mohammed!

The house was lovely and spacious, an old Moroccan house recently renovated, tiled, and plastered, and we wandered about,

Aisha and Kenza and Laura Ann and Laila and I. We greeted the
bride—Rabia looked tired after her long ordeal, but more relaxed—
and she had been settled into her "home," one large room in this extended family household, where her dowry—furniture and pillows
and beds that had gone over on the cart—had been set up. We
watched the dancing and we had tea. Neither Aisha nor Kenza took
off their djellabas here, so we kept ours on, too, while we admired the
beautiful caftans and jewelry displayed, this day, by the women and
friends of the groom's family.

"A proper Arab house," pronounced Kenza for the second time.
"Even the music is properly done. See, Elizabetha, the man, the
violin player, is blind, so he can't see all the women. That man yesterday—" She broke off, shaking her head at the remembrance of the
dark, slim oud player with his crooked smile and his sunglasses.

I decided to risk a joke.

"But Kenza," I said, "he wore sunglasses."

Kenza threw me the kind of look one might cast upon an especially
stupid child. "Oh, Elizabetha!" she said in disgust. "Really! Don't
you realize he could *take them off?*"

Aisha giggled.

By seven o'clock, we were all tired. The bride had been brought
out a second time, the presents shown again, tea and delicious round
butter cookies served, special chairs brought for us to sit on (though
we all preferred the comfortable banquettes), tea served once more. I
was ready to leave. I was worried too about David and Bob, who had
gone fishing at the Amizmiz barrage, and who did not, I thought,
have a key to the house.

"I must go, Aisha," I said, and to my surprise, met with no opposition whatsoever.

"I have to go, too," she said, "and so does Kenza."

We departed, murmuring *"Yom el baraka"* to the brother by the
door, Kenza sailing out with barely a word to him. Aisha produced
two plastic bags of the butter cookies, which had been pressed on us
by the groom's sister, since we could not stay for dinner.

When we got home, we found that David had caught a four-and-a-
half pound pike, the biggest of the season so far, at the barrage lake.
He was very proud. However, the details of catching this remarkable
fish had to take second place to Laura Ann's account of the final
phase of the wedding festivities.

"Oh, and Baba, yesterday I forgot to tell you that the lady announcer with the gold teeth, well, I counted and she had *twelve* gold bracelets. And Baba, you would really have laughed today if you'd seen what that man looked like when he tried to kiss Hajja Kenza!"

I smiled, too, at the memory, and we talked into the night about weddings and fishing and private life and public life on Rue Trésor.

Chapter 8

A Change in the Weather

In the days that followed the wedding, I began to notice subtle changes in the social climate on Rue Trésor. Sometimes, when I went out with my market basket, a veiled, unknown woman would speak to me. At first I did not recognize any of the hooded, anonymous figures, but would recognize the children accompanying them and, with Aisha's help, gradually learned to watch for the details—patterns embroidered on face veils, tattoos, shoes—that distinguished one woman from another. Who were the ladies who spoke? I did not know them all, but they had obviously been at the wedding. Since I had been at the wedding too, I must be socially acceptable for some reason. Therefore, presumably they had decided to speak.

I did recognize Rachida, the plump and cheerful schoolteacher. She was unmistakable by her size, her round, steel-rimmed spectacles, and her cream-colored motorbike, on which she rode briskly home from school at lunchtime and back to the classroom when the lunch hour was over.

"Her boy, Fuad, is the one with the wall eye," Aisha told me, "and her girl is named Laila, like your own daughter."

Ah, yes, the boy with the wall eye, who could not seem to make up his mind whether Laila was friend or enemy and who lay in wait for her whenever we went out of the house.

"*Bon jour*, Laila!" he would call out. "*Bon jour! Bon jour!*" And the smaller children on the zanka would echo, "*Bon jour!*"

Laila, embarrassed, would turn away, but Fuad, unabashed, would walk along beside us, repeating, "*Bon jour*, Laila," until, receiving no response, despite my suggestion to Laila that this would be polite, he would jerk her blond hair and run away, laughing at his cleverness.

David had pointed out, sensibly, that he and Fuad always spoke and told Laila that she should speak, too. "You're just being snobby, Laila," he said, but Laila refused to be led along the path to socializing on Rue Trésor. She did admit that Fuad's sister was nice to her in the French class at Arset el Ma'ach, but she refused to make further overtures.

Aisha's youngest son, Youssef, had lost his earlier shyness and knocked on our door almost too often, asking for his mother. We shook hands in a curious formal way on these occasions, I and seven-year-old Youssef with his tumbled black hair, quick black eyes, and slightly skewed mouth. Aisha had told me that of all her four children, Youssef was the most difficult.

"Boys are harder than girls," I agreed, remembering my own son's early years.

Aisha shook her head. "No," she said. "Some boys are harder to bring up than other boys. It isn't between boys and girls."

I thought this was less a universal statement than a sidelong comment on her poor hunchbacked daughter, Najiya, who seemed to be difficult in both health and temper. Najiya suffered from earaches or headaches or eye strain or sore throats, and it was a rare day when she did not appear at our door, asking for her mother "quickly." Abdul Krim, Aisha's middle son, smiled and nodded to us politely when we passed him on the sibha or on the zanka. He was very good in school, especially in mathematics and sports, Aisha confided, and the manner in which she spoke of him indicated that he was her pride, her hope for the future. Saleh, the oldest son, had been in two different schools and a minor motorcycle accident in the past five months, but Abdul Krim was steady and intelligent, with a good disposition. In Aisha's eyes, his only failing lay in the fact that he refused to accompany his father to the mosque on Fridays. Abdul Krim had told his mother that praying was a useless occupation, a statement that had shocked her. "And even if he thinks that way," she had said to me, "why can't he go anyway, just to please his father?"

At midday, if our front door stood open, Shadeeya and Ali, two of

Zahia's younger children, would pause on their way home from their Koranic school to wave at me before heading into the sibha for lunch. They each carried an old-fashioned slate encased in a plastic bag: Shadeeya, in a blue nylon smock that ended just above her thin, knobby knees; and Ali, with his close-cropped black hair, an outgrown sweater patched at the elbows, and big intelligent brown eyes. The bag was to protect the lesson to be memorized for the following day: a *sura* from the Koran chalked in large-size Arabic script. Shadeeya and Ali went to the *kuttab*, or Koranic school, on Riad el Zeitoon, said Aisha. Her youngest son, Youssef, had gone there too. The teacher's name was Moulay Mustapha.

"Isn't Moulay Mustapha the name of the man who came to tea with Abdul Lateef last night?" I asked Bob.

Bob said that it was.

"Does he run a Koranic school on Riad el Zeitoon?"

Bob affirmed that he did.

So it was Moulay Mustapha, an intense young man with a bad complexion, who wrote a Koranic sura on Shadeeya's and Ali's slates every day.

"The Moulay title means he's a *sherif*, or descendant of the Prophet Mohammed," explained Bob, "and a saint as well."

"A saint?"

"A descendant of one of the saints whose shrines are in the city or near it. In Moulay Mustapha's case, I think his ancestor is Moulay Ibrahim, but I'm not absolutely sure."

To my surprise, none of the children from Rue Trésor attended the government preschool day-care center at the end of the street.

Why? "Because it's very expensive," said Aisha. "At first it was supposed to be free, but that never happened. Who can pay twenty-five dirhams a month to keep their children there, who aren't even learning anything? Only the rich."

"Is it nice?"

"Oh, yes," said Aisha. "Toys and garden and lunch. I'll take you there some day. Lalla Yezza cooks for them, and we all know her."

Lalla Yezza passed by on her way to market one morning when the peddler stood in Rue Trésor, and Aisha introduced her, a cheerful, gray-haired widow with a loud and penetrating voice.

"She's not from here," explained Aisha. "She lives in Sidi Youssef ben Ali district, but she's been working at the center for years and everybody knows her. When her children were small and the weather was bad, the teachers let her bring them to the center, and all of them slept there."

Gradually I began to recognize the children who came from Rue Trésor and those who did not. The day-care center children wore checked smocks. Rue Trésor children, when they wore smocks at all for school, wore blue. The tiny redhead with a ponytail was Mina, Fatima Henna's daughter; the dark-haired child with the faint suggestion of an incipient mustache on her upper lip was none other than a descendant of Thami Glaoui Pasha; the other small redheaded girl, who had cried so at the wedding, was Salima, the daughter of Rakiya, my friend with the goiter; Rakiya was Fatima's sister. Salima came often with her older sister, Hind, to visit her Aunt Fatima while Hind gossiped with Naima, Hajja Kenza's daughter. The two teen-aged girls stood on the corner where the zanka divided, knitting and chewing gum and watching the people who passed by on Rue Trésor.

"Those girls should both be wearing djellabas and veils all the time," announced Aisha disapprovingly one day when we passed them. "That's the way trouble begins, letting them go without."

I knew that Hajja Kenza had been having trouble with Naima ever since the wedding. Two nights ago they had been quarreling so loudly I had heard them through the thick brick wall that separated our bedroom from theirs. Yesterday morning Kenza had appeared on my doorstep looking distraught and asking for Aisha. She had barely answered my greeting. Aisha had gone across to the sibha, Kenza behind her, and in a few minutes the two ladies had re-emerged, and Kenza went back into her own house, a garment over her arm.

"She wanted to borrow Najiya's djellaba and hood," said Aisha, "and since Najiya is home from school with another of her headaches, I was glad to loan it."

"But why?" I was puzzled. "I know Hajja Kenza is angry," I said hurriedly. "I heard them quarreling last night and the night before."

"Well, Kenza has a right to be angry," said Aisha. "Naima tore her best blue djellaba."

"And all the quarreling and crying is because of the torn djellaba?"

"Oh, no, that was just how her mother found out about it."

"Found out about what?"

According to Aisha, Naima, just for fun, had been cruising up and down Boulevard Mohammed Cinq on the back of a school friend's brother's motorcycle. Yesterday they had crashed; Naima had cut her leg, torn her djellaba, but what was worse, had been interviewed by the traffic police! Her mother was furious that her daughter had been riding on a strange young man's motorcycle without permission. The accident had revived an old quarrel between mother and daughter: whether Naima would be allowed to wear her djellaba in the new fashion, that is, with a small pointed hood (essentially decorative) down the back, and a scarf over her hair, or whether she should be forced to wear the djellaba old style, as her mother did, with the voluminous hood folded and fastened over the forehead and with a veil covering the bottom portion of her face.

"Now that Naima has been so foolish, her mother is insisting that she has to wear the hood and veil. Well, it's difficult," allowed Aisha, "to bring up young people these days, and especially without a father."

I began to notice that the women of Rue Trésor did, despite Aisha's denials, talk together informally, not only across the rooftops, but also from the open doorways of their houses, always keeping one foot on the sill, so they could quickly step inside if a strange man appeared on the zanka. But this kind of socializing was not practical for me, since my Moroccan Arabic was not yet fluent enough to take part in these informal, lightning-quick exchanges of information, recipes, gossip, troubles, and the sarcastic joking that I had yet to master, in understanding as well as speaking.

But the rooftops were open, and I continued to spend nearly every sunny afternoon there, reading, writing, and practicing my Arabic. Aisha was there part of the time, and she prolonged her rooftop tasks, I suspected, just because she realized I wanted her to help me in conversation.

The women of Rue Trésor were often on the roofs, to hang or take down laundry, to rest, to sort and dry not only grain but also other crops that arrived regularly from home villages. I had seen olives spread out, in season, on two of the roofs, and one day wool appeared on Rakosh's roof. Khadooj, Rabia's mother, sat there between two enormous piles of raw sheeps' wool, just brought in after shearing.

"*Lebas!*" I called out, following Aisha's example, and Khadooj looked up and acknowledged our greetings.

"*Lebas,*" she replied, rather shortly, and turned back to her task, sorting the wool into separate piles, one white, one brown, pulling each handful apart as she did so, quickly, deftly, to let it fluff and dry thoroughly before it was carded, spun, and finally woven into the rough wool from which so many of the men's winter djellabas were fashioned.

"Hey, Khadooj, what's the matter? I've hardly seen you for a week. Have you been sick?" asked Aisha.

"No," replied Khadooj, "but I guess you might as well know, Aisha. You've been a good friend to me. I'm leaving here. I'm moving to my mother's and father's house."

"Why?"

Khadooj shrugged in reply. "Why not? Rabia's married now. My parents need me more than the family here."

"Well," offered Aisha after a few moments, "they'll still miss you."

"Yes," said Khadooj, again in that abrupt tone. "They'll miss me, all right, they'll miss having somebody to load the work on. They want me to stay till after the feast, but I've made up my mind, I'm leaving Friday."

Three days away. We were all silent. Aisha wandered about the roof, pulling at our clothesline, tightening it. The weather had been uncertain all day, brilliant sunshine alternating with dark clouds blowing across the sun, darkening the seemingly endless piles of wool surrounding Khadooj. The steady rhythm of pulling and fluffing would be interrupted only if she found something unusual in the pile, a burr or a stone that would have to be yanked out.

"What are you finding mostly?" I ventured.

"Dirt," she replied. "Nothing but dirt," and she sneezed twice as she tossed a handful of clods and stones to one side, where they sounded dully as they hit the roof.

"Catching cold?" inquired Aisha solicitously. "Wrap up, Khadooj."

"I'm not catching cold and I am wrapped up," replied Khadooj rather snappishly. She rose slowly, pulling herself erect, tufts of wool sticking to her faded scarlet caftan and the blue one beneath it and her layers of old sweaters and her thick head scarf of wool, a man's plaid scarf tied on gypsy-fashion. "Hey," she called down into the well of the courtyard, "Lateefa! Zahia! Can't you get off your behinds and get up here and give me a hand? Look at the sky! If it rains, the wool will be soaked and we'll have to clean it all over again!"

I watched Khadooj standing by the ladder, haranguing the women below. Her legs, between the bare foot and the knee, showed below her tucked-up caftans; they were swollen and thick as the trunks of the palm trees in the Parc Foucauld.

"Listen to her," said Aisha softly. "She can't keep her mouth shut. She scolds and she nags and she complains all the time. Her legs. Her back. Everybody has troubles. But if we thought about our troubles all the time, there'd be nothing else to think about. She's really a good woman. But would you know that to hear her nagging?"

"Do her parents live nearby?"

"Not far. In the Kasbah. She goes every morning to clean their house and cook their dinner. Her mother is an invalid and her father broke his leg just before the wedding."

Khadooj sat down once more at her station between the piles of wool.

"Are you talking about me?" she asked, not unpleasantly.

"Yes," said Aisha, laughing.

"Well, talk nicely," instructed Khadooj.

"We will if you will," returned Aisha. "Are Lateefa and Zahia coming up?"

Khadooj snorted. "Who knows?"

Aisha sighed deeply. "It's too bad," she said softly so Khadooj could not hear. "Khadooj is worth five of Zahia, look at the way Zahia lets her children run about. Shadeeya's hair is not even combed before she goes to the kuttab, Kamal's nose is never wiped. And look at the roof!"

A head, wrapped in a series of contrasting head scarves, appeared at the top of the ladder. It was Lateefa, and she shouted across to us in her high, sweet voice, before sitting down beside Khadooj to join her in sorting and fluffing the wool.

Poor Lateefa. So pretty, so gay, so bright. Twice married. Twice divorced. Why? Because she was barren, the greatest misfortune that could befall a woman in this society. Rakosh, her great-aunt, had taken her in, and now she was, like Khadija, "Rakosh's child." In a sense, her presence freed Khadooj, Aisha said, though Khadooj would never have admitted it. In her quiet, pleasant way, Lateefa was an efficient and willing worker, as she had demonstrated by her organization of the wedding party.

"Have you heard about the *mesakeen*, Aisha?" she called.

"Yes," replied Aisha. "But what else could they do?"

"Who are the *mesakeen*?" I asked.

Had I seen a little old woman with a crutch who had been hobbling down Rue Trésor every day recently, going in and out of Aisha's sibha? Yes, as I thought back, I had.

"Does she live over there, too?"

Aisha nodded.

"There's a tiny room up above the Glaoui. The old woman and her old husband live there."

"What does the husband do?"

"He's a beggar," said Aisha, "but he's not very good at it."

Lateefa interrupted with some further piece of information about the mesakeen.

"They're all alone," went on Aisha. "They sold their land and came to Marrakech looking for work, but these days you have to know different things to get work, and they don't know much of anything, and the woman is crippled besides. Their son died in the war, he was put in the war by the French."

Which war, I wondered, but Aisha wasn't sure.

"What is Lateefa saying?" I asked.

"What we all know now. The old man looks pretty healthy and didn't do too well at the beginning, and they were nearly starving, I guess. So the wife said, 'let me try to beg, I look pitiful enough,' and she makes more money than he did, and they had meat last night for the first time in months."

"What does the man do then?"

Aisha smiled. "He takes care of the house, since it's his wife who brings in the money. He washes the clothes and shops and cooks, and this morning he borrowed a broom from Lateefa to sweep the room, and that is how we all know."

I could think of nothing in reply.

"It's fair," Aisha went on. "They've divided up the work equally." She sighed, again, unexpectedly. "Let's go down. It's getting cold up here. I'll get the rest of the laundry later."

It was true. The sun had gone, heavy cloud banks covered the Atlas Range, and shreds and fragments of ragged mist swirled about the minaret of the Koutoubia. On the roof opposite, the white wool had dulled to gray, the brown almost to black. Lateefa's and Khadooj's brightly wrapped heads bent over the foams and billows of wool, working faster, faster, to beat the coming rain.

The children's report cards arrived at the end of the second trimester. No report had been given them the first period, because of their deficiency of language, so this was the first written indication we had of their work at the Lycée. To everyone's delight, Laura Ann had made the second honor roll. "My good grade in English brought it up," she insisted, but it was still an achievement. Laila, David, Tanya, and Greg had all received commendations for *beaucoup de progrès*.

Everyone congratulated and embraced everyone else, but Tanya held back. "All that *beaucoup de progrès* is okay," she explained, "but the real crunch is getting put in *Groupe* A or *Groupe* B or *Groupe* C, like all the kids who really speak French. When I get grouped, then you can kiss me!"

Bob invited me to join his evening interview sessions, particularly when Abdul Lateef and Moulay Mustapha came. Bob said he had noticed a certain relaxation in their attitude toward him; were they, too, coming to accept us as something other than oddities?

Abdul Lateef, a small, erect man with keen eyes deep-set into a lean face, owned a bicycle repair shop near the Djemaa el Fna entrance to Riad el Zeitoon; he had been born in a mountain village and had only lived in Marrakech for ten years. "Here I am a foreigner like you, Bob," he smiled.

But Moulay Mustapha, his distant cousin, was a true Marrakshi for five generations back. He had been born in the Kasbah district, where his family still lived, and his father was a *fki*, or religious functionary. Although his father was also the proprietor of a small novelty shop (toys, ribbons, toilet articles), he earned most of his livelihood from his work as a fki: writing Koranic suras and religious prayers and prescriptions for those in need of help and assurance: people with health problems, family problems, career doubts, business difficulties.

"He makes a good living," Moulay Mustapha admitted. "Everybody has some problem they wish him to solve."

"You didn't want to be a fki like your father?" I asked the question innocently, and was not prepared for the piercing, almost angry glance that Moulay Mustapha bestowed on me before he answered.

"Didn't want to? Of course I wanted to. But I cannot be a fki, I do not have the power." He looked mournful and began to pick at his face. "So I opened a kuttab."

"Are there any girls in the classes?" This question was not so innocent, since I knew perfectly well that Shadeeya, daughter of Hassan and Zahia, sat in his classes every day, but I wanted to try to cover up whatever blunder I might have made about the fki.

"Yes, yes." Moulay Mustapha accepted another chocolate chip

cookie (Laura Ann had discovered that the bittersweet chocolate bars from our little store, cut up, made excellent cookies). He dipped the cookie in his tea. "I have fifty-three pupils, Madame, and fifteen are girls. This is since Independence, of course," he added, finishing off the dunked cookie. "And I teach French, too, at night, to adults." He smiled, a pleasant smile that made him look as young as he really was and erased momentarily his perennially worried, anxious expression.

I smiled to myself, thinking that Moulay Mustapha's French classes must be much more interesting than ours, since it seemed unlikely he would spend much time on the dreary Thibault family of the fourth floor, Place d'Italie, Paris! Thus I only half heard the speech that Abdul Lateef was making about independence from the French colonialist regime.

". . . and the average Moroccan has a new pride," he was saying. "We want to educate all of our people, both men and women. Girls go to school now, but almost none went before Independence."

"I think there is a law," murmured Moulay Mustapha vaguely.

"No, no," insisted Abdul Lateef, who considered himself the more sophisticated of the pair. "There is no law forcing people to send their daughters to school. But parents send them themselves. They want their children to be educated. It is a noble aim."

I nodded, hoping that I looked suitably impressed. Apparently I had passed muster, for Abdul Lateef looked at me kindly and said, "Did you know, Madame, that Moulay Mustapha is a descendant of the great Moulay Ibrahim, whose shrine is near here, and whose *moussem* is the most famous in all of southern Morocco?"

We had heard this before, but I tried to pretend this was news, and I asked a question about the *moussem*. What was it exactly?

"Moussem?" Abdul Lateef looked at Moulay Mustapha; Moulay Mustapha looked at Abdul Lateef. "Why, a moussem is . . . a moussem is a celebration, an anniversary celebration of the saint's death, a time of pilgrimage to the saint's tomb to pay one's respects."

"Like a *ziyara* to a saint's tomb, as in Kerbela and Najaf?"

Abdul Lateef looked directly at me for the first time. "You have made a ziyara, Madame, to Kerbela?"

I nodded. "Many years ago, when we were living in the village in Iraq."

"Ahhhh!" he replied and sipped his tea in silence. "Ahhh!" he said again.

The enigmatic silence, which lasted several minutes, was broken by Bob.

"When is the moussem of your famous ancestor, Moulay Mustapha?" he asked.

"In the spring."

"Perhaps," said Bob deliberately, "we can all go together to the moussem of Moulay Ibrahim."

Moulay Mustapha's expression was difficult to fathom. He swallowed some tea. "*Enshallah*," he intoned. "If the good God so wills it."

Later, when the two men had gone, I suggested to Bob that perhaps he had gone too far. Since shrines and mosques were forbidden by law to non-Muslims, had we not put him in a difficult position by suggesting that he take us infidels to such a sacred celebration?

"Maybe," allowed Bob. "But he didn't object to talking about it at first. It's a great source of pride to be related to a saint. They're very important here, you know."

I began to wonder about saints and moussems and fkis. Moulay Mustapha had appeared to be very disappointed indeed when he had been forced to admit that he didn't have the power to become a fki. What power was he talking about? And were there women fkis? I realized I knew nothing whatsoever about this aspect of my friends' and neighbors' lives.

The Iid el Sageer, or little feast following Ramadan, was approaching. We had been visited formally by Hajja Kenza on two occasions during the month of Ramadan; both times she had held forth pompously about the necessity of really fasting as opposed to pretend fasting.

"Oh, we know about those men," she said, "government officials and so on. They turn a pious face to the public. '*Ramadan karim,*' they say, but as soon as they get inside their own houses, they take a bite of this and a bite of that and a little cup of tea. And they call themselves Muslims! It's a disgrace!"

"You'll find people like that everywhere," Bob commented.

"In America they have Ramadan?" asked Kenza in amazement.

"No, no," I answered and tried to explain about Lent, which was, I thought, based on the same general idea, though somewhat less stringent in its application.

Hajja Kenza grunted. "Humph. Ramadan is more, more . . ." she groped for the proper adjective and turned to Aisha, who supplied it after a torrent of words had passed back and forth ". . . more holy!" Kenza pronounced triumphantly. "Christianity is an easy religion. Everybody does what they like."

"Well, at least they don't pretend to fast when they aren't fasting," returned Bob, with some asperity. "Which is better?"

Hajja Kenza started to laugh, stopped, announced she couldn't understand Bob's Arabic, and turned to Aisha for clarification. After five minutes, the subject had somehow shifted to the coming celebration of the feast.

"At Bab el Robb," Hajja Kenza confided, "you can buy a good sheep from the country for about twenty dollars. No more!"

Bob said he didn't think we could afford or would need a whole sheep for our family.

Hajja Kenza exploded. "Nonsense, Mr. Bob! I'm a single widow with one daughter and I am buying one, Aisha is buying one. Everyone who is anyone buys a sheep for the Iid."

"But they're not Muslims," pointed out Aisha.

"Ah, yes," Kenza eyed us ruminatively. "Yes," she repeated absentmindedly, and rose to go.

"Hajja Kenza," began Bob, "I wanted to tell you that David and I are going away for the Iid with a friend of ours. Do you think it'll be all right for B.J. and the girls to stay alone in the house while we're gone?"

Kenza snorted. "Oh, of course, of course. *I* stay alone all the time without a man. Am *I* afraid?"

We both shook our heads; I could not imagine Kenza being afraid.

"The door is strong, solid metal. Of course, if *Elizabetha* is afraid" (she gave me a withering look), "Aisha could always stay with her."

I quickly said that I wasn't afraid at all! But I was annoyed that Bob had decided to go visiting Berber villages on this particular feast. The Harrises were going to Rabat, and the girls and I would be alone. Ordinarily this would not have mattered, but the feast was a time for families to be together, especially, I thought, families all by themselves in an alien environment. However, the game was set. I understood perfectly well the reason for Bob's trip, to get some sense of the villagers with whom the Marrakshi merchants dealt, some picture of the country that was so closely tied to this city. There were no hotels in the villages, and we could not all sleep in the car. Rationally, it was quite right for Bob and his anthropologist friend Don Cole to go, and to take David with them. But irrationally, I resented the whole plan.

Some of my resentment must have been evident, for Kenza, in an untypical gesture, laid her hand gently on my shoulder.

"Ah, we'll take care of her," she said. "Women can take care of themselves and each other. Who needs men?" And she smiled, whether at the situation or my feminine weakness, it was hard to tell.

Kenza and Aisha did take care of us. The afternoon Bob left, Aisha proposed a trip to the sheep market, and Laura Ann, Laila, and I walked with her past the entrance to Arset el Ma'ach, the Hebrew School, the Kasbah gate. The streets were full of people on this, the final day of Ramadan, for at sundown the horns would blow and the drums would sound and the season of fasting would come to an end. A new season would begin, the season of feasts: Iid el Sageer would be followed by Iid el Kabeer, Ashura, the Fête du Trone, the moussems of the saints. Everyone was out doing last-minute shopping, and many people seemed bound in the same direction as we.

We passed under the high double-stone arch of the gate at Bab el Robb to find the *mechouar*, the stretch of land between the city walls and the mountain highway, transformed from an empty plain into an enormous sheep market. As far as we could see, the plain was alive with moving, milling flocks of sheep, and the noise was deafening. Thousands of sheep bleated and baaed: black sheep, gray sheep, brown-and-white sheep, multicolored sheep, sheep with curly horns, sheep with short horns, sheep with long, twisting horns, white lambs, black lambs. And moving among the shifting flocks of noisy sheep were the citizens of Marrakech, men and women in djellabas and hoods and veils, shopping for their festal meal.

"Some of the animals are already bought," said Aisha, "but not completely paid for. The owners have to come before sundown tonight to make the final payment and take the sheep away."

The idea that these thousands of sheep would be absorbed in the next twenty-four hours by the city of Marrakech (population, 260,000) seemed incredible to me, and I said so.

"Oh, they won't all be sold," Aisha confirmed. "Some will just go back to the country. Come on, let's go closer."

At first sight of this wide plain jammed with bleating, moving sheep, Laura Ann and Laila had stopped in their tracks. But gradually, holding each others' hands tightly so as not to get lost in the crowd, and with Aisha leading us, we had maneuvered ourselves into the center of the market, and here the noise and dust seemed somehow less, and the process of buying and selling seemed to be conducted in a very orderly and efficient manner. The sheep within each flock were arranged by size, and the flocks were staked to the ground or bundled in carts, or gathered around a truck, with small boys keeping them in order. The sheepmen in their rough wool djellabas were hard to distinguish from one another; it was only among the women that the difference between city and country was evident: town women wore veils, country women did not. Bargains were being struck all around us; money changed hands.

Aisha and Laura Ann were ahead of us, Aisha testing the fat on the back of a black sheep, examining in a professional way a pair of horns, showing Laura Ann how to look carefully at the wool "to make sure there's no disease." Laura Ann seemed to be talking to Aisha; I had noticed recently that she had begun to understand some of the Arabic; I was glad to see her trying to communicate.

"Oh, Mama!" cried Laila. "Look at the cute black lamb! Let's buy it for a pet."

"Where would we keep it?"

"In the courtyard or on the roof. It could drink out of the fountain."

"But we'd have to tie it up. It wouldn't be fair to the lamb!"

"It would be such a nice pet," she said wistfully.

I shook my head.

"Oh, please," she begged, "and then . . . and then we could fatten it up and give it to Aisha when we leave for her next year's feast," she finished triumphantly.

I acknowledged the inspiration, but continued to say no. Sheep droppings, on the roof or in the courtyard, plus daily fodder and hours of bleating, day and night, were not things I felt like contending with for the months we would be living in Marrakech.

"Let's just walk around and enjoy it all and admire the sheep," I suggested. "Look, Aisha is bargaining."

"I thought she already had a sheep," said Laila.

Aisha nodded. "Yes, that's true. I just wanted to make sure he didn't pay too much." He, meaning her husband, Khaddour. She always referred to him that way.

Prices did not vary a great deal. A big fat sheep might bring as much as $25; a healthy lamb, $4.00 or $5.00. Aisha's husband Khaddour had paid $8.50, Kenza $20, "but Kenza's sheep is much bigger and fatter than ours."

The festal sheep market seemed basically a sound and simple idea. During the summer and fall, the farmers fattened their lambs in the mountains, and in the winter they came down to sell them on the edge of the city to a populace that wanted them. Supply and demand balanced out. Money received from the sale of sheep was turned into city goods not available in the mountains and on the farms: cloth, jewelry, sugar, tea, cutlery, matches. The citizens of Marrakech

benefited in two ways: They had a country-grazed sheep for their annual ritual sacrifice, and they sold their own goods back to the farmers. A fair exchange. The sheep that were not sold walked up to the
mountains and farms to graze for another year or to be eaten in the
summer.

"How long has the sheep market been going on?" I asked.

"As long as I can remember," said Aisha.

Perhaps the festal sheep market had been in progress longer than
anyone could remember, since the walls had first been built, in the
twelfth century, by the Almoravide Sultan Youssef bin Tachfin, to
protect the city from the rampages of country tribesmen.

"Look, Mama, isn't she pretty?" Laura Ann pointed above us to a
plump girl in a golden caftan, running along the ledge of the old city
wall while the young sheep farmers looked up at her in admiration.
Other girls sat on the wall, shouting and flirting with the men. The
last of the Ramadan sunlight caught their shining caftans, sunlight
that had passed over the masses of sheep, was receding slowly from
the old stone walls, and was darkening the mountain peaks on the far
horizon.

Aisha laughed, but she shook her head, too, at that plump golden
girl. Aisha, I decided, was basically a Puritan.

"We must go," she said, taking my hand. "It's time for dinner."

At the gate, rows of small peddlers were ranged together in an
impromptu market, offering items that would be needed for the cere-
monial slaughtering: long knives, knife sharpeners, metal skewers for
brochettes; rope to tie the sheep; blocks of wood in various sizes to be
used as cutting boards; piles of straw and fresh-cut fodder to fatten
the sheep already sold, to keep alive and well those that were still for
sale.

A professional butcher stood there, too, who would, his son was
shouting, for only a small fee, slaughter a sheep for a family without
a male head or anyone able to perform the ritual. While the boy
shouted, a sheep bleated his last, and a horde of children materialized
to see the next steps in the process. Laila hid her head in my shoulder
so she wouldn't have to look, but Laura Ann moved forward with
Aisha. Did she remember, vaguely, similar feasts in Egypt, when, as a
small girl in Cairo, she, too, had witnessed the slaughter of the
sacrificial sheep?

"He will kill ours first thing in the morning, after prayers," Aisha
was saying, as we walked slowly home.

"He?"

"My husband."

"Oh, yes." I was continually confused by Aisha's reference to her husband as "he." She called her sons by their names, Youssef, Abdul Krim, and Saleh; she called the baker by his name, Moussa; her father's name had been Mohammed. Why was her husband simply "he"? Was it obvious to everyone who "he" was? Was he so close to her as that? Did she not want anyone to know her husband's name? I simply did not know.

"Will there be lots happening tomorrow because of the feast?" Laura Ann was asking.

I translated; the girls looked disappointed at Aisha's reply, a firm negative shake of the head.

"The Iid is a private feast," she said.

"Not even in Djemaa el Fna there won't be more dancers or snake charmers or something?" Laura Ann pressed her.

Aisha allowed that there might be, but that had nothing to do with the feast.

She repeated again what Abdul Lateef had told Bob; there were no really public aspects to the Iid in Marrakech, except in the mosques. One went to the mosque, one prayed and gave thanks to God that one had enough of this world's goods to be able to buy a sheep and give a portion of it to one less fortunate; one went home and ate with one's family. Abdul Lateef deplored the fact that people spent more than they could afford on the feast. "Everyone feels he must have a sheep or he's not respectable or self-sufficient."

"We all take some food to the mosque," Aisha was saying, "and we eat together and give a meal to the poor."

"And the second and third day of the feast?"

Aisha looked surprised. "We give on the first day. That is enough."

The doors of the grain market, just inside the Kasbah gate, were closing as we passed, and the flour mill, conveniently located next door, was being swept in preparation for the three-day holiday. We walked to Djemaa el Fna and stood in line to buy fruit before the market closed, with the last-minute shoppers waiting for buses to take them home to Demnate, Azilal, Agadir, Essaouira, Amizmiz, and other places we had not even heard of. They sat patiently beside supplies for the weekend: baskets of fruit and vegetables; bundles of wood and charcoal; a newly polished table; two live chickens: offerings for the feast from one family member to another. Everyone in Marrakech, it seemed, was getting together or going away for the holiday. Everyone but us. I tried to shake off my silly depression when we got home by making a cake and some cookies, in case Pansy, our American friend from Rabat, or Jerry, one of the students from the summer program, appeared.

"This is for the Iid?" asked Aisha, eying the newly baked cake.

"Well, we may have guests. A lady from Rabat and maybe one of my husband's students."

"A man?" Aisha looked disapproving.

"Oh, he won't sleep here, Aisha," I reassured her. "Just eat. But maybe the lady will stay."

Aisha's relief was evident. She was taking seriously Bob's request that she take care of us, and was glad she would not have to deal with the problem of a strange man in the house.

"Come see our sheep, you and Laura Ann and Laila."

We crossed through the sibha to Aisha's courtyard, where a moderately good-sized sheep stood in one corner, masticating some grass and carrot peelings.

"Not bad, eh?" Aisha smiled and patted the animal's flank.

"Nice sheepie," Laila said gently, but the sheep went on chewing his peelings and paid no attention.

Najiya came out of the bedroom in a pink caftan and shook hands with us. The other families who lived around the dingy courtyard were not in evidence this evening, and Aisha seemed very much in charge, and proud of the situation. Youssef ran up and down the passage two or three times to show he was there, and he finally came in and spoke and shook hands, too. His face, badly lacerated in a fight at school, seemed much better since Aisha had taken him to the pharmacy, where they had cleaned and bandaged the ugly, jagged cut and applied some sulfa powder.

"Mama, who's crying?"

We listened. Yes, someone was sobbing nearby. Najiya and her mother exchanged glances and Aisha said, in an annoyed voice, "Oh, don't bother about it. That's just Zahia, crying because Hassan took a sheep to Khadooj and her mother and father and hasn't given her one yet. How silly she is."

The sobbing continued behind Rakosh's door while we stood at the entrance to the sibha, waiting for an elderly man to pass by.

"The qadi," whispered Aisha. "Si Qadi!"

I peered out to get a good look at our most distinguished neighbor before he turned the corner and headed down to his house at the dead end of the small zanka. Tall, self-possessed, clean-shaven, in a rust-colored djellaba of excellent quality, he wore his hood carefully folded over a white skullcap. The qadi's glance passed over us quickly, three foreign females of no obvious distinction, standing with a friend in the sibha.

"You can see the garden in his house from your roof," Aisha told me, still in a whisper. "And he has two television sets."

We went to bed amid the joyous noises signaling the end of Ramadan, that month in the Islamic year that dramatizes the virtues of poverty, humility, the love of God. And at the end of the month comes celebration: The fast is over, and plenty appears once more, if only temporarily.

Early on the morning of Thursday, January 27, we heard the blaring of radios and television sets. King Hassan II had returned from prayers at the royal mosque in Rabat. The Iid had officially begun, marked in Marrakech by a long siren sounding across the city. A great stillness settled over Rue Trésor.

"It's never been so quiet before," said Laila.

"Everybody's killing their sheep, silly," replied Laura Ann.

Laila made a face at her, then forgot everything at the sound of our door knocker. It was Pansy!

"Happy feast!" she cried, and presented the children with a bag full of American candy and cookies.

"Oh, thank you!"

"Look, Laura Ann! M and M's and chocolate peanut butter cups!"

"Come, Pansy, we'll show you the house," said Laura Ann.

We all took the tour, and on the roof, we looked over the edge of the dividing wall to see Hajja Kenza and Naima, with the help of a hired butcher, still at work on their twenty-dollar sheep. They nodded and kept on with their task. The butcher was chopping the meat into appropriate-sized pieces while Kenza laid out the liver and lights, tidily, on a clean slab of wood. Naima was scrubbing the roof, and while we watched, she stood up and helped her mother turn the sheepskin inside out to dry before slitting it to be cured and sheared of its wool.

"The first day we eat the soup from the bones, and the liver," Kenza said, after shaking hands with Pansy. "Then the chops in brochette the second day, and the third day the rest of the meat in tajeen stew."

We waved at Lateefa and Zahia, also up on the roof preparing meat. I decided that Hassan must have brought a second sheep as a peace offering, for Zahia, the second wife, was in high spirits, giggling and calling across, "Happy feast! Happy feast!"

The knocker sounded almost the moment we had reached the downstairs courtyard. It was Naima, bearing a plate of lamb chops.

"For the feast," she smiled, and was gone before I had time to think of how to reciprocate. For reciprocate I must, I felt.

The cake was cut up, and Laura Ann took a plate of slices, centered by a package of M and M's, next door.

"Hajja Kenza expected it, I think," she said, "but they liked it, too."

The knocker banged again. Jerry Weiner stood at the door. We invited him for lunch.

Once more the knocker sounded. It was Aisha, whose broad smile above a plate of grilled liver and her own bread hot from the oven faded at the sight of Jerry. But I introduced everyone, we shook hands, and I ran in to the kitchen to cut some more cake for Aisha's family.

"Laura Ann! Laura Ann!" Naima's voice was calling from the roof.

"Here, Mama." Laila brought in a bag of toffees. "This is for Youssef. Pansy brought us so much."

"A good idea, but it's better to offer it for everyone. Why don't you present the plate to Aisha?"

Laila did. Aisha kissed her and smiled and wished us all a happy day. Laura Ann reappeared just as the door closed behind Aisha!

"What did Naima want?"

Laura Ann laughed. She looked at Jerry. "She wanted to know who the man was and what he was doing here while Baba was away and whether he was going to sleep in the house!"

"Well, Jerry," I said, "fortunately I mentioned you to Aisha yesterday, or my reputation on Rue Trésor would be absolutely ruined."

We went in to a lunch of Aisha's liver and bread, some of Kenza's chops, and the rest of our cake. Except for soup from the bones, our festal menu was surprisingly like that of Aisha and Kenza and Zahia and their families.

Our Iid weekend, which had, in my own mind, begun so dismally, turned out to be pleasant after all. Pansy brought some American friends over, which gave the girls still another opportunity to show off our house, with its splashing fountain and colored lights in the bedrooms. The Harrises returned early from Rabat and invited us over

Sunday afternoon. It was nearly dusk when Bettye and I, drinking tea in her comfortably warm house, were startled by a crash, followed by screams.

"What's that?" I asked. "Did you hear something?"

"Probably just the children," answered Bettye, "hollering around in that half-finished villa the governor is building next door. It's for a new wife, they say."

She poured another cup of tea.

Another cry reached us. "Mama! Mama!"

I rushed outside as Greg and Laila, both crying and screaming hysterically, ran toward me.

"Laura Ann's dead! She's dead!" cried Greg.

"Laura Ann! L-Laura Ann!" hiccuped Laila. Her face was contorted with tears.

"Be quiet, Greg!" said Bettye sharply. "Of course she's not dead."

My heart contracted, and I kept running toward the half-finished villa, then stopped in my tracks. Laura Ann, her face and hands streaming with blood, a dazed expression on her face, was staggering up the walk, supported by Tanya.

"Laura Ann!"

"She fell!" said Tanya. "Fell through the glass bricks of the balcony."

I could see the balcony from where I stood. Twenty, thirty feet above the ground through glass onto a tiled surface below? It didn't seem possible that the child could do that and still be alive.

"Stop that wailing!" insisted Bettye. "All of you. You're not helping a thing!"

Bettye and Tanya and I half carried Laura Ann up to the gates of the Harris house, where Ernest, roused from his study by the screaming, had already backed the car out of the garage.

"We've got to get her to a doctor," he said calmly. "Put her in carefully," and he opened the back door of the car. "We'll go to our doctor. He's French."

Shock. My mind registered that Laura Ann was in shock and had to be kept warm. Where was her jacket? Whatever was the matter with her, we had to keep her warm. It was so cold. I ran crazily all over the house but could not find my daughter's jacket.

"Get in the car, B.J.! We have to get her to a doctor!" Ernest, who had never raised his voice to anyone in my presence, was shouting.

Tanya, without a word, handed Laura Ann's jacket through the car window. It had been in full sight the whole time, hanging on the front gatepost. My mind was a confused mixture of visions: Laila and Greg crying in Bettye's arms, Tanya wiping her eyes, and Laura Ann slumped heavily against me in the back seat of the car, her purple sweater smeared with blood.

The doctor's office was just closing, but Ernest, efficient as usual, ran around to the back door where the doctor was getting into his car and dragged him back to look at our emergency case.

The nurse and doctor, both impressed by the blood, took over quietly. We sat there numbly, Ernest and I, while Laura Ann was laid out, and when the half-hour examination was over, it turned out that my older daughter had cut her hand badly going through the glass, had a surface scratch on her face, a sprained ankle, and that was all.

"*Madame,*" murmured the nurse, "*C'est un miracle! Un miracle véritable! Grâce au bon Dieu, Madame!*" She was holding Laura Ann's hand while the French doctor picked out, one by one, nearly forty splinters of glass.

"Rest and quiet," he said finally. "And a tetanus shot. On Monday bring her back for an X ray of her ankle. I don't think anything is broken, but we should be sure." He shook his head. "*Un miracle,*" he repeated.

"It must have been her clothes that helped to save her," I suggested, and he agreed. Because it was so cold that Sunday, Laura Ann had been wearing two heavy sweaters over an undershirt, tights, heavy socks, corduroy pants, and her new leather boots from Spain. The boots had absorbed much of the force of the fall, for the heels, brand new, were shattered into bits.

By the time we got back to the Harrises, Bettye had calmed Greg and Laila. Bettye fed us all, and, still a little dazed, we were driven home by Ernest, who helped me get limping Laura Ann down Rue Trésor and up the steep stairs to her bed. On Rue Trésor the baker had come out of the shop to inquire about Laura Ann, and Fuad, lounging by the sibha, said something quietly in French. It sounded like "I'm sorry." I could not think of anything to say to Ernest except to thank him and apologize for being so slow-witted about not getting into the car.

Ernest smiled. "I didn't mean to holler, either," he said, his ordinary calm manner having returned. "But I didn't know what was the matter with the child. I thought maybe something terrible. Couldn't think of anything except a doctor, fast."

Aisha came in as Ernest went out, and I burst into silly tears explaining what had happened. This started Laila off again, and Aisha looked alarmed for a moment until I wiped my tears away and held onto Laila until she had subsided.

"Thanks be to God, it is a miracle," Aisha said, putting her arm about Laura Ann and squeezing her affectionately. "Rest, Laura Ann. And thank God, thank God that it wasn't worse."

When Bob and Davy returned, full of their mountain adventures, village life paled by comparison with events in the city. Bob drove over to thank Ernest and Bettye for taking such good care of us, and he looked at the balcony through which Laura Ann had plunged. He came home and shivered. The Monday X rays showed a torn ligament in the sprained foot, which, the doctor said, Laura Ann had to keep propped up for a week. During those days, I was surprised and moved by the reactions of our neighbors, whom two or three months ago I had considered so cold and hard and unfeeling. Hajja Kenza and Naima came to sit by Laura Ann's bed and shake their heads; Lateefa came and brought wishes from Rakosh and Zahia. Fatima Henna's mother sent word, via Aisha, that she was glad of our escape from worse fortune. Moussa the baker and Abdul Kabeer, the shopkeeper, asked after her, and even Mbarak, the sleepy-eyed bath boy, offered condolences.

The first day Laura Ann limped off to school, she came home in a happy mood. It had been rumored in her class, she said, that she had fallen from a fifty-foot balcony and would be in the hospital for a month. "When I came in the gate, Eve and Simy came running toward me and they kissed me and said they were so glad I was back. I think they really were."

In my relief, I suggested to Aisha that we have a *karama*, or thanksgiving party, in honor of Laura Ann's miraculous escape.

"I could invite everyone who has been so good to us."

Aisha shook her head. "Not a good idea."

"Why?"

"It just isn't. Did you make a vow beforehand?"

"How could I?"

"Exactly. It was an accident. You don't have karamas after accidents. Maybe Laura Ann's foot would get worse or her hand get infected. One never knows."

Yes, I thought, Aisha was right. One never knows. One can never be delivered from the possible dangers of accidents or the equally possible blessings of good luck. There was little to be done about either. I dropped the subject of the karama, glad that Laura Ann was safe and sound once more.

Chapter 10

Fatima Henna's House

Her name was Fatima, but Laura Ann had called her Fatima Henna ever since the day she had sat on our roof and decorated Barbara Buchler's hands so beautifully with henna. Since Fatima Henna's mother was also named Fatima, Laura Ann's nickname was a convenient way of distinguishing mother from daughter.

Fatima Henna was the oldest daughter in the family. Her father, Hussain, was a bus driver for the CTM Company. Hussain and Fatima had ten children. Aisha told me.

"Ten children?" I repeated incredulously. "Fatima doesn't look like the mother of ten children."

Aisha laughed. *"Baraka!"* she said and held up her hand, with all five fingers close together.

"What?"

"Baraka! I mean they are blessed, but more than blessed. Enough is enough. *Baraka!"*

Of the ten children, only seven lived at home. The oldest son had died young; another was married and working in a Casablanca factory; a third had returned to the ancestral village of Ait Tamour, where he was farming the small piece of land still belonging to the family. Of the children at home, Benasser was a barber in a shop on Riad el Zeitoon; Brahim had graduated from secondary school to a bookkeeping position in the Marrakech Holiday Inn. Two younger boys were still in school; the second daughter, Jameela, was the pallid half-grown girl who ran to the store without her djellaba every morning; the smallest daughter, still a toddler, was sometimes carried around by Jameela and sometimes played in the sibha with Zahia's children, Shadeeya and Ali and little Kamal.

Fatima Henna's husband, a first cousin, had deserted her more than a year before we moved into our house on Rue Trésor. From that day, said Aisha, "she had become very nervous, although she had not been too happy before." A big, buxom girl in her early twenties, with round cheeks that should have been rosy but were not, Fatima Henna moved with an air of suppressed agitation. I had seen her crossing Djemaa el Fna, holding her daughter Mina by the hand, striding briskly along with a carefully wrapped, flat paper package under her arm, the finished sewing or embroidery she was returning to the merchant who had commissioned it. She strode along too briskly for little redheaded Mina, who protested loudly and dragged her feet and had a hard time keeping up with her mother. But Fatima Henna, lost in her own thoughts, did not seem to even hear her child.

When Fatima Henna had sat on our roof in the sunshine, outlining those designs on Barbara's hands, she had been absolutely calm and still, and the lines of discontent that cut, too early, down both sides of her mouth, had disappeared in her total absorption in the task before her. But afterward, when we sat drinking tea, the lines around her mouth were there again, pulling her face down into an ugly, sullen mask, which was broken only when she smiled at her friend Suad. It was Fatima Henna and Suad who had danced together so suggestively at the wedding, prompting Najiya's insult and precipitating the bitter quarrel that followed. Having seen at close range the unhappiness on Fatima Henna's face, I was not surprised that she had turned to Suad for comfort. For although her natal family had taken her in, they could not help but be somewhat displeased at the course their oldest daughter's life had taken.

"Why doesn't she get a divorce?" I asked Aisha. "Isn't desertion grounds enough?"

"Oh, yes," Aisha assented, "but remember, her husband is a first cousin. To go to the qadi and sue your cousin for divorce is bad for the reputation of the whole family."

"So Fatima Henna has to suffer."

Aisha sniffed. "She has bread to put in her mouth and a place to sleep and her family around her. She has a pretty daughter to raise.

She has a skill; everyone says she does the henna beautifully. You saw it yourself. Many people do not have that much. Her life is not perfect, but whose is?"

Although both Aisha and Hajja Kenza had mixed feelings about Fatima Henna, there was no ambivalence in their attitude toward Fatima the mother.

"Everyone admires and likes her," said Aisha. "She laughs at her troubles!" This, I was learning, was the ultimate compliment, though I ventured that perhaps Fatima could laugh because she had been blessed with good health.

Aisha nodded. "Yes," she agreed. "Good health is a gift from God!"

Fatima was indeed thus endowed. After ten children and a lifetime of continual hard work, she was still a good-looking woman, tall and strong, always smiling, separating the children fighting in the darb, scrubbing her black-and-white-tiled doorstep, hanging up clothes on the roof.

Kenza told me that Fatima had lived on Rue Trésor for about thirty years. "She is from the country, but she tries to understand the ways of the city," said Kenza. "She tries to raise her children decently, to have some manners, and she keeps her roof clean. Look at Rakosh's roof. Those women from Ourika don't have the faintest idea of how to keep house. Neither did Fatima when she first came. But she's learned. And work! Elizabetha, you have no idea how hard she works!" The sidelong glance and the tone told me only too well that Kenza felt I had no idea how hard anyone worked, since I did nothing myself except cook and mend, and the rest of my time I wasted, she said, with books and papers.

"Oh, I know! I know!" I averred. "I've seen her hard at work."

"They didn't even have running water in the house until five or six years ago, and she had to go to the end of Rue Trésor every day and get her water from the public fountain! Think of that!"

I thought of it. My admiration for Fatima increased. A strong character and a strong back. The weak died early here, the strong survived. There did not seem to be much middle ground in this society. Life was hard for both men and women. If you were blessed with health, you embraced life with its sorrows and occasional joys. You laughed in the teeth of hardhearted fate. From what I had observed, children were trained from their earliest years to expect the worst. Babies were little indulged; they cried for long periods before being fed, and few of them were fussed over. Carried on their mother's backs until they could walk, both boys and girls had the comfort of maternal closeness, but they seldom saw their mother's face. Weaned suddenly, they were set on their feet and expected to begin to learn how to behave. How often had I seen toddlers howling outside the closed doors of their houses, crying to be let in. No one paid any attention. When the child stopped howling, the door would be opened and he would be let back in the house. Supposedly he learned quickly not to howl.

One morning there was unusual activity on Fatima Henna's black-and-white-tiled doorstep. Three men—two in suits and one in the white garb of a male nurse—came on motorbikes. Benasser, the brother who was a barber, had collapsed. He was taken to the hospital that afternoon.

"He's yellow as a lemon," Aisha told us. "Not a sign of blood in his skin. He has a liver disease and they say he may die."

Bob and I thought he must have severe hepatitis, and two days later this was confirmed by Kenza, who had discovered that Benasser was in a private room, with tubes putting water and blood back into his body. Five members of his family had already donated blood, and two taxiloads of relatives had arrived from Ait Tamour, expecting his death momentarily. Jameela had even taken two pans of mourning cookies to the oven to be baked, but just as the cookies were ready and the mourners preparing to mourn, Benasser rallied. He would not die, it appeared, but the extra care had been so expensive that Fatima Henna had taken a job in a hotel.

"There's not enough sewing and henna at this season," Aisha explained, "and they have to pay the hospital bills now."

"Where is Fatima Henna working?"

"In one of the big hotels near Djemaa el Fna."

"Poor Fatima Henna."

Aisha nodded. "It's not good for a girl to work in a hotel where she's around strange men. But what else can she do?"

The second floor of Fatima Henna's house had been rented to a French couple. We had met them when we first arrived. The Frenchman's name was Jason, his wife was Gaby, and they were in the import-export business, he said. Gaby cut dresses and shirts and caftans á la Marocaine, which were sewed by Fatima Henna and Suad and then shipped to Paris, to be sold in the moderate-priced ready-to-wear market. But before we had been in our house a month, Jason and

Gaby had departed mysteriously, and the place had been inhabited by the four or five young Americans David talked to through his bedroom window.

The neighbors were very hostile to these young people. Kenza had spoken deprecatingly of them on several occasions and kept asking whether we knew them. We said no.

"Fatima and Hussain are very glad they asked the landlord to brick up the balcony when the French people came," said Aisha. "You saw the walls at the wedding. The work isn't as good as on the house, but at least the family life is private. They were shocked at the way the French people behaved, and the hippies are worse. But they can't see the hippies, and the hippies can't see them."

In the early months we had little contact with these young people, even though they *were* all Americans, David reported. But one morning in January, Bob, sitting on the roof reading, was drawn to the scene on the opposite roof by cackling and squawking punctuated by very loud English swearing. He stood up and saw that three of the young Americans, after finally managing to kill a live chicken they had bought in the market, were now trying to pluck it. In their inexperience, they were pulling off, with the feathers, most of the bird's skin and meager meat.

"Hey," Bob called, "you know if you dropped the bird in hot water first, the feathers would come out easier."

The three looked up, a bare-chested young man in a black pirate turban, a girl in a caftan, and a curly-headed blond boy with glasses.

"Too much trouble, heating the water," answered the curly-headed boy.

Bob, rebuffed, went back to his book, but in a few minutes the curly-headed boy shouted, "Hey, I just realize I know you!"

"What?" returned Bob, somewhat startled.

"I know somebody you know at Goddard College, and they told me to look you up."

Mutual friends established, Bob invited the boy, Alan, for a cup of coffee. When I got home from the market that day, I found them in the dining room. Alan had eaten most of a plateful of cookies and had drunk three cups of coffee, heavily laced with milk and sugar. He was obviously hungry. He also needed a bath. We invited him to stay for lunch, and he told us the story of his life. It went on for quite a while. His father was someone important, it seemed, and so was his uncle. He had gone to the best schools on Long Island, but with the coming of age he had become disillusioned with life in the West. He sat there, a rather pathetic figure in his patched jeans and raveled Abercrombie and Fitch sweater, explaining to us that he had come to Marrakech because that was where it was—the truth, that is.

"The truth is to be found here, in the East," he asserted, "not in corrupt America. Ours is a sick society."

Bob nodded, but pointed out that Moroccan society also had some problems.

"Yet I think you will find they are closer to the truth here," Alan insisted seriously.

"But what truth?" I asked.

Alan was vague. It was something important, something real, it was here, couldn't I feel it in the air around me? What it was exactly, well, that was why he had come, to try to find it. After several hours, he left.

Bob and I looked at each other. We discovered we rather liked Alan and felt sorry for him, but we didn't want to spend our time in Marrakech listening to the story of his life and his friends' lives. However, I had agreed to buy eggs for him from our egg man and vegetables from the vegetable peddler, because he had told us a sad story of local hostility. Almost none of the merchants would sell them food, except inferior produce; people who looked like hippies were always served last, he said.

I knew this was true, since I had witnessed such incidents in the market. The transient population was reasonably large in Marrakech, and the close-fisted Berber and Arab merchants were suspicious and wary of the young drifters from the hard-currency countries: France, Germany, Denmark, America, Canada, Britain. Where were their families, asked Hajja Kenza?

I told Aisha and Kenza and Lateefa and Zahia, who all asked me the same question at one time or another, that these young people were traveling, they were seeing the world.

The good ladies had snorted. "But they live like pigs," said Kenza. "They don't do anything. They wear dirty clothes. They don't take baths, and they take drugs, bad drugs, not just hash, and it is said that they take them for fun!"

"For fun?" I echoed foolishly.

"Yes," repeated Kenza, "for fun, not for a serious reason, to make a husband jealous or poison an enemy or get into a trance for the sake of one's health. And," she leaned closer and whispered, as if this were the final degradation, "they have money! Why do they live like that when they have money? And where do they *get* the money?"

I tried to explain that some of these young people were unhappy in their families, that their families sometimes did not care for them, and so they had left home to find their own way in the world.

Aisha and Kenza and Lateefa and Zahia were incredulous. How could their families not care for them? What was wrong with America? Their families sent them money, didn't they? That meant they cared for them, didn't it?

This argument I found unanswerable, at least in my neighbors' terms. How could I explain to Aisha and Kenza, who pinched every penny to send their children to school so that those children could earn enough money to care for the parents in their old age, that some American parents sent *their* children money just so the children would stay away? The good ladies of Rue Trésor would never have believed me.

It was true that most of the hippies had some money, or could lay their hands on money in an emergency. They could cable home, and the central post office always had a line of young American and European nomads in jeans and Moroccan shirts and back packs, waiting by the cable office to ask for money or receive it. With the exception of a few pitiful bits of flotsam and jetsam who begged outside the post office and in Djemaa el Fna, most of the young people had allowances from home or savings they could draw on. If desperate, they could always go home. But now they were searching for the truth, living poor in the belief that poverty would save them from the corrupt influences of affluence.

For in those years Marrakech was "where it was at," which seemed to mean hash and the truth. Many hundreds of young nomads with those general goals ended up in the medina in one or another of the small cheap hotels in the zankas off Riad el Zeitoon or Rue Bab Agnaou. They found hash and keef, but usually found little else they had hoped for. Expecting brotherly love and international friendship, they were disillusioned by the Moroccans' hassling of them; they were shocked by the poverty they were seeing for the first time at close quarters; and they were annoyed by the local puritanical social attitudes, which they thought they were escaping by leaving home. Some turned hostile in return, a few made friends among young Moroccans, tried to learn the language, and stayed a while, but most moved on farther East after doing Morocco. Truth was hard to find and not always too attractive if discovered.

I bought a dozen extra eggs a day and some vegetables, and our children would deliver them to Alan and Sheryl and Mark. These young people seemed fascinated by our children. They invited the children to have ice cream at the Fruit Shake; they wanted them to play football in the mechouar near Bab el Robb. I was somewhat wary of this relationship, but Bob thought it was not a bad idea for the children to see how these young Americans lived.

"After all the glamor and controversy surrounding hippies at home, don't you think our kids will find the real thing rather sad, just as we do? When it's no longer forbidden, I mean!"

I hoped they would.

Alan's girlfriend Sheryl had studied French at Bennington and used to come over and help Laura Ann with her lessons. She was good with the girls, friendly and firm, and I warmed to her. Lena, however, a sometime member of the ménage, was another matter. Lena, Alan told us confidentially, was a character of some notoriety. Lena was not her real name. No one knew her real name. She had swallowed all kinds of potions and combinations of drugs from the rich variety available on the open market and had emerged alive if somewhat damaged. She had slept alone, on the streets of Marrakech, in her sleeping bag.

"Why did you do that?" Laura Ann asked.

Lena stared. Obviously such a question had never occurred to her. Lena was going to buy a camel and ride alone down to the Mauretanian desert.

"Why?" Laura Ann asked again. "What for?"

Lena looked at her again, but did not deign to reply. Lena's only problem with the proposed camel journey, she said, was that she wanted to have a baby to care for and keep her company while she was traveling in the desert, and nobody seemed interested in giving her one.

"I think that's awful," said twelve-year-old Laura Ann bluntly. "Think of the poor baby! What will it eat in the desert?"

Lena and Sheryl raised their eyebrows while I looked down at the floor. Laura Ann was holding her own quite well, without any help from me. Now Sheryl and Lena were off on another topic, a plan to leave for Essaouira, where they would build a mud-brick house by hand on the beach near Diabet, in a colony of foreign young people. I had the distinct impression that by now Lena was barely tolerating Laura Ann's and my presence, our bourgeois reactions, and wanted to leave suddenly, dramatically, to demonstrate her disapproval. But her cup of coffee was half full, and she was eating a large piece of cake. Lena was hungry, too, like everybody else.

Across from Fatima Henna's house, and next to an empty house, lived Lalla Fadna, the elderly woman in black velvet whom I remembered from the wedding. We saw her sometimes on the roof. Lalla Fadna had bad rheumatism, and the sun helped the pain, she said. Her husband Boushta was an office employee of the railroad; her only son, Hamid, was married and lived on Riad el Zeitoon.

Lalla Fadna shouted whenever she saw us, despite the rheumatism, in a particularly loud and penetrating voice—"because she's lonely," Aisha said. "She doesn't see many people, and her husband, Boushta, is very quiet." I did not quite see the logic of this, unless Boushta was hard of hearing, but I accepted Aisha's explanation, since it seemed perfectly reasonable to her. Had I misunderstood some nuance of the conversation? It was quite possible, for Aisha was taking my comprehension for granted these days and often lapsed into a Moroccan Arabic so quick and short-voweled that I had a hard time keeping up.

Next to Fatima Henna lived Rachida, the plump schoolteacher with the cream-colored motorbike; her husband, Sadiq; her children, wall-eyed Fuad and round-faced Laila. I had often seen a small gray-haired woman standing in the doorway talking to Fatima Henna or Fatima; this, it turned out, was Rachida's mother, who kept house for the family while Rachida taught school and Sadiq worked as an administrator at Sidi Mimoun Hospital.

The house itself belonged to Hajja Kenza, willed to her by her father. Each month she collected the rent, as she did from us, and each month Rachida or her mother would invite Kenza, as we did, to come in and drink coffee.

"The new house" stood beside Rachida's; this was not a totally new house, but had been completely renovated by the owner, the well-to-do proprietor of the only bookstore on Rue Bab Agnaou. His wife was an invalid, Aisha learned, which explained why no one appeared on their newly plastered roof, except for a manservant. Opposite the new house, next to us, lived the assistant manager of the Ramada Inn. (Aisha called it the Ramadan Inn and thought it a funny name for an American hotel, and I had to agree.) This man was young and newly married, but we had never seen his wife, a native of Fez, not even at the wedding.

"They say she doesn't like Marrakech at all and refuses to go out except to take the train to Fez to stay with her family."

At the end of the zanka stood the covered passage that led to the qadi's house. After Aisha's father had died, the qadi had bought the entire sibha, three houses abutting on each other, each with its own courtyard and garden. I had seen the trees in those gardens from my roof.

One day, Laila and I walked to the end of the street, a quiet, clean cul-de-sac in the center of the city. Physically, the qadi's cul-de-sac was only a few steps from one of the busiest and noisiest squares in Marrakech, but in terms of the way it was arranged and entered, one might have been in a remote section of the deepest part of the medina. Kenza had once explained to us that our rent was high because the property was valuable; I believed that she was right; it was valuable as are all protected beautiful spots in the hearts of urban areas.

By February, I thought I had figured out who belonged to what entrance along the street, both Rue Trésor and the small zanka that gave onto it. But one morning we woke to find that the empty house had been turned overnight into a hotel. We had all seen the remodeling in progress, and everyone assumed it would be rented to a family. The hotel sign had been saved until the last moment. Hôtel du Sud.

The women were furious. They thought this was a bad omen for the neighborhood. On the roofs that afternoon, Lateefa told us that Rakosh was going to write a letter to the governor. Fatima shouted from her roof that she would ask Hussain to write one, too.

"It's not good for children to be around a public hotel," she said. "Men tourists and women tourists going in and out!"

I did not know what, if any, action resulted from Rakosh and Hussain's letters to the governor or even whether they were ever sent, but the hotel stayed open. The door had been painted a bright green, "a holy color," Aisha had noted approvingly, but that was before the hotel sign went up. The door, unlike all the other doors on Rue Trésor, stood open, and the women walked past it quickly. The children were encouraged to play on the quieter, smaller zanka, setting up their games of impromptu checkers with stones, bits of glass, and bottle caps. The little girls chalked their hopscotch near Fatima Henna's black-and-white doorstep, and Hind and Naima moved down toward Rachida's house, where they stood knitting, endlessly knitting, comparing nail polish shades, scolding the toddlers, and occasionally taking part in a French version of "Pease Porridge Hot" that began, *"Tirez la gauche! Tirez la droite!"*

Rue Trésor was a mixed neighborhood, not at all what one might have expected from first appearances. The rich religious judge with his three houses; Aisha living in two rooms and sharing her courtyard with four other families; the schoolteacher and the hospital administrator; the extended family from Ourika, one son a repairman, one a waiter; the railroad clerk; the bus driver; a descendant of Glaoui Pasha; a nut seller; a pair of elderly beggars; rich widow Kenza with her three houses; the assistant manager of the Ramada Inn. And now a hotel.

"Mr. Bob," commented our French teacher, Abdul Aziz, with whom we had begun to stop and chat after classes at Arset el Ma'ach, "I know what Westerners think about the medina. Rich people and poor people living in the same neighborhood. What does that suggest to you?"

Bettye and Ernest and Bob and I had looked at each other, at a loss for an answer.

"Why, does it not suggest to you that the poor people are only there to work for the rich people? But that is not the way it is at all. Everyone takes responsibility for everyone else. Your street is a quarter, a true neighborhood, in the ancient sense of the word."

"You mean there aren't some quarters in Marrakech that are mostly rich merchants or mostly artisans or mostly religious persons?" asked Bob. This was what some of the old histories had implied.

"A few, yes," admitted Abdul Aziz. "But most quarters are a mixture of all kinds of people, such as you find on Rue Trésor. That is the true meaning of the medina."

One night, early in February, I had tucked the children into bed and opened David's window for a last look at Rue Trésor, quiet and deserted, except for Marzook, the fat watchman who sat in the lighted, open doorway of the Hôtel du Sud.

"It's cold, Mama, leave the window shut," said David, and I had barely pulled the window to when we heard noise in the distance. Someone, it sounded like a man, was running up the street toward our house, shouting at the top of his lungs.

"What's that?" asked Laila fearfully, sitting up in bed and clutching her teddy bear.

I stood irresolutely in the bedroom as the shouting and the footsteps came closer. Bob came running up the stairs.

"What is it?"

"I don't know."

"Fatima! Fatima!" The man called out the name as he came along Rue Trésor, banging first on one side of the street, then on the other, and not on the wooden house doors that would have reverberated, but on the hard, thick, brick walls, which absorbed the frenzied blows in sickening dull thuds.

"Is he hitting his head?" Laura Ann sounded frightened.

"No, I don't think so," I answered. "I think just his hands."

Bob opened Davy's window carefully and we all looked down into the street. Marzook the watchman, who only a moment ago had sat in the open doorway of the hotel, had disappeared; the light was out and the door was shut. All the doors were closed on Rue Trésor, and the street was empty except for the anguished man who now stood directly below us, screaming and pounding on the door of Fatima Henna's house.

"Fatima!" he sobbed. "What have I done? Oh, my sister!" He repeated this in a voice that rose higher and higher while he continued to pound on the door.

"Allah! Allah!" he called. "Fatima!"

"Is he sick, Baba?" whispered David.

"Drunk, maybe?" I ventured.

"I don't think so," Bob answered. "Let's just be quiet."

The man below us was small, hardly more than a boy.

"Fatima! My sister! What have I done? O God!" His pounding and shouting became more desperate. "Fatima!" he screamed.

But the door remained closed. No light showed in the house. He paused; then, in a frenzy of frustration, he began to rip off his clothes. First he flung his skullcap on the ground, then his djellaba came off, he unzipped a jacket and tossed that down, between intermittent poundings and cries of "Allah! Fatima!" Next came his turtleneck sweater, and he stood there, in his undershirt and trousers, in the bitter cold, sobbing, "Fatima! Fatima!"

Still the door did not open. He leaned his head against the rough wall and wept, quieter now. I was reminded of the toddlers left outside until they had stopped howling; for the door now opened a crack, and the father, Hussain, stood on the black-and-white-tiled sill, a broad figure in a skullcap and djellaba, sinister and large in the cold winter moonlight.

"In," hissed Hussain, but the boy had sunk down against the wall and did not seem to hear.

The father picked up the crumpled form of the boy, took him inside, and returned to pick up the discarded clothes from the street. The door shut softly. In the back of the house somewhere a candle flame sputtered yellow. A woman was sobbing. Someone said, "Shhh." The candle was extinguished. Once more silence reigned on Rue Trésor.

We closed our window. I tucked the children into bed again. Ten minutes had passed.

"What happened?"

"We don't know," said Bob, "but he's all right now. We'll ask Aisha in the morning. Now go to sleep."

Downstairs Bob said it sounded as though the boy were saying he stabbed his sister. I reminded him that Fatima Henna had been working in a hotel for the past month to help pay her other brother's hospital bills. Had she become involved with a man, been discovered by her brother, and then been stabbed by the hysterical boy to save the family honor?

In the morning Aisha insisted she had not heard a thing. "Our house is quite a way in from the street," she reminded me. Later in the morning, she told me that none of the neighbors knew anything. Fatima Henna's mother had made her regular appearance to wash the front step and had said good morning brightly to everyone, as she usually did. The only unusual detail was that the mother, instead of sending Jameela, had put on her djellaba and veil and had gone to the store herself for milk. "We think that was so she could speak to everybody on the street." After a moment's reflection, Aisha added, "Whatever happened, it's a secret," and shook her head. "It's not good to work in a hotel."

"But Aisha," I pointed out, "you yourself said she didn't want to. She prefers sewing and henna. She had to. That's hard. Her life is hard."

"Life is hard for everyone," said Aisha. "But we all try to do our best. Fatima Henna is not doing the right thing. If she were pleasant, she could persuade her brothers to talk to her father, and then maybe her father would agree to a divorce and she could marry again. But oh, no, not Fatima, she has to take the easy way out."

"The easy way?"

Aisha did not answer. She shrugged. "She thinks she's too good for everything," she said finally, rather bitterly.

"Well, I can't help it, I'm sorry for her," I answered, and opened the refrigerator. I thought the subject was closed, but to my surprise, Aisha suddenly burst out,

"Sorry for her? Sorry? You think that's a good way to behave, running around with men, doing God knows what? Would you want Laura Ann and Laila to do that?"

"No, no, of course not," I answered quickly, somewhat taken aback by the sudden change in tactics. "I agree with you that's not a good way to behave, but I still feel sorry for her."

"Save your pity for her mother," she said. "Think of the disgrace. All those years of hard work for your children, and then—" she drew in her breath sharply and stopped.

"They're from the country," I pointed out. "You said yourself that people in the country don't always know how to behave in the city."

"Believe me," retorted Aisha, banging a pot down on the tile drainboard with unnecessary force, "they don't behave *that* way in the country. She's never been any good, that girl."

There it lay between us, the unvarnished statement. I think we were both a little appalled, for we both realized what consequences that kind of talk could have, not only for a girl, but for her whole family.

"It's nothing against the family," Aisha said quickly. "It's a good family. Everyone works hard. But even in the best of families, sometimes there's someone bad. I feel sorry for her little daughter, Mina, and I feel sorry for her mother."

The sound of the garbage man's horn put an end to the conversation. No one ever knew exactly what happened. Moulay Mustapha, who knew Brahim and Benasser, the two sons, told Bob we would probably never know.

"He may have stabbed his sister to save the family honor," he admitted, "or he may have done nothing at all."

"Nothing at all? Then why the hysterics?"

1. Visiting dancers from the south (Sultan's festival)

2. Rue Trésor

3. Fernea house, girls on the balcony

4. Men and women in grain market

5. Over-all view of Djemaa el Fna

6. Acrobats, Djemaa el Fna

7. Gnaoua dancers in Djemaa el Fna

8. Walled shrine

9. Market closed during siesta

10. Koutonbia minaret detail

11. Fortune-teller, Djemaa el Fna

"Well," explained Moulay Mustapha, "he might have seen his sister with a man and become upset and then run home, shouting that he'd done something terrible, to *pretend* that he'd protected the family honor."

Abdul Lateef nodded thoughtfully. "Families work these things out in their own way," he pronounced.

A week passed. Aisha and I saw Fatima Henna's mother in Djemaa el Fna, near the Café des Glaciers. I did not recognize her at first, but Aisha went up and spoke to her.

"I wonder what she was doing in Djemaa el Fna," mused Aisha. "Not shopping. She had no basket."

Was the errant daughter lying wounded in one of the servants' rooms of the hotel on the square? Had the mother come to take care of her? And who was paying so that Mina could go to the expensive day-care center? Aisha looked dumbfounded when I told her I had seen Mina at one of the play tables the day I had gone with an American Peace Corps friend to visit the center and meet the two teachers.

"You're sure, Elizabetha?"

"Yes. Mina waved at me, and I waved back."

"You know the child?" Mary, the Peace Corps volunteer, had asked.

I had nodded and smiled. "Yes, she lives on this street."

"Madame must be mistaken," Farida, one of the pretty teachers, said at the time. "We have no children from Rue Trésor."

And Amal, the other pretty teacher, smiled, "It's easy to make a mistake, all children look so much alike."

I said nothing, and was taken into the kitchen to observe what a good lunch was being prepared for the children.

"*Lebas*, Madame!" old Lalla Yezza, my friend the cook, cried.

"*Lebas!*" I replied.

She gave me a hard stare and went back to stirring the pot of rice. Had she overheard my conversation about Fatima Henna's child?

The hippies, back from Essaouira, had tried to reoccupy their second-floor lodgings, with no success. Sheryl said they had told her the roof had collapsed upstairs, and it was obvious they didn't want anyone there. Had they something to hide? No one could be sure. All we knew was that Mina was in the day-care center, the hippies were locked out, the people in Fatima Henna's house went about their daily business, and no one had seen Fatima Henna.

A week passed before old Lalla Yezza stopped before my open door, where Aisha and I were buying carrots and onions from the peddler.

"*Lebas*, Madame!"

"*Lebas!*"

"I have a good job," she said loudly. "The teachers are good girls. They are kind to me, to the children, to everybody."

"Yes, Lalla Yezza."

She started all over again, repeating the same phrases about the good teachers at the day-care center. Was she warning me not to get them into trouble by telling someone about Mina's presence?

"I understand, Yezza," I answered. "They are kind to everybody, children and mothers."

I hoped she understood that I was trying to tell her I wouldn't dream of saying anything to anybody in an "authoritative" position. She smiled. She seemed satisfied.

"*Bslama!*"

"*Bslama*, Yezza!"

Winter wore on, and Fatima Henna did not return.

Chapter 11

A Way into the Medina

The Western feast of St. Valentine's Day, a source of amusement to the Moroccans in our class at the Mission Culturelle Française, ended memorably. We arrived home to find three children sitting around the heater in the dining room: Laila, Laura Ann, and Greg. Where were David and Tanya? I looked at my watch; it was nearly nine-thirty.

"What happened?" Bettye was asking Greg in a worried voice when the knocker banged loudly, very loudly. In burst a jubilant David and an equally jubilant Tanya.

"They asked us! They really did!" announced David.

"Wait a minute," said Ernest. "Who asked you what?"

"We've been playing soccer with the kids in the square," said David.

"We were waiting for you to come by so you could see us," said Tanya.

Tonight, of all nights, we had driven home with Bettye and Ernest, rather than cutting through the square behind Rue Trésor on foot, as we usually did.

"Isn't that great, Baba?"

"I'm not so sure it's a good idea," interjected Bettye mildly, with a glance at Tanya.

"Oh, Mama, it was fun," insisted Tanya. "They're real good players."

"How come they asked you?" inquired Bob. "They never did before."

"Well, you know me and Tanya've been wanting to play soccer out there for a long time. Some nights we'd go by slowly and hope they'd ask us to join, but they never did, and—"

"Tonight," Tanya interrupted, "Davy thought we should stand closer, so they could tell we wanted to—"

"I had a feeling they might tonight, and Tanya thought so, too, and then I thought I heard one of the big guys say, '*Joues-toi, joues*,' and we ran in. Are they good! Man!"

Bettye still looked dubious.

"Ah, Mrs. Harris, let her play," begged Davy. "She looks like a tomboy, and everybody is real nice to her. She plays good."

As the days passed, Davy's spirits rose. Tanya did not always take part, but David was playing neighborhood soccer almost every night after his French class. The boys on Rue Trésor no longer pulled on his clothes or shouted insults at him. His earlier fishing successes had given him some status, and his new soccer prowess established his reputation, a reputation enhanced (judging from Fuad and Ali's admiring glances) by the surprising variety of French and Arabic swear words that he managed to insert into all of his street conversations. One day he went to the Cinema Marhaba with Aisha's boys, Youssef and Abdul Krim, to see a popular spaghetti Western, *On M'Appelle Trinita*. "You know, Mama," he said thoughtfully, "that was the first time Youssef had ever been to the movies. He really liked it." When he went to the store with Laila she told me no one ever pulled her hair.

Laila, however, remained shy and reserved. She seemed to be making some friends at L'École Renoir; I had heard names dropped: Gail, Malika, Anne Marie. But she also reported continued irritation at one French child who waylaid her on the playground daily with one or the other of the two English sentences she knew: "Do you speak German?" and "Do you eat corn flakes for breakfast?" Bob remarked that those sentences were certainly far more polite than the gutter curses that were David's first venture into Arabic. But on Rue Trésor Laila held back. With the plump schoolteacher's daughter she would exchange "*Bon jour, Laila*" 's, and the two little girls would smile conspiratorially at the coincidence of each other's identical names. And one Wednesday afternoon I heard the unmistakable chant of Laila's favorite skipping-rope rhyme rising from the small zanka.

"Polichinelle! Écarter!"

"Polichinelle! À sauter!"

"Why don't you go down and play, Laila?" I suggested.

"No, no, Mama, I don't want to!" and she went into her room and shut the door, obviously to keep Mama from making any more untoward suggestions about her social life. Yet, fifteen minutes later, I was certain I heard my younger daughter's voice raised in the chorus. I tiptoed to the window to see Laila, curled up in her window sill, calling down verses of her own!

"Polichinelle! Mangez la soupe!"

"Polichinelle! Touchez parterre!"

The little girls in the street below repeated the new verses in thin, childish voices, joined by Laila, chanting from her vantage point on the window sill. But that was as far as she would go.

This was not true of Laura Ann, who would stop on her way home from school to speak in French to Naima and Hind, as they stood knitting against the wall of Rachida's house. Laura Ann carried on regular window-to-window conversations with Khadija, in broken but understandable Arabic. At school she found friends, a little group of girls who ate lunch together: Eve, Simy, Marie-Jose, Dalila. Laura Ann announced that she wanted to have her ears pierced and would like a caftan to go under her djellaba. When I suggested that we might get Lateefa to make the caftans, Laila timidly added she'd like a caftan, too.

Occasional bursts of hostility still erupted in the evening French classes. Sentiment about the Americans seemed to be divided, David said, between the boy who would toss a rock at him and another who took pains to greet him formally at the beginning and end of each class. But the crowd harassment had generally stopped.

Like their parents, our children were beginning to feel more at ease in the larger area of the city as well as on Rue Trésor.

One day when I was ill, Laura Ann and Laila had gone to the Gueliz market alone to buy bread and cheese and fruit, and had bargained for and ridden home a horse and buggy, which had deposited them conveniently (according to Laura Ann's instructions) on the corner of Rue Trésor and Rue Bab Agnaou. David went to have his hair cut on Rue Bab Agnaou. The barber asked five dirhams, David offered two. They settled at 3.25. Laura Ann invited the son and daughter of her French tutor to play, and all five children went together to Djemaa el Fna. Although the French children had lived all their lives in Marrakech, they had not spent much time in Djemaa el Fna, it turned out. Our own children were rather pleased, I thought, to show their French schoolmates the secrets and wonders of the medina. And as their fluency in French increased, their confidence grew accordingly.

Bob's work was going well, too. Abdul Lateef and Moulay Mustapha continued to visit, and several other Marrakshi men had joined them, including Omar, our old friend the djellaba merchant. Omar was enrolled in a modern bookkeeping class at the École Pigier, and since he was looking at the family business for the first time in a new way, Bob's interest in the traditional marketing patterns of Marrakech seemed to hold a special fascination for him. He came to tea frequently, and he brought relatives and friends involved in other aspects of the local market system: a wholesaler in sheepskins, a dyer, a manufacturer of embroidered slippers, an auctioneer of rugs.

The cold increased. Most of the entertainers on Djemaa el Fna had disappeared, except for one or two old men who stood in the beggars' chorus at the entrance to the Semmarine. The Saharan dancers were still there, and the man who drank boiling water; a new peddler, a medicine man whose liniment (in brown bottles) would, he said, cure backache, rheumatism, headache, shortness of breath, stomach cramps, and dizziness, held forth in the nearly empty square. Each week the lines of ragged men and women grew longer in front of the two pious merchants on Rue Bab Agnaou, the tailor and the soft-drink seller, who fulfilled their duties to the fourth pillar of Islam by distributing bread to the poor every Friday morning. Moussa, our own baker on Rue Trésor, began to give away his day-old bread to women and children who asked for it.

Very early one morning, I heard Kenza clanking her pail down the wall outside our bedroom window, and when I looked out, I saw the pail going back up on a rope, filled with hot water from the public bath across the street. A moment later the pail went down again and came up with a pot of glowing charcoal inside it. Kenza turned and caught me staring at her.

"What a good idea!" I murmured. "Do you think the bath boy would give us some for cooking tajeen?"

Kenza, for the first time since I had known her, looked slightly embarrassed, and Mbarak, the bath boy, laughed raucously from his niche in the door to the public bath fires.

"Yes, yes, Elizabetha," answered Kenza, and she shut her window quickly, as though she had been caught in an illegal act.

"She gives him cigarettes and sometimes home-cooked food and tea," said Aisha when I inquired about this new phenomenon. "Mbarak gives her hot water and charcoal in return. But that's only because the boss is in Casablanca. He wouldn't dare otherwise."

"Is Mbarak from Marrakech?"

"Oh, no, he's from the Sahara. All the *fernatchies*, or boys who stoke fires, are from the Sahara. Poor boy, who knows if he will ever go back. No work there. He doesn't mind a taste of Kenza's good couscous, and cigarettes are expensive."

The next time I bought lamb chops I asked Aisha whether we could buy some charcoal from Mbarak. Wouldn't it be better to have it on a straight business basis?

Aisha shook her head. "Then he wouldn't do it. But to give some in exchange for a present of cigarettes, that's different."

So we exchanged, Mbarak and I, a pot of charcoal for a pack of cigarettes. The exchange worked to our mutual convenience. But I could not help smiling to myself when I thought of Hajja Kenza's pails of hot water. So much cheaper to buy a few packs of cigarettes and give Mbarak some leftover couscous than to purchase an expensive hot-water heater!

The Glaouis bought a television set. No descendant of Glaoui Pasha was going to be put down by Hajja Kenza and the qadi! Aisha smilingly told me that Glaoui had invited them all to watch TV, an invitation that Hajja Kenza had yet to extend! The hospitality of the country was more generous, Glaoui had said, than the hospitality of the city.

The egg man, the vegetable peddler, and the tall, blind beggar in olive drab stopped regularly at our house now. Lalla Yezza, the cook from the day-care center, passed by regularly, and one day she brought interesting news, which inadvertently confirmed my guess that she had had something to do with Fatima Henna's little daughter Mina's presence in the day-care center. Fatima Henna, she said, was coming home. Two days later, Aisha and I saw her on the darb. She greeted us briskly. The screaming in the night, the pounding on the walls by her hysterical brother might never have happened. The family, as Abdul Lateef had suggested earlier, had worked things out in its own way.

Bob remarked that Hajja Kenza had been turning coquettish lately when the representative of the electricity office appeared to collect our bills. Was it possible she was looking for another husband? Aisha had laughed at this suggestion.

"Oh, Kenza'd like that, but she'll never get another man!"

"She's already had two!" I protested.

"She drove the first one away, though," Aisha confided. "He was a *khalifa*, or neighborhood representative, for the pasha. A good man, with another wife from Fez. Kenza and the Fazzi woman fought all the time, even though they lived in different houses. Out the windows, on the street corner, it was awful! Kenza lived here, and the Fazzi woman lived where Kenza lives now. You'd think Kenza would have been happy, having the bigger house. Oh, no, not Kenza. She wanted to be the one and only, and she tried to get her father to let her divorce him. But when the khalifa found out, he left first."

"And the second one?"

"Naima's father? A good man, gentle, the *muqaddam* of the mosque on Djemaa el Fna, where they're putting up the new minaret now. But he had bad health, and he died when Naima was a baby. Kenza was so upset all her milk left her and I had to nurse Naima."

So the tie between Aisha and Kenza was stronger than the associations of childhood. It was a tie of milk, a tie that made their children unsuitable as marriage partners; it was the tie of sisters.

"Maybe she doesn't want to bother with men any more," I suggested. "She keeps saying they're no good, and who needs them!"

"I don't know," mused Aisha. "She doesn't know how to treat men. Men like a woman to be pleasant in the house, but all Kenza ever did was scream and take their money. Is that the way to keep a man?"

I was quite aware of the domineering, sometimes shrewish, and penny-pinching aspect of Kenza's character, but had chalked it up to bitter experience and the need to make it alone as a woman in a male-dominated society. I said this to Aisha.

"Yes," she agreed reluctantly. "But it makes some people harder than others."

For me, too, in a different way, the medina was beginning to open up unexpectedly. Lateefa had agreed to make caftans for Laura Ann and Laila, and we all went to the suq to select material, sky blue for Laila, purple for Laura Ann. We walked for hours, from one cloth market to another, through narrow, covered passages to cubbyholes that offered braid, buttons, zippers, thread. We plodded through markets of furniture, china, primus stoves, pots and pans, more cloth, more zippers. We tacked back and forth until Lateefa was satisfied with price and color and quality, but by this time I was tired and thoroughly confused. Aisha took us by the hand into an alley so narrow only two people could walk abreast.

Where were we going? I was so tired I only wanted to go home and shut my metal door with the hand of Fatima upon it, sit down, and have tea; the girls, too, were stumbling with weariness.

"Aisha . . ." I called tentatively, but she was ahead, and we had no choice now but to keep walking, for I was totally lost. At a jog in the alley, we emerged at a public fountain where a workman in a blue coverall was dousing his head under the tap. Another half turn and I realized where we were: in the square behind Rue Trésor, where David played soccer. The day-care center was on my right, the tuberculosis clinic on my left, my own house straight ahead.

I stopped and looked back. The street on which we had traveled seemed to have disappeared, hidden in the jog by the fountain.

"That's Aisha's way," said Lateefa, smiling at my confusion, "but it's not mine."

"Ah!" said Aisha, also grinning, "everybody has his own way of getting where he wants to go."

This, I discovered, was literally true. When I went to the market with Kenza, we never came home by that alley, which jogged at the fountain. Kenza had her own special route, as had Lateefa, and Naima too, Laura Ann reported.

The next time I went out with Aisha I suggested we follow "her" way from the opposite direction, so I could see where it came out.

"It comes out different places," said Aisha kindly. "You have to try and see which one you want."

I did. If I turned left at the end of the alley and walked straight, I arrived at Djemaa el Fna. If I turned right, I ended up at the gold market and the Bahia Palace. Very interesting. Gradually I began to explore the medina by myself, and when my courage faltered I would devise excuses to ask Aisha to accompany me.

We shopped for the special ingredients necessary to make tajeen, which Aisha was showing me how to concoct. The ingredients for tajeen were available everywhere in the market: meat, onions, pickled lemons, turmeric, coriander, sesame seed, fresh lemon verbena, parsley, raisins, nuts, prunes, ropes of garlic. But some merchants had more piquant pickled lemons or fresher lemon verbena than others.

Couscous, too, varied. Every housewife had her own couscous merchant, the quality and size of whose stock of grains harmonized with the housewife's particular way of handling it. I was interested in learning about couscous, but glad I did not have to prepare it. A whole day, Kenza insisted, was necessary to cook a perfect couscous, washing the grain, semicooking it, handling it, buttering it, and then starting all over again. As rice is a staple for the eastern Middle East, so couscous signals home for the North African. But one mistake, and the semolina degenerates from a pile of fluffy separate grains, lightly spiced and salted and steamed in chicken and vegetable broth, into a mush not too different from porridge!

"This is the pharmacy," Aisha announced, stopping before a corner, deep in the suq, occupied by old-fashioned wood-paneled shops, filled with shelves of boxes and bottles. Dried herbs—gray, dull green, brown—hung down in bundles from the ceilings of the pharmacies; dark and light plants seemed to flower, rootless, in bottles of alcohol and formaldehyde. Stoppered glass bottles and vials were filled with yellow sulphur, and white, brown, and flesh-colored powders. These were all mysterious and magical ingredients; alone or in combination, they could cure anything, or kill anything, Aisha said.

"But they can be dangerous," Aisha cautioned me. "Only people who know, like curers and cutters and witches, should use these things."

I remembered Sheryl's story about some mixture that Lena and her more adventurous hippie friends had ingested. From their description of its effects, it sounded like watered-down deadly nightshade, à la Agatha Christie. One of the group that had sampled the potion had been paralyzed for two days and troubled by horrible hallucinations for weeks afterward.

Near the pharmacies a few old women sat beside small bundles of dark purple roots. "*Fuwa*," Aisha identified the roots. "It's very hot but gives meat a good flavor."

"A pinch of fuwa is like a shot of French brandy," Abdul Lateef told Bob. "It will pick you up."

Other roots, bound into packets with tree bark, were used as toothbrushes. *Helba*, small white seeds, were added to bread or cooked with beans for flavor. But one must beware of *hubb el rasheed*, Aisha warned, a tiny black seed used by both men and women in making magic. Hubb el rasheed could be used as a poison, or it could be used beneficially. Mixed with two or three other spices, chosen by the *sahra*, or magic maker, it was thrown onto a fire of charcoal, and the sick person breathed the fumes of the seeds which, in such form, had healing powers.

"Ah, yes, magic!" Abdul Lateef explained to us in some detail about magic and its use throughout the city. "There is good magic and bad magic, black magic. It is *very* bad. Everyone fears it."

"It is forbidden by law to practice magic," Moulay Mustapha added, "but everyone does it."

Abdul Lateef nodded in agreement and abruptly changed the subject.

Entire sections of the market were devoted to beauty preparations and personal toilet articles used by women: *Ghaseel*, gray lumps of clay, were melted in water, and this paste was applied before shampoos, to give the hair body and sheen. Small circles of pumice, stamped with inscriptions, were used to soften heels and elbows in the bath; slightly more expensive heel and elbow softeners were covered with decorative circles of crocheted string. The insides of dried gourds made effective *lufas*, or bath brushes. A whole array of bottles provided the basic materials for a hundred perfumes and oils. Tiny glass bottles filled with gray or black powder and sealed with a silver cover turned out to be kohl, the universal eye liner.

Henna, too, was available everywhere: henna, pounded to fine green powder or loose in dried herb form, to be pounded at home by the more particular housewife. Henna was not only used on the hair and as a paint for designs on hands and feet, as Fatima and Aisha had demonstrated with Barbara Buchler; henna was also rubbed all over the body and then washed off in the bath; this way it cleaned the pores and improved skin tone. And henna, like dates, had a ritual association; the first present a groom's family offered a prospective bride's family always included henna.

If one preferred to dye one's hair black rather than reddish, one mixed henna with *hejra*, black crystals that were brought to a boil, cooled to lukewarm, and then applied, like a thick soup, to the head and left overnight. Washed out in the morning, the soup left a black, glossy color on the hair.

That evening, when Abdul Lateef came to tea, was it my imagination, or was his hair a little shinier and darker than last week?

"Oh, yes, men use hejra," Aisha responded when I inquired. "Of course. Even he uses it sometimes." He. Khaddour, her husband.

In the market, near the beauty preparations, were items to ensure that the beauty one worked to create was not destroyed by the envy of an enemy. Charms against the Evil Eye came in all sizes and shapes, in shiny plastic triangles decorated with sequins, in the shape of the hand of Fatima (oilcloth or cloth or metal), or in simple circles, outlined and covered with yellow or black plastic. Most charms contained bits of yellow sulphur, reputedly the strongest antidote against the influences of evil spirits. There were also money bags, small purses strung on ribbons, to be worn around a woman's waist, under her djellaba.

The suq was full of things I had never even imagined, which made the beauty counters of our Western department stores seem impoverished and limited by comparison.

I began to notice one particular woman who always sat quietly alone, in Djemaa el Fna, a little distance from the flamboyant pigeon man's "place." She wore a green veil wrapped around her head, and on a towel in front of her was posed a single white egg.

"She's a *shuwafa* from Bab el Doukkala," Aisha explained. "She tells fortunes. She breaks the egg and then reads the pattern made by the egg as it spreads."

I remembered the old Egyptian practice of reading the future in blots of ink, which Lane recorded a hundred years ago, and in my enthusiasm had taken a tentative step forward before Aisha pulled me back.

"We don't know her," she whispered, and propelled me on, past the lines of embroidered shirts swinging on hangers in the cold February wind, the stalls filled with leather belts, belts with brass buckles, red and blue belts embroidered with flowers, caftan belts encased in plastic and closed with huge metal hooks and eyes.

I thought a moment. "Couldn't you find a shuwafa you know," I suggested, "to come to the house? I know Mrs. Harris would like to have her fortune told, and maybe Lateefa would want to come, and Kenza."

We passed on, beyond the display of belts, the few disconsolate Gnaoua dancers, the boy hawking hot soup. We stood on the corner near the Café des Glaciers, waiting for the traffic to pass so we could cross toward home.

"All right," Aisha said finally. "Before you came, there was a shuwafa who lived on Rue Trésor. She's a friend of Lateefa's. She's reasonable. We could trust her."

A shuwafa, it seemed, was like a doctor, a psychiatrist, a bloodletter (like Hajja Kenza's), a butcher, or a vegetable merchant. Everyone to his own, and it was better to be recommended by a friend.

"In Iraq the shuwafas tell fortunes with coffee and tea cups. Do they here?"

Aisha was dubious. "They work with sugar, flour, eggs, but I never heard of coffee. They read hands, though."

Abdul Lateef told us that the really powerful and important shuwafs—that is, men—worked with "traditional materials," which he defined as mixtures of small stones washed up by the sea, snail shells, the clavicle and other bones of the sheep, dates, and the upper and lower jaws of the hedgehog. The mixture had to be exact, he said, or the fortune would be worthless. These materials were put in a basket, covered with a silk scarf, and mixed carefully, but if anyone uncovered the basket or saw the way the bones and shells were falling, it had then to be discarded. After a time, the shuwaf threw the mixture out onto the floor or onto clean sand, drew a cross through the mixture, and looked at the patterns and forms made by the materials as they had fallen. As the bones and stones and shells fell, so fell the future.

A week later, Lateefa called me across to the sibha to say she had sent for her shuwafa, through a mutual friend, and would let us know as soon as she appeared.

Whenever Aisha and I went together through the medina, we never walked far without seeing a saint's tomb or shrine, those niches and arched doors I had noted long before in my solitary visits to the historic sites of Marrakech. Rows of shoes marked the holy places, and it seemed logical that Aisha, who had explained so much to me, might talk about the shrines. She never did, but something about the way she sucked in her breath as we passed these sacred points in our journeyings indicated that they were important to her. How important? And why? Did she visit them when she was not with me, her Nasrani friend?

Gradually, as I began to find my bearings, my first fearful impressions of the medina began to change. Rather than a warren of forbidding alleys, where lurked unknown and possibly unpleasant experiences, the medina began to appear as an individualized, rather personal place. I came to understand Abdul Lateef's reluctance to move into a new apartment in the modern Daoudiate section; he did not want to leave the security and intimacy of the medina, where, as

Aisha said, he had long ago found his own way of getting where he wanted to go.

I began to construct my own metaphors about the divided city in which we lived. The French had felt the very form of the medina to be a suffocating influence, stifling modern growth and progress, as it meandered about without design or plan, unable to be comprehended or mapped in any logical fashion.

But now I began to wonder whether the medina did not have its own logic, its own structure, apparent only to those who lived within it and who had learned their own private ways of traversing it. I began to envisage the city of Marrakech as a giant and fanciful tree. If one thought of Gueliz, the modern, Western part of the city, as a trimmed and shaped topiary tree, such as one finds in the gardens of Versailles, then Boulevard Mohammed Cinq was the trunk of the tree. And at the end of the trunk lay the roots, the thousands of tiny, tendril-shaped streets and alleys and zankas and sibhas and darbs that converged in some fashion of natural growth rather than imposed design upon larger tendrils, which emerged at last into the trunk again, nourishing, invisibly, the artificial topiary growth beyond. As an alien and a stranger, my own attempts to trace the connections I thought I was beginning to see seemed rather feeble, for any eight-year-old child of Rue Trésor would have recognized the connections instinctively. However, I continued, fascinated, to explore the very labyrinth that had so bewildered and antagonized me in the beginning. At first, the high walls and shuttered windows and the stout, impenetrable doors had put me off, suggesting, to my Western eyes, coldness, isolation, imprisonment. The covered, veiled women and the hooded, covered men had reinforced that initial impression. And the high-walled houses stood on twisted, narrow streets that did not come out fair and square (in my definition) so one could see where one was.

When had my basic attitude changed? The wedding had marked a turning point, and Aisha's trust and goodwill had helped from the beginning. But my own inner resistance and hostility to this alien labyrinth had also begun to melt, as I began to be able, in Aisha's words, "to find my own way to where I was going."

I learned also, at long last, to deal with another kind of supposed hostility. One morning I marched up to the coffee merchant on Rue Bab Agnaou, the one who so disdainfully ground my coffee finer than

I wanted. I had brought a sample, and I showed it to him and ordered a half kilo of coffee, to be ground "like this one," I repeated, in
French and Arabic, pointing again to my sample. He barely glanced
at it, and proceeded to grind the beans. I knew the grind was going to
be too fine, and it was. I looked at the bag of coffee he had handed
me, and I handed it back. I showed him once more the sample of
coarse coffee in my hand. He leaned across the counter and glared at
me and demanded his money. I refused and glared back. He said
something, very loud and insulting, which I did not want to understand. For another split second we glared at each other. I was afraid
he might hit me or I might hit him. What could I do? I had gone
this far, and I couldn't give up now. I laughed. Instantly, the atmosphere changed. The boy who helped in the shop laughed, too, and
although the coffee merchant did not laugh, he ground some more
coffee for me, coarsely. I paid. He said good-by. I said good-by.

When I turned away from the shop, toward the Bata shoe shore, I
felt I had won a major battle. In a way, I had. So *that* was how it was
done! Laugh in the teeth of hardhearted fate, Aisha had told me long
ago. But be tough. I thought of Kenza and Omar. Yes. That was the
way to survive, but as Aisha had pointed out, it made some people
harder than others.

The cold hung on, and the rains descended upon us. Aisha arrived
one morning, distraught, to ask for the morning off. The drains in
their courtyard were clogged, and water lay on the floor of the room
where Fatima el Kabeera and her son Abdul Moumin lived. Who
were they? Aisha was too upset to enlighten me.

She went off to find a plumber, and when he came, a great
hullabaloo ensued as the five families whose houses gave onto the
court argued as to who was to pay which share of his fee. Aisha felt
she should pay less, as she had walked nearly a mile in the drizzling
rain to find him. By noon the affair had been settled through
Rakosh's mediation, but not very amicably. Still, the drain was un-
stopped, and fortunately so, for in the afternoon, another cloudburst
poured into the courtyard, and as I stood in my narrow kitchen mixing a cake for supper, I was startled to feel cold water swirling
around my ankles. Water was rushing in under the door of the
kitchen, a step down from the level of the rest of the house, and thus
for the moment the only room affected. I ran to the front door, and
there, across from me, stood old Rakosh, staring, as I was staring, at

the drain in the center of Rue Trésor; it was working perfectly well, but too much water was coming too fast for it to be carried off, and several houses along the street were flooded.

Rakosh and I communicated our mutual dismay. She lifted up her knobbed old hands, and the wide sleeves of her dove-gray djellaba fell back to reveal an intricate bracelet tattooed on her wrist, a real silver bracelet on the other wrist, and heavy silver rings on two of her twisted fingers. Her thick glasses were rimmed with tortoise shell, and the lenses were tinted with rose.

"What to do?" she called out in a thin, cracked voice. Khadija came out, and Rakosh spoke to her great-grandniece in a gentle tone and gestured across to indicate that Khadija should speak to me. I remembered the story of Khadija, whose dying mother had begged Rakosh to take the baby. Khadija's mother had known her husband would probably marry again and that a stepmother would not be much interested in the three-month-old daughter of a former wife.

"Rakosh," Aisha had said, "is kind. She cares about people more than anything else. Everyone on the street respects her. All of her sons' wives, Khadooj and Zahia and Fadhila, have tried to get her out of the house, but the men won't agree. They know it's their mother who keeps the place comfortable and watches the children when Zahia and Fadhila aren't paying attention. And Rakosh manages the money so everyone has enough to eat."

The rain continued to pour down and we continued to gesture at each other over the rising river on Rue Trésor. Khadija leaned against the doorway of the sibha and chewed gum vigorously; Rakosh simply stood, her arms raised up in the sleeves of the dove-gray djellaba. Was she praying?

"Rakosh wants Khadija to be a teacher," Aisha had said. "She's good in school, like Abdul Krim." Abdul Krim, Aisha's favorite child, was the boy the French people who had once lived in our house had offered to take to Paris and educate with their own son.

"But I couldn't do it," Aisha had confided, wiping tears away. "Some people said I should send him. Some said I shouldn't. He was only seven. I couldn't. I knew he would never come back to us, and if he did, he wouldn't be the same. Did I do right, Elizabetha?"

I looked down at the water swirling in the street. What was it I'd said to Aisha? I'd told her Abdul Krim was getting a good education right here in Marrakech.

"It was because we knew some people whose son went to France,"

Aisha had explained. "He never came back. He sends his parents money, but he lives in Casablanca and doesn't visit them. They're strangers. What good is a family of strangers? Did I do right?"

I had assured her again that she had.

"Ha! Elizabetha!" I looked up to see Aisha and Lateefa, crowded in behind Rakosh in the sibha. "What to do?"

We were all obviously helpless before the elements. Another hour, I thought, and the court and the downstairs rooms will be flooded.

"It will be awful in the village," shouted Aisha. "All mud."

She had sent her youngest son Youssef off only yesterday with his father, Khaddour, who had volunteered to repair his sister's house in their grandfather's village, Sidi ben Slimane. "Youssef," said Aisha, "will help his father and his aunt. She takes in washing, for the land doesn't yield much anymore. Youssef can hang up the clothes. It'll be good for him!"

Bob had been roused from the study bedroom and leaned over the balcony. I explained about the river rushing by our front door. "Nothing to do until it stops," I said. "Let's hope the children don't get caught in this on their way home from school."

Bob was Bob to me, but Khaddour was "he" to Aisha. It was strange. I knew that Aisha ran her house, as Rakosh ran hers, but I knew also that Aisha deferred to her husband and was proud of him in some way. "He" was not used at all in a derogatory sense. Even Hajja Kenza, scarcely a champion of the male sex, had grudgingly admitted once, "He's a good man. Big and strong."

"He" did seem a pleasant, good man, and he certainly was big and strong. But he had no education, and the few times I had met him on the street, lifting boxes and cartons for a daily wage on Rue Mellah, or wandering about, a tall man in a brown, woolly djellaba, he had the absent expression of one who is bewildered by life. He smoked a lot of hash, he worked when he could find work, he butchered the family sheep on feast days, he went to the mosque to pray regularly on Fridays. He was certainly not a mean father or husband. He was a good, simple man for whom life had become too complicated. He.

The rain seemed to be letting up somewhat. Finally, the last of the river was absorbed by the street drain, and the flood was over in an hour, as suddenly as it had begun. Rakosh and Lateefa and Aisha and Khadija and I nodded and went indoors to repair whatever damage had been caused. I'd been lucky. The water had overflowed from the kitchen into the court only a few minutes before, and had run off into our drain. Only the kitchen was left to mop up.

But cold winds continued to blow. "Too much rain this year" was Kenza's comment, and she took her fern in from the upstairs window sill. Abdul Lateef and Moulay Mustapha said that everyone was worried about the winter wheat. Marrakech was close enough to the land so that the state of the farms was a matter of general concern; a drought or wet crops that rotted in the field produced an immediate and devastating effect: Less grain meant less trade, which meant hungry nights next winter.

People were also worried about the continuing strikes in the schools, though Abdul Lateef and Moulay Mustapha were reluctant to discuss this potential political bombshell. Politics was apparently not a safe topic for men at any time, but the women had no such qualms, and Aisha and Kenza talked about them almost every day.

The strikes had been in progress for the past two weeks. We had seen policemen at the gates of Arset el Ma'ach when we went for our evening French lessons. And fresh revolutionary slogans had appeared, chalked on the walls, the gates, the blackboards.

La grève pour toute ma vie, said the slogan cut into the surface of my desk. *Pourquoi pas?*

Why not indeed? Since Independence in 1956, thousands of young Moroccans had thronged to the newly opened free government schools, and now, sixteen years later, the government had not been able to provide enough jobs to absorb this rush of educated citizens. But the government's difficulties did not mean much to the unemployed high school graduates who roamed the streets of Casablanca and Fez and Marrakech and Meknes. *La grève pour toute ma vie. Pourquoi pas?* (I'll strike all my life. Why not?) expressed only too well the bitterness and disillusion of the young people who had been promised a better future in the new independent Morocco.

How had the strikes begun? "Over food," said Kenza.

"Food?"

"Yes, the students in the *internats* or dormitories complained the food was bad."

Neither Bob nor I could believe it was that simple. With help from Aisha and Kenza, articles from the opposition paper, *L'Opinion*, and hints from Omar, Abdul Lateef, and Moulay Mustapha, we pieced together the sequence of events that now threatened the political future of the present regime.

Until recently, the government had been providing full board, room, and tuition for all country boys who maintained A, B, or C averages when they enrolled in the secondary schools in the cities. But as the job market shrank, the Ministry of Education had decided only to support the best students, those with A averages. Others had either to pay for their schooling themselves or withdraw and return to the villages. Neither alternative was acceptable to the boys who had anticipated a life different from the semiserfdom of the farm as their fathers had lived it under the French protectorate government and under the sultan's leadership before that.

The government opposition party picked up the student grievances and was using them to promote general strife and confusion. *La grève pour toute ma vie*, as a slogan, spread over Morocco.

In the middle of the third week of the strikes Aisha and Kenza attended a parents' meeting at Arset el Ma'ach.

"Kenza got a lot of people to go," said Aisha, "and they say the ministry of education representative is coming. If the schools stay closed, the children will lose a whole year and have to *redoubler*, or repeat. Think of all that money for books and paper, wasted!"

The meeting was a success, Aisha reported. Many women and men had come, and Kenza had made a long, angry speech! The ministry representative was moved to promise that Arset el Ma'ach would be open the following Monday.

"That's what they say about all the schools!" Kenza was supposed to have replied. "I don't believe you!"

And in the hue and cry that followed, the ministry representative insisted that whatever happened in other schools, he, personally, would promise that Arset el Ma'ach would open.

And so it happened. Najiya was turned back from her school by an angry mob. No one could say exactly who was in the mob, but windows were broken, and the police had come and taken several boys away in trucks. Youssef's school did not open at all. But at Arset el Ma'ach a solid line of police formed a cordon around the school gates, and the pupils filed in one by one. "A lot of people shouted," said Aisha, who had gone with Kenza to watch, prepared, as the other mothers on Rue Trésor were prepared, to march on the ministry and seek out the representative if the school did not open as promised. But after all the pupils had filed in, the shouting died down, and the mothers went home.

Arset el Ma'ach stayed open, and a week later, Youssef's school reopened, but Najiya's school remained closed. The strikes spread across Morocco: There were riots in Rabat, and in the period of resulting tension, King Hassan took to television to announce that all schools were being closed "to give the pupils a holiday." They would reopen, His Majesty said with a smile, after Ashura, the tenth day of the month of Muharram, and the Feast of the Throne.

It rained again that night, after the King's speech. Thunder pounded above the courtyard, and the fountain, with its orange goldfish swimming around and around in the blue-and-yellow basin, was lit by flashes of lightning. We woke to a gray Sunday. After breakfast, Aisha had still not appeared, and Laura Ann went across to inquire whether she might be ill, for Aisha had been suffering from a toothache for the past week.

Aisha came, a towel thrown over her head, looking terrible. Her teeth?

"No," she said, "I thought you would have heard the noise during the night."

"The thunder?"

"No, the wailing and the crying. It was very loud. My neighbor Fatima el Kabeera died at midnight."

"Died?"

"Of TB. She's had it for years. May she rest in peace."

"May she rest in peace!" I repeated.

"What is it, Mama?" Laura Ann asked, and I explained.

"Tea, Aisha?"

She shook her head. "I have to go back, I promised to help make tea for the mourners," but she did not refuse the cup I poured for her.

"Oh, Elizabetha, it was terrible. We could hear her coughing and coughing, and two or three nights ago bubbling in the lungs, too, and so we sent a telegram to her daughter in Essaouira because her son is blind and couldn't, but the daughter didn't get it till yesterday, and her mother died just before the daughter got here."

Aisha was sipping the heavily sugared tea as she talked. "I have to go. People are coming all the time."

"Shall I go and call?" I asked, wondering if it were important for a neighbor to appear.

"Yes," said Aisha, "but not now. Too many people. I'll tell you when."

"Should I send food or money? In America, people often take food."

Aisha shook her head. "Money. They have nothing. Everyone will have to contribute for the funeral and the burying and the food and tea and the *talabas*, who will come on the third day to say the *fatiha*."

"When will the woman be buried?"

"Today," said Aisha, rearranging the towel over her head. "May I borrow your tea kettle?"

"Yes, yes," I answered, glad to be able to offer something, since my presence was apparently not wanted.

"You should go anyway," said Bob. "Aisha probably wants to make sure you have a proper reception, but it would be more neighborly and probably more interesting to just go."

I resisted. As in the wedding festivities, I felt a certain constraint in this urban atmosphere, which discouraged just "appearing" at someone's house. To go to Aisha or Kenza or even Fatima Henna's or Rakosh's house, that was something else, but I had never even met the dead woman.

The skies were dull that morning and the street seemed more hushed than usual. Kenza, in her best brown djellaba piped with black, came out and went along the street, knocking on every door, collecting from each neighbor so that the poor old woman could be given a decent burial and not be put in a pauper's grave.

Before noon, several old men came and were seated by Zahia on a strip of sacking, laid like a carpet on Rue Trésor in front of Rakosh's house. They were distant relatives of the old woman from the Souss, Aisha told me, and now lived in Riad el Zeitoon. One couldn't serve them tea inside because the women were there, but Lateefa brought out a tray, and the old men sat there, sipping the clear glasses filled with mint. They went away and returned later with a litter of four scalloped planks, which bore the marks of recent scrubbing. It was laid against the wall to dry in the pale early-afternoon sun, and the old men sat down again.

At about one o'clock, the sound of women sobbing could be heard, and I waited for the louder wailing and ululation that I expected would follow when the body was brought out. There was none. Silently the body, wrapped in its white shroud, was carried out, placed on the litter, and covered with the *mahram*, the ritual tomb coverlet of green. On the shoulders of men from all parts of Rue

Trésor—Hassan, Boushta, Hussain, Glaoui—the old woman was carried silently to the cemetery at Bab el Robb.

Aisha came afterward, insisting that she wanted to work, to get away from the house where she had been mourning for more than twelve hours. And she wanted to talk.

"Poor woman! Poor thing! How we admired her, but how glad we were not to have her terrible troubles!"

The dead woman's husband had earned a modest living sewing braid on djellabas, but he died young, leaving her with almost nothing except two small children. Her own family was too poor to provide for three more persons, so Fatima el Kabeera had gone to work.

"She made very good bread and soup," said Aisha, "and took it to Djemaa el Fna and a man sold it from a cart and gave her part of the profit. She kept her family alive until her son was apprenticed to a djellaba maker, and her daughter sewed at home until she married her cousin, a good man with a steady job in the post office. The post office cousin married a second wife, because the first gave him no children. But the wives lived together pretty well.

"They're of the same family and they're good people and it works," Aisha said. "The daughter's husband was transferred to Essaouira two years ago, and then the son's eyes went bad. He couldn't see whether the braid was sewed on straight or crooked, and he lost his job. But the daughter and her husband sent them flour and oil and rice and sugar, and when the daughter came to visit her mother, she would clean and do the laundry and take her mother to the doctor.

"But by then the TB was too bad. There was nothing the doctor could do. And now she's gone; she was so courageous, so hard-working, such a sweet disposition." Aisha's voice rose at the end of each phrase. She was very agitated.

"Did the neighbors all contribute for the funeral?" I asked.

"Yes," said Aisha proudly. "Even the qadi."

"How much did the qadi give?"

Aisha drew herself up. "The qadi gave something more valuable than money. He loaned the *mahram*, the green coverlet for the body, the one he brought from Mecca when he made the pilgrimage."

Abdul Lateef and Moulay Mustapha, when they came that evening, described again, rather proudly, as Aisha had done, the neighborhood's response to the crisis. "A proper funeral," said Abdul Lateef, "is the responsibility of the quarter, the neighborhood." A friend of Moulay Mustapha, as his contribution, had volunteered to serve in the group of *talaba* who would chant the *fatiha*, or prayers for the dead, on the third day after the funeral.

The next day, having received my go-ahead from Aisha, I went to pay my condolence call and offer a small gift of money. When I entered that dark, windowless room, bare except for some pillows and quilts and a small chest with a broken hasp, I understood only too well why the neighborhood had rallied. Lunch was just over (courtesy of Glaoui, I remembered), and some empty bowls and bits of bread lay on a tray on the worn matting that covered the earth floor. The people sitting on the mats, bundled up in all their clothes against the cold, looked as worn as the room, ravaged from the days of weeping, but beaten down by life long before.

Aisha explained that I would have come yesterday, but we had company. Since Bettye Harris had come over briefly, this was technically true, but Aisha and I both knew I could have come at any time. For some reason she felt compelled to keep up the fiction, and I decided to go along. After all, Aisha knew more about the etiquette of such matters than I did.

The dead woman's middle-aged daughter shook my hand, accepted my contribution and my condolences. (Coached by Aisha, I had gotten out, "May God grant the soul of your poor mother eternal rest.") They all thanked me. The second wife offered tea. Aisha fixed me with an eye, and I remembered I was to refuse.

I did so. My husband was waiting. I had wanted to say simply how sorry I was for their trouble. We sat silently for a moment or two. Aisha cleared her throat loudly. I rose on cue, shook hands with the daughter, the tired-looking husband, the second wife, the blind son with casts, white and gray, on his eyes, and I fled from the darkness in that sad, bare room.

The third day after the death, all the women of the sibha—Aisha, Rakosh, Lateefa, Zahia, Fadhila, and Glaoui—prepared lunch, and then the *talabat*, the Koranic students, filed into the narrow passage off Rue Trésor, in their formal robes and newly wrapped turbans. The ritual wailing, like the call to prayer of the muezzins from the minaret, continued all afternoon through a light drizzle. We could hear the chanting and the intermittent wailing and ululation over the soft, steady fall of the rain.

On Saturday, the daughter and her husband locked up the bare room and took the blind son to Essaouira, where they would stay, Aisha said, for a week or two until they decided what to do.

Chapter 12

The Feast of Accession to the Sultan's Throne

The first days of Muharram were complicated by further strikes, not only by the students but also by the butchers, protesting a government order to lower meat prices by nearly 50 per cent. However, the seriousness of the butchers' strike, which had begun in Marrakech and was sweeping the country, was blunted by the holiday on the first day of the month of Muharram, the beginning of the Islamic New Year. Schools and offices and food markets were closed, and people thronged through Djemaa el Fna, eating and drinking, watching the entertainments, and buying drums for their children.

Drums, it seemed, were a sure sign that Muharram had begun. Bob had counted more than seventy shops that had been set up overnight in the square to sell nothing but drums, filling this special annual demand.

Along Rue Trésor, as on all the streets in Marrakech during these days, the human percussion of hand-clapping was being replaced by the drums. Every child seemed to have one or two; Shadeeya and Ali and even little Kamal sat in the entrance to the sibha all day, drumming, drumming, drumming. Hind and Naima organized drumming among the groups of girls, and the rhythmic patterns of beats punctuated all the daily activities on the street. In the square by the clinic, the teen-aged boys had switched temporarily from soccer to percussion, and the group finished each evening with a walking drumming procession through Rue Trésor.

"Oh, Mama, why can't we get drums, too?" asked Laila.

Why not? I took them to Djemaa el Fna to choose from the hundreds of drums for sale: the big cylindrical glazed pottery drums that the women had beaten so skillfully at the wedding party; the wide wooden skin-covered drums, open on one side, used by the Gnaoua dancers; drums in the shape of a rough hourglass, used for more private festivities. But the majority were children's drums, manufactured especially for the Ashura holiday, cheap clay overlaid with shiny paper; the paper, pasted on in shades of hot pink, blue, green, and gold, cleverly simulated the famous pottery of the Safi drums.

"Oh, look, Mama!" Laura Ann had discovered a collection of tiny drums suitable for a dollhouse. We bought several, plus three medium-sized children's drums (at twenty cents each), and wandered through the other temporary stalls where walnuts, almonds, raisins, and ropes of figs were for sale. These, Aisha told us, were the ingredients for *kooreeshaat*, special sweets to be made and given to children on Ashura.

Abdul Lateef and Moulay Mustapha explained that Ashura was like Christmas, when children received presents, new clothes, and sweets.

"Just as the Prophet's birthday is a special holiday for men, so Ashura is special for women and children," they said.

But no one seemed to know the religious origins of Ashura, which commemorates a famous battle between the forces of two clans of early Islam, a battle that split Islam into the two major sects that still exist today: Shi'a and Sunna. In the village in Shi'a Iraq where we had lived, the first ten days of Muharram had been days of penitence, and Ashura, the day of the battle, was a day of sorrow and mourning. Here, in Sunna North Africa, Ashura was a day of triumph and success, transformed over the centuries into a cheerful holiday for children.

That year in Morocco, however, the drumming, though outwardly gay, had an ominous undertone. The butchers' strike was in its fourth day, and skirmishes between students and police were reported from Rabat and Casablanca. Bob had come home early from the market, after a crowd of students yelling, "Strike! Strike!" had run through the suq, followed by the police, not far behind, yelling, "Don't be afraid! Don't be afraid!" But the merchants of Marrakech, having become accustomed over the years to the inevitably disastrous personal results of civil disorder, had quickly pulled down their metal shop doors and gone home. As meat disappeared from the market, the price of fish rose to almost a dollar a kilo, an unheard-of figure, according to Kenza.

"I'm not eating anything but plain old couscous until the government decides to stop this foolishness," she announced from her window sill as I passed.

Ashura was marked by drumming competitions among the different quarters of the city. Families outfitted their children in new clothes; Aisha stood outside her sibha, in djellaba and veil, handing out kooreeshaat to every child who passed.

"My father always did it when he was alive," she said, smiling. "I'm glad I can still do it."

"What are we going to do on the Fête of the Throne?" Laura Ann wanted to know. "Lots of my friends at school are going to Casa or to the beach."

"Let's go to the mountains with the Harrises," suggested Bob. "It may be the last time we can ski at Oukaimeden. We'll have a picnic."

But when the Fête du Trône dawned bright and clear and warm, Bob was in bed with bronchitis. I drove over to the Harrises and offered to take all the children to see the great festivities promised by the newspapers and television to mark the fête, an old feudal ceremony, in which the rural people came to the city to renew their allegiance to the Sultan. This year it was to be celebrated particularly lavishly, Omar confided, to calm the people and put an end to the strikes, without further violence.

Almost every shop in Marrakech sported a token decoration for the Feast of the Throne—red buntings, Moroccan flags, pictures of the King. Rue Trésor had also modestly bedecked itself: A narrow red bunting and a Moroccan flag were pinned above the store; the bakery sported a string of lights, as did the Hôtel du Sud; and a wide red banner stretched across both the ladies' and men's entrances to the bath. Upon the bunting was pasted a large picture of the King on horseback, in his traditional white djellaba and hood.

The warm weather and the clear air after the recent rains had helped put everyone in a languid, holiday mood. But Bettye, like Bob, was in bed with a cold. Greg wanted to stay home with his mother, and Ernest had work to do, so David, Laila, Tanya, Laura Ann, and I set off for the mechouar, the plain near Bab el Jadida, the newest gate, which stood at the eastern end of the city. Here, according to newspaper and radio announcements, great festivities—dancing and singing and fantasias, those classic demonstrations of equestrian skill—were scheduled to take place.

We drove past the post office, where a large Berber tent, beige appliquéd with black, had been set up. A reception seemed to be in progress, but we did not stop, proceeding instead down Boulevard Mohammed Cinq, decorated splendidly for the occasion with swaths of red bunting and clusters of Moroccan flags. On the square between the post office and the Koutoubia mosque, a giant crown of lights had been erected above the fountain, and flags flew from posts set all around the circle.

By the time we reached the Koutoubia, the scheduled cannon salute to the King had already been fired, but the phalanxes of policemen on motorcycles were still holding back the crowds of excited children and tourists so that the governor of Marrakech could broadcast his formal greetings to the people from in front of the mosque.

The mechouar beyond Bab el Jadida, ordinarily a flat plain with a slight depression in the middle, had been transformed into a gigantic campsite for the days of the fête. Near the street, just across from the city walls, five large Berber tents had been pitched, and within yellow cordons, groups of country people in the costumes of their villages were dancing, drumming, clapping, singing. Long lines of men in white robes and turbans, their curved silver swords held close to their hearts on colored silk ropes, moved in opposition to the women, in glittering caftans and amber beads, their pink-and-silver scarves floating behind them in the sunlight.

These were dances, songs, beats I had not seen or heard before, special to the mountains, the women's high, sharp voices sounding in strange yet curiously satisfying discordances against the chant of the men.

Bread and circuses, I thought vaguely, as we watched the dancing, the crowds standing nearby and clapping appreciatively, the vast mechouar filling up with citizens of Marrakech come to see the King's entertainers. Bread and circuses to quiet the people's unrest.

Beyond the dancing areas, families were camped out for the feast in small tents, mere triangles of material struck on poles to give shelter for a night or two. Cushions and blankets had been spread within the tents, where their owners were resting or cooking over charcoal; pack donkeys were staked out near the tents; and the show horses and saddles from the Ouarzazate area, home of Glaoui Pasha, were everywhere.

"Oh, let's go look at the horses," suggested David, a horseman since the age of six, and highly excited at this massive display of purebred horseflesh.

"That's an Arab! Look at his neck!" he told us. And, "You can tell this one is well bred by the big blood veins in its legs!" And, "This horse is young, Mama, his testicles are real small!"

We admired the handmade leather saddles, some finely tooled, some embroidered in bright colors, some bound with real silver.

"You see, none of the stallions are gelded," David explained professionally, "and that's why their penises are so long. In America, stallions are gelded early. But here, they say that they're fighting horses, so they have to be full of zip! Have you ever ridden an ungelded stallion?"

The girls and Mama shook their heads.

"I have," he said, "and it's not easy."

"Davy, did you read all this in a book?" asked Tanya.

"Nah! Ginger, my riding teacher in Austin, she told me most of it," he admitted, "but one of the boys at school told me about the stallions. Boy, I can't wait to see these fantasias. When are they supposed to start, Mama?"

I didn't know. The paper had not specified time, only indicating that "great displays of indigenous dancing and horsemanship would be seen, in tribute to the accession to the throne of His Majesty, King Hassan II, of the Alaouite dynasty, ruler of all Morocco!"

A horse was being shod nearby, and we gathered around to watch while David explained what was happening. I noticed that we were attracting, among these country people, more attention than the beautiful horses: four foreign children, three white and one black, and their mama in strange Hush Puppy shoes and sunglasses.

"Can't you ask somebody when the racing starts, Mama?" Laura Ann suggested. I tried. But my inquiries, in both French and Arabic, did not seem to even register on the faces of the men. Perhaps they only spoke Berber?

"I'll ask," David volunteered, and he looked around until he saw a boy, somewhat taller than he, wearing the baggy pants and short jacket of the mountains, his head shaved except for one long lock of hair in the center. The boy was holding a beautiful chestnut horse, its blond mane clipped.

We waited while David walked up to the boy, nodded, walked around the horse, patted it gently on its flank, its chest, its head, until he had reached the boy again. He made several gestures that even I could see were meant to register his unqualified admiration for the pedigree of the beautiful horse. The other boy smiled. When, then, was the horse to gallop, asked Davy, with an eye on the sun and a hand held up in questioning.

The boy held up his hand, all five fingers. Five o'clock. Or the sign to ward off the Evil Eye? I could not be sure, but the two boys nodded at each other and David returned triumphant, until we realized that we had an hour and a quarter to wait.

"Oh, no," Laila cried. "That's too long."

"Well, there's nothing else to do," I pointed out, "unless you want to walk home. Our car is completely boxed in by other cars. Look at the crowds; there are thousands of people here. We might just as well find a place to sit, buy a Coke, and relax."

The center of the plain was clear of tents and dancers and horses, and this depression, I decided, was probably the racing field. The best idea seemed to be to climb the opposite bank, the bank closest to our imprisoned car, and sit at the top where we could have a view of the entire mechouar. We settled down, with Cokes and peanuts, while the February sun beat down on our heads. It was so hot that I found it hard to remember how I had shivered in the flooding rain of a week ago.

A whole battalion of policemen, in trucks and on foot, had moved onto the racing field, scattering the people streaming across and pushing for places on the banks. Was it possible the fantasias were about to begin? It was not even four-thirty.

Four horsemen in white moved slowly down the field. Policemen followed and took up their positions at the bottom of both banks. In the distance, up on the hill where the tents were pitched, we could still hear the boom of drums and the high voices of the women and men singing; they clapped in syncopation as they moved in the measured dances of their grandparents.

"Look!" Horsemen had gathered at both ends of the field. Would there be music to begin, drums, a master of ceremonies, a representative of His Majesty?

"Bang!" At the sharp crack of a pistol shot, four horsemen were off. They rode slowly at first, then gathered speed, and at a shout and signal from the leader, they broke into full gallop, streaming down the field, their rifles held high, twirling them like batons, and suddenly fired straight up into the air, on cue, while in full gallop. The horses were pulled up short and stopped dead. David leaned over to say something, but his words were drowned out by another shot. A group of three horsemen charged from the other end of the depression. Run, gallop, twirl the long silver-chased rifles, shout, fire into the air. Laura Ann pointed at the gunsmoke, three perfect smoke rings rising slowly upward together above the crowds of people, toward the red walls of the ramparts of Bab el Jadida.

Bread and circuses *par excellence*, I thought. Everyone was enjoying himself. Political differences seemed to be forgotten. The King was smarter than anyone realized. Bang! Bang! Bang! The fantasias went on and on, the Berber warriors in white, standing up in their silver stirrups on bay, gray, black, and chestnut stallions, firing their silver-chased rifles in perfect unison into the air. They charged across the mechouar to demonstrate, as in the past, their allegiance to Hassan, Alaouite ruler of Morocco, whose right to the throne, even Omar had admitted, was religiously derived.

"It is on the Sultan's *baraka*, or good grace, that the welfare of the whole country depends," Omar's father had told him.

After all, the King was a saint, too, like Moulay Mustapha, and the King had, presumably, the power of a great fki, like Moulay Mustapha's father.

The men cheered and the women ululated as each successful fantasia run was completed. The clapping erupted, too, clapping for joy. Against the blue sky above the mechouar, the peaks of the Atlas gleamed white with snow, and the mountain village homes of the proud Berber warriors lay like dark coins among the snowy crags. If the sunny weather continued, the wheat crops would be saved, and the citizens of Marrakech would thank God and their good King for another year of plenty.

"David, wouldn't Ginger love this?" Laura Ann asked.

He shook his head. "She'd be furious. She'd be thinking of the horses. Why if she were here, I bet she'd be saying, look at that, Davy, look how tight they're holding the horses' heads. That's bad for their mouths!"

"Well, it's pretty spectacular anyhow," allowed Laura Ann.

Throughout the fantasias, our children were surrounded by children from the countryside who scrutinized them intently, but had not touched or pulled on their clothes as the children on Rue

Trésor used to do. Except once, David reported later, when one boy, after staring at all of our children for some minutes, wiped his hand quickly across David's white hand and Tanya's black hand and then looked at his own palm. "Tanya and I think he was trying to see whether our colors would come off, so he could tell whether we were fake or real."

We reached home at dusk; the decorative lights had been turned on, and even narrow Rue Trésor had a festive air. Sounds of drumming and clapping echoed and re-echoed. It had been an exciting Feast of the Throne, I told Abdul Lateef, who came that night, having heard from Moulay Mustapha, via Shadeeya and Ali, that Bob was ill. I described the dancing and fantasias in glowing terms. But Abdul Lateef merely nodded and said flatly that the horsemen and the dancers were probably rented for the day.

"In the old days," he pontificated, "the people danced and rode for nothing, because they wanted to show affection and support for the Sultan. Afterward the Sultan would give them presents to show his affection for them."

"But what's the difference?" asked Bob, sitting up in bed to drink his tea.

"There is a good deal of difference," said Abdul Lateef with dignity, "between being *rented* like a piece of furniture, and giving your talents, as a free person, and being offered a gift afterward. It is then an exchange between a King and his people, not a commercial transaction between master and slave."

The day of bread and circuses had come to a successful conclusion, it had seemed to me, although perhaps Abdul Lateef's opinion was more widespread than we realized.

But the strikes had ended. The government capitulated to the butchers and sentenced three students, described as ringleaders, to six-month terms on the prison farm near Rabat. Most of the schools opened on the day after the Feast of the Throne, and meat went back up to its original price of two dollars a kilo. The national crisis had been averted, the sun continued to shine, and spring was coming.

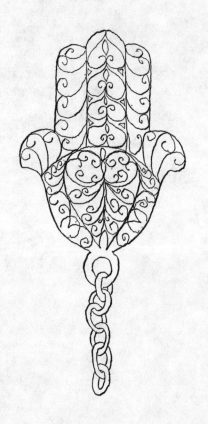

Part III

Chapter 13

Spring Comes to Rue Trésor

All along Boulevard Mohammed Cinq, from the Parc Foucauld to Gueliz, the orange trees were budding.

"Soon," said Aisha, "the blossoms come and it will smell wonderful. And then it will be time for the Prophet's birthday, and after that the *moussems!*"

"*Moussems?*"

"Didn't Moulay Mustapha tell you about them? You said he is a saint, related to Moulay Ibrahim."

Yes, I did remember. Moulay Mustapha, half proud, half embarrassed, confessing that one of his ancestors was Moulay Ibrahim, the saint whose great festival, or moussem, attracts thousands of pilgrims to the mountain near Marrakech each spring.

"Maybe we can go," I suggested. "Moulay Mustapha says it's for everyone."

"Oh, yes," said Aisha. "I would love to go. I haven't been to Moulay Ibrahim since I was a little girl, smaller than Laila. But," she added, "it's not time yet."

The weather was changing, however. Little girls' flowered dresses and men's short-sleeved shirts were displayed in the French shop windows, and the Bata store on Rue Bab Agnaou showed its first shipment of sandals. Now, every morning, Mbarak the bath boy closed the door of the furnace room against the heat of the fires, and lounged in front of the bakery instead, where Moussa sat in the lightweight tan gabardine djellaba, which had replaced his rough woolen winter garment.

Spring really seemed to be on the way: Hajja Kenza retired her fern and replaced her white geranium on her second-floor window sill. When we filed off to French classes in the evening, the sky was full of clouds, dove gray and crimson above the rosy walls of the tuberculosis clinic. The soccer game started at sunset, and it was now more fun, Davy said. "You can see better where the ball's going."

Our lemon tree showed a few tightly closed leaves, and occasionally the goldfish surfaced, blowing bubbles on the water in the blue-and-yellow-tiled basin of the fountain, as though they, too, could sense a change in the season. Against the back wall of the courtyard, the oblong of morning sun illuminating the tiles and the panes of colored glass and the mirrored cupboards grew larger and stayed longer. One could sit in the courtyard in early afternoon without feeling a chill to the bone.

But it was still more comfortable on the rooftops in full sunlight, and I continued to spend my afternoons there, mending, writing in my notebook, reading, and sewing innumerable buttons on the children's school *tabliers* or smocks. On the roofs about me my friends were hanging up washing and airing the bright-colored quilted comforters, filled with good sheep wool from the countryside, which had warmed the families on Rue Trésor all winter in the cold, tiled rooms of their high-walled houses. Fatima Henna's mother swept her roof and swabbed it down and scrubbed it. Hajja Kenza cleaned out her storage area, pulling out bundles and boxes from under the tin-roofed lean-to, sweeping the area, turning over the bundles and dusting them, rearranging everything, all the while tossing caustic remarks in the general direction of the neighborhood eyesore, the cluttered roof of the family from Ourika.

"Ah, Hajja Kenza, forget it!" Zahia returned crisply one afternoon, stung to reply after days of Kenza's nagging. "The children like to play with the junk on the roof! Mind your own business!"

Kenza snorted. "Bugs and rats are attracted to messes like that," she said, "but of course if that's what you want . . ."

Zahia shrilled something back, and Kenza subsided, but went on muttering about bugs and untidiness and how some people never learn, until she finally ran down and finished covering her boxes and bundles in silence. She had placed a new sheet of flowered plastic on the floor, "to keep off the damp," she explained to me. Then she replaced the boxes and bundles, tucking the plastic all around and over her belongings, securing the whole conglomeration finally with three large stones carefully placed over the plastic so that obviously nothing could be played with or get out of place on *her* roof.

"If a burglar or a big rat comes, I'll hear a stone fall," she said, nodding as if pleased with her strategy.

I wondered idly what valuables lay in those carefully tucked-up bundles. Gold pieces? Blankets? Rugs? The dried sheepskins from a dozen festal sacrifices? Kenza, with her three houses and her white geranium and her chic djellabas, remained, despite her loud and forthright comments about nearly everything, somewhat inscrutable to me. Bob suggested that she was a miser, in the classic sense of the word. She was indeed obsessed with care for money, and her own house, which I had visited by now several times, did not display any evidence of spending: no comfortable banquettes, no curtains, no rugs, no silver ornaments. She and Naima lived rather frugally, it appeared, in two rooms, one a narrow kitchen, the other a small room with two beds and a single cheap wooden table. I knew Kenza had recently been disputing with the plump schoolteacher Rachida over the unbelievable raise in their rent. According to Lateefa, who had it from Rachida's mother, Kenza had tried to get Rachida and her husband to pay a whole year's rent in advance, so that Kenza wouldn't have trouble scraping up her yearly property taxes. Rachida, no fool, had taken the case to the qadi, who had come up with a classic compromise: Rachida and her husband would take their rent to the qadi's office each month, where a clerk would deduct a certain percentage to lay away against the taxes. The rest went to Kenza. One certainly had to give her A for effort. But where did all her money go?

"Elizabetha!" called Lateefa across the roof. "Did you know that Rabia is pregnant?"

"No, but that's wonderful," I said.

Kenza raised herself from her kneeling position, where she had been giving final pats and tucks to the plastic storage area. "About time!" she hollered.

Lateefa looked annoyed. "Hajja Kenza," she said reproachfully, "you know she's only been married three months!"

"And it's taken her three months of love-making to make one baby!" Kenza retorted, laughing hilariously at her own quip. Her golden teeth flashed in the sun.

"Is she coming to visit?" I asked Lateefa. Ordinarily a bride, in other Middle Eastern countries, visited her natal family forty days after her wedding.

"Oh, no!" said Aisha quickly. "She may not come now till after the baby is born. Or maybe not at all, now that her mother has moved out. But Rakosh has been to see her. She's fine."

"Did you know the new summer materials are in, in the Semmarine?" called Fatima Henna's mother. "Fatima Henna says there's very pretty stuff, silk from Japan, and cheap." (Laura Ann's name had stuck. More and more people seemed to be calling her Fatima Henna.)

"You want to go, Elizabetha?" asked Aisha.

"Yes, why not?" The girls had been pleased with their own caftans, which Lateefa had finished beautifully, and they now wanted to take caftans back as presents for cousins and friends in America.

We set out late that afternoon, Lateefa, Aisha, Laila, Laura Ann, and I. Laila held tightly to my hand, but Laura Ann forged ahead with Lateefa, wearing a navy djellaba. Aisha was still in her old brown one (the new djellaba I had given her as a present for the feast was put away "for best," she explained). Laura Ann had become increasingly more independent, often going to the suq alone, with Naima, or occasionally with Eve and Simy, her friends from school. No one bothered her anymore, she reported, and actually, I realized as we pushed through the crowds on Rue Bab Agnaou, no one bothered any of us anymore. Not long ago I had taken a house guest to the market, and in the spice bazaar she had gotten ahead of me while I stopped to buy walnuts. Almost immediately a teen-aged boy in a black beret materialized beside my friend, wheedling, "I be your guide, Madame, through marvelous market of Marrakech!" As she called me, a second boy said, audibly, "The other's a Marrakshi, forget it," and the pair of would-be guides melted away. We had, it seemed, after nearly a year in Marrakech, been tagged as residents.

"Oh, I'm glad winter is nearly over," sighed Lateefa, as we paused on the street corner by the Café des Glaciers to wait for the traffic to pass.

"Mmm," agreed Aisha.

"Rakosh feels the cold so," said Lateefa.

"Oh, I understand," I put in. "I do, too."

We moved with the exuberant late-afternoon crowds thronging through Djemaa el Fna, crowds that had changed their winter dress and their winter wares with the change in season. The handcarts offering hot soup and boiled potatoes had been replaced by the peddlers of cold drinks. The performer who had drunk boiling water had disappeared, but a second contingent of Gnaoua dancers had taken his place. A new spring line of the popular tourist shirts, elaborate white braid swirling across the faded blue Tuareg cloth, bobbled above our heads on a long stick, held by the peddler like blue fish on a pole. Ahead of us a crowd had gathered to watch someone high on the scaffolding around the new minaret. It was finally completed after nearly six months of work. But what were they doing up on the scaffold now?

"The decoration," said Aisha. "Like in your house, the cut-out plaster."

Ah, the cut-out plaster designs. Were they embellishing the minaret with a verse from the Koran, or were they applying the leaf, stem, flower design that decorated the walls of our house? It was difficult to see, as the men were so high above us and we were separated from the scene by a larger-than-average group of bystanders.

"The first man has the drawing, he marks it on the wet plaster," Aisha was saying. "The second comes after him and cuts out the pattern with a knife, and the last one puts a bit of paint here and there, so one can see the design better from a distance."

We watched the three men in baggy trousers and skullcaps moving quickly along the scaffolding high above us, quickly, quickly, drawing, cutting, tinting. All the way around the base of the minaret a band of design in plaster, the Marrakech specialty, was being applied for posterity to the mosque of Djemaa el Fna.

"He has to work fast," Lateefa added. "The plaster gets hard in a few minutes."

"Come *on*, Mama," urged Laila. "I thought we came to look for caftan material."

Aisha laughed tolerantly. "She's so small, she can't see anything," she said, squeezing Laila's arm affectionately, apologizing for my daughter's lack of interest in plaster bas-relief!

Past the beggars' chorus we marched, into the spice market, through the carved gate of the Semmarine. The spring materials were indeed "in," bolts of bright printed silk unrolled tantalizingly across one narrow counter, another, ten, twenty! We walked and walked, sometimes in a single group, sometimes Laila and I together, Laura Ann and Lateefa and Aisha ahead. We went from stall to stall, pricing the "silk" from Japan. We looked at nylon shot with threads of gold and silver. We looked at filmy see-through underskirt material. Laura Ann found some clear blue she liked, but after extensive and unsuccessful bargaining, Aisha insisted it was too expensive. After 2½ hours of exciting "shopping," I had bought only a spool of black thread. Aisha and Lateefa had purchased two lengths of heavy cotton ticking, in stripes of black and brown and gray, to make the skirts which, Lateefa said, were the newest "at home" fashion. I had noticed Fatima Henna wearing one on the rooftop; Glaoui had one, even Zahia.

"Oh, yes, Fatima Henna," said Lateefa. "She wore it first. She always knows what's à la mode." She giggled slightly at her use of the French expression. "And it's so practical. Easy to wash, wears like iron, and saves your caftans!"

"Mama, let's go home!" Laura Ann, I could see, was disappointed with the results of our expedition, and Laila hung on my arm in fatigue.

"Did you know Fatima Henna is joining a *zaweeya*, Elizabetha?"

"A *zaweeya*? What's that?"

Aisha and Lateefa looked at each other and giggled again, no doubt at my unbelievable ignorance. Aisha patted my arm.

"I'll tell you all about it later," she said.

"Mama!" It was Laila.

"Yes, we're going, we're going!"

"Can we get some chick-peas, please?"

"Yes, yes."

Aisha was saying something, but her words were lost in the noise of people and carts and animals, a mixed sound echoing through the great vaulted passage of the Semmarine, reverberating from the tin that had replaced the wooden roof after the disastrous fire of a generation past had nearly destroyed the ancient market. Tin had replaced the wood and doubled the noise, but in the narrow lanes where slatted plastic had been laid instead of tin, it was quieter. Here, as we passed, light fell in stripes upon the wooden carts, the dark, ragged sacks of the porters, the bright geometric designs of the rugs, the thick, wild loops of red and yellow wool hung out to dry before the dyers' shops, the copper and brass, the bright ribbons and sequins and amber, the multicolored and scented goods of many countries.

"There he is!" The children were already running toward the stall where the chick-peas were smoking and popping like corn in a great tin cake pan set over charcoal. Full of protein and vitamins, I told myself as I paid the proprietor, and we walked home slowly, munching the warm kernels from the twist of paper, Aisha, Lateefa, Laila, Laura Ann, and I.

Zaweeyas. I had read about zaweeyas, religious brotherhoods or lodges for men, often associated with shrines and saints' tombs not only in Marrakech but also in other cities and in rural areas throughout North Africa. But I had not realized that there were sisterhoods in the zaweeyas. Or were the organizations unsegregated? And how did they relate to the moussems?

The next day, Aisha did indeed tell me about zaweeyas and moussems. She warmed to her subject. It seemed as she described them that the zaweeyas were like clubs or ladies' auxiliaries attached to some of the *murabits* or *seeds*, the shrines and tombs that were found all over the city.

What was involved? Regular weekly meetings, said Aisha, prayers, an appearance at the annual moussem or celebration for each saint, and an occasional *erss* or dance party, with music and food.

"Do you belong to a zaweeya, Aisha?"

"No, I haven't time. But I try to visit the murabits. Some people call them *seeds*, the tombs of *sidis* or saints. The visits help me."

"Some day when you go, will you take me?" I asked rather timidly.

Aisha nodded. "Of course."

"When can we go?"

Aisha looked at me hard, putting her head on one side slightly, while she rearranged the faded red print head scarf over her curly, slightly graying hair. She wound the scarf around her head carefully, tied the knot in front, then shook her head, as if to see whether the scarf would come off.

"You have some reason you'd like to go soon?"

"Well . . . I guess I have," I answered, telling myself that Laura Ann's uncomplicated recovery from her fall from the balcony of the governor's house certainly made some kind of pilgrimage appropriate.

Aisha nodded. "Tomorrow, in the afternoon?"

"Yes," I answered, delighted.

I told Bob about our plans and confessed I was a bit surprised at Aisha's openness.

"Why?" he asked.

"Well, since all the mosques are forbidden to non-Muslims, wouldn't you assume that saints' shrines would be, too?"

"Perhaps," answered Bob, "but maybe the rules are different for shrines. Anyway, Aisha knows about these things better than you or I. If she's ready to take you, I'd assume it's okay."

Tomorrow. I found I was looking forward to our visit to the murabit with a great deal of anticipation. Aisha's enthusiasm, and her satisfaction at Fatima Henna's decision to join the zaweeya, seemed to indicate that this religious interest was an important element in my friends' lives, an element of which I had been totally ignorant. It was clear from what I could see on Rue Trésor that the women did little entertaining of each other in their homes, and the chitchat of rooftop visiting hardly fostered a warm enough camaraderie with which to face the tangible difficulties of everyday life. Did the experiences of the zaweeyas and moussems fortify the ladies of Rue Trésor? I was very curious to find out, and glad that Aisha had offered to take me along on one of her visits.

But the next day Najiya had one of her bad headaches, which Aisha feared might develop into an ear infection. The day after that I was scheduled for a parent-teacher conference at the French school. All the children were doing well, said the principal, and Laila, overcoming her early ignorance and timidity, had been promoted to *Groupe* B.

"It is incredible, really," he said. A short, fair man with brooding eyes, he was known for his strict academic standards, standards that had kept the performances of his students on the national examinations so high that the Marrakech French school was flooded with applications from all over Morocco. "What a pity Laila will not be able to continue in a good French lycée."

I agreed.

"And, Madame," continued M. *le provisoire*, "if she only had French in the home. . . ." He sighed.

I smiled to myself. The children's French education had been worthwhile, but it was obviously never going to be perfect without French parents! The five American children had successfully passed and surpassed their probationary period. It had not been easy. Bettye Harris and I often wondered aloud whether we would have asked our children to go through it all if there had been an easier way out, a nice, convenient English school, for example.

Every day something kept coming up to prevent Aisha's and my visit to the murabit. After my parent-teacher conference, Aisha's husband arrived home unexpectedly. He had finished repairing his sister-in-law's village house, and had brought back with him not only Youssef, delighted to be home and teasing the smaller children on Rue Trésor once more, but a niece. Little Aisha, as she was called, had never been in Marrakech before, and "he" had thought it would be fun for her. I had noticed the child, small, thin, dark-haired, standing shyly just inside the entrance to the sibha, hands clasped behind her back, watching from big dark almond-shaped eyes the exciting comings and goings on Rue Trésor. I had tried to speak to her once or twice, but she had shrunk back into the passage, away from my gaze. The day Aisha, standing beside me in our open doorway, observed this, she had laughed.

"Ah, little Aisha," she said gleefully, "tiny Aisha," she added playfully, "speak to the lady. She's not a . . ." A what? I didn't catch the word, but from the context and the rather kindly look she leveled at me and the way the child turned, finally, and nodded in my direction, I gathered that Aisha must have been assuring her that I was not a bogey lady. I remembered the day Laura Ann and I, during one of our first weeks in Marrakech, had smiled at a toddler on the bus and then found ourselves being used by its mother to frighten the child into behaving. Perhaps our image was improving.

Aisha felt her niece's discomfort and mine, for she slipped across the street and took up a handful of tiny Aisha's skirt.

"Look, Elizabetha! Isn't Aisha's new skirt pretty?"

"Oh, yes!" I cried enthusiastically, and the child smiled and looked down proudly at her skirt, of the familiar striped ticking we had bought in the market a week ago. I had seen Najiya wearing one and realized that Aisha had probably cut her own length of skirt material in two and asked Lateefa to make them up for the girls. It was like her.

"Ha! Madame!" Lalla Yezza, the old cook of the day-care center, plopped her basket down at my door and hailed me through her veil. "How are you?"

"Fine. And you?"

"Ahh, not so bad. At least I didn't get the flu, all the children at the center are getting it. But then, I'm tough. If I weren't, I'd have been underground long ago."

"Right you are!" answered Aisha, and slipped back across the passage. "Thank God for health!"

"Madame," cried Yezza, "do you know why Moulay Mustapha is having trouble with his landlady?"

I shook my head, surprised that Yezza even knew Moulay Mustapha.

"The lady's brother has come from Casablanca and wants to live in the schoolroom, that's why she wants it." Yezza nodded triumphantly, aware that she had given me a bit of new information.

Fatima Henna's mother called to us from her own doorway.

Aisha translated. "She says that Fatima Henna is trying to decide which zaweeya to join: Moulay Ibrahim or Mul el Ksour."

"Ah, both are good!" shouted back Yezza. "Mul el Ksour has fine *erss*, I hear. And one very good drummer."

Before I had time to ask about the drummers and the erss, Youssef had zoomed out of the passage, scaring little Aisha and Khadija with a "snake," the spring from a ball-point pen he had obviously plucked out of the trash. Little Aisha screamed, Khadija struck out and missed, and Youssef, laughing, ran up the street crabwise, to make things more interesting. His mother shook her head.

"Well, he's got spirit!" said Yezza kindly. "He'll get along."

"I hope so," said Aisha, and turned into the passage as Yezza picked up her basket and bade us good-by.

"Elizabetha!" It was Kenza, now hollering from her window sill. "I hear you want to visit the murabits."

I nodded. News got around fast. And the way Kenza was shouting, everyone else on the street would soon know, whether they were interested or not.

"That's good," said Kenza. "Everyone should go regularly."

"Why don't you come along, then?" I queried, boldly. "Maybe it will help your stomach."

Kenza prissed her mouth. "Hmmm! Listen to her," she said, spreading her hand out to the street in general. "Telling *me*, Hajja Kenza, to visit the murabits! My! My!" She leaned her head on her hand and grinned her golden grin.

"Well, why not?" I craned my neck so I could see her properly on the second-floor sill. She did not look well, dark circles under the eyes, the chin tattoo standing out clearly on the sallow skin.

"Well, why not?" repeated Kenza pertly, imitating my intonation in an irritating way. "Maybe I will. Tell me when you and your friend Aisha are planning to go."

Was there an edge of sarcasm in her voice? I was not certain.

But, when, after many delays, Aisha suggested we go to the murabit the following day at four o'clock, I could hardly wait to run up to the roof and tell Kenza, who, I thought, would be just finishing her afternoon siesta. When I reached the roof and leaned over the wall that separated our two houses, I saw Kenza was still asleep on a red-and-black-striped blanket, her feet in the sun, her head and torso arranged under the shade of the storage lean-to. Naima sat beside her, crocheting a pink sweater.

Naima looked up. In the split second before she saw me at the wall I caught an unguarded expression on her face, a look of bitterness, anger, a look that shocked me. But almost immediately her face changed. She smiled brightly and put her finger to her lips to indicate that her mother was not to be wakened. I whispered my message, which Naima promised to deliver, and withdrew, but the girl's bitter look stayed in my mind. Was it going to satisfy Naima, the life her mother had led, in two bare rooms, outliving two husbands, a daughter to raise, couscous to prepare daily? A white geranium in the spring? A fern in the winter? I did not think so. It was true that Kenza had successfully managed to make the accumulation of money part of her conservative existence, and this no doubt absorbed a good deal of her time and energy. But Naima, at fourteen, had been brought up differently, to expect different and more interesting things. In her miniskirts and crocheted sweaters, she was clearly bored and restless. I felt it would be touch and go between Hajja Kenza's desire for a good marriage for her only daughter and Naima's growing tastes for the adventures that her sexuality could provide. The incident of the motorcycle and the djellaba was not an isolated one. Boys passed by her door every day, calling up to the window; the quarrels between Naima and her mother did little to discourage them.

The next afternoon, four o'clock came, but no Aisha. It was cold. The courtyard tiles lay gray and dull under the cloudy sky. The goldfish seemed to be sleeping in the bottom of their blue-and-yellow-tiled basin. The kerosene in our heaters was low, and Bob set out to get a new supply. Four-fifteen. What had happened to the spring? Four-twenty-five. Aisha was obviously not coming.

A click in the lock testified that I was wrong.

"Let's go, I'm ready," said Aisha.

"Shall I wear my djellaba?"

She shrugged.

I decided not to bother and tied my scarf over my head and buttoned up my coat.

"Hajja Kenza isn't well enough to go," said Aisha.

We set off, back along Rue Trésor toward the clinic, through the narrow street that led to Arset el Ma'ach and the school where we studied French every evening. Aisha did not speak, nor did I. We plodded along, behind Arset el Ma'ach, guarded by police against the bands of students still trying to close the school, past the Hebrew School, into a large street, to the right, through the gate of the Kasbah. Where were we going? Sun flashed and disappeared, casting shadows on the city walls, the stone stanchions of the Kasbah, the bicyclists, the children gathered in small knots on the corners, the merchants in front of the great mosque of Yacoub el Mansour beside the Saadian tombs. The Saadian tombs? Was that where we were going? My heart sank. This was one of the major tourist attractions of Marrakech!

"This is a very famous murabit," said Aisha, her voice sounding muffled behind her veil, as, yes, indeed, we headed toward the false passageway that led into the great tombs of the Saadian rulers. Few people were visiting on this cold day of our false spring; the vines, leafless in winter, hung down bare tendrils over the walled passage.

"Najiya and I used to come here in summer when she was small," Aisha was continuing. "But she was frightened by this passage, and so we stopped coming. I still come alone sometimes on feast days. It's a nice garden."

I agreed that it was a nice garden and tried to swallow my disappointment as we walked past the massive tombs, the vaulted chambers rich with stalactite carving, the elaborate tiles, the rare woods carved in patterns of great and marvelous complexity to mark the burial place of the Saadian Kings and their families. When Moulay Ismail conquered the Saadians and drove their descendants from Marrakech, he destroyed their palace, the El Badi, but apparently did not want to desecrate their tombs. He contented himself with bricking them up so their only entrance was from a narrow place in the wall of the El Mansour mosque. The tombs were rediscovered in 1917 and opened to the public then. I had seen them at least half a dozen times, alone and with visiting friends.

"See, this is written from the Koran," said Aisha kindly, pointing out to me several inscriptions carved into the tomb faces.

"Yes, I see," I responded, a bit numbly, feeling that Bob had indeed put his finger on it when he had said that Aisha knew better than I what was appropriate; I admitted to myself that she had solved the situation very neatly. She had not wanted to disappoint me further, and she had indeed brought me to a murabit, or tomb, the greatest one in Marrakech, which was open to all, tourist, infidel, child, believer. Even me.

Storks flew above us, from wall to wall where their nests perched on the tops of the pillars. Bits of dry grass drifted down from one of the nests. I looked up at the shifting clouds in the sky. The wind was chilly.

An elderly European couple sat on the steps at the far end of the garden, in berets and scarfs and heavy coats, sketching. Now a loud French voice was heard as a small, guided tourist group entered.

"Everyone finds this murabit beautiful," said Aisha in a pleased way.

"Yes," I said meekly. What else was there to say? She was quite right. I was the intruder, the pryer, the peeking Thomasina, the curiosity seeker. I felt vaguely embarrassed. It was time to go.

"Does Abdul Kabeer also visit the murabit of the Saadians?" I asked, feeling as though some comment was required.

"He visits wherever and whenever he wants," said Aisha shortly.

We passed through the gate of the Kasbah without speaking and were walking along a narrow street heading toward home when Aisha suddenly stopped and took a deep breath.

"We are going to Allala Arkiya," she said.

And before I had time to ask her who or what Allala Arkiya was, she was pounding on a whitewashed arched wooden door covered with five locks of different sizes and ornamented with several hands of Fatima.

"This is a small murabit," said Aisha quickly. The door opened a crack, and an old woman peered out at us. She was large and fat, in a full dress and long sweater, with a green scarf wrapped around her bright hennaed hair, tattoos clear on her chin and between her eyes. Her eyes widened as she took me in, foreigner, obviously, Christian, probably, as I wore no djellaba, no veil like Aisha, but only a red scarf and a plaid coat and black stockings and shoes.

"Well," said Aisha peremptorily, "let us in."

The woman still stood there staring at me, and Aisha, taking another deep breath, said something to the effect that "This is my friend, she is Christian but she wants baraka from Allala Arkiya, believe me, she is in need of baraka, and who knows, she may need it more than we do, since she is a Christian."

The old woman raised her eyebrows, nodded at Aisha's words, and opened the door so we could slip inside.

"Welcome," she said. "We have plenty of baraka here."

"Take off your shoes," whispered Aisha.

I did so.

Aisha glanced around quickly. Only two other people, both women, were visible in the stone-flagged courtyard, irregularly shaped, and cut now by the afternoon sun into spaces of light and shade. The women knelt beside a tomb, a tomb covered with a kind of mosaic of small chips of red-and-blue tiles. They did not look at us, but went on with their business, kissing the tomb and then climbing down to a lower level, where they took a drink of water from a large clay water jar set in an iron frame.

We stood there, waiting, while they put on their shoes and departed. Three more women came in as the old, fat woman let the first ones out. When the door had been shut, the fat lady, apparently an assistant, led us to a reception room, a small, dark cubicle hung with rugs and curtains, where a woman sat on a flowered cushion, surrounded by baskets filled with different objects, which were difficult to identify in the dimness.

"It's the *muqaddama*," said Aisha. "The keeper of the shrine. Speak to her."

"*Lebas*," I said weakly.

"*Lebas*," responded the muqaddama, staring at me, but not with quite the open astonishment I had engendered in the doorkeeper. The muqaddama looked at me, I thought, rather as one would scrutinize an especially odd child or animal. She was not old, the muqaddama, perhaps forty, the outlines of what must have been an ample figure masked by layers of voluminous garments, flowered and striped, in pink, red, yellow, rust, blue. She wore a white headscarf, but her black hair hung long and loose below it, and the heavy kohl outlining her eyes gave her the look of a seated statue. But her eyes flickered, and the expression in them was not that of a statue.

"The room is full of baraka. Can't you feel it?" whispered Aisha.

I swallowed and nodded, wondering what was going to happen next.

"Does she have some special person she wants protected or some special need?" asked the muqaddama, speaking to Aisha, but with her flickering eyes on me. I, somewhat flustered, could suddenly not remember the Arabic word for accident, to explain about Laura Ann, and I wanted desperately not to disgrace Aisha.

So I stammered out, "No, thank you," adding that any baraka would be just fine and fulfill all needs if it came from Allala Arkiya.

The kohl-rimmed eyes crinkled. The muqaddama was smiling. At my reply? Who knows? From the several baskets in front of her, she selected pinches of salt and black seeds, and four small tied and beribboned sacks, like tiny sachets. These were wrapped in a scrap of newspaper and twisted at each end, like an oversized cigarette.

"Give her a dirham," instructed Aisha.

I decided to take a chance, and said, directly to the muqaddama, "May I have one for my friend, too?"

Those clever eyes crinkled again, and she made up a second packet. I placed two dirhams into her large, well-shaped hand, decorated with dots and lines of orange henna.

"Allala Arkiya blesses you," she intoned, pocketing the coins somewhere within the voluminous colored layers of her clothes. She nodded. The interview was over, but as we turned she said to Aisha, "Show her our quarters and give her a drink from the sacred well."

Those eyes flashed at us and then she looked down at her baskets full of powders and seeds and salts and sachets. Aisha said thank you, I followed suit, and we went out into the courtyard toward the tomb. The fat assistant escorted us down a short flight of stairs and pulled aside an orange curtain to show us the set of two neat rooms where she lived; a pair of man's shoes sat beneath the bed. Her husband? In a woman's shrine?

"The muqaddama lives up above," explained the assistant in a thick, lispy voice, indicating another curtain two levels above, this one of printed plush. "I live here with my husband, near the well." I looked at the rock-lined aperture near us, which had a bucket beside it. "No, the drinking water is there, in the jar; it's from the well, don't worry," she said.

Aisha and I followed her up to the jar, where she poured us a cup of holy water. Aisha drank first and handed the tin cup to me.

I looked down into the brackish water and hesitated.

"Drink," whispered Aisha. "It is full of baraka."

The fat assistant was eying me. There was nothing to do but drink it, hard water with a strange metallic taste.

"Bless you," murmured Aisha.

"Bless you," I repeated.

"You don't have to kiss the shrine," said Aisha, in the way one explains etiquette to a child. I stood beside her while she knelt down before the tomb, passed her brown, work-scarred hand across the smooth blue-and-red mosaic tiles of Allala Arkiya's resting place, and then bent and quickly kissed it. After a moment she rose and pulled up her veil; we put on our shoes and headed out.

"*Bslama*," she said to the fat assistant.

"*Bslama*," I repeated.

"*Bslama*," responded the assistant, and the big wooden door swung shut behind us, the five locks clanking together against the wood. A donkey cart clopped by and a motorcycle varoomed behind us. The kebab stand on the corner suddenly turned on its pressure lamp, and the smoke from the fire billowed up into the sunset.

"It's late," said Aisha. "We have to get home."

By the time we had walked quickly and in silence the half mile to Rue Trésor, the daylight was gone. Laila's blond head peered around the big gray door of our house, and I waved to her.

"Thank you, Aisha."

"*Bslama*, Elizabetha," she said.

From what happened that day, I began to realize that I had misinterpreted the purpose of the murabits, the tombs of saints and the saints' shrines in general. Visits were not so much to say "thank you," as I had expected, but to ask for help, to make a vow that if such help were given, some task would be performed by the suppliant: a karama or party of thanksgiving; a return visit to the shrine; a contribution for candles or toward the upkeep of the shrine; a gift to charity.

"We'll go one day to Sidi Bel Abbas," said Aisha, the day after our visit to Allala Arkiya. She seemed pleased with our packets of baraka, and our visit in general. "He is the patron saint of Marrakech and one of the seven, and now that you live here, you must visit him and pay your respects."

"Yes, Aisha."

"One day. But of course then you must wear your djellaba."

"Of course."

We went upstairs to shake the sleeping bags out, and I decided to ask more about Allala Arkiya.

"She was a holy woman, very good and kind."

"And her tomb or shrine is only for women?"

"Yes. Men aren't allowed, ever. On Fridays you should see, it is filled with women."

I said I was surprised to see such young women, that I'd expected only the old patronized the shrines.

"No. No," answered Aisha. "Everyone goes who lacks something." She sighed. "And which of us does not lack something in our lives?"

"True." We tucked the aired sleeping bags in under the mattresses, plumped up the children's pillows, and went down into the cold courtyard together.

Bob told Abdul Lateef about my visit one evening, which annoyed me, as I felt somehow that it was a private matter between Aisha and myself.

"But Abdul Lateef is a good friend now," he insisted. "Why shouldn't you trust him? Besides, I'd like to understand more about how the murabits and zaweeyas fit into the life of the city."

So I agreed to sit down the next evening and talk about the shrine.

"I was taken by a woman friend," I explained to Abdul Lateef.

"Ah, yes, a friend." He paused. "Of course, Allala Arkiya is a women's shrine. That makes a difference. But with the other, larger shrines, or with the rural shrines, I do not think, Madame, that you should enter them. People are very conservative here in Marrakech. It might be . . . unpleasant, both for you and your friend."

"Are there many small shrines like Allala Arkiya?" asked Bob, shifting the focus of the conversation.

"Oh, yes, dozens," answered Abdul Lateef. "Every quarter, almost, has a shrine, not necessarily for women only. There are the big shrines as well, such as those of the seven saints of Marrakech. There may be a hundred murabits in the city; what do you think, Moulay Mustapha?" Abdul Lateef always deferred at some point to Moulay Mustapha's supposedly greater religious knowledge.

Moulay Mustapha, whose mouth was full of cake, simply nodded.

"You see, Madame," Abdul Lateef smiled, a bit patronizingly, I thought, "here we are more concerned with religion on an everyday basis than you are in America."

Stung by obscure motives of patriotism or religion or whatever, I could not resist replying that we had many shrines in America, too.

Abdul Lateef opened his eyes, and Moulay Mustapha stopped chewing and stared.

"In America? Really? But we have heard that America is not at all a religious country. Isn't that so, Moulay Mustapha?" Another nod from Moulay Mustapha.

Bob was eying me, too. Why had I gotten into this ridiculous argument in the first place? I swallowed hard, and found myself saying that, yes, of course there were many people in America who did not actually practice their religion, "just like in Marrakech," but many others were very devout, according to their individual beliefs.

"But they don't have murabits there!" Abdul Lateef's tone was close to scathing.

"Oh, yes, they *do*," I insisted, and rushed on, finding myself in an impassioned description of roadside shrines in Mexico, great pilgrimage shrines like Ste. Anne de Beaupré in Canada, the grotto in my own hometown of Portland, Oregon.

Bob was smiling. I was furious, suddenly, at him. How dare he smile?

"And people go to those places to make a vow, to receive baraka?" asked Abdul Lateef.

"Yes, in a way," I answered. "They say a prayer, they light a candle. The baraka is not always something you can hold in your hand, and pay for, like the packet I received from Allala Arkiya . . . but . . ."

"Yes," said Abdul Lateef sharply. "Well, what is it, then?"

What was it? Well, *what* was it? I groped, trying to explain something I had not really conceptualized for myself. "Well, it's more like a feeling one has afterward, a . . . sense of well-being, comfort, of peace. In English we call it grace." And suddenly I had an inspiration. "There is this song that says it better than I . . ." and I found myself translating into bad French that old hymn,

> Amazing grace, how sweet thou art,
> To save a wretch like me,
> Oh, once I was lost, but now I'm found,
> Was blind, but now I see.

I looked up. By now everyone was smiling, probably for different reasons. Moulay Mustapha was murmuring, "But that's the same idea! Grace is like baraka! Yes! Yes!"

Abdul Lateef frowned at Moulay Mustapha's enthusiasm. I found I had nothing more to say and was glad of the excuse to get more hot water for the tea.

When I came back with a new pot of tea, the subject had been changed to Moulay Mustapha's trouble with his landlady, who wanted the schoolroom back. I felt I had been gently snubbed by all three gentlemen. For a moment, I rebelliously wanted to break into the conversation and explain that I knew all about Moulay Mustapha's trouble with his landlady, and further, I knew why she wanted the room. But I did not. I said good night.

Abdul Lateef looked up. "Baraka is complicated, Madame," he said. "It is both visible and invisible."

"I think I understand," I said.

"Do you?" The question hung in the air. Did I?

"Abdul Lateef, I don't know really," I said. "I am only trying to learn."

Abdul Lateef smiled. He nodded his head vigorously and exchanged a look and a few words of Berber with Moulay Mustapha. "Well," he said, "that is the way to begin."

I felt that he was giving me a pat on the back, as friendly as it was patronizing. I cleared the tea table, stacked the dishes in the kitchen, and climbed the steep stairs, past the tiled walls of the balcony, to our elaborately plastered, tiled, and colored bedroom. It was the middle of April, but the cold had descended again. Perhaps the orange trees on Boulevard Mohammed Cinq would be blighted by the unseasonable frost. I shivered and turned out the light, lying for a long time in my bed, watching the shifting patterns of color on the floor and ceiling, along the walls with their plaster border: stem, flower, vine, calyx. Why was this idea of baraka considered so difficult to grasp? Basically, it seemed simple enough, in the way Aisha had first explained it to me. But perhaps Abdul Lateef and Moulay Mustapha's and even Bob's conception of it was different from Aisha's and mine. Grace? Blessing? Certainly amazing grace.

Chapter 14

Baraka

Baraka. Now I seemed to hear the word everywhere. Why hadn't I noticed it before? *"Baraka-llahufik"* said people, thanking one, a dozen times a day. The bath boy's name, Mbarak, meant, simply, blessed.

"Baraka!" Aisha had laughed when I said Fatima didn't look like the mother of ten children. "They are blessed. More than blessed. Enough is enough. *Baraka!"*

"Yom el baraka" (day of grace and blessing) we had said in greeting on the day of Rabia's wedding. *"Mabrook!"* (You are blessed!) one said in compliment if someone had a new dress, a new job, a new scarf. *"Alf mabrook"* meant "You are a thousand times blessed." *Baraka.* "It is on the Sultan's *baraka,* or good grace, that the welfare of the whole country depends," Omar's father had said on the occasion of the Feast of the Throne. Was it chance that in other parts of the Middle East people used different words to say "thank you," that Mbarak was not a common name? Or did it go deeper? As Abdul Lateef had said, all life, everything in Marrakech was tied together. Every day, one lived by manipulating the fragile ties of different lengths and widths, which joined man and woman to God, man to woman, man to commerce, man to man. Was baraka the extra ingredient that subtly changed the atmosphere in which the operations of life took place, as a drop of salt in the solution changes litmus paper from white to blue? Did baraka provide the benevolent

ambiance within which one could mediate more easily the often discordant spheres of human life, encourage good, keep evil at bay?

"Ah, and don't forget *na'ama*," said Aisha. Now that we had
begun to talk about baraka, she seemed eager to discuss it. She had
thought about it a lot, it appeared.

"Na'ama is like baraka?" Now I was confused again.

"Na'ama is a kind of baraka, a gift of God to the people in this
world, food, water, things like that," Aisha explained. "When Si
Qadi loaned his tomb cover from Mecca for the poor woman's funeral, he was giving away some of his baraka, and thereby he got
more baraka."

I nodded, hoping I understood.

"Now, karama," continued Aisha, "is close to baraka, too."

"How?"

"Well, it's a party, like you thought. But it kind of tells people
that the hostess has asked for and received baraka and wants to
share that baraka by fulfilling her vow and feeding her friends."

"Now," said Aisha, "you can see why I didn't want you to have a
karama after Laura Ann's accident, can't you?"

"Yes."

Aisha nodded in the same patronizing way as Abdul Lateef had
done, but unlike him, she did pat me on the shoulder. I expected her
to say, "Well done," but she merely said, "You're beginning to understand."

That evening Abdul Lateef had more to say on the subject.

"Baraka can be like an investment," he said, "as in the market.
You give something and get back something more, if it is properly
and thoughtfully done, with the proper intention or *niyya*. If you
don't have the niyya, it's no good, whatever it is."

"We say the same thing in Christianity," I answered, "about the
intention, the niyya."

"You do?" Abdul Lateef looked at me, seemed about to say something, then changed his mind. He glanced at Mustapha and resumed
his tutorial tone.

"Since you are so interested in baraka, Madame, you should go to
the moussem of Moulay Ibrahim, the celebration of the ancestor of
our friend here, Moulay Mustapha." Abdul Lateef winked. "We all
know it is the biggest and the best moussem. The biggest camels, the
biggest crowds, and most distinguished saints!"

Moulay Mustapha blushed, but he was pleased.

"Oh, yes," I said. "I'd like to. Is it for everyone?"

Moulay Mustapha nodded eagerly. "Yes, for everyone. Bob must come, too."

"Thank you," said Bob. "Maybe we will."

Abdul Lateef smiled again in that satisfied way, then was serious. "However, Bob, as I said before, the shrine and the zaweeya are only for believers, though the spectacle is public. Am I not right, Moulay Mustapha?"

Moulay Mustapha nodded and smiled.

"Are there any special preparations for the moussem of Moulay Ibrahim?" I asked.

Abdul Lateef actually laughed, then covered his mouth with his hand and pretended to clear his throat. "Oh, yes, Madame," he said, with a twinkle in his eye. "You'll see."

We did not have long to wait. On Saturday, David, Tanya, and Laura Ann rented bicycles in Gueliz and went off on an "exploration expedition," complete with picnic lunches and bottles of *raybi* for everyone. "That strawberry yogurt is real good for quenching your thirst," David told Tanya, who tried raybi and agreed. Laila and Greg were not interested in exploring, however, so I brought the two younger ones back to our house, where they took a new batch of American comics up on the roof. They were sitting up there in the sun reading when the drumming and singing began.

"Mama! Mama!" cried Laila from the roof. "Some people from Djemaa el Fna are dancing in our street!"

I looked out the window on the landing. A billowing purple flag, three men, two drums, somebody dancing. It did indeed look like the square of Djemaa el Fna had descended on Rue Trésor.

"It's the *naga*," said Aisha, smiling.

"The naga or the na'ama?" I was confused again.

"No, the naga, they are the people who announce the moussems."

We opened our front door and stood on the doorstep, as our neighbors were doing, Zahia peering from the second-floor window, Lateefa from the roof, Glaoui, wiping her hands on her striped skirt, from the sibha, around which the children had clustered, tiny Aisha, Khadija, Mina, Ali, and little Kamal. But Youssef would not be still and watch, and he pranced after the naga, keeping time clapping to the beat of the two drums. He pranced gaily, as the first drummer pranced, a small, wiry man with close-cropped black hair and leathery skin whose eyes shone as he swung his round, open-ended drum, nearly as big as a wheel, high above his head, then brought it down to knee level with a little joyous jump, all without missing a beat. Up and down and around circled the wide drum, but the second drum stayed in place, as well it might, I thought, for it was a massive instrument. Longer than it was wide, it was almost as tall as the old man who carried it on a thong around his neck and beat upon it with a pair of curved sticks.

"*Sidi Bel Abbas! Ah-ah!*" The old man sang, the little jumping man sang. Ali and Mina clapped to the drumbeats, and the young standard-bearer swirled the purple flag of the naga across our narrow street so skillfully that we could see the embroidered slogans clearly. And as the flag moved, the brass bauble at the top of the pole caught the sun, and all the smaller decorative flags and scarfs and the tassel of new lambs' wool fluttered in the mild breeze.

"*Allah-ah-ah!*"

The drums increased their tempo. The little man jumped faster, and Youssef, in a burst of enthusiasm, leaped up to try to grab the flag.

"Youssef!" Aisha called at her youngest son mildly, without really expecting him to obey, and he did not. Instead, Youssef kept clapping and leaping, counterpointing the drums and the songs until the man with the flat drum ran up and down the street, calling for contributions.

"They want money for Sidi Bel Abbas," said Aisha, "to help pay for the decorations so it will be a good moussem."

"Can we give them something, Mama?" asked Laila. I asked Aisha, who nodded, and Laila ran to get a coin and dropped it into the wide drum, where it thunked resonantly against the stretched skin.

"*Baraka-llahufik,*" cried the little jumping man, and the standard-bearer dipped the flag in our direction before moving on to Fatima Henna's black-and-white-tiled doorstep.

"Ho, Elizabetha, so now you're giving contributions to the patron saint of Marrakech?" Kenza shouted down in a loud, grating tone.

For some reason, I was irritated. "Why not?" I returned.

She nodded, absently. Perhaps I had overreacted to her tone. Perhaps she had had another bad quarrel with Naima, or her stomach was giving her trouble. Impulsively I said, "We're thinking of driving to the moussem of Moulay Ibrahim. Would you like to come? The car is very comfortable."

Kenza's face changed, softened. "Thank you," she said. "But," she added, reverting to the old harsh tone and indicating with a grand gesture the drummers and the flag-bearer who were now singing and drumming before the entrance to the Hôtel du Sud, "those people are the naga for Sidi Bel Abbas, Elizabetha, *not* Moulay Ibrahim."

"Yes, yes," said Aisha. "I told her."

"Hmph," responded Kenza ungraciously.

"Mama, what's she doing?" Laila was prodding me gently.

One of the maids at the Hôtel du Sud had stepped out into the street, had reached for the flag and buried her head in its folds.

"The flag has lots of baraka," said Aisha. "The girl would like to have some, to make her feel better."

I translated this for the children, who looked at each other.

"Maybe she's got acne," suggested Greg, "and she thinks that will wipe it off?"

"I don't know," I said. "I think she just feels better if she touches the flag. She thinks it's holy."

"You believe that stuff, Mrs. Fernea?" asked Greg.

"I don't really know," I answered, as truthfully as I could. "But I think it means a lot to many people here, Greg. It's certainly true for them."

"Aisha believes it, doesn't she, Mama?" asked Laila.

Aisha turned to me expectantly at the sound of her own name. I chose to translate the comment rather obliquely by saying that Laila was asking whether Aisha thought there was much baraka in the flag.

Aisha nodded and smiled and then unexpectedly picked up a handful of Laila's soft, fine, blond hair. "Just like in this," she said. "That's what people are saying when they see Laila or touch her hair. They're not insulting her, they're saying '*shi baraka*'—'this is a thing full of baraka.' "

Laila seemed singularly unimpressed by this explanation. She'd heard all that before. She didn't care what they said, she didn't like people to pull her hair or touch her. I said I couldn't blame her, but she had to realize that people did not mean bad things by it. She sniffed, unconvinced.

The naga had reached the other end of Rue Trésor. Youssef followed them, still clapping; Kenza banged her shutter to. I noticed she had not dropped any coins into the skin drum.

When I took Greg home and picked up Laura Ann and David, they were very pleased with themselves. They had bicycled to a nearby village, they said, had played kickball with some of the children, and then found a bottomless pit.

Bettye and I looked at each other dubiously. "A bottomless pit? How do you know it was bottomless?"

"We threw stones in, and we never heard them splash!"

They were pleased with their secret afternoon.

"Well," returned Laila, "*we* saw some holy men drumming, and a girl wrapped her face in the holy flag."

"Yeah," asserted Greg.

The older children nodded absently. Bottomless pits were obviously more fascinating than holy flags, especially if you had discovered them yourself.

Nagas began to appear regularly along Rue Trésor. Many moussems, it seemed, were in preparation, and even in Djemaa el Fna, new such groups could be observed.

"But," said Abdul Lateef, "the nagas or people like them are always there, in Djemaa el Fna. There are just more of them at the time of the moussems."

Moulay Mustapha and Abdul Lateef took turns explaining in great detail that many of the performers in Djemaa el Fna were actually doing more than just performing for coins. For the most part, they were members of particular zaweeyas or brotherhoods and were "demonstrating" the miracle or baraka associated with their zaweeyas.

"Drinking boiling water, walking on glass, handling poisonous snakes, are they not miracles of a type, Madame?"

I agreed that they were.

"So the performers are proselytizing or preaching just as the preachers themselves. Each in his own way."

"Each in his own way is demonstrating baraka?"

"Exactly." The two men smiled. "You are coming along," said Abdul Lateef with his infuriating smile.

Mark and Alan came to say good-by. The group of young Americans had not been living in Fatima Henna's house since the altercation between her brother and her father, but they had dropped by our house occasionally for coffee. Now, they said, the group had decided to split: Mark and Alan were off on a motorcycle for Tangier and a boat home; one of the girls was going to Spain; Lena was off to

Mauritania. Sheryl was staying until she had a letter from home with her passage money.

Two days after their farewell visit, Bob brought me the French-language newspaper. "Look at this story," he said. "No wonder everyone took off so fast!"

The police had broken a drug and smuggling ring operating out of Oujda, near the Mediterranean coast and the Algerian border. A French doctor, with a private plane, was flying back and forth to France and was identified as having a son named Jason who had lived in Marrakech, who was missing and for whom the police were still searching.

The missing man, it appeared, was "our" Jason, who had told us he was in the import-export business, and who had sublet his apartment in Fatima Henna's house to the group of young people soon after we had arrived on Rue Trésor.

"No wonder the kids cleared out. They probably heard things were about to break and were terrified they'd be implicated," said Bob. "As well they might. The doctor paid thousands of dirhams in fines without batting an eye! Everyone must have made a fortune!"

"But were the kids really involved?"

"I don't think so. Do you?"

I shook my head. They were too innocent, somehow, in their searching for the good. But how had they known the raid was coming?

Sheryl came by, looking frightened, to say she was hiding out with some friends, and pleaded with us not to tell anyone that we'd seen her. "I've been in jail once in Casablanca, and I don't want to go back."

We both looked at her curiously. "Oh, not for this kind of big jazz, the million dirhams, and so on," she said quickly. "They put me in jail because once on a bus I didn't have my passport, but I did have some *keef*, and the police searched everyone who had no I.D. But that Jason—we might have ended up in the local clink forever, just for living in his apartment! It's gross to think about!" And she disappeared, with our promise that we would not breathe a word to anyone, though we doubted anyone would ask us.

That weekend Laura Ann and I were shopping for jewelry in the silver market when the sound of drums was heard again.

"Is it the naga?" I asked the silver merchant.

"Not exactly," he said. "It's the camel to be sacrificed at the moussem of Moulay Ibrahim. A gift from the city of Marrakech."

I rushed out just in time to catch a glimpse of the procession, for unlike the nagas, groups of three or four at the most, this was a real procession, passing directly before the door of the market, and pausing before the Bahia Palace gate, while the drummers gathered a crowd with their music. The good-looking young camel pranced about in his finery, shaking his shiny red-and-green satin blanket. The leader of the group began to preach.

"*Ya innaas!*" (O people. Believers!) he cried in an impassioned voice, though most of his words were lost in the noise of the clamoring children trying to get closer to the jaunty camel. He was protected by three sturdy flag-bearers, their pink, green, and orange banners all embroidered with slogans and all decorated with scarves and brass knobs, like the purple flag of Sidi Bel Abbas.

The drummers circulated among the crowd for contributions, and the procession moved on, down toward Dar Si Said.

"He is a fine camel, is he not?" said the young silver merchant. "The city always gives a good one to be sacrificed for Moulay Ibrahim." He was young and wore Western clothes.

"Will you go to the moussem?" I inquired timidly.

The young man looked up and smiled. "Perhaps," he answered. "Much baraka is to be gained by going."

Laura Ann and I saw the camel procession again on Rue Bab Agnaou, just before we turned onto Rue Trésor. The flag-bearers had folded up their silken flags and were hurrying toward Djemaa el Fna. For lunch? And where was the camel?

Just before the Prophet's birthday, the sun came out and, as Aisha promised, the bitter orange trees on Boulevard Mohammed Cinq blossomed. In Gueliz women gathered to pluck the blossoms for perfume, their skirts tucked into their waistbands, their hair tied up. The Prophet's birthday dawned bright and warm. Aisha brought us *msemmen* (the buttered ones), a kind of fried pancake made of flour, salt, water, and yeast. Shadeeya and Ali and little Aisha wore new clothes, and Lateefa and Zahia took all the small children "for a walk," they said, greeting me as they passed our door. All along Boulevard Mohammed Cinq, families were out promenading in their new clothes, and the scent of the orange blossoms filled the air.

The morning after the Prophet's birthday I was startled by a loud pounding on our door, and when I opened it, there stood two burly policemen with billy clubs and revolvers. I gulped.

"Y-yes?"

The two burly policemen eyed me and looked over my head into the courtyard. What had I done? My mind jumped to Sheryl and the drug raids. Did they want her?

"The water! The water! Madame! Throwing dirty water into the street? Is that a good way for a citizen to behave?"

Aisha suddenly materialized beside me. "What are they talking about?"

"Oh, the water." Aisha laughed gleefully. "Just a bit of wash water, officer, see, I throw it into the drain here . . ." and she pointed to the big manhole in the middle of Rue Trésor. "It's better than dirtying the house, now, isn't it? Doesn't your mother throw her wash water out?"

The two policemen, blustered, were silent. "You have to realize, Madame, we have to check up every so often to keep people from littering the streets with garbage!"

No wonder the streets were so clean, I thought, if the policemen made regular calls like this.

"Garbage, yes! Of course!" Aisha was indignant and righteous. "Anyone who would throw garbage into the street deserves to be scolded . . ." Was she going to say something about our untidy friends from Ourika? No. I breathed a sigh of relief. "We understand. But water . . ." she spread her hands and smiled. "All it does is run into the drain."

"Just checking," murmured the policemen, and moved next door to Kenza's house. I wanted mightily to stand there and listen to Kenza light into them, but, alas, she was not home!

The streets were filling up with pilgrims. When I went to market, the buses clogged Rue Bab Agnaou, clustered in Djemaa el Fna, buses marked Moulay Ibrahim. Families sat on the street corners near the Cinema Marhaba, across from the dry cleaners, before the coffee store; they sat with picnic baskets and blankets, come from villages all over the Souss for the moussem of Moulay Ibrahim, the first and most important moussem of spring, the moussem called "the Mecca of the poor" in North Africa.

"It marks the beginning," said Moulay Mustapha. "Moulay

Ibrahim is, as we have said, the biggest and best" (a smile to Abdul Lateef), "but there are many others: Moulay Durain in Essaouira; the Ait Oumghar, in the mountains; the moussem of Moulay Abdallah bin Hussain in Tamslouhte; Lalla Fatima in Ourika; Sidi Rahal above Marrakech; Sidi Ahmad Oumoussa in Agadir . . ."

I nodded pleasantly, but I had lost count. I hoped this did not show on my face. Apparently not, for Moulay Mustapha was still enumerating moussems and saints. "And these are only the moussems in the area of Marrakech!" he finished triumphantly. "It is very important and interesting for everyone!"

"Perhaps Moulay Mustapha will accompany you to the moussem of his famous ancestor," suggested Abdul Lateef.

"I . . . er . . ." Moulay Mustapha looked uncomfortable. "Of course, I would be delighted, but I have to be there early, to march in the procession with the other saints." He said the word quite casually and matter-of-factly, and Bob, who had looked surprised for a moment, nodded to himself.

"Of course, we understand," Bob said. "Besides, I have to drive the ladies!"

The three men laughed together at the foibles of the world, and the Destiny that leads to such eventualities!

"It begins on Monday, I think," I said. "Didn't you say the sixth day after the Prophet's birthday?"

"Yes, but it begins on Tuesday," said Moulay Mustapha.

Since he was a saint, we figured he must be right and our calculations wrong, and secretly I was glad, for Monday was a horrid, cold, rainy day, almost like midwinter.

"You have to come see the workers' parade!" Aisha announced after breakfast as Bob and I sat in the dining room over coffee.

Bob and I glanced at each other.

"I thought there wasn't to be one," said Bob. We had heard that the traditional May Day parade was to be canceled by the government.

Aisha snorted. "Well, there will be. We'll be able to hear them from here."

By ten, flags of all colors, columns of workers, floats, soldiers, soccer teams in uniform, and marching bands were plodding down Rue Bab Agnaou in the pouring rain.

"We want a better life for our children!" announced a banner.

"Bulldozers—not picks and shovels," said another.

Moussa the baker said to Bob, "They're writing about your government," and pointed to the sign, "End racial discrimination in the United States and South Africa!"

Bob nodded.

The marchers looked damp but cheerful, and the spontaneous shouting and singing and clapping went on among the different *huntas* or organized groups of workers, from the mines, the olive oil factory, the dairy, the hotel workers, the charcoal workers.

And the women! Scores of women marched in djellabas and veils, shouting and laughing. Aisha laughed, too.

"What are they saying?" Bob asked.

"Baraka min inneefak
Esha'ab kullu fa'ak," chanted the women.

"Baraka?" I couldn't believe my ears.

"Oh, yes."

I stared. Aisha stared back. "You know, Elizabetha, *baraka*, enough is enough. They want more money, more food. There're lots of people who have no work. *Baraka!"*

"Yes," I said. "I think I see."

Bob said later that he was surprised to see so many women marching.

"Why not?" returned Aisha. "They work. Why not march? But lots of women who work weren't there," she went on, "the servants, the shuwafas, the curers, the midwives—*they* work, they should march, too. They will, you wait and see, maybe next year."

Baraka could be used in many ways I had never suspected, then, even as a modern political slogan.

That evening when Moulay Mustapha came he confessed he had made a mistake about the moussem.

"I'm very sorry," he said, "I don't know how, but it started today."

My heart dropped. No moussem? After all this?

"You see, Madame," said Abdul Lateef mischievously, "even saints make mistakes. Is that true in America, too?"

I felt quite crushed, and realized how much I had depended on this excursion, not only to help bring me closer to what seemed one of the central interests in my friends' lives, but also to compare the experience with other pilgrimages I had taken. Would the comparison help me to see and understand some of the things that made this society different from that of Egypt, Iraq? I had hoped so, but apparently now it was not to be.

"B.J.! You're not listening. Moulay Mustapha says the most important day is that of the camel sacrifice, and that isn't until tomorrow. We might still go."

"Really? Do you mean it?"

"Well, yes," said Bob, "I'd be willing to try if the weather isn't too bad. The mud will be awful, though. Think of that."

"A true pilgrim," intoned Abdul Lateef, "sees the mud and the other difficulties as advantages, for they improve the quality of the pilgrimage." He gave me another of his mischievous looks. "But that isn't true in America, is it, Madame? There everything is supposed to be easy."

"No." My voice was pettish, and at the quick look in Abdul Lateef's eyes I consciously suppressed my irritation. "No, Abdul Lateef, it is the same with us."

"Ah, is it now? Did you hear that, Moulay Mustapha?"

But Moulay Mustapha was not paying attention. He and Bob were discussing the muddy roads. "I have no decent boots," Moulay Mustapha mourned. "I will ruin my one good pair of shoes."

I looked at my watch. Nine-thirty. I had better alert Aisha to the fact that we had already missed the first day, so she could tell everyone else. I excused myself and let myself out the door into a silent, rain-sodden Rue Trésor and into the dark sibha. Someone was arguing in Rakosh's house; Zahia's querulous voice rose higher and higher, and little Kamal was crying. The television was going full blast at Glaoui's, but the door to Aisha's court was locked. I banged on the door until a man's voice called out. "What? What do you want?"

"Aisha!"

She came, finally, a towel thrown hastily over her head, and held a lantern up to my face. When I apologized for Moulay Mustapha's mistake, she said it didn't matter, we could go for the camel sacrifice, "the day which is full of the most baraka." She would tell the others that we should go by seven-thirty, after the children had left for school.

By the time I had let myself back into our house, Abdul Lateef and Moulay Mustapha were leaving, pulling up their hoods before venturing into the cold.

"We must get Moulay Mustapha home so he'll be ready to participate in the celebration of his ancestors tomorrow," winked Abdul Lateef. "He gets a more concrete share of the baraka even than the pilgrims who have come a long, difficult way."

We knew that the income from the shrine and from the zaweeya, the coins offered annually by the pilgrims, for candles, for curing, for fortune telling, for prayers, was divided among the direct descendants of the saint. Bob had a theory, supported by Abdul Lateef, that the whole system of moussems and zaweeyas might be tied to the economic systems of the small towns and cities. Everything tied together, but in different ways and at different levels, Abdul Lateef had said. A complete institution, the zaweeya.

"Perhaps this year you will receive enough to get married," I joked gently. Moulay Mustapha's desire to marry was well known, but he complained that his salary as a Koranic teacher would not allow him to do so for many years.

"Oh, no!" he sighed. "Marriage becomes more expensive all the time. And there are so many descendants of Moulay Ibrahim now that by the time the income of the zaweeya is divided among all of us, it is a very tiny amount."

"Enough to buy us a glass of tea tomorrow?" smiled Bob.

"*Enshallah,*" said Moulay Mustapha. "A *bientôt!* To Moulay Ibrahim! Bslama!"

We woke to a cold, steady drizzle. Aisha came to say that Najiya's ear was worse, that Rakosh was poorly, and that Lateefa had to stay to take care of her. And Kenza, who had been more desirous than any of us to come along in our Peugeot with its padded blue seats. What about her?

"She said she'd let us know this morning."

Bob looked out at the rain in the courtyard and said nothing. I, too, said nothing, in case too great a show of eagerness on my part might make him decide not to go at all. I gave the children breakfast and told them we might be going to the moussem and would be back by suppertime. In case we were not there when they returned from school at five, they were to get the key from Najiya.

"Kenza has her stomach trouble," reported Aisha. "She asked us to bring her some baraka. But I'm ready!"

Well, then. Aisha and Bob and I. Why not? Aisha had her lunch tied up in a large scarf. I put ours together and made a thermos of coffee. Bob went to get the car and we finally set off at seven-fifty-five, in a fine rain that stained the red walls of the houses of Marrakech. Fog lay on the ramparts of the city, and the mountains to which we were headed were not even visible.

"Poor prospect," said Bob, "but I'm willing to try if you really want to."

We drove in silence through the fog and rain.

Chapter 15

The Moussem of Moulay Ibrahim

Moulay Ibrahim. Where was the village? It was not on any of the major signposts, but we had been told to follow the road toward Asni, up from the plain of olive trees and palms surrounding Marrakech, into the foothills of the Atlas.

Today, the second day of the *moussem* of Moulay Ibrahim, thick, swirling fog covered everything. Bob strained to see ahead in the gray mists that veiled the mountaintops, the grasses, and the wild flowers along the narrow strip of asphalt road that wound up, up the side of the mountain.

I stared out at the blackness, asking myself whether Bob might have been right in wondering if we should have come at all. How could one see even the camel procession if the fog was this thick?

"When I came with my father and mother, long ago, it was a hot day, like summer," said Aisha. "It took us all day on the bus."

"*Enshallah* the weather will improve," I said.

Bob made noises of skepticism. It was not easy to drive up the slippery switchbacks in the rain and mist. But gradually the visible strip of gray-green grass on each side of the road seemed to widen. I glimpsed dots of red poppies and yellow buttercups. Soon we could see the roofs of a village, though the steep valley below us was still filled, like a cup, with fog. The mists lifted slightly the higher we climbed.

"I wonder . . ." Bob was musing to himself as we came in sight of

rows of buses and taxis, parked ahead of us, off the road, beside tea
and food carts set up in a meadow. "This must be near the turnoff up
to the shrine. Moulay Mustapha says no *public* transport is allowed
in the village, everyone has to stop below. But maybe private transport can go on?"

We inched along behind an old and battered Chevrolet filled with
people. Clouds of hot steam rose from the tea shops to swirl and min-
gle with the cold fog above the heads of pilgrims huddled by the
road, just as they had sat on the street corners in Marrakech. But
here they looked miserable. Although the rain had stopped, the mist
still hung over us. Occasionally it rose briefly to display the edges of
trees and the ravine on our right where the mountain stream roared
over its stony bed; then it would descend again to veil us all in dank-
ness and anonymity.

"Where the hell . . . ?" The ancient Chevrolet crept by the knots
of pilgrims resting by the side of the road, the buses and taxis, grinding slowly on and on. "We must be close to the turnoff," said Bob.
"But I can't see it!"

The battered Chevrolet stopped dead, and Bob braked suddenly
and skidded across the wet highway. The Chevrolet backfired
violently, which made Aisha jump; then the old car turned sharp
right, and we followed. Five feet up the steep, narrow road was a
signpost: "M. Ibrahim," it said, like a doorplate announcing the
presence of a great gentleman.

"He couldn't go faster," said Aisha, who had sensed Bob's annoyance at the Chevrolet's performance. "Look!"

The road, like a tunnel in the fog, was lined on both sides by
pilgrims, family groups, men in pairs, single men, climbing the last
miles to the shrine; a solid line of cars plodded ahead of our
Chevrolet, at the noble speed of perhaps ten miles per hour. A
woman in a dark green djellaba carried her tea kettle in one hand,
her child by the other, and a baby in a striped red sling across her
back. Donkeys ambled in and out among the pilgrims on foot, skirt-
ing the ditch, carrying burdens of tent poles, tents, bedrolls, and bundles of belongings.

"People are actually coming up here to camp in this weather," Bob
shivered. "What a ghastly festival!"

He was right. The weather was terrible. An occasional sodden-look-
ing pilgrim was heading down the hill, and from the strained and
unhappy expressions on these poor persons' faces, the whole ritual
seemed more like a wake than a festival. Why had we come?

Without warning, the tunnel road ended. The mist rose slightly, and we found ourselves in a muddy meadow clogged with cars and carts and donkeys and motorcycles. A large man, his skullcap topped with a peaked plastic bag to keep off the rain, displayed his brass traffic director's armband close to Bob's nose and directed us energetically around and around the muddy meadow until we found ourselves heading down the hill again!

"Oh, damn!" Bob cursed. "Let's just go home, B.J. We're headed in the right direction."

I held my breath. I wasn't in total disagreement with Bob, since Moulay Ibrahim, now that we'd reached it, presented such a depressing prospect. We could see nothing but the tunnel road and the muddy meadow and the traffic cop, in our rear-view mirror, shaking his fist at us since we had somehow not followed his directions properly! Where were the jaunty camels, the famous shrine, the descendants of the saint in their festal finery? Lost in vistas of mud and mist, obviously. Aisha, however, broke the impasse by opening the car door and starting to get out.

"Just a minute, Aisha, I'll park," Bob said and eased down the hill several meters, before pulling our Peugeot over into the ditch to get out of the traffic flow.

"Well, here we are! Now what?"

Aisha was not fazed at all by Bob's tone. "We should go by ourselves and let Mr. Bob go where he wishes," she said crisply.

Bob nodded. He knew only too well that, with his fair skin and hair, he looked very Western, very much the stranger, and no less so in his burnoose, which we had given him for Christmas. In my green djellaba and head scarf, I was more anonymous, particularly in Aisha's company.

We agreed to meet at the car at noon. Bob started climbing directly up over the brow of the hill, but Aisha took my hand and guided me along the road, across the trampled meadow of the parking lot, and over the wooden bridge, which spanned the Wadi Moulay Ibrahim, where the holy stream flowed down through the rocky gorge, past the foothills, and onto the plains below, watering the land where grew the grain and olives, the oranges and tomatoes and beans that we bought in the market of Marrakech. A stream full of baraka, as my neighbors had told me.

"Gypsies," said Aisha. "They'll probably dance later," nodding toward a family sitting by the bridge, smoking and drinking tea.

The women wore shawls and fringed towels over their heads; one of the men was beating on a drum in a halfhearted way. He did not seem very lively, but then who was, in this mist?

Aisha grabbed my arm. "The *qubba!*" she cried. "Look up there!"

The modest green dome of Moulay Ibrahim's tomb emerged from the fog for a moment, and then the clouds descended again.

"Let's go on up," said Aisha.

But where to? The dome might have been a mirage, for all we could see now, below the walls of mist, were stone steps leading up to the sloping, narrow, cobblestoned streets of the village. Three or four hundred people lived here, Moulay Mustapha had said. Today there were many more than that already, hundreds of pilgrims thronging the narrow street at nine in the morning, pushing and jostling us. We passed the whitewashed walls of the houses spotted with damp. The overhanging wooden roofs dripped with the night's rain; we struggled up past the market stalls along the narrow lane hardly wider than Rue Trésor, which led to the shrine.

I assumed that Aisha would visit the shrine and I would browse in the market while I waited for her. But we were being propelled along more quickly than we would have wished, shoved with a group into a small open circle where two guards stood, keeping an uneven line of pilgrims moving in and out of the shrine's entrance. In the crush my hand slipped from Aisha's, and I panicked.

"Aisha!" I called desperately. What was she doing? She was heading toward the entrance, but I had no plans to go in at all.

She turned, fighting against the stream of traffic to do so.

"Come on!" she shouted through her veil. "You've come all this way to make the pilgrimage! You'll feel better when you're inside." And to one of the guards, eying me curiously, she added, "My friend isn't feeling well."

The guard waved me on, and, full of trepidation, I had no choice but to follow. To go back now would be worse than to go on. We had come for the public spectacle, Bob and I. I had never expected to enter the shrine; in fact, Abdul Lateef's warning seemed to ring in my ears: "The shrine and the zaweeya are not open to nonbelievers," he had said. What was I doing here then, being guided along this corridor, the gateway to the shrine? It was a narrow hallway lined with rows of neatly dressed men in turbans and djellabas; they sat with their backs to the whitewashed wall, lost in contemplation, apparently unaware of the disorderly procession of pilgrims from all over Morocco that was passing and pushing by within inches of their crossed bare feet. Did Aisha realize I wasn't supposed to be here?

Would she get into trouble if they discovered that I was not just another Moroccan woman in a green djellaba come to pay her respects to Moulay Ibrahim?

At the end of the hall the line stopped, and my heart was beating so loudly I was certain Aisha would hear and wonder. It was one thing to enter a shrine or some other forbidden place accompanied by a government official, I thought, a person of importance who could explain and arrange things if something went wrong; it was quite another matter with someone like Aisha. Oh, I hoped she would not suffer on my account.

"Bang! Bang! Bang!" It wasn't my heart, but the pair of wooden paddles clapped together by the shrine's functionary as each contribution was dropped into the shrine box by a departing pilgrim. The box was locked. Presumably it was from this accumulation of small coins that Moulay Mustapha would, at the conclusion of the moussem, receive a minute share.

"Ssst! Elizabetha! Take off your shoes."

I did as I was told, bending down and nearly being knocked flat by an enthusiastic mustached gentleman behind me, who was rocking back and forth, calling out to himself and the world in general "Allah! Allah! Allah!"

"Hang on to your shoes!" I could hardly hear Aisha above the noise from the shrine, the cries of women, the swishing of garments, the clacking of the wooden paddles, the rise and fall of many voices intoning prayers.

We were pushed forward into the qubba, and I prayed I would not make some dreadful mistake and disgrace Aisha. I thought of the two hefty guards and the functionary with his wooden clappers. They looked rather thick, those clappers. Were they for chastising nonbelievers? I shook my head to clear away my apprehension, but it only increased. My hands were shaking, the shoes knocking together, but no one could hear, for within the shrine the noise was even louder. Rows and rows of men and women stood together on the other side of the sarcophagus of Moulay Ibrahim, set apart from the pilgrim procession by a low railing; were these the members of the zaweeya? They rose and extended their arms toward Mecca; they fell to their knees, they prostrated themselves on the mats that covered the floor.

"Allah! The most merciful! The most compassionate!" they prayed. "Hear my prayer!"

What was I to do? I felt my head scarf slipping. Aisha knelt and pulled me down beside her. I set down my shoes, jerked my scarf back up over my hair, and tied it tightly under my chin. We were kneeling, with a dozen other people, men and women, beside the sarcophagus, a raised tomb over which had been fashioned in stone the contours of a human body. This in turn was covered by a beautiful old Kashmiri shawl, its faded crimson wool embroidered with the lotus, one of the oldest symbols of fertility. I wondered whether the shawl, or tomb cover, had come from Mecca, like the qadi's green tomb cover that had been loaned for the poor woman on Rue Trésor. At the end of the tomb, where the head of Moulay Ibrahim presumably lay, a turban of some stiff gold material had been placed.

A woman next to me suddenly stood up and threw herself across the tomb, kissing and embracing it passionately, and weeping as she did so. Several other women broke from the ranks and followed suit. But Aisha, who had pulled her veil down to her chin, did not. Her lips moved in prayer. She seemed enclosed in a moment of silence; and as I watched her, so intent, for a split second all around me the voices and sounds of prayer and the clapping of the wooden paddles faded, and I knelt there, too, in silence. It was uncanny. I felt quite alone, with Aisha, in the shrine of Moulay Ibrahim, and I quickly said a prayer, begging that we be allowed to make the pilgrimage together, without difficulties for my friend, who had brought me here, I thought, because she believed I was in need of help of some kind, help that might be provided through the baraka to be gained by our pilgrimage to the moussem.

"Which of us does not lack something in our lives?" Aisha had not spoken, but her voice echoed in my ears. I told myself that the hysteria of the women throwing themselves on the tomb, combined with my own nervousness, made me think I was hearing voices. I lowered my gaze. There were my shoes, Hush Puppies bought in Austin, Texas, mud-caked, sitting beside the old Kashmiri-covered shrine. Aisha knelt beside me, within her own circle of silence, but for me the split second had passed. The qubba had become once more a vaulted whitewashed room, crowded with men and women, guarded by a tall man wearing a white turban and holding a pair of wooden paddles.

I looked about me, waiting for Aisha, not wanting to disturb her solitude. Several clocks lined the walls of the shrine. I noticed a French ormulu clock, gilded and ornate, and a clock in Roman numerals with an Arabic inscription lettered across its face, which had stopped at some point in time at seven-ten. There were photographs of the present King Hassan and of his father, the late beloved Mohammed Cinq. My hands stopped shaking. Perhaps it was going to be all right. The Kashmiri shawl, I saw, was old and worn; near where we knelt a tiny mend showed near the fringe, a mend done carefully in the wrong shade of red. It stood out like a stain under the bare electric bulbs that lit the shrine, the sarcophagus, the rows of men and women praying, the pilgrims outside shouting to come in.

Aisha stood up. I did, too. She bent forward and kissed the tomb. I knew I should probably do the same, but I could not. Instead, I placed my hand next to hers for a second on the side of the tomb.

Holding our shoes above our heads, we made the tour of the tomb, the new arrivals shoving us forward at a breathless rate. We dropped our offering into the wooden box, and with a ritual "bang" and "clack," we were ushered, pushed almost, out of the qubba.

In the corridor, we paused to put on our shoes. Again someone pushed me, I dropped a shoe, cursed myself for my clumsiness, peered down into the darkness, but could not see it anywhere. People jostled me on all sides and Aisha was calling me, but I could not find my blasted Hush Puppy in the piles of shoes that were coming off and going back onto the feet of the pilgrims: feet in black socks, feet in lacy tights, a child's bare small feet, red from cold; feet in pointed yellow leather slippers; hennaed feet; bare feet with broken toenails and calloused heels.

"Elizabetha!"

"Coming!" But how could I come and walk through the mud with only one shoe? I groped around on the floor and there, looming out of the darkness, was my one shoe, and next to it, a single foot, a terrible foot. I pounced on my Hush Puppy and found myself, close to the ground, staring in horror at that foot, twisted and grotesque. I saw, as I sucked in my breath, that the foot was calloused on the wrong side, not where an ordinary foot would have been worn, for this was the foot of a one-legged, club-footed cripple. I closed my eyes, opened them. The foot was gone, but the cripple was visible, sliding along the floor of the corridor, swish, swish, along the mat on his behind, propelling himself along with that single deformed yet useful foot.

"Yallah!" The guard was pushing Aisha out. She beckoned to me urgently and I bent quickly, tied my shoe, joined her in the corridor, and in a moment we were out in the enclosed area around the shrine once more.

"Bang! Bang!" The clappers sounded in the distance. It was over.

"There! Now don't you feel better?" Aisha asked cheerily, and I said fervently that I certainly did. We were in open air and daylight again, and now it looked as though the sun might even come out. And a fragrant, familiar odor was wafting toward us.

"Let's have some mint tea!" I suggested gaily, and we had gotten all the way to the shop before I remembered that I had locked my purse in the car. A trip down to the road showed no sign of Bob. It was nine-forty. The dramatic moments in the shrine had been merely moments; they had seemed much longer. Two and a half hours until noon. How stupid of me to lock up all my cash!

"Let's get a seat on the wall for the camel procession," Aisha suggested.

We trudged back across the parking lot, over the bridge, up the stone steps slippery with mud to the beginning of the narrow street that led one way to the shrine, the other way along a broader mountain road bounded by winding stone walls.

"The procession has to come by here," said Aisha. "I'm sure of it."

We sat down on the wall.

I felt exhausted, drained from the intensity of those brief moments in the shrine. Aisha, too, was silent. We sat together on the wall, huddled in our djellabas in the damp cold morning. Gradually the aroma of tea reached us, in our dazed state, and the smells of boiling soup, the sight of men cutting onions and potatoes and carrots into sizzling pans in the shops at the entrance to the narrow street. I was aware that I was hungry. Aisha must have been, too, for without a word, we moved up the wall, away from the tantalizing sights and smells. We sat on the wall, waiting for the camel to appear, the procession of saints, for Bob, for mint tea, for lunch. The minutes ticked by and the mists burned off, layer by layer, as the sun rose higher in the sky. Across the deep gorges and up over the road we had come, the high peaks of the Atlas slowly emerged from their veils and shrouds of mist. The pilgrims came out of their tents, crawled from their beds, unfolded blankets, and spread them out to dry in the sun. A few family groups were packing to leave, but more were arriving, and on the dark slopes and rocks above us the trees were gradually being hidden by new tents: tall white ones; blue-and-yellow French camping tents, makeshift lean-tos of plastic and sticks; old army pup tents, olive-drab and gray. The ramparts, too, were slowly filling with bystanders; as far as I could see up the mountain road where the procession was to march, there was scarcely an empty place on the wall. The sun waxed hotter; I sat up straighter as the warmth reached through my damp djellaba. Aisha sat with her eyes closed, taking in the sunshine. As the sun touched the highest peaks in the circle of mountains surrounding the grotto, I could see the new snow gleaming silver in the sunshine, the drops of water glistening on the scrub pines, the clumps of wild thyme bright lavender in the dark undergrowth that covered the sides of the mountain. The puddles shone along the road below.

Who had called Moulay Ibrahim "the Mecca of the poor"? He had been misinformed, I thought; for every level of Moroccan society seemed to be represented in the growing hundreds of pilgrims gathered on the slopes and the ramparts to watch the annual sacrifice of the camel, that scapegoat upon which all the evil of the year would be placed and erased. Dignified gentlemen in sober djellabas, of excellent cut and material, their wives in equally sober djellabas, sat in the tea shops with their children and servants, sipping mint tea. The young men in turtlenecks and safari jackets and French-cut blue jeans mingled with the men of the mountains, in white turbans and djellabas, their knives carried over their hearts on bright-colored silk ropes, like the riders in the fantasia or the feast of the King's accession to the throne. Little girls in plaid skirts and navy blue sweaters walked with their veiled cousins in djellabas. Some of the women of the countryside wore *haiks*, lengths of white wool, wound about their colored skirts and shimmery blouses; their hair, puffed and braided over white head scarves and tied with silver pins or ropes of amber and sequins, was not covered by the hoods and veils of the town women. Even a few women and girls could be seen without djellabas, wearing short coats and head scarves. Everyone had come to Moulay Ibrahim, and many carried white flags on sticks, flags decorated with dots and patterns of henna.

"The ladies with the scarves and no hoods are from Fez," said Aisha, and then looked at me and smiled. "Just like you. Maybe they think you are from Fez, Elizabetha, though why should a Marrakshi go to the moussem of Moulay Ibrahim with a Fassi?" She smiled again. The traditional rivalry between the two ancient imperial cities of Morocco was still alive and seemed to reach not only into economics and politics, but also into friendship, art, food, and religion.

The woman next to us, in a dark brown djellaba, cleared her throat and pulled down her purple veil. "It's going to be a beautiful day after all," she said to me, in a slow, deep voice. I looked at her and smiled at the old face, a face full of humor, age, experience, her tiny blue tattoo an arrow between her eyebrows. But I was afraid to speak for fear that my accent would betray me as a stranger, someone who had no business here.

"Yes, it is, *el hamdillah!*" Aisha answered, breaking in and pulling down her own veil, presumably to demonstrate friendliness.

"See, even the young people are coming back," commented the old woman, nodding in the direction of a trio of boys in Western clothes, each carrying a flag for the moussem.

Aisha was silent. Was she thinking of Abdul Krim and Saleh, her own sons, who refused even to go to the mosque with their father because they said there was no point in it?

"Ah, Alalla, do you remember the story of the woman who couldn't climb El Khalwa?" continued the woman.

"Which one was that?" Aisha responded.

"Well, she was a woman who wanted a child," said our newfound friend, "but for seven years she did not conceive. She came to Moulay Ibrahim, and they told her she should climb El Khalwa, the sacred mountain, up to the tree there." (She pointed to a large tree with widely spread limbs just visible on the peak across the gorge.) "But she was not well, and although she tried to climb, she couldn't make it. Her husband was with her. They prayed together at the shrine, and her husband said, 'Don't be afraid, I am strong, I will help you.' And he carried her up the mountain on his back. And when they got to the top, they prayed in the same spot where Moulay Ibrahim himself prayed, on El Khalwa, they say, right by the tree there . . ." (We gazed across again to where the tree stood out black and clear against the blue sky.) ". . . and then they came down again. Forty days later she conceived and bore a fine son. And guess what?"

"What?"

"The next year the woman came back to the moussem and she climbed El Khalwa by herself with her baby on her back! Such is the power of Moulay Ibrahim!"

"Such is the power of Moulay Ibrahim," said Aisha, "if one has the proper intention, the niyya."

"Ah, yes, if one has the proper intention!" repeated the old woman in the brown djellaba.

There was a pause. "Where are you from?"

"Marrakech," answered Aisha, "and you?"

"Beni Mellal. And your friend?"

"She's from Egypt," said Aisha quickly. "That's why her Arabic sounds strange."

"Ah!" smiled the old lady. "That's nice! Is there anything as beautiful as this in Egypt?" and she took in with one sweep of her arm, the rocky grotto, the valley full of pines and wild thyme, the green-domed shrine, the crowds of pilgrims, the mighty peaks of the Atlas rising high around us.

"Well, not quite the same kind of beauty," I temporized.

"Hmph!" she commented. "Is she a schoolteacher or something?"

Aisha laughed. "No, no . . ." she said, but the old lady interrupted her.

"Who is *that*?" she whispered, quickly pulling up her purple veil at the sight of fair-haired Bob approaching in his dark glasses and his black burnoose.

"My husband."

"And is he Egyptian, too?" she returned, eying him closely and, I thought, rather skeptically.

"Oh, no," said Aisha, quick as a wink, "he's American!"

"Ahhh!" said the old woman. Her brow furrowed, and the tiny tattoo between her eyebrows disappeared in a wrinkle. "American!" She seemed highly amused. She touched me on the arm. "Well, they say all the world comes to Moulay Ibrahim!"

"That's because the whole world is in need of baraka!" returned Aisha.

"Ah, you speak rightly," said the old woman. "*Bslama.*"

"*Bslama,*" we replied, as she moved off.

"Well," said Bob. "I didn't mean to scare your friend away. Aisha, how long do we have to wait for the camel procession?"

Aisha told us it would not be much longer, but we should not move now or we'd lose our seats. "The camel has to come around three times," she said.

Something did seem to be happening down there in the parking lot. It was the camel prancing up the muddy stairs in his draperies of pink and yellow satin, his garlands of scarves and tassels and ribbons,

his retinue of young men carrying flags. The camel was the traditional gift of the tanners of Marrakech, Bob had been told, a symbol
of their own conception of their relation to the earth; for in taking
the dead skins of animals and transforming them into beautiful shoes
and purses, the tanners were rejuvenators, the proper symbolic mediators between life and death.

Aisha suddenly took off down the stairs, running beside the camel,
trying, as everyone else in the crowd except us seemed to be doing, to
touch the sacred animal, to tear a thread from his tassels or scarves.

"It's *our* camel," she explained breathlessly when she came back to
the ramparts, and the way she said it made me think for a moment
that yes, it was her camel, she'd been keeping it all these months
hidden away in the storage cabinet of her tiny courtyard, and that it
had emerged on the proper day, like a genie from a bottle, this sacred
magic animal that was to take all the ills from the thousands of
pilgrims all about us and blot them out with its death.

"I touched it, I really did," Aisha told us elatedly, and rearranged
herself on the ramparts. "Oh, yes, thank you," she said, and accepted
one of the glasses of mint tea that Bob had brought us.

I found I was vaguely uncomfortable at Aisha's run after the
camel. Should I have congratulated her? Or what? Perhaps nothing
was necessary, for she was nodding to herself while she sipped her tea
and seemed pleased at her success.

I looked about us and thought I spied a familiar figure in the
crowd opposite us.

"Aisha, isn't that Rakiya?" I pointed to a tall, stately figure opposite who did indeed resemble Rakiya, our friend with the goiter
who had sat next to me at Rabia's wedding. There was no mistaking
the red hair of her younger daughter, nor the brand-new djellaba of
her teen-aged daughter (it was the same blue as Laura Ann's).

We waved and ran across the street. Rakiya pulled down her veil
and said we were lucky we hadn't come yesterday, because it had
rained all day and the rooms for sleeping were very expensive and the
soup was watery and if it hadn't been that she was to meet her sister
here, she would have gone right home.

"Do you want to ride back with us this afternoon? There's plenty
of room in our car," I offered.

"Oh, thank you, I don't know whether my sister wants to stay or
not. If we're not here by four, we're staying, all right?"

It was agreed. We wedged ourselves back into our places on the ramparts, which Bob had adroitly occupied during our moments of absence.

By now, the rocks and slopes were filled with people, waiting. On all the roofs of the village houses, men and women and children stood, or sat or leaned over to get the best view of the festivities still to come. The camel, which had been circulating throughout the crowds on the slopes and lined along the narrow streets, was to pass in procession once more before being led to sacrifice, Aisha explained. Two policemen ran up and down the street leading to the shrine, trying to keep a passage clear. Below, near the muddy parking lot, two men in suits and some men in djellabas stood, waiting. We also waited.

"What's going on?" Bob asked impatiently.

Aisha shrugged, and shifted on the rampart. The two policemen had stopped running back and forth, and simply stood, unable to control the crowds that pressed behind them, filling the street leading to the shrine. The camel, focus of the entire day's activities and ritual, seemed to have disappeared.

Now the people on the rooftops moved forward and seemed to rustle in anticipation. Could they see something we couldn't? We heard a faint chanting; then, from below, we could see a procession approaching, a procession of men who paused at the parking lot to be greeted ceremonially by the two waiting men in suits, the group of men in djellabas.

"Who are they?" I asked.

"The qadi and the mayor, I think," said Aisha.

Up the stairs came the procession, following the prancing gay camel, going around for the last time, with his retinue and flag-bearers. But hadn't Aisha said earlier that the camel went around three times? I turned to ask. Too late. Up the stairs, chanting, behind the sacrificial camel came "the saints," said Aisha. These were the living male descendants of Moulay Ibrahim. We looked for Moulay Mustapha along the lines that passed before us, rows of men of all ages in white djellabas and hoods, in suits and ties and tarbushes, in striped djellabas. No Moulay Mustapha. Chanting, they followed the camel, his neck in its fringed and colored scarves arching in pride and disdain, his flags of purple, pink, green, white, unfurled. The children waved their smaller white flags, dotted with henna, saluting the procession of saints, and the camel who was going to bear away their troubles with his death. The saints passed us. The camel passed us. But there was no sign of Moulay Mustapha.

"They'll sacrifice the camel below, in a special place in the rocks," said Aisha. "We can't see it from here."

"That's all?" asked Bob. "Is it over now?"

"Oh, no, there's much more. The camel will be back. I told you. Just wait."

Bob and I exchanged uneasy glances. What was Aisha talking about? The camel was on its way to its death. She had said so. How could he come back for the third time?

"The beaters! The beaters!" Shouting and ululation could be heard in the distance, somewhere up near the shrine, and Aisha leaped to her feet and ran to the edge of the road, where she stood, clutching a handkerchief in her hand. Fleetingly I wondered, Why the handkerchief? To dry the ritual tear one was supposed to shed at the death of the camel?

"The beaters!" But the police came first, clearing the way for whatever was to follow. The ululation and shouting increased. All along the rooftops and the ramparts where we sat, the women were sounding a greeting, though it was hard to tell whether their voices were calling in sorrow or in joy. Half a dozen young men followed the policemen, waving the white flags of Moulay Ibrahim from side to side, clearing a definitive path; after them, running fast, came two young men, pulling a rope, a rope to which something was tied. What? I bent forward to see better, then recoiled at the sight. For it *was* the camel coming around for the third time—the dead head of the sacrificial camel, its proud eyes closed, its haughty neck severed.

Along the dried mud of the street, they dragged the head of the camel, gray, dusty, and dead. And the women ululated and shouted loudly, and I shuddered as the head disappeared. At the end of the ramparts, the two men, still running, headed down a narrow path toward the gorges of Moulay Ibrahim, their grisly burden jerked along behind them, over bushes, brambles, clumps of lavender and thyme.

Bob and I turned and watched them go down into the gorge, getting smaller and smaller, the two men leaping, crossing the stream, their sacrificial burden no longer visible. We saw the tiny, doll-sized figures climbing up, up the opposite slope toward El Khalwa, toward the tree at the peak where Moulay Ibrahim had prayed, the tree the old woman had pointed out to us earlier in the day, where the barren woman had been carried by her husband.

"The legend of the camel's head," Moulay Mustapha had explained, back in Marrakech, "is that it disappears miraculously the seventh day after the sacrifice."

And I remembered Abdul Lateef's sarcastic reply, "And is it any wonder that the head disappears, with all the buzzards and squirrels about?"

Moulay Mustapha had half smiled, but instead of agreeing with Abdul Lateef, as he usually did, he had said, "Yes, of course, but that is a kind of miracle, too."

Now, as the tiny figures, still presumably dragging the sacrificial head, reached the top of the mountain and the outstretched branches of the saint's tree, a kind of murmur passed through the crowd. The spell was broken. The sacrifice had been made. The ritual was finished. Rather anticlimatically, after all the drama, people climbed down from the rooftops, filled the cobblestoned streets, and pumped up their primus stoves to make tea.

When Bob and I turned back from the gorge, Aisha had disappeared. I looked quickly, all around. No Aisha.

"There she is," said Bob, pointing to a figure, kneeling in the street with many others. Disturbed, I ran to her, thinking she might be ill or faint. She looked up at me calmly, however; nodded, and went on with what she was doing. I realized then that she was carefully blotting up with her handkerchief, like half a dozen other women, a spot of the blood of the sacrificial camel, which had dripped into the dust as the young men ran by.

"It's baraka," said Aisha, folding her dust and blood-besmirched handkerchief and tucking it carefully into her djellaba pocket. "It's for Najiya. Maybe it will help her headache; we've tried everything else."

We walked back to the car slowly and sat inside to eat lunch, savoring our hard-boiled eggs and cheese with pieces of Aisha's good bread, carefully peeling our oranges. The coffee from the Thermos was still warm and tasted marvelous. It was nearly two o'clock.

Aisha said she would like to buy souvenirs for the children, so we left Bob and headed back up to the market stalls on the main street. These were small shops carrying small items: plastic toys for children; flutes, whistles, headbands of plastic flowers; white canes and flags; change purses, key rings, tin pendants in the shape of a teardrop, bearing a verse from the Koran stamped upon them.

"No," muttered Aisha to herself, "no," and we walked along,

fighting the crowds of people still pushing toward the shrine. "We'll buy from the Ait Bamra."

"The what?" I asked in bewilderment, but Aisha did not answer, and I followed her toward a row of black-robed women, sitting before baskets of charms.

"The Ait Bamra has the best charms. They're from the desert," Aisha said. And indeed these women did look as if they had come from another region; they were not dressed like any of the other pilgrims I had seen. They looked more like my old friends from the deserts of southern Iraq; their black garments might have been all-enveloping *abbayas*. I watched as Aisha bargained, unsuccessfully, for a charm against the Evil Eye, a pink-and-yellow plastic hand of Fatima decorated with sequins.

"Come on, let's go," Aisha said in a disgusted tone, and the lady tossed her head and put the hand of Fatima back into its basket.

We moved on a few steps. We were standing beside a wooden door, like the door of a modest house, two stone steps up from the street when, to my surprise, Aisha knocked.

"Where are we going?" I whispered.

"The zaweeya," she replied.

The zaweeya? My morning nervousness returned. I had never planned to enter the sacred tomb earlier in the day; now I had no desire to go uninvited to a zaweeya. But the door opened, and a young man in baggy trousers, white shirt, and skullcap, with one eye whitened by trachoma, surveyed us.

I shrank back. I was just opening my mouth to say I would wait right here for my friend, when Aisha took my hand and led me across the threshold. The door shut behind us.

I reached for Aisha's hand. We were in a dark room of some kind, completely unlighted. My own eyes might as well have been whitened and blinded by trachoma, for I could see nothing. Aisha and the young man were whispering, as she led me along a seemingly narrow passage. The ground, which felt like rocks under my feet, sloped upward.

As my eyes gradually adjusted to the darkness, I could see the dim outlines of another door ahead. The young man was unlocking it. I clung to Aisha's familiar rough hand as light burst through the door, and noise, a rush of sibilant sound like the hum of bees or the rise and fall of waves beating on the shore of some bright and unknown sea.

"Step up," Aisha cautioned.

We did so. I saw the young man who had led us talking to another young man in the half-open door. They turned and looked at us; some kind of cursory inspection was under way, before the doorway filled with the blinding light and rush of sound.

"Step up again," said Aisha.

I blinked as I moved into the strong light, and the hall door slammed behind us. We were in the zaweeya.

"Aisha, wait," I pleaded. But she had already pulled me into a large, open courtyard, filled with women. I felt stunned, dazed, as though I had been hit on the head and emerged, like the wanderer in old fairy tales, in another time, another place. Where was I? I let go of Aisha's hand and stood still. Everything seemed out of focus in the sudden strong light.

We were in the zaweeya of Moulay Ibrahim, and whatever I had expected, it was not this. The qubba or tomb we had visited in the morning had been a shrine with overtones of a church. I had known shrines and churches all my life. What lay before me now, however, was a great, sunny, multileveled courtyard with whitewashed porches and pillars and passageways and blue and green doors leading off in unknown directions.

The courtyard hummed and buzzed with the sound of women's voices. Women in voluminous robes and hoods moved across the courtyard or sat in groups, gesturing and chatting together; the outlines of their figures were vivid yet curiously flattened, etched by the strong, clear sunlight falling on the pale flagstones and reflected from the dazzling white walls and pillars. What did it all remind me of? A woodcut, an illustration from an old book? But what old book? And what was it an illustration of? A women's market? A cloister in a convent? No familiar images came to my rescue so that I could compare, put together, relate to something within my own experience.

Clearly there was order, a plan of some kind operating in the crowd, for there was no pushing or jostling. Peace, order, but of some pattern I did not recognize.

"Come," Aisha whispered urgently, and I grasped her hand, took two steps forward, and stopped. The feeling of strangeness, or disorientation, came over me again. Think, I told myself sternly. Look around. Observe. Organize your thoughts. Pull yourself together.

Yes. I took a deep breath. I looked around. A great religious market in progress? A women's refuge? It was to this zaweeya, Aisha had said, that women came who lacked something in their lives, the sick, the barren, the defeated, the abandoned, the sorrowing women. The initial rush of strangeness faded. I looked to my left, where a long, wide passage sloped downward away from me; all along this passage, new mats had been laid down on both sides, and here women lay or squatted cross-legged, drinking tea. Some reclined on cushions, under swaths of material of many colors, white, green, flowered, which, like curtains, served to separate one woman from another, in small, enclosed cubicles. Some of the long, colored draperies had been caught up and tied back, tentlike. Others fell full, to mask the sleeping or sick woman beneath. The women wore loose caftans of white, their heads and throats also bound in white. I breathed more easily again. I was seeing, observing.

"They've come to sleep for three nights in the zaweeya," said Aisha, coming back for me, standing near the entrance, looking down the corridor of cubicles. "Rich women can have rooms." She gestured to the row of green and blue doors that had been cut out of the whitewashed wall on the opposite side of the courtyard. One of the doors opened as we watched, and an old woman, also in white, hobbled forth with a cane. "The dreams they dream in the little homes here will tell them what to do about their sickness or sadness.

"Come on," she said, taking my hand again, and we headed toward the center of the courtyard, where women walked to and fro, toward the pillared porches on the right, in and out of the passages and corridors that sloped upward beyond the porches. It was a very large zaweeya, I was thinking, when Aisha pulled me up short.

"Be careful!" She warned. I looked down at a slab of stone, covered with . . . could it be . . . blood?

"Where the camel was sacrificed. It's very bad to step there."

The camel? What camel? I drew in my breath, perplexed again. Hadn't Aisha herself said the camel had been sacrificed down below the ramparts, in a special place? Was there another camel for the women?

I held on to Aisha, who paused before another row of women sitting on individual mats. Each held a pen and had a pile of small squares of paper beside her; most were busy, writing.

"The *talabat*," said Aisha. "They write suras from the Koran. I'm looking for one Rakosh told me about."

"Where's she from? Is she a *sherifa?*"

"No, no," said Aisha, "but Rakosh says she's good. She's from Ourika."

A cry of pain rose above the soft, peaceful humming of the women's voices in the zaweeya. I turned to look. The cry had come from the pillared loggia, a level above us, where rows of women sat on the paved stones or on wooden benches. It seemed to be a young girl who had cried out, a young girl in a skirt and a green sweater, with a diaphanous green scarf fluttering from a twisted and useless arm. She cried out again, and I saw an older woman holding the girl's useless arm, massaging it gently.

"The *mateeyalum*," said Aisha. "That is their porch."

Ah, yes, the word made sense now. I had heard of the *mateeyalum*, or curers, those men and women to whom God had given a special ability to ease pain and disease. Hajja Kenza had spoken of them; so had Fatima Henna and Lateefa and Moulay Mustapha.

Here in the zaweeya, they had assembled in their own loggia. The mateeyalum were of all ages. Some simply talked to their patients; others massaged arms and legs or walked their clients up and down the length of the shady loggia, its high, whitewashed pillars grown over with ivy.

One was spitting on her patient. Could it be?

"Oh, yes, some people like that, the saliva of the mateeyalum is supposed to be very holy. I don't care for it, myself," said Aisha.

The mateeyalum we had noticed first was still massaging the useless, twisted arm of the girl in the green sweater; the mateeyalum forced the arm out, the girl screamed, and then the old woman took her in her arms, patting the girl's back while the girl hiccuped with sobs.

"The talaba I wanted is just not here," said Aisha, returning from the row of scribes. "They say she didn't come because of the rain." Aisha looked disappointed. "Let's go."

But I didn't want to go. Now that I had overcome my panic and nervousness, I found it pleasant and peaceful in the zaweeya—the murmuring of the talabat, the subsiding cries and soothing noises of the curers and their patients, the prayers of the women in the little homes, waiting for a dream, the dream that was to be an omen of their future. The different sounds and images that had seemed so overwhelming at first sight now blended together and fitted into a pattern, unforeseen and unexpected, but clear. I wanted to stay longer in this harmonious women's world.

Aisha pulled me out, however, as quickly as she had pulled me in, and we sidestepped the bloody stone and knocked on the inner door.

Again, the man in baggy pants opened the door and asked Aisha something. She giggled and shook her head. He gestured off in another direction, toward another passageway; she shook her head again and laughed her hearty laugh. The dark passageway ended, the second door opened and shut behind us. We were out in the small open square before the shrine once more.

"What did he say, Aisha?"

"He asked if we wanted our sons circumcised. That dark passage is where women go if they want their sons circumcised in the zaweeya, a holy place to do it, and the doctor's good."

"And what did *you* say?"

"Oh, Elizabetha!" Aisha paused and laughed again. "I told him our sons were far too old for that, that had been taken care of years ago, and he said we looked too young to have grown sons." Her eyes lightened. She was pleased.

I smiled back. "Let's go buy the charms, Aisha, and some walnuts for the children."

From the baskets of the Ait Bamra women we selected two big hands of Fatima, cut of yellow plastic on a red ground, decorated with sequins, centered with a core of sulphur. Sulphur, said Aisha, was the best deterrent of the Evil Eye. I also chose a tiny cross of cowrie shells sewn into black felt, struck by its anomaly in this Muslim setting. And from an old man, we bought some bundles of thyme and lavender from the mountains. Aisha protested at the price.

"You get these for free just by walking around here and picking them off the mountainside. Then you sell them for that much money?"

"We sell them because they come from the *holy* mountain of Moulay Ibrahim and are full of baraka," returned the man sharply. "You want the baraka at this price or not?"

I asked him to throw in two bags of walnuts and offered a reasonable price for the combination. He grumbled but nodded. My watch said almost four. Time to look for Rakiya and her daughters. Time to look for Bob and head home. We went down the stone stairs, over the wooden bridge where the gypsies sat drumming and singing for coins, which their children picked up and cached in a smaller drum. Clouds of incense and the smoke of hashish and tobacco perfumed the air.

The mood of the moussem had lightened and changed. The great drama of the sacrifice was finished. Pilgrims sat in clusters on the rocks, looking at the splendid view of the mountains, eating bread and cheese, sipping tea, making a last leisurely visit to the qubba now that the crowds had decreased. The sound of tympanies and pipes and drums came from a wide white tent, ornamented with tassels, which had been set up below the ramparts. A group of young men clustered near the entrance to the tent.

"*Chleuh* music!" said Aisha. "Somebody's dancing."

We waited for Rakiya and her daughters. The drums and tinkling tympanies from the tent were playing a different tune from the drums and pipes of the gypsies, but no one seemed to mind.

"I don't think they're coming," said Aisha. "Now where is Bob?"

We found him sitting on a rock above the car, wrapped in his burnoose, admiring the mountain panorama, the mists swirling in again across the peaks as evening approached.

"You all right, B.J.? You're very pale."

I stared at him, familiar, solid Bob. "I'll tell you about it later," I said, surprised that the effects of my experience in the zaweeya still showed on my face as they lingered in my mind—the porch of the curers, the women in their little homes, the bloody stone—like the fragments of mist once more descending on the holy mountain.

At the turn in the road at the bottom of the hill, where the Wadi Geghaia flows down from the peaks, Aisha asked Bob to stop. She stepped down the stony bank and filled a plastic bottle with the rushing water of the blessed stream. Silent and weary from the total effect of the long day, we drove home through shifting fog and sunlight, toward the red ramparts of Marrakech.

An hour later I banged on our silver door knocker in the shape of the hand of Fatima.

"Mama! Baba! Was it fun?" asked Laila.

"Did you see the camel?" asked Laura Ann.

"When're we going to eat?" asked David. "I want to go play soccer."

The next morning Kenza appeared to ask about the moussem.

"I took her into the qubba," said Aisha happily.

"You did, eh?" Kenza pursed her lips and eyed me appraisingly. "Good, good. I wish I could have gone with you, but oh, my stomach." She pushed irritatedly on her front, which did seem to be protruding more than usual. "Ah, my poor stomach. How I could use some of that baraka you got up there in the mountain." Her face twisted in pain.

"Well, we brought you some," I answered, and gathered into a bag some of the thyme and lavender from the shrine.

Kenza's eyes shone. She smiled, and the rim of gold teeth reappeared. "Ah, thank you, thank you," she said, taking with real eagerness the packets of herbs. "You," she said, shaking her finger in my face with some of her old spirit, "you will benefit from this baraka, too!"

I nodded.

"She's on the right path, hey, Aisha?"

And Kenza and Aisha chuckled together over my good fortune.

Chapter 16

Mul el Ksour and the Fortune Teller

It was late afternoon, several days after Moulay Ibrahim. The front door opened. It was Aisha. I was surprised to see her, for we had parted only ten minutes before, until the next morning, I thought.

"Elizabetha, the moussem of Mul el Ksour begins tonight. You want to go?"

"Now?" After lunch guests and two hours in the market, I was tired. Further, Bettye Harris was bringing some friends from Rabat for tea.

"Yes, now. Zahia's already gone with the children, and she said we were to come with Lateefa and Khadija and meet her there."

I hesitated. I was really tired. And what about the Harris's friends? But on the other hand, when would I have another chance to go to the moussem of Mul el Ksour?

"There'll be dancing in the women's zaweeya," Aisha added.

"Go on, B.J.," urged Bob. "I can take care of the guests, and Laura Ann can make the tea. Bettye will understand."

"Wear your djellaba," Aisha counseled. I ran upstairs to put on my trusty green djellaba, and when I came down, Aisha and Lateefa were spooning up yogurt and eating bananas.

"Laura Ann offered us some," said Aisha in a pleased way. "A good idea. The dancing goes on for hours! So you better have some too."

We finished off our yogurt, the ladies pulled up their veils, and I kissed Laura Ann good-by and thanked her and Bob for taking over my duties. Outside the door Aisha's son stood at the entrance to the sibha. At the sight of me, in my djellaba and head scarf, he laughed aloud. I was embarrassed.

"Abdul Krim is laughing," I said nonsensically to Aisha. Obviously he was laughing. What did I want Aisha to answer? To reassure me and tell me I looked no different from Lateefa and herself? Ridiculous.

Aisha simply snorted. "Abdul Krim doesn't need to come to the moussem! He doesn't believe in them, remember?"

This seemed a *non sequitur*, and yet I realized somehow that Aisha was trying to relieve my embarrassment at her son's rudeness or to reassure me in some way about the coming evening. Going to a moussem brought one baraka. So why should one worry about the gibes of nonbelievers even if they were your own kin? But Abdul Krim's derision had stung, for my own motives were complex. I was also not certain what to expect, and the old fears and uncertainty attending our visit to Moulay Ibrahim settled down over me again.

The colors in the evening sky cast a strange pallor over the low roofs, the red walls, and the black horse-drawn carriages on Rue Bab Agnaou. All day, storm clouds had been massing and breaking up. We had had a few sprinkles of rain earlier in the afternoon, but nothing to resemble the downpours of early spring. Now the banks of clouds hung low over the square of Djemaa el Fna, moving above us, around the minaret tower of the Koutoubia, above the bus station and the little mosque with its new band of plaster decoration. Sudden bright shafts of light flared between the clouds, to be covered just as quickly by new clouds; the quick shifts between light and shadow were like the sputtering of giant candles.

A group of men sat near the edge of the square, flanked by flags. Three of the men were drumming, and a fourth stood in the middle, exhorting us as we passed by, his black hair wild and matted, his djellaba ragged, in contrast to the other members of the group, who were neatly attired in turbans and ordinary djellabas. The hiss of the yellow pressure lamp punctuated his cries, and as Lateefa moved forward to drop a coin in the drum, I instinctively drew back.

"It's only the *naga*," said Aisha, "for another moussem. They are gathering converts for the group. They always do it at the time of the Seven Saints. You know, Mul el Ksour is one of the Seven."

We walked between the ranks of cabs and carriages, and the line of fruit stalls, which marked the outer boundary of the square. A carriage full of tourists pulled out of line suddenly, and we jumped to avoid it. But Khadija, trying to sidestep a pile of orange rinds that had not quite reached the gutter, was nearly caught by the back wheel.

"We tour the beautiful garden of Marrakech," said the guide in English, to his carriage full of fashionably dressed English ladies. "The beautiful gardens at sunset."

From the aspect of the clouds, the tourists would have a strange sunset. I turned around to look at them galloping off toward the Koutoubia, its noble minaret, usually so rosy, pale and muted in the uncerain gray and yellow light from the sky. They had not, I realized, even noticed Khadija's narrow escape.

Raindrops caught us. Aisha called, "hurry, hurry," and rushed us through a pair of heavy wrought-iron gates into what seemed an enormous warehouse. Mattresses, pillows, bolts of upholstery fabric, black and yellow cut velvet, maroon plush, and flowered cretonne lined the walls from floor to ceiling.

"The khan of Mul el Ksour," said Lateefa.

Did this storehouse of rich fabrics belong to the zaweeya, or had it merely been named that because it stood in the same general area? I did not know. Neither did Aisha.

By the time we'd passed through the khan and through the second pair of iron gates, we were in a quarter of the medina I did not know. The brief flurry of raindrops had ceased, and the sun still alternately flashed and disappeared between rags of clouds; Lateefa's striped djellaba glowed fluorescently in the light, and Khadija's one thin silver bracelet flashed.

We walked along, from one dark covered street into another, out into the open for a brief moment, then into another passageway. When I stumbled for the third time and reached out to the nearest house wall to steady myself, I realized we must be in a very ancient part of the city, for the wall was rough under my hand, and the bricks were crumbling and broken. Occasionally the rounded remnant of an arch, long since collapsed, showed in the light between houses. The lurid sky of ragged yellow-and-gray clouds still glowed above us, and we could see the high delicate silhouette of a minaret, the tops of green-tiled roofs. Candles lighted our way down the last dark passage, candles held by small boys, whispering, "Mul el Ksour, Mul el Ksour," and ushering us into an open space around the old and noble building of the mosque complex.

"Here we are!" said Lateefa in her high, sweet voice. "Where's Zahia?"

"Probably in the zaweeya," replied Aisha. "She loves the dancing, doesn't she, Khadija?"

"Ahhh!" agreed Khadija, who had been totally silent during our journey, except for the cracking of her bubble gum, an irritating and yet cheerful sound, somehow, down the dark, unlit passages, under the strange sky.

Aisha and Lateefa pushed through the crowds milling in the square around the mosque, the shrine, and the zaweeya. I hoped they would not try to take me into the mosque, for whatever the rules might be for the shrines, I knew perfectly well what they were for mosques. But no, we were going to the shrine, Aisha said firmly, and she stopped at the door to buy candles. Again my heart began to beat loudly, but there was no difficulty. The three of us in djellabas, and Khadija in her sweater and skirt, stepped down three steep steps, from the debris of many centuries onto a floor paved in the distant past, just as one enters the buildings of ancient Rome by stepping down several feet from the modern streets.

We were in a large, spacious courtyard, paved with white-and-blue tiles, centered by an old dry fountain, from which no water splashed. "Your shoes! Your shoes!" Aisha reminded me, and I took them off, as my friends had done already. And they led me to an old tile set in the side of the wall, an arch-shaped tile with inscriptions in green and blue.

"It is from the time of Mul el Ksour," whispered Aisha in the same hushed tones she had used in the Saadian tombs.

The crowds were modest, compared with the pushing throngs at Moulay Ibrahim. I began to feel more relaxed as we crossed the courtyard and passed the silent fountain and the rows of women with babies who sat all around the walls of the courtyard.

"They are waiting to have the babies circumcised," said Lateefa. "It's free at Mul el Ksour, and they have a good doctor."

The women looked as though they had settled in for the night, with pillows and blankets and snacks, the babies wearing green paper caps with the star of Morocco emblazoned upon them in honor of their approaching circumcision.

And here we were in the shrine, with no fanfare. There were no guards, no clappers, no enthusiastic, semihysterical pilgrims knocking us about. We were in a moderate-sized room, recently whitewashed, where stood a plain, raised catafalque, perhaps three feet high, its heavy green moire cover newly edged with green braid, the same braid I had seen in large spools in the suq when the girls and I had shopped for caftan material. Instead of circling the tomb, we sat down cross-legged on the red-and-green woven mats. Aisha and Lateefa prayed in a traditional way, cupping their hands upward in supplication. I gazed steadfastly at the ground, wondering how long excitement and interest would triumph over my real fatigue. Sitting, I realized that my shoulders were sore, my head ached, my stomach was rumbling. Fortunately Khadija beside me was fidgeting and cracking her gum again, so presumably my rumblings would not be noticed.

I did utter a prayer, another supplication that I not cause trouble for Lateefa and Aisha and Khadija. So far my prayers had been answered, but I did not know how many more hours we would spend here, and hadn't Aisha said there'd be dancing in the zaweeya? Aisha finally stood up and kissed the shrine, as did Lateefa. But Khadija did not, which made my own omission less noticeable, I hoped. As in Moulay Ibrahim, the other side of the catafalque was lined with men and women, holding a kind of congregational prayer meeting, reciting together the sunset prayers of the devout Muslim.

We put on our shoes in the white, uncrowded courtyard and stepped up into the square again. It was almost night, and above the green-tiled roofs and the high, slender minaret, the yellow-and-gray sky was darkening. Rags of pink clouds fluttered against the ominous blackness like the flags of the nagas we had passed in Djemaa el Fna.

Aisha and Lateefa were arguing about going to the zaweeya. Khadija and I stood apart, waiting for them to make the decision for us. We watched the growing crowds entering the shrine and the building next door, which presumably was the men's zaweeya, for here, clearly visible through the great wrought-iron windows, sat many men. Their djellabas and their green-and-white turbans glowed in the light of scores of bare electric bulbs, hanging from the high, green roof on long, thin, shining chains like strange upside-down candles.

"I told Zahia we'd meet her there," Lateefa was insisting, and Aisha, with one eye on the stormy sky, and the other, I thought, on the guard at the entrance, nodded and said, "Yallah!"

We entered the zaweeya without any further ceremony, and I told myself that it was my own fatigue combined with the dramatic evening sky that had created my sense of foreboding. It had all been a trick of space and light, the murk of shifting bright and dark clouds reflecting my own unfamiliarity with the dark and light zankas of an unknown part of the medina; for Aisha and Lateefa seemed very lighthearted, as though on the way to a party.

"Hold my hand and look at the ground," Aisha said in my ear, crisply, brusquely, and at her tone my sense of foreboding returned, my nerves twinged once more. In a moment we had dropped from the lighted green square into a dark tunnel, barely higher than we were, a long one that wound around and around into, I thought, nothingness. I held onto Aisha and thought that at least in the dark no one will notice me, but at the third or fourth turn, the tunnel opened up into a brightly lit foyer where an armed policeman stood, and an old man sat at a table full of candles. I involuntarily drew in my breath, but Aisha simply held up our candles to demonstrate we didn't need any; we passed inspection. After the foyer came a long corridor; here, too, women sat in rows, their babies wearing the same green paper caps as they had in the shrine, settling in for the night in the zaweeya to await the morning ceremony of circumcision.

This women's zaweeya in Marrakech was very different from the zaweeya of Moulay Ibrahim. There, in the mountain refuge, the rooms of different levels had been built according to the topography of the mountain; in the course of the centuries, the shrine extended into loggias and courts and passages as further room was needed. In contrast, Mul el Ksour's refuge for women might have been a large and comfortable town house. The rooms were built around its well-paved courtyard, which was shaded by bitter orange trees in bloom. The trees stood stiffly in plots of earth circled with blue-and-green-tiled borders. They gave a festive garden air to the rather damp courtyard, covered with a dark night sky sprinkled with stars among the shifting clouds. The scent of the orange blossoms blended curiously and pleasantly with incense being burned somewhere in the rooms and with the perfume of the women visitors to the zaweeya.

"There's Zahia!" Lateefa cried delightedly, and she ran forward with Aisha to where Zahia stood, in a large crowd of women near one of the orange trees, watching something . . . the dancing, perhaps? The sound of drums was loud.

Khadija waited for me, and we ambled across to the crowd. Yes, it was dancing. The noise came from five large skin drums, alternately booming alone and coming together in a combination of rhythms.

"You came, and you brought Elizabetha!" Zahia was chattering happily and very loudly in order to be heard above the music and over the children who were whining and hanging onto the folds of her djellaba—Kamal, little Ali, Shadeeya, and Aisha's small niece, who was to return to the village next week. "Just in time, too. Everybody was afraid of rain, and the drummers took a long time getting started."

I could hear the drums, and the ululating of women in the audience as they expressed their pleasure in the performance. But the crowd was so dense I could not see the performers themselves.

"Get up here," suggested Zahia, and she pulled me up onto the tiled rim of one of the tree plots.

She was right. I could see the whole scene from my new vantage point: The drummers, in white, with pale blue scarves tied around their heads, were seated inside the circle of spectators; and a girl danced alone, a dark-haired girl just entering puberty, one might have said, from her immature body, her legs too long for the short skirt she wore under her blue nylon school smock, a *tablier* just like Laura Ann's.

"Hold onto the tree," instructed Zahia. "See, isn't that better?"

I agreed. But Zahia's cheerfulness seemed at first out of place. The dancing girl looked to me as though she had reached a state of trance and was almost out of control, her head lolling back and forth, her arms limp. An older woman in a gray djellaba and hood stood close behind, clutching the back of the girl's tablier, keeping her on her feet, or the girl, it appeared, would have fallen to the ground. At that moment the dancer's head dropped forward onto her chest, the drummers ceased abruptly, and the woman in gray grabbed the girl under the armpits. The drums began another beat, slower, softer. Although she seemed to have collapsed in the older woman's arms, the dancing girl gradually straightened up and began to move to the new beat, not in the jerky, lolling manner of before, but simply and gracefully.

"Isn't it nice?" Lateefa whispered happily beside me.

I nodded, though "nice" was not the word I would have chosen for what I assumed was a religious experience. But perhaps I had brought with me my own ideas of trances and therapeutic group dancing as serious business, for everyone else seemed to find the spectacle pleasing. Lateefa was lifting the children up, one by one, so they could see, too. Khadija had wandered away, looking for an open

place. She had found one and worked up to the front row of spectators, where she stood, arms folded, as she did in the sibha, watching
the girl in the blue smock. Khadija nodded her head in time to the
drums, and her mouth worked steadily at her bubble gum.

"Look at that girl!" said Zahia in disapproving tones. "Wait till I
tell Rakosh. She looks so rude!"

By now more women had joined the dance, and smaller girls
stepped forward, shaking their childish heads and torsos back and
forth, moving in the gentle but insistent new rhythm of the drums.

Zahia poked me in the ribs.

"You want to dance?"

I smiled. "No, thank you."

"But you can dance, can't you? Don't they dance in America?"

"Oh, yes," I answered, "but that's not my music."

I smiled again, but Zahia did not smile back. She stared at me for a
few seconds and then passed my remark on to Lateefa and Aisha,
who then also stared at me. Had I made some blunder? I went back
over the conversation but could not remember anything I had said
that seemed particularly unusual.

Aisha was nodding wisely. "It's true that they may dance all
night," she said, "and we see now that you would like to stay, but we
have to go home pretty soon. We could come back tomorrow
though, so you could dance, couldn't we?"

"Oh, yes," said Lateefa. "Would that be all right?"

"Yes," I said. The conversation was vaguely perplexing, but in my
fatigue I simply registered the word "home" and said I'd be ready to
go whenever they were and would be happy to come back tomorrow.

"First we have to show her the *diwan*," said Zahia, and I was led
around the dancers, past the orange trees, to a brightly lit room on
the other side of the courtyard, where women sat or reclined on cushions and banquettes, smoking and drinking tea.

"Those are the *shorfa*," said Aisha excitedly. "The descendants of
the Prophet Mohammed and of Mul el Ksour. Would you like us to
take you in and introduce you?"

I peered in at the room full of elaborately attired ladies, at their
silver- and gold- and rose- and blue- and wine-colored caftans, their glittering jewelry, their embroidered slippers in rows by the door, their
hair fashionably arranged in the manner of the time. What would I
say to the shorfa?

"No, thank you, Aisha. I prefer to stay and watch the dancing with you before we go."

Aisha and Lateefa exchanged satisfied glances. We joined the circle of spectators once more, clapping and ululating as the central girl in her blue smock continued to turn, gracefully, accompanied now by several other women dancing in different ways, but to the same beat. We passed the rows of babies waiting to be circumcised. A few were asleep in their mothers' arms. The ululation continued above the drums, the clink of glasses could be heard in the diwan of the shorfa, and an occasional child set up a wail. Clouds were covering the stars above us; in the smell of the coming rain, the scent of the orange trees seemed stronger than ever.

We left the courtyard of Mul el Ksour by another route, through a large, bare room with a stone slab in the middle, covered with darkening blood. A sacrifice had been made here today, obviously, on the first day of the moussem.

"Be careful of the sacrifice stone!" called Zahia, but I had already carefully stepped around it.

"Wasn't it fun?"

"Did you enjoy it?"

"Do you think your husband will let you go tomorrow? We'll go with you."

"Yes, yes," I answered automatically as we walked back along the worn, narrow streets, between the crumbling walls of the old houses. My green djellaba felt heavy on my shoulders; I stumbled now from fatigue, and when we had traversed the khan of fabrics and cushions and were passing the fruit stalls, I realized how hungry I was. Food! I bought oranges for everyone.

"You don't need to do that, Elizabetha."

"Oh, yes, I do," I insisted boldly, between mouthfuls of orange sections.

"But why?"

"Because," I stammered, then rushed on . . . "because today is a day of baraka."

Aisha grabbed my arm. "See, didn't I tell you all the moussems would do her good? Some of the baraka of Mul el Ksour has stayed with her, and with us, too."

We stood in front of the stall, in the light of the pressure lamp, peeling our oranges.

"Oh," said Zahia, "but you didn't need to buy them for the children, too."

Perhaps fatigue had loosened my tongue, for I found myself saying, in appropriate phrases I did not realize I knew, "Oh yes, I do, because children are baraka every day and should be remembered."

The ladies burst into delighted exclamations. A trio of young men in jeans, all foreigners, drew near us and stared into our faces.

"The one in the green djellaba, with the scarf," said one of the boys in perfect English, "she must be English."

"No, no," said the second, "she's Russian, maybe a spy in disguise." They laughed together.

I kept my gaze on my orange, hoping no flick of eyelid would betray me. After a few breathless seconds, the third boy said, "How can you be so sure? She didn't even react to your English. She must be from Fez. The women there wear scarves like that instead of hoods. My Moroccan friend told me so."

We waited until the boys had moved off before heading toward home.

"Let's give something to the naga, too," I said, thinking of the circle of men under the strangely colored sky, their flags fluttering like clouds, the tall, tattered preacher with his shock of wild hair exhorting us to leave the way of evil and join the pathway of pilgrims toward the good. But the wild-haired preacher was asleep on the ground, and when Khadija put my coin into the contribution box, the men did not look at us. "*Baraka-llahufik*," murmured one.

"All right, now let's go, my husband will be angry," said Zahia, and we walked quietly across the nearly empty square toward Rue Bab Agnaou. We had gone only a few steps when a loud French voice said, "*Bon soir*, Madame Fernea!"

I started in surprise. The ladies turned, too, in fright. There stood a group of men in winter djellabas, but one, the tallest, was smiling at me; it was the policeman from our French class at the Mission Culturelle, the policeman who, in a suit and tie and vest, discussed with us almost every evening those boring events in the lives of Madame and Monsieur Thibault of Place d'Italie, Paris! I had not recognized him in his djellaba.

"*Bon soir, monsieur*," I replied quickly.

"Who was *that*?" asked Lateefa in a coquettish voice when the men had passed by.

I told them. They hooted with laughter. Zahia clouted me on the shoulder. "Come on. Tell us. Who is he really?"

"I am telling you. Honestly. That's who he is."

"And your husband knows you know him?"

"Yes, yes."

"And you've never taken a walk with him?"

I knew very well what that meant. "Of course not!" I said indignantly, perhaps a little too indignantly.

The ladies giggled behind their veils. Khadija stared at me and smiled and cracked her bubble gum loudly.

"Well, well," said Lateefa, again in that arch, coquettish tone.

"Really," I insisted, "that's all there is to it."

Aisha laughed. "Oh, Elizabetha, you're so serious! We're just teasing!"

"Hmph!" said Zahia. "Well, I'm not teasing when I say that any time you don't want your handsome husband, we'll take him, won't we, girls?"

"Oh, yes," burbled Lateefa, and the ladies laughed and the children shuffled beside us, the last steps to our houses on Rue Trésor.

"*Baraka-llahufik!*" I called out, as I reached my door.

"Listen to her," cried Zahia. "One minute a man, the next minute she's talking about baraka!"

"Quiet!" shouted a loud, unmistakable voice from a second-floor shuttered window above us.

Zahia was not to be put down. "Good night, Kenza!" she hollered and dissolved into laughter as she headed down the dark sibha with Aisha and Lateefa, the children hanging onto their mother in weariness. Khadija was the last, and she turned and waved goodnight.

In the morning, I discovered from various books that Mul el Ksour was the surname of a great mystic of the fifteenth century, Sidi Abdallah el Ghezwani. Or his surname may have been Sidi Moulay el Ksour. He had come to Marrakech, according to the books, to become a disciple of the great Sidi Abdul Aziz. When Sidi Ghezwani's mystical education was completed, he went to Fez, but his fame became so great that the Sultan of Fez had him thrown into prison. There he died in 1528, an old man, and his body was brought back to Marrakech to be buried; he is now one of the seven patron saints, the *sabá'at rijal,* one of the mystical seven who supposedly guard and protect the city.

Omar, our djellaba merchant friend, told Bob how pleased he was that I had visited the shrine of his ancestor. He was a direct descendant, he said, of Mul el Ksour, but this saint was a merchant. not a mystic. His name, Mul el Ksour, literally meant master of the palaces. The French books were obviously wrong.

Abdul Lateef and Moulay Mustapha agreed with Omar that the books were certainly wrong—Mul el Ksour was a great merchant and the patron saint of merchants. Sidi Moulay el Ksour, who was he?

Aisha said she did not know about merchants and mystics, but that everyone agreed that Mul el Ksour was one of the seven. But, I asked, why is the oratory, the tower of the minaret, called el Ksour when it was built almost 150 years before Sidi Ghezwani el Ksour was buried in Marrakech? Did other members of the Ghezwani family live in Marrakech in the 1300s and give money for the tower to be built? Was it possible that Sidi el Ghezwani wanted to visit his family as well as complete his mystical education when he decided to migrate to Marrakech? Or was this a different el Ksour? These were questions no one could answer for me, and, indeed, no one seemed to have any interest in answering. Mul el Ksour was a great saint; he was one of the seven. That was all one needed to know.

Further, said Abdul Lateef, I had obviously gotten a totally wrong impression from the dancing in the women's zaweeya. For some reason he had been very curious about my reactions to the occasion. Did I find it moving?

"Yes," I said, and went on to describe the occasion as interesting and pleasant.

"Pleasant, Madame, pleasant? You describe the great mystical trance of the derdaba or religious dance as merely pleasant? I think perhaps you are mistaken or were not paying proper attention."

His tone irritated me, that same patronizing tone, but I tried to keep calm. "Really, Abdul Lateef, everyone behaved as though they were at a party, having a good time. Really they did. You can ask my friends."

He pursed his lips. "The derdaba is a serious, a psychological experience, Madame. It is deep and important."

"But—" Bob was trying to catch my eye, willing me to be quiet. But I didn't want to be quiet. I knew that this kind of dancing and music session had often been described as therapeutic, cathartic, full of intensity and drama, but my whole impression of the occasion had been that all were in a gay and lighthearted mood and enjoyed themselves thoroughly. "It was fun, Abdul Lateef," I finished boldly.

Bob winced; Mustapha looked scandalized. Abdul Lateef opened his mouth, then shut it again. My last remark had apparently placed me beyond the pale, someone to whom nothing more could be said.

Moulay Mustapha tried to make peace. "But, Lateef, maybe the women's derdaba is different? Who knows what the women do in their zaweeya?"

"Yes, Mustapha," agreed Lateef. "Who knows? Who knows indeed?" He shook his head mournfully. "Only God knows!" And he raised his gaze upward, as if asking God to give him patience and understanding of this strange unknown world of women.

The moussem of Mul el Ksour was to continue for three or four days, and on the third day Aisha announced that since it had not rained, the women would be going to the zaweeya about five. Was I coming?

I did not know quite what to answer. We were expecting guests for dinner, Laura Ann's French tutor and her parents from Le Havre. How could I go off to the zaweeya at five and be certain of being back home in time to cook and serve the meal?

"Let's see, Aisha," I temporized.

After lunch the clouds opened and rain poured into the courtyard, beating on the tiles, making fine inroads into the basin of the fountain, surprising the goldfish, who jumped and plunged in the pelting drops.

"Maybe it will stop," said Aisha disconsolately.

"Maybe," I agreed. But did I want it to stop raining? "Do they only dance at the moussems, or could we go some other time?"

"Oh, we could probably go another time. The zaweeya meets regularly, and at different people's houses. Somebody brings bread and somebody brings tajeen and the hostess provides the mint tea. But it's easier at the moussem. Everybody's there and they don't have to look for drummers and nobody has to cook."

Aisha was preparing vegetables, and I was making a sponge cake for dessert.

"Did you recognize the beat the other night?" she asked.

"What?" I asked.

"You said, 'that's not my music' when we asked if you wanted to dance. I just wondered if you recognized the later beat."

"No." I folded the egg whites in the batter and put the cake in the oven.

"Each person has his own beat, his own tune," said Aisha quietly. She washed the egg beater, and I dried it. "One will recognize it."

"Ah . . ." I said. "That's why—" and then stopped. I had been about to say that was the reason the drummers had stopped halfway through the dance and started over on another beat. Obviously they were searching for the right combination to suit the dark-haired girl in her blue school smock.

"And it is bad to dance to the wrong tune, the wrong beat, one's spirit becomes confused."

"Yes, I can see that."

"And every saint is different."

"Yes."

"So people only go to one zaweeya, regularly, so the spirits don't become confused."

"Yes."

"Rakosh goes to Lalla Sitti Fatima; Lateefa and Zahia go to Mul el Ksour. You know, Fatima Henna may be going there, too, or to Moulay Ibrahim. Glaoui goes to some moussem in the mountains. Kenza would like to go, but she doesn't want to spend the money. No wonder she's beginning to feel poorly all the time."

I stood still in the kitchen, holding the egg beater in my hand. It was well dried, the cake was in the oven, the vegetables were ready to cook, but I did not want to leave the kitchen, for never had Aisha become so personal with me. She stood there, too, hanging and rehanging the dishcloth on its rack.

"And you, Aisha?"

"I have no time, Elizabetha. When the children are finished with school, I will join Sidi Bel Abbas. That is where my mother belonged."

The door knocker banged.

"Some foreign man wants Mr. Bob."

The moment was over.

All afternoon the rain continued to beat down on the tiles in the courtyard. I had mixed feelings, for I knew my friends wanted to dance, and yet I was hoping against hope that it would rain until after five and thus release me from the need to choose between my French guests and the moussem. Yet I thought I knew what my decision would have been. Why was I kidding myself?

Bob came back from the market to say that everyone was expressing apprehension about the harvest. The rain had been good earlier, but now it was bad, for the winter wheat was ripe and needed to be cut before it rotted in the fields.

At six o'clock it was still raining. There would be no dancing in the zaweeya of Mul el Ksour tonight, Aisha reported sadly. Zahia had gone and come home, saying that people were leaving, and the moussem was ending early because of the rain, a bad omen for the harvest.

The children arrived home from school, soaked to the skin. Bob had gone to pick them up but had missed them. We all changed for dinner, and our evening went off well. Everyone seemed to enjoy himself, Laura Ann's tutor complimented her on her progress in French, and the lady from Le Havre took two pieces of sponge cake. Yes, I said, it was an American recipe. What, I wondered guiltily, would I have done if it had not rained at all? I decided not to think about it.

Next morning the sun came out and dried up the puddles in the courtyard. Bob, after his morning trip to Djemaa el Fna, said that many men, in work clothes and carrying scythes, had gathered in the square, waiting to be picked up by the farmers to help harvest the wheat crop quickly. Aisha's husband had gone, too, she said; it was usual for him to pick up occasional wages as a day laborer during harvest time.

Aisha also said that Lateefa had received a visit from her favorite shuwafa. Did I still want a shuwafa to come and tell our fortunes? I looked at Aisha. For the past eight months I had been asking regularly whether a shuwafa might be engaged. Then I had seen the shuwafa's visit as a way in which I might logically invite my neighbors to tea, so that I might begin to know them better. That reason was meaningless now. But yes, I said, of course I still wanted the shuwafa.

"When?" asked Aisha.

"Maybe tomorrow, Wednesday. The children will be home, and the girls want their fortunes told."

Aisha nodded.

"And Lateefa should come, if she wishes."

Aisha turned. "Najiya?"

"Of course. And Mrs. Harris will want to come, too."

Aisha looked surprised. "Does she really?"

"Yes, yes. We have shuwafas in America, too."

"You do?"

"Of course."

In the afternoon I drove over to tell Bettye. She was excited, and I found that I was, too. After having heard so much about this particular shuwafa from Aisha and Lateefa, I was anxious to see what she was like. Laura Ann and Laila loved to have their fortunes told, and we all waited the lady's arrival with anticipation.

The shuwafa's appearance was rather unexpected. After the months of buildup, I suppose I had expected an old woman, or at least one of some experience with life. Certainly I had not anticipated this rosy-cheeked girl, looking scarcely more than twenty, draped in a white haik and carrying a small baby, also wrapped in white. Was she from the country? No, she wrapped her haik in a city manner, winding it around the neck and head so that her hair was completely covered. She had an open face, an easy smile and laugh, and she dandled her pretty baby on her knee and looked around at us while we sat in the salon and bargained for a price for seven fortunes: Laura Ann, Laila, Aisha, Najiya, Lateefa, Bettye, and me.

"Agreed!" said the shuwafa in a bored voice. She stood up, walked around the room while we all watched, asked if we could have tea when the work was finished, and being told yes, deposited her baby on Laura Ann's lap and sat down again. Laura Ann looked pleased, and the baby jumped up and down in delight at all the attention.

Now the shuwafa sat down in one of our blue canvas chairs and, while we continued to watch her every move, pulled from a pocket somewhere inside her clothes a kind of bracelet or charm, a cluster of three cowrie shells strung between knots on a strip of braided leather.

"Can I go first, Mama?" Laura Ann asked eagerly.

The shuwafa nodded and smiled. Laura Ann passed the baby to Laila and moved to the chair beside the shuwafa. She took my oldest daughter's hands in hers, strong, large hands for such a small woman. Drawing the string of cowrie shells down over each of Laura Ann's palms, she murmured something to the click of the cowrie shells, then closed her eyes.

Laura Ann looked at me, quickly, her eyes excited. We all waited for the shuwafa's vision or inspiration to come.

"Waaaaaaa!" The baby let out a long, piercing wail.

The shuwafa opened her eyes as Laila stood up hastily, a dark stain of urine spreading across her dress. "The baby's wet on me, Mama," she said simply, looking distressed and holding the baby out at arm's length.

The shuwafa laughed and reached for her baby. I ran to get a towel and told Laila to go up and change; Laura Ann offered to take the baby, and the shuwafa, looking closely at her, nodded and smiled and said she would tell Laura Ann's fortune later.

So we started all over again. First Lateefa, who sat quietly while the string of cowrie shells clicked across her hand and the shuwafa murmured again and closed her eyes. I looked at Lateefa, whose face showed, in the bright light from the sunny courtyard, lines of tension and worry. She was beginning to lose her fragile good looks, from the concentration and hard work of sewing the fine seams of braid onto djellabas, from her own disappointment after the collapse of her two marriages.

"I see, yes, I see . . ." The shuwafa droned on. I found it difficult to understand what she was saying, and no one seemed interested in translating for me. Najiya and Aisha were staring rigidly at the shuwafa, who muttered something about a man, not a good man, and a woman, a very good woman. A few quick words, very low, made Lateefa smile. Her face relaxed.

"Now for Madame!" The shuwafa gestured toward Bettye, who by now had the same anxious, tense expression I had noted on Lateefa's face as she waited for her future to be outlined for her.

We were silent. The cowrie shells clicked, the shuwafa opened and closed her eyes, paused, and began to speak clearly so I could hear and translate for Bettye.

"In a short while your husband will receive a great opportunity. He must not take that opportunity, or there will be trouble. He must wait until a second opportunity arises, after some months."

The young shuwafa in white abruptly withdrew the cowrie shells and said, directly to Bettye, "You have three children and you worry about them all the time. Your husband is the one who needs your attention more."

When this was translated, Bettye stared fixedly at the shuwafa. I thought the shuwafa was going to say something, but another wail from the baby interrupted whatever she had been about to do. The baby was busily wetting again, but this time Laura Ann had managed to blot it all up with the towel before her own lap had been stained.

"Well," said the shuwafa, "I see I must read this girl's hand before anything else happens," and proceeded to outline a wonderful future for Laura Ann.

"What's she saying, Mama?"

"You're lucky in everything. You will be successful in whatever you

do, you will marry a man who is rich and intelligent, and he will love
you very much."

Laura Ann grinned. "Will I love him, too?"

I translated this for the shuwafa, who shrugged in reply. "I don't
know," she said. "Is it important to the girl?"

Laura Ann said that it was.

The shuwafa looked perplexed. She shut her eyes, opened them,
and looked at my oldest daughter's hand once more. "I'm not sure,"
she finally said, "but he will love you, and that is all that matters."

Everyone smiled. We shifted in our seats. I took the baby, who
jumped up and down on my lap and crowed happily. It was Najiya's
turn. I tried to listen carefully, for this was bound to test the ingenu-
ity, I thought, of the shuwafa. What could she say to the bright-faced
girl, with her pitiful hunched back?

"Many men will offer to marry you," I heard, "but you do not wish
to marry them, and your parents agree with your decision."

"But why?" the words burst from Najiya. "Why don't I want to
marry them?"

The shuwafa looked displeased. "Because they are not of your family," she said in a tone of just barely veiled scorn. "You do not wish
to marry an outsider because you know that the family takes the best
care of its daughters."

"Of course, of course," agreed Aisha. Najiya continued to look
doubtful.

"So," finished the shuwafa, her eyes closed, "you wait at home
until your cousin is ready to give you a good home."

Najiya withdrew her hand and looked sullenly at the ground. The
shuwafa reached quickly for the girl's hand, held it tightly in her own
for a moment, and added, "and this marriage will take place as soon
as your headaches and earaches are finished."

She gave Najiya a brilliant smile, and Najiya smiled vaguely in return. I mentally applauded the shuwafa's masterful diplomacy. We
all knew that Najiya's health problems would probably never be over.
But the shuwafa's words offered a shred of hope, and might even encourage Najiya to think less about her illnesses and make some effort
at recovery, for that, I had thought for some time, was part of the
problem. No matter what medicines and charms and doctor's
prescriptions were offered, Najiya did not want to be well, for she had
decided already that her future was bleak.

I did not hear Aisha's fortune, delivered in a low monotone; I dandled the baby while Laila put her small, pale hand into the shu-wafa's. My youngest daughter was told that she, too, was to have a pleasant and lucky future, like Laura Ann. Great talent, a good mar-riage, all was sufficiently vague and pleasant until the final moment, when our shuwafa spoke quickly and announced that we must take Lalia to Sidi Bel Abbas and light a candle there for her. This seemed a bit strange, even ominous. Why should I take Laila to Sidi Bel Abbas, and not David or Laura Ann?

"Did you understand, Elizabetha?" asked Aisha.

"I think so."

"The shuwafa says it's very important, and even if Laila herself doesn't go, you must go and buy a candle and take it to the shrine, and say a prayer and then everything will be all right."

"What did she say, Mama? Is my fortune bad?"

"No, no, dear, the shuwafa just says we should go to a shrine together and light a candle to make sure everything turns out well."

Laila shook her head. "I don't *want* to go to one of those shrines."

"Well, maybe Aisha and I can go instead." Laila looked upset. The afternoon had begun so well. The shuwafa tightened her grip on Laila's small hand and clicked the cowrie shells. Laila pulled her hand away. The fortune teller looked annoyed; she frowned.

"Mama, can I go now?" Laila asked.

"Yes, dear. Why don't you take the baby out in the court?"

I felt vaguely uneasy as I extended my own hand to the young shu-wafa in white. But in a moment I heard the baby gurgling and my daughters laughing, as they played with her. I told myself it was nothing, that sense of unease. Then I realized that I was sitting there, rather foolishly, holding out my hand, but the shuwafa had not taken it. She had put away her string of cowrie shells and was looking at me in a rather hostile way.

"Well," I said brightly. "What about me?"

"You know I can't read your palm," she answered.

I was perplexed, a bit annoyed. "What does she mean, Aisha?" I asked, wriggling my hand and trying to speak lightly. "Why can't she?"

Aisha, too, looked perplexed, and before she could answer, the shu-wafa burst out, "Don't be silly. You know why."

I shook my head.

"We don't compete," she said.

"Compete?" I echoed.

"Compete," she repeated firmly. "Don't tell me you don't read hands. I know you do."

I opened and shut my mouth. I was thoroughly startled, and the vague sense of unease I had felt when Laila withdrew her hand from the shuwafa's returned to me. It was true that I occasionally read palms, as a diversion at parties, but how could this young woman in white possibly know?

Aisha tried to intervene. "Madame has paid for seven fortunes," she began.

"Never mind, Aisha," I said quickly, and stood up. "It doesn't matter. Let's have some tea."

When I recounted the events of the day to Bob, he was pleased by the girls' behavior.

"They were both good sports," he said approvingly, "the baby wetting, and all. Maybe she was testing them, and when she found they were good-natured, she decided to give them good fortunes."

This had occurred to me, too. "It's funny that she knew I read palms, though," I mused. "I'm sure I never told Aisha or Lateefa or anyone here."

"A lucky stroke on her part," responded Bob, "or maybe a flash of intuition?"

"Yes, but if you could have seen the way she looked at me . . ."

"Oh, B.J., come off it. How did she look at you? You know perfectly well there's nothing to it."

"Yes," I said uncertainly, and tried to laugh. "Well, it was interesting, anyway."

But Aisha did not take the events of the day so lightly. "Why didn't you tell me you read palms before I brought the shuwafa?" she reproached me.

"Well . . . er, I don't know, Aisha. I didn't think it was important."

"Oh, but it is. It will help you."

"How?"

"To understand. To gain baraka."

I nodded, partly because I didn't want to get into another discussion of the whole subject right now.

Aisha smiled. "There will be another moussem soon. Maybe this time it won't rain and we can all dance together. Won't that be wonderful?"

"Yes," I said.

"And we must go to Sidi Bel Abbas soon and light the candle for Laila."

"Yes." I thought back. It had been Sidi Bel Abbas where I had first asked Aisha to take me, many months ago. And now we were going by order of the shuwafa, Lateefa's favorite shuwafa, who would not read my palm. Life on Rue Trésor had taken a strange turn.

That evening, Bob managed to direct the conversation to shuwafas. Abdul Lateef found my afternoon experience amusing.

"Bob, women are not proper shuwafas. They cannot be. I will take you to a real shuwaf, a man, if you are interested in such things."

I felt myself bristling, bridling again at Abdul Lateef's familiar, patronizing tone. "But our shuwafa was very good, very interesting."

Bob smiled tolerantly. "My wife is very impressed, because the shuwafa refused to read her hand."

Abdul Lateef's expression changed. "But that is ridiculous when one makes a contract. What reason did this so-called shuwafa give?"

"She said she didn't want to compete."

"Compete?" Abdul Lateef's eyebrows rose.

Bob graced us once more with his tolerant smile. "B.J. has always read palms, but only for fun. She thinks of it as a game."

Abdul Lateef frowned. "Such things are not games," he said. "Not . . . precisely reasonable or reliable perhaps, according to modern scientific thoughts, but they are not . . . games."

"Certainly not." Moulay Mustapha shook his head vigorously in agreement and went on to explain that his father had been having an affair with another woman until his mother visited a powerful shuwafa, and after that the whole business had stopped.

"That was magic, though," said Abdul Lateef, "*shu'ur*. We are talking about fortune telling here, Mustapha. For example, when I first came to Marrakech from the village, I went to a shuwaf. He told me what to expect, whom I would marry, how many children . . ."

Moulay Mustapha almost giggled. "Was it only from your hands he could tell?" he said.

Abdul Lateef did not respond to his friend's joke. He extended his palm. "Would you care to read my hand, Madame, just for fun, as you call it?"

I shook my head. I did not want to be pulled into whatever game was in progress, a game I did not understand.

"On your terms," he insisted. "For amusement only."

I was uncomfortable at his insistence, at the intent look in his eye, but I did not want to hurt his feelings.

"I only read women's hands," I said lightly. "Remember, you have said yourself that only men are proper shuwafs!"

"Aha!" Abdul Lateef smiled with satisfaction and withdrew his hand into the sleeve of his djellaba. "She admits it! She's a wise woman, your wife, Bob!"

Bob looked at me with some amusement, I thought, but I did not feel amused. "Will you get us some more tea?" he asked, and I rose, glad of an excuse to leave the room.

Some days later, Aisha presented me with a gift, a packet of paper in which were a walnut meat, a square of peanut candy, and a single date.

"Thank you, Aisha, but what is it for?"

"My neighbor returned last night from the moussem of Moulay Durain. She sent it to you."

I was surprised. "But why? Do I know her?"

"You have seen her. But she knows you've been going to moussems, that you read hands, that you gave Kenza some of your baraka from Moulay Ibrahim. She wants you to have this."

The importance of this gesture, which seemed minor to me at the time, was made clear by Abdul Lateef, who told Bob that I should consider the neighbor's gift a great honor. I was surprised at his interest; Abdul Lateef the skeptic, talking seriously about gifts of baraka to me, the foreign lady?

"Nobody gives a gift of baraka like that except to one who is a close friend, to a shuwafa one wants to placate, or to someone who needs it," he had said. Since I was not a shuwafa and not a close friend of this woman, had I publicly expressed some personal need?

I did not know whether I had or not. Certainly I had told Aisha that I wanted to visit murabits. It was no secret on the street that we had attended the moussem of Moulay Ibrahim and that I had expressed an interest in other moussems, in having the shuwafa visit. Now, as if to further my spiritual education, Abdul Lateef had told Bob twice that he would be glad to discuss religious subjects in general with me. But I had lost my taste for such arguments. Events were proceeding in directions I had not expected or planned, toward ends I could not visualize. To reassure myself, I reasoned that the trips to the moussems, the shuwafa's shrewd guesses, and the gift of baraka from an unknown neighbor were not significant except that they indicated kindness and compassion of my friends on Rue Trésor. Perhaps they had begun to accept me as a person, someone more like themselves than as a figure, or an object, a representative of the foreign colonialist infidel. And thus, then, as a person, I was in need, as they were, of baraka, that touch of amazing grace that would help me through the difficulties of life. Surely that was all there was to it.

And yet when I paused on Rue Trésor the next day, shifted my market basket from one hand to another, and fished a coin out of my purse to drop into the blind beggar's chipped enamel bowl, Kenza called out to me.

"It is helping," she said. "You are learning."

"Learning?" I stood, staring up at her, beside the white geranium in its pot on the second-floor sill.

"You are learning what our duties in this world are!" she said enigmatically, as though I were being initiated, prepared for something, and were making progress along the expected path. But what path? Whatever it was, I was not at all sure I wanted to continue in the indicated direction, but I did not know what to do, or whom to tell about my change in plans.

The cycle of moussems continued, and the spring sun waxed hotter. It was nearly June, close to a year since we had come to Rue Trésor.

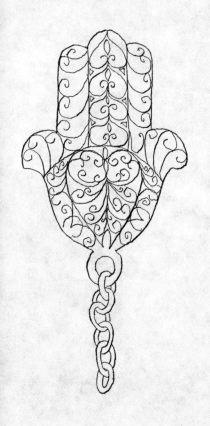

Part IV

The heat came down upon us with the violence and suddenness of a thunderclap. After the days of spring rain, followed by relatively mild weather, we woke one morning to suffocating heat: A *shargi*, or hot, dry wind from the southern desert of the Sahara, had blown in during the night. The slamming of doors and window shutters could be heard all up and down Rue Trésor; our neighbors were sensibly closing up their houses to retain whatever freshness remained in the air, and we followed suit. In the courtyard, the lemon tree and the fountain loomed through a haze of dust. The baker covered his loaves of bread with a faded blue cloth; Mbarak the bath boy stayed inside, and even Zahia's toddlers did not come out to play in the entrance to the sibha.

From the rooftop where we climbed the first evening to try to get a breath of relief, the city looked deserted. As far as we could see, the rooftops, where so much of the women's social life took place, were empty; only foolish foreigners like ourselves, obviously, ventured out into the shifting miasma of dust and heat that, overnight, had clouded the clear air and blue skies of Marrakech. The peaks of the high Atlas were no longer visible; the green-tiled roofs of the Saadian tombs and the stately minaret of the Koutoubia mosque were wrapped in veils of blowing dust so thick they might have been banks of swirling fog.

"How long will this go on?" Bob asked Aisha. Laila, our only child with allergies in Austin, had begun to cough for the first time since we had arrived in Marrakech.

Aisha shrugged and blinked her reddened eyes. Mine hurt, too.

"Who knows? It's too sudden. It's a bad one."

On the second day the children came home from school exhausted. They dropped their school bags just inside the front door and sank into the canvas chairs where they sat, transfixed with fatigue, staring at the floor tiles. Even the goldfish lay at the bottom of their blue-and-yellow basin, hardly moving for the bits of food sprinkled on the dusty water.

On the fourth day, we woke to find that the shargi had gone, blown away by northeast winds from the Atlas Mountains almost as quickly as it had blown in. We could literally taste the difference in the air. It was hot, yes, but dry and clear, not close and gritty, like the days of the shargi.

"Summer is here!" said Aisha.

And as the summer season began, the routine of Rue Trésor changed. The vegetable peddler came early, after the garbage sweepers, but before the carts bringing sacks of flour to the bakery, stacks of firewood to the bath. The workers in the dry-cleaning shop, the garage mechanics from Bab Agnaou, and the students on their way home from school lunched earlier at the grocery store, washing down sandwiches (cheese, jam, or sardines) with bottles and bottles of raybi, the popular strawberry-flavored liquid yogurt. They leaned against the walls of the bakery, on the shady side of Rue Trésor, joking with Moussa, the baker, or Abdul Kabeer, the clerk.

"The heat!" they complained. "The heat!"

"Better than the shargi!" Moussa returned. "Anything is better than the shargi!"

At noon the grocery, the bakery, the bath, and the tile store closed for a two-hour siesta, as did the garages and the dry cleaners. Moussa and Abdul Kabeer went home, like the students, but the workers would nap on the cool cement floor of their garage, or lie down behind the counters of the dry cleaners.

Moulay Mustapha let his pupils out half an hour earlier, and Ali and Shadeeya would arrive at the sibha, panting, their slates, inscribed with the daily Koranic lesson, smudged with sweat.

When the sun began to sink low on the horizon, the women would come up on the rooftops to breathe in the coolness and gossip about the events of the day. The dignified blind beggar with the enamel bowl chained to his wrist appeared irregularly, and Lateefa thought he might be sick. Our neighbor El Mesakeen no longer limped out to Rue Bab Agnaou, but merely shuffled as far as the door of the bath, where she sat with her hand lightly extended to receive the coins of the faithful.

In Gueliz, the jacarandas were blossoming, their purple petals flaring out against the red walls of the houses, adding a fierce brilliance to the more everyday beauty of the pink and scarlet bougainvillea. The yellow flowers of the palm trees in the Parc Foucauld and the Menara gardens, past their prime, dropped to the pavements, and collected in golden piles by the bus stops. Along the wide avenues families promenaded in the evening: djellabaed and veiled ladies carried babies on their backs and held small children by the hand; fathers walked with sons; groups of schoolgirls in pigtails and short white dresses filled the sidewalks beside the city walls.

Djemaa el Fna bloomed, too, in the morning and the long summer evenings, offering a program of new and old entertainments and spectacles; but during the hottest hours of the day it was almost totally empty, except for peddlers asleep under their carts or propped up in the narrow shade of their tiny stalls.

"Clank! Clank! Clank!" The red-costumed water sellers arrived first at sunset, jingling carved brass cups, tossing the tassels on their straw hats. "Water, fresh cool water!" they called.

Gradually the acrobats would emerge, and the Gnaoua dancers, the preacher, the rebaba player, the African lady and her husband selling perfume and slices of fresh coconut; the pigeon man and his partner with their cages of birds; the snake charmers carrying pails full of drowsy adders and boa constrictors. All would awake from their afternoon snoozes, to be followed finally by the chorus of ancient beggars, seemingly more fragile and bent than ever. But their cry echoed across the square as loudly as it had in winter.

"Alms!" they pleaded. "Alms for the love of Allah! Allah is pleased by a gift of alms!"

The refreshment menu had been totally transformed. Gone were the steaming boiled potatoes, the hot mint tea, and the thick vegetable soup of the cold days. Cucumbers, hard-boiled eggs, salted nuts, and cold broad beans were offered instead. An ice cream man with an embroidered skullcap pedaled a bright yellow-and-blue freezer; a Coca-Cola vendor clinked his posh bottles against a tray of expensive ice. For those who could not afford the luxury of iced water or Coca-

Cola, there was still an old man with a waterskin over his shoulder, its black hair matted with the wetness of its contents; he carried a brown glazed pottery cup in his hand to serve his customers. Prickly pears were in season, and Laura Ann and David (but not Laila) would buy one for a franc, munch out the pulpy orange fruit, and toss the green peelings into the gutters like all the other citizens of Marrakech.

The young men who poured out of the Cinema Marhaba sported light cotton robes, or *ganduras*, over their pants and shirts, ganduras of white batiste or faded blue Tuareg cloth, embroidered in yellow, white, or black. Bob admired them so much he bought one for himself from Omar. Kenza broke out her peach sharkskin djellaba and her tortoise-shell sunglasses. The dark, sober djellabas of winter were put away. Lateefa wore a pale blue check and a purple veil for her trip to Ourika; she was to accompany Rakosh, she said, who was returning to her native village on business. The division of the family crop was about to begin and Rakosh, as a landowner, albeit an absent one, felt she must be present to oversee the activities.

"We missed a moussem yesterday," Aisha said to me casually one morning as we prepared lunch in the kitchen. I looked at her, startled.

"Why didn't you say something?"

Aisha shook her head. "You had to go to the French Mission. And I had an awful toothache. I still do."

She looked pale, and I urged her to go to the dentist. "Yes," she said, "I will, when Najiya is better."

"Najiya's sick again? Didn't the charm from Moulay Ibrahim help?"

Aisha sighed. "Yes, for a while. But I don't know what to do next."

"Would she like to go to our doctor?"

"Maybe."

"Should I make an appointment?"

Aisha looked at me. I had caught her looking at me in the same way several times in the past few weeks. I had told her long ago that we would be leaving in the spring. But spring had passed, summer had begun, and we showed no signs of leaving.

"My husband is considering staying in Marrakech a while longer," I said. "Do you think Kenza would mind?"

"Ask her," Aisha answered shortly. She finished peeling potatoes.

Then she looked at me again. Are you really leaving, that look seemed to say.

"Do you want me to make an appointment for Najiya?"

Aisha nodded. "Yes, thank you. Next week," she added, "I should be finished with this toothache. The heat makes everything worse."

I knew that Aisha was also discouraged about the approach of the end of school, for this year many students would be forced to *redoubler* or repeat, because of the weeks of classwork lost during the winter strikes. Najiya would have to, since her school had been closed since February; Abdul Krim probably would also, though the fate of Saleh, the oldest, and of Youssef, the irrepressible youngest son, was not yet certain.

"So this year's all wasted, all the money and books and paper, and next year they'll make us buy different books, and how can we afford it? Sometimes I don't know, I just don't know whether I can go on."

A tear splashed down onto the tiled drainboard. Aisha crying? I had never seen her cry.

"Maybe I should have sent Abdul Krim to Europe with the French people when I had the chance," she added, very low. "But I couldn't, Elizabetha, I just couldn't."

I put my arm around her. "I know, Aisha. Of course you couldn't."

She pulled up her skirt and dried her eyes on the hem. "It's my teeth and Najiya and the end of school all coming at once, that's what it is. We should have gone to that moussem last night."

"Yes," I said. But how could we have gone?

"There'll be another soon. Maybe we can go then."

"Yes. I hope so."

Aisha cleared her throat loudly and sniffed. "I don't know how Abdul Krim will do if he has to repeat. It's a great shame."

"He'll manage, I'm sure. Think of Kenza, Aisha. She doesn't even have sons like you do!"

"True. True." She laughed suddenly, harshly. "And now her only daughter, Naima, is sick."

"I didn't know."

It was true that I didn't know that Naima was ill, but everyone on the street was aware that things were not at all as they should be in the bosom of Hajja Kenza's house.

During the shargi, Mbarak had disappeared. After two days of confusion, the owner of the bath had found another boy, whose name was Thami, Laura Ann informed us. Thami was younger than Mbarak, lighter-skinned, and he wore sporty pink trousers, somewhat spotted, and a wrinkled yellow shirt that bore marks of past style. In contrast to the silent Mbarak, Thami was a friendly and expansive person, and within twenty-four hours he had captivated Naima. At almost any hour of the day or night, one could hear them bantering, Thami from his stance against the wall of the bath, Naima from her upstairs window. They tossed coins and flowers and sweets back and forth; they giggled and flirted. When Hajja Kenza went off to market, Naima came downstairs almost too quickly and stood in her open doorway, chattering, and batting her eyes at Thami.

"That girl was wearing a transparent nightgown today," Bob said, in bemused tones one afternoon. "I tell you, I passed right by, and it left absolutely nothing to the imagination!"

Soon all the neighbors on Rue Trésor were clucking about Naima's behavior with Thami.

"It's not decent," said Lateefa.

"Who is he?" asked old Yezza. "Nobody. He has no family."

"Hajja Kenza should take better care," said Zahia. "He's only a boy of the streets."

Kenza would come home, order Naima upstairs, and slam the door and window shut. But she couldn't keep constant watch, and after about two weeks, she finally capitulated. Our window was surreptitiously open, like that of Rakosh, the day Kenza called down to Thami, the boy of the streets who bore the name of the great Glaoui Pasha. She invited him inside; for tea, couscous, a lecture? No one knew, but Kenza hardly spoke to anyone after that, and for days did not even bother to bargain with the vegetable peddler. When she ambled out in her peach djellaba, her stomach was protruding in a most alarming manner, and she seemed to have shrunk visibly in stature.

I hesitated to approach Kenza, since she seemed so upset, but our lease was running out, and other arrangements would have to be made soon. Bob and I had talked about our own feelings of regret at the prospect of leaving. We had just become acquainted with our neighbors and had begun to understand the mechanics of life on Rue Trésor. The market system, Bob said, was starting to unfold for him, with the help of new friends and old ones, and already it was time to go.

Laura Ann and David had mixed feelings also. Laura Ann had

found a kind of niche; she had her friends at the Lycée, and her associations on Rue Trésor, however slight, were reasonably pleasant. She enjoyed going to the suq and had become an expert bargainer. She had even had an offer of marriage, from a young merchant whose shop was next to Omar's.

"He is half serious, Bob," Omar reported. "He asked me to approach you."

Bob shook his head. "She is still in school."

Laura Ann was indignant. "I'm supposed to tell him, Baba," she said. "Not you!"

Bob smiled. "They do things differently here," he said.

David, too, had managed to work his way into the soccer game on the square, to go to the movies and swim with Youssef and Abdul Krim, as well as with his friends at the French school, and with the Harrises.

Only Laila seemed somewhat uncomfortable. She was still shy about going out on Rue Trésor alone; she had not wanted to find any of the neighborhood girls compatible, and she flinched when Kenza clasped her in that classic grip of iron and bussed her soundly on both cheeks. Only in the house, with Aisha, did she relax, but she felt far more at home at the Harrises', or with her French schoolmates. Invitations to play, to attend birthday parties, these came more often now from Gueliz, and Laila seemed to spend most of her free time away from Rue Trésor, in the French section of town. Laila, Bob and I decided, showed strong signs of decamping to the side of the colonialist French!

"Oh, Baba, when are we going home to Austin?" Laila asked, wistfully, one evening at dinner. "It's almost June."

Bob considered. "Well, I'd like to stay as long as possible. I'm learning all kinds of new things about the city, Laila. Did you know that Marrakech is divided into many different little quarters or neighborhoods, like ours, each with its own bath and bakery, and some even with a mosque?"

Laila sighed deeply, with the "Baba is going to be boring now" look that she assumed whenever Bob tried to explain to her about the city in which she was a transient, if reluctant, resident.

"But you said we'd go home when school was out," Laila persisted, "and that's only twenty-eight more days!"

"I'd like to stay another year, really!" Bob began.

"Oh, no!" cried Laila. Her eyes filled with tears.

"I wouldn't mind. I'd like to," Laura Ann announced.

"Well," temporized David, the diplomat, "it wouldn't be so bad, now we can understand the language."

Laila said nothing, but her eyes were fixed on her father, and her lower lip was trembling.

"We can't," I put in briskly, "and that's that, whether we want to or not. Your father has to be in Austin by September 1 to meet his classes at the university."

Laila blew her nose, snuffled once more, and was silent. We set into our supper of tuna fish sandwiches and cucumbers.

"But I *would* like to stay until the last possible moment," said Bob, between halfhearted mouthfuls of his sandwich. Our ravenous winter appetites had dulled in the heat, and it was difficult to get anything down. "Do you think Kenza would object to our staying in the house until August?"

"Why should she? She'd be delighted for the extra rent. She's very annoyed we haven't found her a family from America to move in just as we move out."

"Well, you'd better talk to her then."

"But," Laila objected, "August's more than sixty-nine days away!"

"Oh, it won't be so long," her father tried to comfort her. "Soon school will be out, and then you can swim in the Menara pool. Omar says it's a fine pool, very clean."

"Don't want to," mumbled Laila.

Laura Ann looked at me, then down at her plate. We had gone to the Menara pool, Bettye and I, with all of our children. It had not been a smashing success. "Really, Baba, it was too much," Laura Ann said. "You should see it. The pool's okay, but there were so many boys, about a thousand, and maybe five girls, including Laila and Tanya and me."

Bob looked unconvinced. "Well, I'll take you myself and then we'll decide," he said.

Soon posters announcing the annual Marrakech folklore festival began to appear on the red walls along Boulevard Mohammed Cinq, on the bus kiosks in the Parc Foucauld, in the store windows of Gueliz. Tourists came from all over the world to view the spectacle, arranged first by French and now by Moroccan officials to demonstrate the indigenous songs and dances of the countryside. We went with the Harrises and mutual visiting friends, and were greeted by two of the ushers, pretty girls in colorful caftans.

"*Lebas, Madame! Lebas!*" It was Farida, and her coworker Amal, the teachers from the day-care center, who, I was nearly certain, had taken in Mina when Fatima Henna lay ill, wounded or ostracized during the past winter. Farida and Amal found us lovely seats and fussed over our programs.

We sat in improvised bleachers, overlooking the walls and ramparts of the ruined Badi Palace, lighted by scores of lamps that glowed along the walls, around the base of the ornamental pools. Two white-robed and turbaned horsemen, on finely caparisoned white horses, guarded the sixteenth-century gates, while the tourists watched the Gnaoua, the acrobats from Amizmiz, the Berber dancers from the mountains, the stick dancers from the plains.

The folklore festival brought visitors to Rue Trésor, too, for Glaoui's sister, her sister's husband, and their daughter were dancing in the troupe from Telouet. The neighbor women crowded into Aisha's and Glaoui's common courtyard to meet the mother and her daughter, broad-shouldered women with rosy cheeks, their dark hair drawn over their white head scarves, clumps of amber encircling their throats.

"They went to Algeria last year," whispered Lateefa. "In an airplane."

"Did they get paid well?"

"Oh, yes, five hundred dirhams [about a hundred dollars] for ten days of performing, and they got all their trip and their room in the hotel and the food free."

The mother sipped a glass of mint tea and smiled at her daughter. "She's saving money for her wedding day," she said.

The daughter looked down modestly, smiling too.

I rushed home to get Laura Ann, who had much admired the dancers from Telouet, but she was not back from school yet, and by the time she returned, the mother and daughter had left to prepare for the next performance.

During the days of the folk festival, painters and a carpenter and a mason arrived on Rue Trésor. They set up ladders in the small zanka against the walls of Fatima Henna's house, and the door stood open all day while the workmen passed back and forth across the black-and-white-tiled doorstep.

Fatima Henna's mother communicated the news to us, via Aisha and Lateefa, that a "good family" was moving into the second floor of their house, the apartment vacated by Jason, Mark, Sheryl, Alan, et al.

We had wondered about the apartment, which had stood empty for more than two months since the day, following the drug scandal, when the police had arrived and confiscated what possessions remained in the empty rooms.

"The people coming in are distantly related to us," confided Fatima Henna to me across the rooftop. She spoke a bit proudly, I thought. "The mother of the family is a cousin of my mother's mother."

From the children's window we could see the walls being plastered white, new curtains being hung on the windows: a print of gold ferns on forest green. A red rug from Chichaoua was delivered, and one day a cartload of red-and-black plush cushions and banquettes arrived, as well as a television set.

"Four TVs on Rue Trésor now," Laila commented. "Hajja Kenza, Glaoui, the qadi, and now the new people. Can't we get one, too?"

"We're leaving, remember?" her father pointed out.

"Oh, yes, how could I forget?" said Laila.

The oldest daughter of the new family attended a French school. She and Laura Ann took to conversing back and forth through their windows and across the roofs. Her family had been living in Daour el Askar district, the girl told Laura Ann, but were delighted with the new apartment, which was more convenient to the city center. Since Jason had been six months behind in his rent, the present occupants had obtained the apartment by paying half the back rent and agreeing to redecorate. The family was pleasant, greeting the neighbors regularly and politely. Fatima Henna and her mother appeared relaxed, even gay, in the presence of ready confidantes and resident relatives. Rue Trésor was changing.

A party at the French Mission ended the evening classes. With our fellow travelers in our journey through the dull lives of Madame and Monsieur Thibault of Place d'Italie, Paris, we sat stiffly on chairs in a circle, drinking Coca-Cola and Judor out of bottles and nibbling madeleines and Marie biscuits. We had been into the Thibaults' linen closets together (twelve sheets, six pillow cases); we knew they had a radio, but no television; we knew that the daughter was learning to sew and the son had spent his vacation with his grandparents in the country; we even knew what the Thibaults ate for breakfast (no jam with their baguette of bread, only butter). But we still knew almost nothing about each other, one Hungarian, four Americans, and nine Moroccans (a clerk, a policeman, a judge, a girl who helped her father in his watch repair shop, a couturier, a tailor, a housewife, and two schoolgirls).

The director cleared his throat and presented us all with a certificate stating that we had completed an audio-visual intermediate French course satisfactorily. We clapped. The post office clerk whom I had met on my way home from Mul el Ksour that strangely lighted evening grinned at Bob and clouted him on the back. Bettye Harris and I shook hands with the couturier and the girl who helped her father in the watch repair shop. They giggled. We giggled. Ernest Harris formally thanked our teacher for his efforts. Everyone clapped again. We invited Abdul Aziz, our teacher, to dinner. He accepted, and then, to our surprise, asked if he could bring his wife.

"I have married a Berber girl," he explained seriously to Bob. "I have done this purposely. For only if all Moroccans, Berber and Arab, join together, can the divisions created by the French be healed, and Morocco be a truly united country."

Bob expressed his further surprise to me over Abdul Aziz' sudden confidence. Not only had we not realized that he was married, but we had also hardly expected such a personal revelation to be made on the spot.

Thus we were somewhat nervous the evening of the dinner. What language would be spoken—French, Berber, or Arabic? And how would the Berber wife relate to our foreign household? Would my dinner seem appetizing?

When they arrived, a few minutes early, Abdul Aziz was nattily dressed in a dark blue blazer and gray flannel trousers, but his wife was hooded in a voluminous djellaba and veiled to the eyes. Even the children gathered around, rather tentatively, as she shed veil, hood, djellaba, and stood revealed, a perfectly beautiful dark-haired girl in a silver and turquoise caftan. She smiled. We smiled.

"This is Zainab," said Abdul Aziz simply.

Zainab spoke no French, and appeared to speak no Arabic until, after dinner, I took her upstairs to see the house. There, out of earshot of the men, her husband and mine, she began to talk, in Arabic, very rapidly, about my house, my furniture, her house, her furniture, my mother, her mother, her sisters, her wedding. She talked constantly, all the while we toured the bedrooms and the balcony and the roof together, and then, as we descended once more into the courtyard where the men were sipping coffee, she grew silent. She sat in one of our blue canvas chairs in her silver and turquoise caftan, and smiled enigmatically at us, the tiles, the lemon tree, the little pool where the goldfish swam around and around. Abdul Aziz could hardly keep his eyes off her, and Bob, too, seemed to have trouble focusing elsewhere than on that particular blue chair.

"And the liberation of the Maghreb began the moment the French first set foot on our soil!" Abdul Aziz was declaiming.

"How is that?" I asked curiously.

"We realized immediately they wanted our souls," he said. "The French always do. But they did not get them. Algerians, maybe, Syrians, yes, but not the Moroccans. That is because we never invited them into our houses."

"But you teach French, Abdul Aziz," Bob pointed out. "Surely you have French friends."

Abdul Aziz shook his head vehemently. "It is not possible to be friends with a Frenchman."

Bob looked dubious. "Why not?"

Abdul Aziz ran his hand through his curly black hair in exasperation. "How can I explain it to you? How? Let me tell you a story. When I first was appointed, I often talked with one of the other French teachers, from Toulouse; he was young and pleasant. Occasionally we went to cafés together and to the movies. I began to think I had a real French friend."

"And . . . ?"

Abdul Aziz looked distressed. "One day, he came to me and said some friends of his needed a servant, and could I recommend someone from my entourage."

He paused, and when we did not respond, he said, "Don't you *see*, Bob, he was insulting me, assuming that my *family* were servants who would work for *him*, the Frenchman!"

"But he didn't say your family," I pointed out mildly, "he said your entourage."

"La *famille*, Madame, means the small family, as in the West; the entourage means the larger or extended family, as we have in Morocco."

"I thought entourage just meant the people around you," I persisted.

Abdul Aziz spread his hands. "And who would they be, Madame, except the members of your family?"

We nodded. What else could we do? Abdul Aziz looked at Bob. "I was furious, of course, when he said that, but I controlled myself, because I did not want him going around saying I was one of those nervous Moroccans always flying off the handle and not to be trusted. But I never went to have coffee with him again. And I certainly never invited him to my house."

Bob opened his mouth to protest, but Abdul Aziz was ahead of him.

"I know what you're going to say, Bob. Politicians, the King, a few rich men had Frenchmen in their homes. For business purposes. Not friendship. I would wager very few people in Marrakech have *ever* asked a foreigner into their homes."

So that was it. Of course. Inside was private, the heart of Moroccan life. The outside was different; it was public and commercial, open to everyone, as we had already observed, the beggars, the boys of the street, even the foreigners.

Chapter 18

Lalla Fadna Takes a Stand

Every day the weather seemed a little hotter. Bob's temper was short. The children were cross and picked at their food, but they arrived home early one day, full of excitement. "The Lycée went on strike today!" Laura Ann announced. "We all sat down on the grass and nobody would move. It was kind of fun!"

"What did they do that for?" asked Bob, with a side glance at me.

"The kids said we were the only school in Marrakech that hadn't gone on strike against the bad King, and we had to show sympathy for our comrades."

"And how long will this go on?" Bob asked warily.

"Oh, it's over," said Laura Ann lightly. "The director came out and said we could strike today but exams start tomorrow, and anyone who wanted to take the baccalaureate should be back in class then. But it was fun while it lasted!"

The children could hardly wait for school to end. Bettye and I went to see Greg in his class play, *L'Histoire de Christophe Colomb*. A ship had been built of lathe and papier-mâché, a ship with a mast, painted in bright colors, and on its "deck," the floor of the schoolroom, the French and Moroccan "mariners" acted out the tale of the Italians' and Spaniards' discovery of America.

Bettye and I sat formally with the other parents, the morning breeze blowing through the window banked with scarlet bougainvillea, waiting for Greg's key line. Standing at the lookout, and wearing a pirate scarf to indicate his mariner status, with a toy telescope in his hand, Greg raised his hand, snapped his fingers, and in a suitably loud voice, called out, "*Un oiseau! Un oiseau!*"

He then turned around and grinned at his mother. This nearly broke us up, but by that time all of the mariners were jumping up and down on the "deck" and shouting, "*Alors! Un oiseau! Voilà!*" so that Greg's break in stage etiquette was lost in the commotion.

The children had distinguished themselves. Laura Ann had made the honor roll, and all the younger children were promoted and received commendations.

"So if we stayed another year, you could go on to the next grade. How about that?" said Bettye.

"I wouldn't mind," Laura Ann replied.

"Me neither," said Tanya.

"It'd be okay," David allowed.

Laila's eyes filled with tears. "I want to go home," she said firmly.

"Me too, Laila," Greg agreed. "And soon."

The children formed lines, and singing their traditional song, "Les Écoliers sont sur les vacances," they marched out of the gates of the Lycée Victor Hugo and L'École Renoir, the only schools in Marrakech where the students had gone on strike, not for all their lives, as the Moroccan students had carved in their desks, but for a single day. But though the strike lasted only for a day, Bob and I noted with interest the fact that the student strikes, traditional form of protest throughout the Third World, had finally reached even to the French section of Marrakech, once the hallowed and respected ground of colonialist administrators. Marrakech, like Rue Trésor, was changing.

The days of June drew slowly to a close. Laura Ann and I met the bride Rabia on Bab Agnaou, very pregnant, with a woman we did not know. Rabia pulled down her veil and smiled, as we conversed briefly in front of the dry cleaners'. She had not visited Rue Trésor since her marriage in January. Would she come after the baby was born?

"Well," said Aisha, "I don't really know, but Rabia may not feel it's really her own home anymore. Her father lives here, but Khadooj, her mother, has moved out. The other wives won't be too delighted to see her."

The heat had some good effects, too.

Moulay Mustapha was jubilant, or as jubilant as Moulay Mustapha ever would be. At long last, he had settled his trouble with his landlady. "Her brother couldn't stand the heat," he said. "He went back to Casablanca and now she doesn't want my room anymore. But," he added, rubbing his nose worriedly, "he'll probably be back, and what will I do then?"

"Get her to sign a lease now," suggested Bob.

"Yes," agreed Abdul Lateef. "Then you'll be set."

"She won't, I'm sure," Moulay Mustapha said. "Then she won't be able to pick a fight with me anymore. She likes to fight, like all women."

Abdul Lateef glanced at me and smiled. "Watch it, Mustapha," he warned.

But I didn't rise to the bait. I was too miserable, with a toothache, a throbbing in the lower jaw that made even the daily shopping more of a trial than a pleasure.

"Isn't the heat great!" beamed my friend, the Berber merchant in Djemaa el Fan.

"Great!" I echoed. "No, it's awful!"

"You're wrong, Madame," he returned. He slipped his skullcap down a bit onto his forehead and rubbed his hands, in glee. "The strong get stronger and the weak get weaker. It all works out for the best."

I stared at him. My dress was sticking to my sweaty back. My jaw throbbed with pain. The merchant was smiling. But he was serious, too. I decided to laugh back.

"Well, what about the rest of us?" I said brightly. "The ones in the middle."

"Ho! Ho! Ho!" The merchant thought that was rich. He repeated my *bon mot* to two customers, a man in a Western suit who stared at me, and an older woman in a veil and djellaba who whooped with laughter. "Did you hear what Madame said? What happens to us in the middle? Well," he turned to me, the smile gone. "That is up to God, and Moulay Ibrahim. They can go either way. It is written so," and in a moment he had straightened his skullcap and was making change for my purchase of cheese and jam. The philosophy lesson was over for the day.

My tooth became so painful that I was finally obliged to go to an Algerian dentist recommended by Abdul Aziz. The dentist wanted to wait till the infection receded before extracting my tooth. But two days later I was back in his office. "Pull it now, please!" I begged him, and he complied, somewhat reluctantly. Afterward, I regretted my impatience, for I lay upstairs in the multicolored bedroom for days, a hot-water bottle on my swollen and painful jaw. Through the window I could hear Zahia arguing with the peddler over a missing ten-franc piece, and Fatima Henna scolding Mina. Youssef seemed more nervous than ever, and knocked on our front door every few minutes, asking for Aisha.

Even Aisha quarreled with Kenza, "about nothing," she said. This did not bode well for my own scheduled visit to Kenza, to see whether we might extend our stay. "It's her stomach, I guess," said Aisha, "and she's worried about Naima. But why does she have to take it out on me?"

Bettye Harris came to see me; visiting friends from Rabat wanted to hire our fortune teller. They had heard the astounding prediction the fortune teller in white had made about Ernest Harris—that he would soon receive a good job offer from an unexpected source and should not accept. That prediction had come true.

"Well . . ." I shifted the hot-water bottle from my jaw and played for time. I could not say exactly why I was reluctant to bring the shuwafa back. Was it the ominous quality of her insistence that Laila needed to go to Sidi Bel Abbas? Her refusal to read my own hand? Or what? What was I afraid of?

Bettye must have sensed my thoughts, for she said quickly, "Never mind. I'll just say you can't find her. I'm not sure I want to see her again anyway."

I nodded gratefully. We had talked earlier about this part of Marrakech life, the "pharmacy" of drugs in the suq, the presence of the occult, the importance of witches—our gradual awareness of the magic that seemed to permeate all of Marrakech life in some strange way we could not understand. I felt that the magic was the opposite of the beneficial baraka, the other side of the coin. It was the shargi or destructive wind from the desert, as opposed to the clear air of the mountains. But how could we explain all this to the visitors from Rabat? They would think we had taken leave of our senses.

"I don't know," I said truthfully. "Aisha could ask and see if the fortune teller's around."

"Forget it," said Bettye, rising. "I'll just say you don't know your neighbors too well."

But we both knew that wasn't true anymore. Without realizing it, our family seemed to have become a part of Rue Trésor, a fact that was to be demonstrated sooner than we expected and more dramatically than we might have wished.

Bob drove the visitors to Rabat, and the night after he left I went to bed early with the children, only to be awakened by confused noises. A whole corps of motorcycles seemed to be revving up outside my window, preparatory to racing up and down the street. Men were shouting and calling through the warm summer night. I opened the window and looked down. Rue Trésor was indeed full of men and motorcycles. Marzook, the fat doorman at the Hôtel du Sud, stood before the door, gesturing wildly to several other men nearby. Most wore djellabas, but one was in a suit, and two wore uniforms. Policemen? Army officers? By the bath stood another knot of men; Thami was talking loudly, but I understood nothing. Perhaps the whole scene would become clearer if viewed from a higher vantage point? I climbed up to the roof, where I could see that at the end of Rue Trésor, near the day-care center and the clinic, cars and trucks were parked; from the color and height of one, it might have been an ambulance. Was someone ill or dying? After watching the scene for several minutes, I decided I'd never be able to figure it all out, and I went back down, locking and bolting the roof door carefully behind me. It was two o'clock in the morning. The cars drove away, the voices subsided. I was just sinking back into dreams when the noise erupted again, louder, more agitated.

Footsteps sounded above my head. Was somebody on our roof, about to break into the house? For a moment I cowered under the sheet, too frightened to move. But hadn't I just locked the roof door? Even if someone was up there, they could not get into our house unless they decided to jump the forty feet down into the courtyard, which might be fatal. The footsteps sounded again, lightly, then the shouting grew louder. I opened the window shutters, then drew back. I was looking, for a split second, directly into the faces of three strange men, who were crouched on the roof of Rakosh's house.

"Well, what next? Where'd he go?" The words sounded clearly, almost in my ear, the men were so close, but, by peeking warily around the shutter, I could see that they were not actually looking in my direction, but down into Rue Trésor itself. One of the men stood up; his legs, framed in the window, were big and thick. The faded khaki of his trouser legs was curiously lustrous in the glare of a searchlight that the third man was flashing up and down the walls of our house.

Something clinked. An end of chain appeared in view. The standing man was moving the chain, weighing it in his hand, swinging it about in an ominous, experimental fashion. And the man shouting into the street below was flailing a stout stick back and forth above the roof.

The men were obviously looking for someone, someone presumed dangerous, if the length of heavy chain and the stout stick were any indications. Still . . . I shivered in sympathy for the unknown fugitive, as the searchlights flashed, crisscrossing along the rosy walls of the houses, illuminating the heavy, hairy arms of the three searchers on the roof, glinting on the dark chain, glaring on the heads of men milling down below on the street, flickering off figures running, running on other rooftops.

"Mama! Mama!"

I ran across the balcony to the children's room, ducking low under the windows raked by searchlights.

"What's happening?" whispered Laura Ann fearfully.

"I don't know. But I don't think we need to worry. The roof door's locked, and nobody could break down the front door."

At least I didn't think so, I told myself, but did not confess my fears to Laura Ann, whose window revealed another frame of the street, the entrance to the sibha. Abdul Krim and Saleh and Rakosh's eldest son, Hassan, stood there in their nightclothes, arguing with the searchers.

"What are you doing?" cried Abdul Krim.

"Go away! Go away! We need to get some sleep!" shouted Hassan.

The searchers paid no attention whatsoever, not even to the unmistakable rasping voice of Kenza. "Be quiet, you fools!" she was calling from her second-floor window. "Shut up, or I'll call the police."

Her words were almost drowned in the noise of motors running, men shouting. But Kenza was not to be put down.

"Police!" she hollered, and then still louder, "Police!" and she kept hollering until a man's voice answered.

"I *am* the police," said a voice. "Now be quiet, please, Alalla, and close your window so we can get on with our work."

The shutter slammed, and the second searchlight began methodically scanning the walls of the houses once more; Laura Ann and I drew back as the beam passed over the window, nearly getting us in the face.

"Whang!" The chain hit our roof, a sickening sound, and the metallic echoes were muffled in the tufts of dry grass that grew in the bits of earth between the roof tiles. The chain was jerked up again, and clanged against itself, horribly, loudly.

Suddenly the whole street seemed to erupt in sound. Men, shouting, ran across the rooftops, and the search beams joined, focusing on Lalla Fadna's roof, where, incongruously, a djellaba swung on the clothesline, gently, like a ghost in the night breeze. The chain in the big man's hand hit Lalla Fadna's roof. A woman screamed, again and again. We clung together, Laura Ann and I, hardly daring to breathe as we crouched on her bed while the screams died and relative quiet descended.

"Look, Mama! Look!"

A procession of men was passing beneath us from Lalla Fadna's house, along Rue Trésor toward Rue Bab Agnaou. We saw two uniform hats with gleaming badges, several skullcaps, a few bare heads. There was little noise, only the chain hitting the wall, then the metal of our door, then, at a sharp word from someone, withdrawn.

On Rue Bab Agnaou, a waiting car slammed its door and drove off. The murmur of voices diminished, the searchlights were darkened, and the hotel light was abruptly snapped off. In five minutes Rue Trésor was almost as quiet as it had been when I first dropped off to sleep. I tucked Laura Ann back into bed. It was three-thirty in the morning.

I shut the balcony windows calmly enough, but back in my own bed, I began to shiver. Why hadn't I stayed in my room with the shutters locked tight? Was it more comforting to know something definite than to lie in bed, imagining even more terrible goings-on? But after all this, what did I know? I concentrated on my favorite border pattern in our multipatterned room and tried to breathe regularly. The white plaster leaf, stem, and flower gleamed faintly in the moonlight, which shone through the stained-glass window panes: rose, green, blue. Stem, flower, leaf. . . . I fell asleep.

The next morning I could hardly wait to ask Aisha what had happened, and she apparently could hardly wait to tell me, for she arrived nearly half an hour early.

"Wasn't it awful?" she began. "We couldn't sleep for hours. Coming and going across the roof, even somebody in our court!"

"I was scared," I said, "but I got up to make sure the door to the roof was locked."

Aisha nodded approvingly. "I was worried about that," she

confessed. "I thought I'd locked the door after I brought the laundry down, but I wasn't sure."

"What was going on, Aisha?"

"Well . . ." An Army officer, name unknown, had, it seemed, picked up a pretty girl and headed for the Hôtel du Sud, where he had taken a room for the night. Then into the picture walked Hamid.

"Hamid?"

"You know, Hamid, he's the son of Lalla Fadna, who lives in the second last house from the end of the street, near the tile store."

I shook my head. I remembered Lalla Fadna from the wedding. I had talked to her across the rooftops, but I didn't think I had ever seen Hamid.

"Hamid grew up on the street," said Aisha. "He was always wild, but since he got married, he's settled down some. But last night, after visiting his mother, he went to the café on Bab Agnaou. That's what Abdul Krim says, anyway. He saw the officer and the girl and decided he was going to take the pretty girl away from the officer."

I must have looked as puzzled as I felt, for Aisha laughed and said, "Yes, yes, I know. It sounds silly, when he's got a good job and a good wife and two nice children, but some men are like that. You wouldn't *think* he'd need to run after pretty girls in the middle of the night. But Hamid . . ."

"So what happened?"

"Hamid followed the officer into the hotel, walked up to the room and knocked, boldlike. When the officer came to the door, Hamid said, 'Hey, that's my girl, and I'm the one who's going to sleep with her tonight, not you!' No one knows exactly what happened then, but they say the girl laughed and the officer laughed, too, and then Hamid pulled a knife and stabbed the captain in the chest."

"Hamid must be crazy!"

"Oh, yes, he is, just like all men are crazy, but he's sillier than most. And what a nice wife! I mean, Elizabetha, even if he doesn't enjoy sleeping with his wife, he should think of his children before he starts stabbing Army officers, don't you think so?"

I nodded. "And then . . . ?"

"Well," Aisha continued, "when the girl screamed, everybody in my house woke up. He [meaning her husband] and Abdul Krim say the hotelkeeper came and Marzook the doorman . . ." Here Aisha gave a short laugh. "But you know that Marzook, he's big and strong but he can't stand blood, and he fainted, so Hamid got away."

I had an image of the scene, suddenly, the girl screaming, the captain collapsed, bleeding, and big fat Marzook tumbling to the floor, providing just the diversion crazy Hamid needed.

"The doctor came," said Aisha, "and the captain was taken to the hospital in an ambulance. But they couldn't find Hamid."

"Where did he go?"

"They finally figured out he'd gone across the roofs to the big café with the band, and he climbed a tree in the garden and hid in its branches and kept very still, and no one could see him. The colored lights covered him up.

"But you know, Elizabetha, the officer was an important man, they say, so his brother got the police and his relatives to help search, and that's when all that awful commotion started. Everybody was looking for Hamid, except Marzook, who said he was so weak he couldn't move." Aisha snorted with derision.

When the search party moved toward the café, Hamid took off again across the rooftops to his mother's house, where he let himself down into the court.

Aisha stopped and I poured coffee for us both. The children had come down and were eating their breakfast in the kitchen while Aisha continued her story, and I went on translating.

"Poor Lalla Fadna! What could she do! We all have trouble with our children, but Hamid is too much! He's supposed to be a man!"

"So what did *she* do, finally?"

"Well, she's a good, respectable woman, and she gave up her only son to the police." Aisha sipped her coffee reflectively.

"Now Hamid's in jail and the captain's in the hospital?"

"Yes, and they don't know if the captain will live. If he dies, it will be bad for Hamid. It'll ruin him and his family and kill his mother. She adores him. Too much," added Aisha. "She spoiled him."

David and Laila looked disappointed. "Why didn't you wake us, Mama?" asked David.

"What for?"

"So we wouldn't miss the fun!"

Fun! For a second I was indignant, thinking of the captain in the hospital and Hamid in jail. Then I remembered my own avid curiosity. Who was I to criticize?

Aisha went home to get her children's breakfast, and I was just pouring myself another cup of coffee when the door knocker sounded.

Lalla Fadna herself, the mother of Hamid, stood there on the threshold, in an olive djellaba, the hood folded across her forehead and the black veil up to the bridge of her nose failing to hide eyes swollen from weeping and fatigue.

"Ah, Elizabetha!" She put her hand on my arm and launched into a long monologue of which I hardly understood a word, so punctuated was her speech with tears and sobs and imprecations and florid arm gestures in the general direction of the hotel.

Kenza leaned far over her window sill and started shouting at Lalla Fadna, wagging her finger warningly at the old woman. Thami drew closer, and the vegetable peddler stopped his donkey.

"What's going on?" asked Laura Ann. "What's she saying, Mama?"

"It's hard to tell," I answered, "but she seems to be telling me about last night again, and saying something about how bad the hotel is."

Lalla Fadna continued her tirade, with first a gesture toward Kenza, then another toward the hotel. Rachida the plump schoolteacher stopped to listen, then Fatima Henna in a new rose-and-gray striped djellaba, and old Lalla Yezza on her way to market, the rope handles of her shopping basket almost as worn as her hands.

Aisha pushed out of the sibha, a towel over her head, and came to stand beside me. Thami hovered on the edge of this growing cluster of women before my door, and farther down Rue Trésor, Moussa came out of the bakery, and Abdul Kabeer craned his neck over the counter of the grocery to see what was going on. Zahia was calling down from her window, interrupting Lalla Fadna, and Lateefa and Rakosh came out of the house and stood just inside the sibha. I had never seen so many women congregated in the street before, let alone in front of my house!

"It's all because of that place!" Lalla Fadna shouted, pointing at the hotel, where fat Marzook retreated inside. But the girl who cleaned for them looked around the door, a rag in her hand, listening.

"Yes, it's bad! A bad place!" agreed Rakosh.

"Bad for children!" said Rachida.

"Should be closed up, by the police!" Kenza called from her window.

"Yes!" shrieked Zahia, from hers.

"Hey, Kenza says they should close the hotel!" Thami called down toward Abdul Kabeer and Moussa. The cart of firewood stood half unloaded, but two of the baker boys walked toward us, listened a moment to the women, then turned back to their task. Daily bread had to be baked, no matter how many men were stabbed on Rue Trésor!

"No reason we have to put up with such goings-on!" Rakosh continued. Her voice was not loud, but everyone turned to listen. "We must go to the police together. After all, this is independent Morocco!"

"Yes," Rachida asserted. "This has always been a respectable street, as long as I've lived here, until that terrible place opened."

"Years and years respectable," nodded old Lalla Yezza.

"How can we work if we can't sleep?" complained Fatima Henna.

Lalla Fadna produced a handkerchief from inside her djellaba, blew her nose loudly, and then proceeded to describe what she wanted us to do. If the police came to question us, we were to say that the Hôtel du Sud was not a tourist hotel, but quite another sort of place. We had seen men with women going in at all hours, hadn't we?

"Yes," shrieked Zahia. "Yes! I'll tell them!"

"It's a corrupting influence on the young," said Lalla Fadna. "And you know what?"

"What?" we all chorused, and Thami drew closer.

"The hotel said that Hamid didn't come to seduce the girl, but to rob the till, and the captain was wounded while trying to protect the hotel's cash box!"

"No!"

"Can't believe it!"

"The hotel told the police Hamid's a robber, not a skirt chaser!" Thami shouted to the men farther down the street.

Kenza hooted. "Lies! Lies!" she cried. "That boy wouldn't have the sense to—" She stopped in midsentence as Lalla Fadna rolled sad eyes up toward the window with the white geranium on the sill.

"We'll do what we can," said Rachida, saving the situation.

"Don't worry, Lalla Fadna," Fatima Henna added, pressing the old woman's hand.

The women dispersed, and Aisha and the children and I came in and closed the door, as the cry of the vegetable peddler sounded, a bit later than usual, on Rue Trésor.

"Turnips!" he called. "Nice white turnips for your couscous!"

I explained to the children what had happened, and told Aisha I'd be glad to do as Lalla Fadna asked.

"Good," Aisha replied. "For if Hamid is convicted of robbery, he might get six years, but if the captain lives, maybe only two or three years in jail."

"More time for robbery than assault?"

"Yes," Aisha insisted.

"But what if the captain dies?"

Aisha shook her head. "Let's hope he lives."

That evening, Abdul Lateef and Moulay Mustapha were also interested in discussing the events of the past twenty-four hours, and I was glad Bob had returned in time to receive them. The most recent news was that Lalla Fadna had hired a lawyer to draw up a petition to the governor of Marrakech, asking for clemency for Hamid. Would we sign the petition?

Bob looked dubious. Abdul Lateef said he would not sign. Moulay Mustapha said he would, that life was hard enough for young men these days, what with the high cost of getting married, without the additional temptations offered by hotels like Le Sud.

"We're not policemen. We're not God. Who are we to judge?" said Abdul Lateef. "Why should I ask for clemency for Hamid? He's never been worth anything."

Moulay Mustapha shook his head. "Abdul Lateef's lost his faith, Bob. He has no sympathy for anyone."

"No, no," Abdul Lateef protested. "*That* is not my point. But it is interesting," he added, changing the direction of the conversation, "that the women on the street are so united on this issue, don't you think?"

Bob nodded.

"They are thinking about their children's future," put in Moulay Mustapha. "That's what my mother says."

"And you, Madame," Abdul Lateef asked, "will you sign the petition of the good Lalla Fadna, whether or not your husband does?"

"Yes," I answered.

"Women," Abdul Lateef said, in his old patronizing tone. "They stick together, yes. That is part of their power."

He laughed lightly, and I was not certain at that moment whether I should laugh, too, at Abdul Lateef's pompous tone, or be pleased that he had placed me briefly with the other women on Rue Trésor. No, I did not feel like laughing; his tone was pompous, but there was bitterness, too, in his voice, an echo of other conversations, on other subjects, at other times. Women do not understand much; they are ignorant; they cannot control themselves; they stick together; one cannot trust them. They are nothing, really, and yet in this society in which they have no power whatsoever, one must still take care. They always get around a man, by deceit or perfume or feminine wiles or magic or witchcraft or religion or some way. Women, it seemed, powerless though they were, were dangerous, especially in groups. That was their power.

"Well," I said brightly, "I admire Lalla Fadna's courage and initiative. Her son's future is at stake. She's decided to act rather than sit about and weep and wait for her husband to do something."

Abdul Lateef nodded at Mustapha, at Bob. "Watch out, Bob!" he warned jokingly. "Soon your wife will be marching in the street, like the djellaba workers on May Day!"

Bob smiled and I poured more tea.

Laura Ann reported next day that she had noticed two small, carefully dressed, and unfamiliar children standing against the wall on Rue Trésor, watching Ali and Shadeeya playing hopscotch, eyeing Youssef in his zooming rides up and down the zanka.

"Oh, yes," Aisha said. "Those are Hamid's children. Lalla Fadna has taken them in, for they've postponed the trial till they know whether the captain's going to live. He's bad, they say. Hamid's wife cries all day."

A week later the captain took a turn for the better. He was going to live. Lalla Fadna's son was given a sentence of a year and a half in jail, the absolute minimum. Lalla Fadna dropped her petition, but Kenza and Rakosh began to talk of circulating a petition of their own, asking the governor to close the Hôtel du Sud.

"Why not?" Aisha asked me. "It can't hurt. It might help. Maybe we'd get rid of that awful place forever."

Kenza's spirits had revived considerably during recent events. Now she appeared more often at her window, took up bargaining fiercely with the vegetable peddler once more, and pressed my hand warmly when we met on Rue Bab Agnaou, each with our own market basket. Naima seemed to be less obtrusive in her behavior, at least about appearing in her transparent nightgown. But perhaps that was simply because Thami had disappeared as mysteriously as he had come, and the silent, dark Mbarak, who had failed to find work in his family village in the South, was back in his accustomed place by the bath.

Chapter 19

Friendship on Rue Trésor

Lalla Fadna's efforts to save her son had exhausted us all, and we settled back into the routine of daily life on Rue Trésor, with some relief. However, only two days passed before I was disturbed one morning by shouting from the general direction of Rakosh's house. Now what was wrong? I went downstairs and opened my front door to be greeted by the sight of a great crowd of women in the sibha, pushing, shouting.

Lateefa stood on the threshold, twisting her hands in her striped skirt. She looked across the street at me.

"Oh, isn't it awful?" she cried.

"What is it?"

"Aisha and Glaoui. Fighting about water."

A new burst of screaming interrupted us.

"Can I help?" I called, uncertain whether I should stay where I was or try to make some gesture of assistance.

"No, no, we're sending Khadija to get Kenza. Maybe she can do something with Aisha."

Do something with Aisha? Aisha, who was usually so calm and organized and even-tempered. What was wrong?

Khadija had re-emerged with Hajja Kenza, who had thrown a towel hastily over her head. She nodded as she passed by. She was stooped, her stomach still protruded, her complexion was pasty, but her eyes were alight with interest at the sounds issuing from the sibha.

"Here! Here! What's this? What's going on?"

The women who had crowded into the passage parted so that Kenza, stooped and sick as she was, might, as recognized authority, pass through.

The voice of Glaoui was heard, screaming, "What do you mean, to talk to me, a Glaoui, a relative of the pasha, like that? You work as a servant for foreigners! You are nothing, nothing, nothing!"

Aisha interrupted, and I scarcely recognized my friend's voice, heightened, raucous. "Nothing!" screamed Aisha. "If it's nothing to work and support your family and keep them decent so they don't have to beg, then I'd rather be nothing. And who was the great Glaoui Pasha? Nothing but a butcher!"

"Shhhh!" Someone was trying to stop the words, but Aisha pressed on.

"A butcher!" she repeated. "His dead hands and the hands of his descendants are covered with innocent blood!"

By now, Mbarak, Moussa from the store, and the old cart driver had gathered near the passage. They were joined by the suave old man in a gray djellaba who owned the bath. Half smiling, they shook their heads together.

"Women."

"They just can't control themselves!"

"Listen to them! A scandal! A shame for the street!"

"They need a man in there to tell them what's what."

"They need a good beating!"

I stood a few feet away, at my open door, mute and furious, wanting to shout at them, "What do you mean? What about Hamid stabbing the captain? What about the men who beat on the doors and rooftops with their chains when they couldn't find Hamid? Was that control?" But I realized, even in my anger, that such a speech would be ridiculous, the men would turn and stare at me and shake their heads in the same infuriating way as Abdul Lateef. All women (and perhaps foreign women more) obviously have trouble controlling themselves.

Kenza pushed to the front of the passage, her face pink with excitement and concern.

"Can I help?"

"No, thank you, Elizabetha. It's not your problem. I . . ." At this moment she spied the little group of men, and she turned toward them, saying loudly, "It has been *settled*. I settled it. Now it's time for everyone to go home." And she fixed the men with a stare so intense that after a few seconds they shuffled away, the driver to his cart, Moussa to the bakery, Mbarak to his furnace, the owner of the bath to the bath.

But Kenza's triumph was short-lived. That was the moment Glaoui decided on one last gratuitous act. A great bucket of water whooshed out of the sibha, scattering the women like angry, frightened chickens and spattering Kenza's clean house caftan from waist to hem.

"If it's water you want," Glaoui shouted, "take it!"

"Oof!" cried Kenza. "That . . . !"

The epithet was drowned in the cries of the women.

"Come, let's mop it up!" That was Rakosh's gentle voice, and, together with Zahia, Lateefa, and Aisha, she swept the cascade of offending water down into the street.

"It's finished! Finished, all over. Now everybody go home," said Rakosh.

I beckoned to Lateefa. She ran across and shut my door behind her.

"What was the trouble?" I asked.

"It was all about water, the water tap."

Aisha, it seemed, had no running water in her house, but many years ago had come to an agreement with Rakosh: Aisha would draw water from Rakosh's tap (for her and her family) and in exchange would pay one third of the monthly water bill. Since there were six in Aisha's family and fourteen in Rakosh's, this was considered fair. All was well until Glaoui moved in and discovered that it was very expensive to install a water system. To hire a plumber to simply attach a new pipe to Rakosh's installation was much cheaper. Rakosh assented, with the understanding that Glaoui would pay half the bill remaining after Aisha had paid her share. Glaoui had agreed. But, said Lateefa, each year at the beginning of summer, Glaoui began to complain that Aisha was taking more than her share of the water. Since Glaoui was powerless before Rakosh, however (Rakosh could simply have the attachment removed if Glaoui refused to pay), Glaoui took her frustration out on Aisha.

"And now it is finished for another year?"

Lateefa sighed. "I hope so," she said, twisting her hands again in her striped skirt. "It's no fun. Glaoui has a mean tongue." She smiled. "But Aisha doesn't do too badly either. Butcher!" She nodded. "She got Glaoui there. For all her airs, it's true that the pasha was a cruel man."

"But powerful."

Lateefa nodded. "Powerful because he had the French behind him," she said scornfully.

I was surprised at her tone. Was Lateefa, usually so sweet and yielding, really that concerned about the politics of the past, the days of Thami Glaoui, or was her feeling due to loyalty to Aisha?

"Lateefa!"

"It's Rakosh! I have to go." And in a second Lateefa was out the door again and across the zanka.

Aisha went to visit Kenza, perhaps to thank her for her good offices? I was not sure, but it seemed to restore good relations between them. Accordingly, I went to Kenza's door one morning, was invited up, and we talked about our staying for another two months.

"But you'll pay rent."

"Yes, of course, Kenza."

We stood in the dim "salon," nearly empty of furniture, except for a bed, a round table, and the shrouded figures of extra mattresses and chairs in dust covers. I waited, for what? For Kenza to ask me to sit down and drink tea? I knew that was foolish. Kenza did not do such things spontaneously.

"A cup of tea?" she asked, uncertainly, clearing her throat.

"No, no, thank you," I said, turning to go.

Kenza looked relieved. "Everything costs money these days. Now they're saying even mint will go up in price! Think of that! We'll have to cut down on mint tea."

I smiled to myself, wondering what Kenza would have done if I had said yes, please, I'd love some tea.

"How is Naima?" I asked politely.

Kenza's eyebrows contracted. Her face twisted. My question, intended to be merely polite, seemed to have struck an unexpectedly raw nerve. "Naima," she said, "is much better, but she has to keep taking the medicine. She doesn't have to stay in bed anymore."

I was confused. I had heard Naima was sick—a bit, said Aisha—but we did not know that Naima had been in bed.

"She caught a disease at the swimming pool," explained Kenza quickly. "But she'll be all right."

Startled, I did not know what to say. First, we had no idea that Naima was going to the public swimming pool, five girls against several hundred boys, the pool where, after one visit, Bob had decided it was not a good idea for Laura Ann and Laila to spend time. And a disease? The word sounded odd in Kenza's mouth; one did not use such words in this society unless someone were really ill.

"I'm sorry," I said. "I didn't know."

I had turned to go, but Kenza grabbed my arm in a close imitation of her old grip of steel.

"What can I do, Elizabetha?" she hissed in my ear. "I forbid her to go to the pool, but she goes anyway. What can I do? She just goes! What's happening to the world? Your girls go to the pool, too. How can you let them?"

I hesitated. I certainly did not want to tell her Bob had decided the girls should *not* go. Naima was ill. Kenza was visibly distressed and worried. Obviously I had to say something to ease her mind, not make things worse. But what could I say?

"It's difficult," I temporized. "One doesn't know exactly what to do. The world is different now than when we were growing up. People behave differently."

"Yes. Yes!" Kenza was still gripping my arm. "But what will happen *afterward*? Who will want to marry our daughters? Who will take care of them when they're old? Who'll take care of *us*?"

We stared at each other in the dimness of the shrouded room. Kenza's eyes, dulled by sickness and worry, glowed suddenly with a wild light. For a moment, the grip of steel on my arm, that strange glaze in her eyes, frightened me. Outside Zahia was calling Shadeeya. The beggar shouted, "Allah!" My children would soon be coming home from visiting the Harrises.

Impulsively, I put my other hand on Kenza's shoulder, and at the gesture her grip on my arm eased. The light in her eyes faded. She became once more only a pathetic, ill old woman.

"Oh, Kenza, how do we know? We do the best we can, that's all we can do. And trust to God," I reassured her.

She nodded and let go my arm. "And trust to God," she repeated. Then she looked directly at me, old Kenza again for a moment, her gold teeth glinting in the dimness. "You'll pay month by month as usual?"

"Yes," I said, starting down the steep cement stairs in the darkness. "Yes."

"Good." She grinned at me from the top of the stairs, the old golden grin. "And another day you must drink tea."

"*Enshallah*," I replied, pushing open the outside door. She had not come down with me, unusual for her. "Shut the door," she called. "Shut it tight!"

I was already out on the street when she called me from the open window. "Elizabetha!"

I turned to see her, smiling down at me from her old familiar place next to the white geranium.

"Why don't you take me and Naima on one of your picnics, hey?"

"Why not?" I answered. "How about Sunday, is that good?"

"Yes, yes," Kenza said. "And since your husband knows so many rich merchants, maybe one of the young unmarried ones would like to come, hey?" She laughed uproariously, but, I thought, a bit too loudly.

"I'll ask him," I promised. "*Bslama*, Kenza."

Kenza did not reply, but she disappeared from the window. I drew a deep breath. The street was hot. Dust rose in the air from Youssef's continual passing, as he rode his bicycle up and down, up and down the narrow zanka. Khadija stood against the wall, sewing a button onto Ali's trousers. Glaoui and Aisha were quiet. El Mesakeena, the old beggar woman, limped toward me, and I reached for a coin. It was the same old Rue Trésor, and yes, the geranium was still there in Kenza's open window. Poor Naima. Poor Kenza, I thought, and went inside to make chicken salad for supper.

That evening Bob announced that Omar had invited us for dinner, all of us, the following Wednesday evening, a week away.

"How nice!" I said, quite seriously. "Are you sure he wants the children and me, too?"

"That's what he said. His mother and sisters want to meet you, B.J., and now apparently his father has warmed to the idea, too. His father would have had to give permission before he invited us at all, Omar says."

I was pleased. So was Bob. But we were unprepared for the fact that everyone on Rue Trésor apparently knew we were going to Omar's for dinner almost as soon as we did.

The next day, when Lateefa brought the caftan we had ordered for a gift, she sat down to tea with Aisha and me. After a moment, Aisha glanced at Lateefa and said to me,

"Kenza is furious you've been invited to dinner at Omar's house."

"How did she know? And why is she angry?"

"Oh," said Lateefa, waving a hand, "everybody knows."

"Kenza says she took you to his shop first and he should have invited her, too."

Could they be serious? I looked at them and decided they were. "But Omar and Bob are good friends. Why shouldn't he invite us for dinner?"

Lateefa shrugged and giggled. When she smiled, her face assumed the old sweetness and beauty that had undoubtedly made many men and many men's mothers select her as a prospective bride! If only she were not barren.

"Of course," she said in her gentle voice. "But Kenza doesn't think of that. She only thinks about the free meal."

"Well, we all like a free meal now and then," Aisha allowed.

They were waiting for me to say something. But what?

"Is Omar's family a friend of Kenza's family?"

"No."

"Then . . . why . . . ?"

"Well, she knows you've bought a lot of things from Omar and you've taken other people there, and he's gotten a lot of business because of her, so he owes her a dinner."

"Business."

"Yes. Business. She gave him you, now she wants dinner in return."

Well, if one accepted Kenza's point of view, it seemed reasonable enough. We thought differently about this social occasion than she did. But maybe Omar didn't.

"I could tell Omar how she feels."

Aisha nodded. "Yes. That's a good idea."

I had gotten my cue. So I mentioned it to Omar. He laughed.

"Why the hell should I want that old hag for dinner?" he said rather rudely. "She's a witch! She uses bad magic."

My face must have shown some annoyance, for I felt slightly nettled. After all, Kenza had been my first friend on Rue Trésor.

"You're right to say something, Madame," Omar said quickly, "but let me tell you, that woman has made my life miserable this year. She wants me to marry her daughter, first, because she can't handle her any longer. That's bad enough, but then she expects me to give her a lower price on everything just because she once brought you into my shop!" He threw out his hands imploringly. "I ask you.

And I'm supposed to invite that witch for dinner? I look forward to Wednesday as a pleasant occasion."

"Oh, we do, too," I answered quickly. "I shouldn't have mentioned it. Please forgive me."

Aisha told me that another reason Kenza was so annoyed was that "it isn't our custom to have people for dinner, just for fun. There should be a reason, like a wedding or a circumcision or a funeral. Or maybe business. Nobody understands why you have people all the time. The teachers of the children, maybe yes, but others? Why? And so Kenza is killing herself trying to figure out the reason Omar's asked you to dinner, and why his father allowed it. It's a good family, a rich family, and very conservative. They don't have truck with foreigners."

"I see," I answered. "But our customs are different."

When I mentioned this conversation to Bob, he laughed at first, then, reflecting, said, "I guess our behavior must seem strange to our neighbors, particularly these last weeks when we've been so deluged with visitors. Omar asked me if Bob Hamilton was my cousin. They probably think we're either really rich or just crazy.

"But, B.J.," he went on, "I forgot to tell you that Omar, too, asked me why we fed so many people. I explained that when we were traveling and poor, many people had fed us, and since we could not repay those particular families, the only solution was to pass on their kindness to others."

"And how did Omar react to that?"

"He looked at me strangely, and then said, 'Aha! Now, Bob, you are beginning, like your wife, to understand the meaning of baraka and na'ama and niiya.'"

Could I explain it in the same way to Aisha, in the hope that she might pass it along to Kenza? Something else had to be cleared up first. We had set the following Wednesday for our long-postponed pilgrimage to the shrine of Sidi Bel Abbas, for we had missed the second moussem Aisha had told me about. Then Aisha had been in bed, recovering from her visit to the dentist.

But now I realized the following Wednesday was the day we were to go to Omar's.

"Never mind, I understand," Aisha said, "but when *do* you want to go?"

I looked at her guiltily. How long had it been since the young shu-wafa in white had advised me to make this pilgrimage? How many visitors, appointments, dinner parties, and shopping trips had intervened since that day?

"Soon."

She nodded. "Yes. It's important for Laila that you do it before you go, even if you don't want to bother yourself."

"Oh, but I do. I'll do it before I leave, really, Aisha, I promise."

She looked at me sharply, then looked away.

"Did you say something to Omar?" she asked.

"Yes."

"Well?"

"He still won't invite Kenza."

Aisha sighed and walked out.

Early the next morning the noise began outside the door, and continued while I heard the key turn in the lock. Aisha and Kenza were in my house. They were arguing about something. What? I dressed quickly and looked over the balcony to speak to them, but they had disappeared. Into the kitchen? The salon? The dining room? I did not know, but it seemed odd that they should both arrive in early morning without saying a word to me. I had not seen much of Kenza lately; the picnic we had planned had fallen through because Naima was not yet recovered from her "disease." Kenza had suggested another day, but Bob had already promised to visit some *suweekas* or little markets in the outlying suburb of Sidi Youssef ben Ali; he did not want to change the appointment with the young tanner who had offered to take him. Kenza had looked miffed until I explained that Bob needed the car for his work. At that she had nodded absently and gone out.

But a quarrel between Aisha and Kenza? This I had not foreseen. What would they be quarreling about?

I discovered them in the bathroom, Aisha washing sheets and towels in the bathtub, Kenza standing by the sink, haranguing her.

"Good morning, Aisha. Kenza," I said pleasantly. "Anybody want a coffee?"

They both said no and turned back to their argument as though I were not there. Kenza was speaking so fast I could barely understand a word here and there, but it seemed to have something to do with me. What were they doing arguing in my house? I was annoyed. We were not leaving for nearly a month. Kenza was now tapping on the hot-water heater, and she turned to me expectantly. There was a pause. Aisha stood up, wiped her hands on the sides of her skirt, and said clearly,

"Kenza wants me to tell you that she hopes you'll let the hot-water heater stay in the house as a present for her when you leave." She lowered her eyes and blushed.

I stood for a moment, gathering my wits, while Kenza stared at me, and Aisha gradually raised her head. I noticed, abstractedly, that Kenza was biting her lips nervously, one over the other, while she watched me.

I decided to be as pleasant as I could. I didn't want to alienate her just before leaving; after all, she had helped us a great deal in the beginning.

"I'm happy to leave the kitchen cupboard and table as a present, and of course some other small things," I said, and smiled fulsomely. "But the hot-water heater is too expensive. We can't afford it."

Kenza snorted; she expelled her breath loudly; she drummed on the green sink in an irritating way. She opened her mouth to speak, but I was not to be deterred now.

"After all, Kenza," I continued, "everything costs money, as you yourself have said. I'm sorry, but we've had to buy our tickets home to America, and pay for our baggage and for the children's school this year, as well as food and rent and electricity."

Aisha was looking at me full now. Was there a mischievous gleam in her eye? Or was it a warning? Kenza was staring at the floor.

"But I thought we were friends, Madame," Kenza said formally, "and friends often give each other presents."

"True," I said, "and that is why I brought you the inlaid box from Egypt and why I'm giving you the kitchen table and cupboard, which cost us fifty dirhams, and why I've saved the electric coffee pot for you, since I know you like coffee so much and have electricity in your house."

"Mmmm," murmured Kenza. She turned her head away and began to pick at the loose plaster on the wall. At that I could not resist one more gibe.

"And remember, you promised that the kitchen was to be freshly plastered before we moved in. It never was."

She stopped picking at the plaster and shook her head in an absent-minded way.

"All this water—" Kenza gestured toward the tubful of sheets and towels.

"We pay for it," I put in quickly. "We have always paid our bills promptly."

Kenza said nothing. She clasped her chin tightly, as though she would erase the tattoo. She wiped a hand on her old, worn house caftan and grabbed at her chin again. Aisha rinsed the sheets and wrung them out, fiercely turning them tighter, tighter, getting that last bit of water out of their lengths.

"Shall I give you the last month's rent now, then?" I asked. "And subtract the cost of the hot-water heater? Would you prefer that?"

"Yes," she rasped. Her voice was high and squeaky, and she cleared her throat again. "Yes," she went on in an unexpectedly vicious tone, "bring it to me, the pittance it is."

"I'll go and get it."

I was barely out of the room before the quarreling began once more. I stood on the balcony, the money in my hand, listening. No words reached me, only the rise and fall of Kenza's voice, magnified by the tiled walls and floor of the bathroom. What was going on now? Why should Aisha have to listen to this? After all, it was hardly her fault that I had decided not to give away our expensive hot-water heater.

Now they were out in the courtyard, standing at the door. I ducked back into our bedroom. Through the window I could see the gestures, the wide-armed gestures that Kenza was making, encompassing the house, her heart, the world, who knows what, while her expanding abdomen rose and fell with the force of her statements. She was speaking very quickly now, and shouting, something about presents and Aisha and friendship. She sniffed loudly and explosively, and Aisha's voice interrupted.

"Ya, Kenza, what are you talking about? She has given me old clothes for my children to wear, because she doesn't need them. Do you need them? Friend? Of course she's my friend. So are you."

"Ha! Friends!" Kenza's voice was piercing. "Nonsense! You go to moussems in their car and I stay at home."

"You could have come. She asked you."

"I was ill."

"Is that my fault?"

Kenza's voice rose in a scream. "No one cares! No one! I work, I slave, I save my money, I fulfill my duties, and what do I get? No friends, no presents. No one cares about me."

The hysterical note was just barely under control. Aisha started up the stairs, Kenza following, and I came out of the bedroom, deciding I was a coward to stay inside. We met on the balcony, beneath the beautiful traceries in plaster, the gracefully turned columns, the blue-and-green tiles.

"What's the matter, Aisha?"

She looked at me. Tears were streaming down her face. "Nothing," she managed, and started up the last flight of stairs, past me, to hang the laundry on the roof.

I held out the sheaf of bills to Kenza. "Here is the rent," I said.

She would not look at me, but her hand shot forward for the money and proceeded to count it, ostentatiously.

"Is it the correct amount?"

She still would not look at me, nor reply. She simply counted the bills, over and over.

"Is it right?" I persisted. "Or have I made a mistake?"

Kenza nodded, and ducked down the stairs. By the time I had reached the bottom, she was already out the door. It clicked shut behind her.

The next day I asked Aisha about this quarrel, because I was genuinely troubled by it.

"Oh, Kenza is very upset. She's unreasonable, Elizabetha. She wants everything for herself, and nothing for anyone else. I don't know what's happening to her. She was always tight, but not like this."

"She's not well," I pointed out, "and she's having a lot of trouble with Naima. She—"

"Yes, but we all have problems. My teeth kill me sometimes, but I don't holler and scream at my old friends. She's getting very nervous. She accuses me of the most awful things, stealing from you . . . and—"

"Stealing?" I was shocked.

"She says you were her friend first, and I stole you away by taking you to the moussems and now you don't give her anything."

"But we asked her to go with us to the moussems."

"I know, I know. She should join a zaweeya and dance, it would be good for her."

"Why doesn't she?"

"I told you, she doesn't want to spend any money."

We were both silent. Again the tears came, silent tears that splashed onto the kitchen drainboard. I couldn't bear it. I put my arm around her. "Aisha, don't!"

Aisha sobbed loudly and covered her face with her hands.

"How could she say those things to me? I nursed Naima, we were children in this street together, her father used to drink coffee with my father."

"She's sick, Aisha. She's not responsible."

"I don't know." Aisha sniffed and wiped her nose and eyes on a corner of her skirt. "Who am I to talk, but if you have mattresses up to the ceiling and money to fill the post office savings account and your heart is like Kenza's, so tight and miserable, what good is it?"

"Yes," I answered. "Rakosh isn't like that."

"No, she's a good woman, Rakosh. She has room in her heart for everyone."

"Yes." I turned away. Aisha had pulled herself together and was attacking the tiled walls of the kitchen with a soapy cloth. Things seemed to have returned to normal.

"But when you're gone . . ."

"Yes?"

"I'll have no work."

"But . . . won't Kenza . . ."

"Hmph," Aisha snorted. "Kenza wouldn't give me the time of day now. Didn't you hear her?"

"I'll try to find you work, Aisha."

"But I have no work permit."

"Couldn't I help you get one?"

"Maybe. Thank you. When?"

"We could go to the office tomorrow."

"Mama! Mama!" It was Youssef, knocking on the door and calling for his mother. A flash of a smile appeared on Aisha's troubled face. "Youssef! What now? That boy!"

She went out to deal wtih Youssef's latest problem, but I stood in the kitchen, appalled and upset. What had I done, without knowing, to the long-standing friendship between Kenza and Aisha? I had meant well, I told myself. We had come to live on Rue Trésor and, partly to help Bob in his research but also partly out of my own interest, I had tried to make friends with my neighbors, to learn about the part of Marrakech found on Rue Trésor. I had not meant any harm. Kenza and Aisha had both been kind to me; now what had I done to repay their kindness? Kenza and Aisha had been friends since childhood, daughters of a mosque official and a grain merchant, more or less equals. Now Aisha was poor and Kenza was rich, and yet they were still, I had thought, friends as well as neighbors. It was Kenza who had brought Aisha to us when we had first arrived, and we had provided Aisha with a new source of income. She had managed to clothe all her children this year, keep them in school, buy a new stove, and cover the beaten-earth floor of her two rooms with new linoleum. It had seemed obvious, from the beginning, that Aisha needed whatever extra help I could offer more than Kenza, the mother of only one daughter and the owner of three large houses.

I realized now, too late, that other kinds of help had been needed as well, by both of the women: affection and warmth and support, and, wittingly or unwittingly, I had given more of these to Aisha than to Kenza. Aisha herself had responded, and we had become friends. But the friendship was proving to be a liability as well as an asset for Aisha. Terrible words had been spoken yesterday morning. I feared that Kenza's and Aisha's relationship would never be the same as it had been before we came to Rue Trésor. And the only tangible act I could think of to ease the situation was to get Aisha a work permit so that she could find another source of income. But what of the other needs?

I began to wonder about my own motivations and ultimate responsibilities in the situation I seemed to have precipitated. I had wanted to be accepted, obviously. I had wanted to learn, but now I was leaving, and those who had accepted me and taught me what I knew—Aisha, Kenza, Lateefa, Lalla Fadna, Zahia, Fatima Henna—would be left behind. We had all been changed by the encounter, but was it worth it, to me, to them? Was it fair, human even? I could not answer my own questions.

Before we set out for Omar's house, Bob delivered a short lecture on the importance of the occasion and the necessity for polite behavior.

"Oh, Baba, you know we'll be good," Laura Ann said.

"Yes, but just remember," added her father, "this is a very traditional household. They're not used to entertaining foreigners, and although the way they behave may seem strange to you, the way we behave will seem even stranger to them."

Aisha arrived just as were leaving, ostensibly to get something she had forgotten on the roof, but actually, I thought, to see what we were all wearing for our venture into this new stratum of Marrakech society; for, Aisha had confided to me, Omar's family had lived in Marrakech for as long as anyone could remember—his mother was a *sherifa*, or descendant of the Prophet. "It's not just their money, but their history," she explained. "That's what makes Kenza so angry. She'd love to be invited there."

I resolved not to think about Kenza during the coming evening, and, giving a last pat to Laila's hair, followed Bob, Laura Ann, David, and Aisha out the door. Zahia waved to me from the window, Lateefa from the sibha; Fuad, the schoolteacher's son, could not resist putting a hand on Laila's arm; and Youssef zoomed past us, shouting, "Watch out! Watch out!"

Mbarak lounged at the door of the bath, smoking. He nodded, but his boss, the owner of the bath, stepped forward and greeted Bob formally. Bob was thoroughly taken by surprise. "In all the time I have been in his bath and passed by, this is the first time he has greeted me, B.J. We are becoming respectable!"

Omar was waiting for us in the djellaba shop, smiling a bit under his well-tailored mustache, and we wrung each other's hands before we started out, along a way I did not know, through narrow market alleys, into a covered darb, a quieter street.

"Look!" David pointed to the single rows of bricks that rose above us, like miniature arches every few feet, joining one house to another. "What are they for, Baba?"

"Supports to keep the walls apart," explained Bob, after asking Omar. "Omar says this is an old street, maybe hundreds of years. Some of the house walls are weak."

We wound around carefully for five or ten more minutes, under the narrow supporting arches, until we had reached a heavy wooden door, with polished brass studs, a door that arched at least two or three feet above our heads. No tiny window like Zahia's, no shutters like ours, gave onto the street. The front of Omar's house was a high wall, recently plastered with reddish Marrakech clay, and except for the arch of the door, it was totally blank.

Omar rang a bell, and the door swung open as if by magic. A dark, shadowy passage extended ahead. Laila held tightly to my hand while we navigated several steep-tiled steps leading down and then stopped, for we were now at the real entrance to the house. From the dusty narrow streets we had emerged into the peaceful open spaces of a vast, well-kept courtyard, its tiled and whitewashed walls rising high to crenelated parapets. A bird called softly to us from the trees grouped in one corner of the spacious court, much bigger than our own.

"It's a very old house, isn't it, Mama?" whispered Laura Ann, "but nice."

"Yes, very nice."

Omar ushered us across the court to a large room on our left, where, following his example, we took off our shoes before walking on the Persian carpet.

"Please make yourself comfortable," Omar said. "My house is your house. Please!" And he gestured toward the sumptuous cut-velvet banquettes and pillows, until a cheerful commanding voice made us all turn.

This was obviously Omar's mother, Lalla Nezha, a stout but still shapely woman, who smiled broadly and came forward with arms outstretched to greet us. "Ahhh!" she pronounced, her gold and jade pendant earrings swinging and tinkling gently as she bent forward in a shimmery watermelon-colored caftan bound with gold braid, to embrace Laila, Laura Ann, and me, and to shake hands with Bob. She patted David on the shoulder, not the head, exclaimed delightedly at the quality of the material in Laura Ann's dress, and urged us to sit down.

"So this is the family!" she said, looking at us again, one by one, as we shifted rather self-consciously on the flowered velvet cushions. Laura Ann was smiling in appreciation of Omar's mother's undoubted good looks and obvious enjoyment of life, but I had to nudge Laila to break her fascinated stare at the lady's hair style, *à l'Empire,* a gold scarf tied over the front to accentuate a high dark chignon in the back.

"Didn't I tell you, Mama?" Omar was saying, his hands clasped tightly between his knees, a smile all over his face. "Two girls and the boy in the middle. Aren't they nice?"

"Aren't they, though? This one's a bit too shy, though," answered his mother, tweaking Laila's skirt, and then Lalla Nezha got up and left, abruptly, without excuses, leaving us with Omar.

"Be comfortable," she called back from the courtyard.

There was a silence. Omar smiled. We smiled back.

I cleared my throat. Bob seemed disinclined to conversation and leaned back against the soft cushions. Omar eyed us amiably but said nothing. There seemed to be no need. The bird trilled in the tree outside. A saucepan clattered in a distant kitchen. Otherwise it was quiet in the room, a pleasant, comfortable room, the door- and windowframes decorated with intricately carved and painted wood, a craft that was one of the specialties of the artisans of Marrakech. Over the carved wood hung swaths of "glass" curtains, as my mother would have called them, pale gray nylon printed with dark blue flowers to match the cushions. From a tapestry valance above the "glass" curtains hung different lengths of ball fringe, orange, red, and blue, fabric baubles that moved gently in the slight drafts of air. The singing bird flew across, out of the tree, and up into the sky until we could no longer hear it.

Now it was Bob's turn to clear his throat. He pulled himself upright on the banquette.

"Go look for the other children," he said briskly to Laila and David.

They shook their heads.

"Come on," he said. "I'm sure there are other children."

"No, Baba," said Davy. "I don't want to."

Omar stirred. "Can I get you something, Bob?"

"I'm telling the children to go look for your younger brothers and sisters. Don't I hear a baby? Laura Ann loves babies."

Laura Ann frowned. Omar looked dubious, but he rose obediently, beckoned, and we followed him across the courtyard. We had barely approached the opening of another room when we heard muffled exclamations of annoyance. The voice was female. Someone was getting dressed.

"Can't I have any place to myself?" the voice said loudly.

We all beat a hasty retreat, and I, for one, was furious with Bob for getting us into an embarrassing situation when the evening had scarcely begun.

Once more we arranged ourselves on the Spanish velvet cushions. Omar smiled. We smiled. After what seemed a very long silence Omar suddenly rose and left the room.

"Hey, Baba, when're we gonna eat?" asked David.

"Shhh!" Bob admonished sternly.

A silence descended once more. Even Bob yawned as the moments stretched. When was something going to happen?

Eventually a pretty dark-haired girl came in, bearing a ewer and a basin, so that we might wash in traditional style before eating. This was Malika, Omar's seventeen-year-old sister, who was an honor science student in secondary school and lovely in a satiny caftan the color of a cultured pearl. Before presenting the basin and ewer, she greeted us, speaking good French. "*Bon soir*," Malika said, smiling, holding the basin and pouring the water over our hands. In her gold slippers, gold bracelets, and pearly caftan, she was lovely, but she looked unwell, with deep, shadowy circles under her dark eyes, circles less noticeable when she laughed at Laila, busily patting water over her face! Not strictly according to etiquette, but, it appeared, quite acceptable.

When we were all washed and dried, Omar brought in a large tin table and a set of folding legs that he set up in the corner of the banquettes so that we might dine in comfort.

"*Quel bon repas!*" Laura Ann enunciated when Malika brought in a great tray of salads centered by two roast chickens and a dish of sauce.

"See, Bob, I told them to make the sauce separate from the

chicken," Omar was explaining eagerly. "I have seen them do that in the restaurants in Gueliz."

We paused expectantly, but Malika exited, and Omar urged us forward. "Come, come, eat, you must eat alone, as our guests, that is our custom," Omar laughed a little.

Bob, however, clapped him on the shoulder and said it was our strange custom to enjoy eating more when our host ate with us. So, a bit shyly, Omar moved in to the table, and smiling at the absurdity of it all, nibbled a bit of food.

"What's this?" said Laila in English in a very loud voice.

Bob frowned.

"Lettuce," I answered promptly. "You can see that, Laila."

"But what's on the lettuce?" she insisted, and indeed I had some difficulty myself in deciding. Cinnamon? Could that be it? Yes, it was cinnamon. Carraway? Yes, it was carraway, and cinnamon and pepper on the lettuce. Unusual, but not too bad.

I nibbled. Laila left it untouched on her plate.

"Maybe she doesn't like cinnamon," said Omar.

"No, no, she loves it," said Bob brightly. "Don't you, Laila?"

"Yes, Baba," she said obediently, adding under her breath, "on toast."

I chose to ignore this remark and noticed Laura Ann making a valiant effort at the cinnamon lettuce, after her younger sister's presumed gaffe.

"The carrots vinaigrette are excellent," I murmured, and indeed they were, as was the traditional Moroccan salad of fresh green peppers and tomatoes finely chopped together. We had wedges of bread, round raised wheaten bread like the product of the bakery on Rue Trésor, only this was better, crisper, undoubtedly made at home, like Aisha's.

We ate the chicken with our fingers, the salads with spoons, and we dipped pieces of bread into the olive and lemon sauce. Laila acquitted herself well with the chicken, as did David, and I thought we had done respectably, eaten enough but not too much. I was mentally congratulating myself on the children's good manners when Malika entered and removed the tray.

We all smiled again and breathed a sigh of relief.

"Now we have the *specialité!*" announced Omar.

Bob looked alarmed.

"Oh? But Omar, we've already eaten more than enough," Bob protested. "You honor us too much this way."

Omar laughed. "This is very special, Bob. You know I asked Aisha whether you'd had prune tajeen, and when she said yes, I asked my mother to make something else, really special that you'll never eat in a restaurant."

Bob looked interested.

"Oh? what's that?"

"*Voilà!*"

Malika set down another tray. We all leaned forward and stared. What was it? It looked like meat, but it also looked as though it were covered with cinnamon and granulated sugar, freshly spread on with a lavish hand.

"What is it?" from David.

"A very special tajeen," said Omar.

"Yes, very special," added Malika, looking pleased with herself. Had she made it? Perhaps so, for she stood by to see how we liked it. What was there to do but eat it?

"Mmm, very special," murmured Bob, though I could see he found it heavy going.

"More cinnamon in funny ways?" Laila's voice seemed unusually loud and penetrating.

"Hush," Bob said ominously and glared at Laila.

"Try a little," I said.

"It's very good," smiled Malika, and more, I thought, to please pretty pearly-gowned Malika than her father, Laila picked up a bit of sugar and cinnamon-covered meat and managed to swallow it.

"*Très bien!*" Malika patted Laila's blond head and went out in a graceful movement.

We all tried. It was indeed a very special tajeen, but somehow not to Western tastes. Omar nibbled. We finally gave up, protesting that we were really full, it had been such a delicious dinner.

"Good carrots!" offered David.

"And chicken!" piped Laila.

"I liked it all," said Laura Ann politely.

I looked at Bob, signaling that they really had been polite, and pleading with him not to urge them to eat more of the special tajeen.

"Ah, we are all full," he remarked graciously. "You honor us too much."

Omar, very pleased, went out to get Malika. She brought a platter of marvelous fruit, upon which we all fell with great relief and pleasure.

The colors! "Look how pretty!" said Laura Ann. On the silver tray were white-and-blue-flowered plates of red plums, yellowish figs, watermelon cut into squares for easy eating, and surprise, surprise, tiny green artichokes!

After this refreshing ending, we washed again, and then, as we settled back, replete upon the Spanish velvet cushions, the members of the family came in, one by one, to greet us and have tea. Omar's younger brother Mohammed shook hands—Mohammed, whom we knew from the shop; and Ibrahim, with his beard and brooding eyes (he wanted to go to Rabat to school, but his father wanted him to stay in the djellaba business). Another younger brother in secondary school brought in Faneeda, the baby, a fat toddler in a white embroidered shift.

Laura Ann got down off the banquettes and began to smile at the baby.

"Come! Come!" Faneeda came, smiling, and tumbled onto the carpet. Laura Ann picked her up and turned her around. "Come! Come!" called Ibrahim, and his face lost the brooding look while he picked up that marvelous plaything, his baby sister Faneeda, and tossed her into the air! Faneeda crowed with delight.

Now Davy got into the game and he was down on the floor, on his hands and knees, crawling slowly toward Faneeda. She looked at him suspiciously for a moment, then toddled over and stared at him full in the face. "Faneeda?" said Davy coaxingly.

She chortled with glee and sat down hard in front of Davy; he pulled her up and headed her back toward the younger brother.

Omar laughed. "You know what her name means, David?"

Davy shook his head.

"Little *bonbon*. It is a modern name."

"Blessings on the child and keep the Evil Eye from her," I offered to Omar's mother, who had sat down beside me to preside at the great tea ceremony.

She nodded. "The same for your children," she murmured, in a ritualistic way.

I nodded in return.

We knew the tea ceremony was about to begin, for Si Abdullah, the father of the family, entered, wearing his white summer djellaba, and his white skullcap a little rakishly placed on his balding head.

Steel-rimmed spectacles covered the small eyes, but they were shrewd eyes, and they looked quickly at everything. He greeted us all while Malika brought in two big silver trays bearing the tea paraphernalia, pots and glasses covered by tea cloths of net embroidered with white daisies.

That evening I saw clearly demonstrated before my eyes a story that had been told me many times. Tea-making in Moroccan society is a purely personal thing, it is said, totally creative and inventive. No cup of tea is ever the same, and no rules can be given for making it, for everyone's taste is different, and each person's hands make it in their own way and give it a unique flavor.

Every eye in the room, except Faneeda's, was focused on Lalla Nezha, the mother. She sat on the blue velvet cushions in her golden and watermelon-colored gown, presiding very formally over the tray of teapots, sugar bowls, and tea containers, over the three-tiered silver cake stand, and over the tray of perfumes: silver dispensers of rose water and orange flower water to perfume the guests.

First a handful of mint, fresh and fragrant, was crammed into the silver pot, then a large uneven lump of sugar, then boiling water from a teapot offered by a servant girl, plump and well-fed in this good traditional household. Lalla Nezha tried the tea. It did not suit her. It waited. It steeped. She smiled at us all while it steeped.

The girl was summoned to bring the hot water again. More water went into the silver pot, a few more leaves of tea, a small dot of sugar. Another sip. Lalla Nezha sighed and nodded her head with satisfaction. She poured the tea into a set of glasses with different-colored rims, poured it out from a great height, and the tea, steaming and fragrant, was passed around by Malika. Cookies followed.

Ibrahim of the brooding eyes rose and wheeled in a large television set. Everyone looked at us to see what our reaction would be, and Laila quite unaffectedly oohed and aahed with pleasure, the perfect response. We watched a soap opera about a middle-class housewife whose three best gold bracelets had been stolen from her jewelry box.

While the soap-opera characters flounced through their parts, Laura Ann and Malika began to converse in French about the effects of the strikes in the schools. I was surprised at Malika's tone, serious, even fervent when she spoke of a cousin who had gone to jail and been tortured. I tried to catch Bob's eye, but he was absorbed in talk with Ibrahim.

David and Faneeda and Mohammed made a pleasant threesome

on the floor. Laila sat close to me, and Lalla Nezha, the lady of the house, squeezed my hand.

"Is the tea all right, Madame?"

"Perfect!"

Lalla Nezha poured me out another cup, yes, yes, she insisted despite my polite refusal, and then offered me the silver flagon of orange flower water. She sprinkled a few drops on my hands and on Laura Ann's and Laila's hands, and we were instructed to rub it in vigorously and dab some behind our ears.

"Come, come, Malika! Laura Ann! Forget that nonsense you're talking. Look at the TV. Isn't this a sweet scent?"

"Mmmm!" Laura Ann responded. "It's nice." She smiled at good-humored Lalla Nezha, but in a few seconds she and Malika had resumed their political conversation in low voices.

Si Abdullah stood up, opened a finely carved silver incense burner, and, gesturing that the TV was to be turned low, he lit the powdered incense within. Omar rose quickly to do his father's bidding, then turned to Bob and said, "My father wishes you to know that in your honor he is burning incense he bought in Mecca when he made the pilgrimage, the *haj*."

We exclaimed with pleasure.

"Thank you, we are honored!" intoned Bob, his hand on his heart in the old Iraqi tribal fashion. The old man's face changed. He stared. Then the old man placed *his* hand on his heart. He smiled and bowed his head. All was well.

After a moment, Si Abdullah said, "Why is there no *luisa* in the tea, my dear?"

"Ah!" the mother smiled. "I forgot. I always forget you like it with luisa."

He took her place at the tea urn, next to me, and asked for luisa, long, slender stalks of lemon verbena, which were brought by the servant girl. He plucked the soft green almond-shaped leaves, one by one, the best leaves from the stems to be placed in a clean silver pot. The servant girl brought boiling water. The sugar and mint. While the tea steeped, Si Abdullah offered me a leaf to smell.

"Isn't it nice?"

I nodded. The tea was poured, we all drank the new brew prepared by Omar's father, and I congratulated him on the subtle flavor.

"Lemon verbena is wonderful when one is tired," he said simply, sipping the fragrant tea, and gazing around him at his sons, his lovely elder daughter talking politics with Laura Ann (a slight frown here); his chubby, rollicking baby, Faneeda; his handsome wife entertaining foreign guests in his peaceful house, the house, Omar told us, in which his father had been born.

I was not totally deceived by the peace and the calm; I knew from what Omar had said that there were problems in this family, too; brooding Ibrahim, quarreling with his father and refusing to stay in the family business; Malika, who wanted to go to the university, though her father would not agree; even Omar, who wanted to improve the old-fashioned accounting methods of the business, against his father's wishes.

And still I followed Si Abdullah's gaze, thinking to myself, this is it, this family warmth, this shelter, this sense of protection, this is the prized secret that ideally should lie behind the shuttered windows and locked doors of the high-walled houses.

This is what Aisha struggles to keep together, what Kenza wants desperately for Naima; what Fatima Henna's mother hopes will eventually be Fatima Henna's, if only her husband will return; what Lalla Fadna has tramped back and forth to the lawyer's, the police station, to keep intact for Hamid and his children. This is the family ideal for which everyone hopes and works. Lateefa will never have it, for she is barren, but she is luckier than some, she is part of a unit, the unit created and held together by the firm, kindly hands of Rakosh.

Si Abdullah rose. Bob also rose. Si Abdullah smiled faintly and placed his hand on his heart, inclining his head in Bob's general direction. He bowed and asked that we excuse him, as he had not yet had his dinner.

Omar's mother stood up, rustled forward in her watermelon gown, placed a hand under the arm of her husband and went with him, gently and with dignity, out into the court, where a small table had been set for him.

"My father always prefers to eat alone," Omar explained.

Baby Faneeda lay on the carpet, rubbing her eyes. The television play was almost finished. The housewife, it turned out, had "stolen" the bracelets herself because she wanted to buy her lover a gift for the feast. It was time to leave.

I stood up, and everyone else leaped to their feet immediately. No one urged us to stay, a l'Egyptienne, or murmured that it was yet early. Definitely the time for departure had come. We nodded at Si Abdullah, sitting cross-legged on a cushion in the courtyard eating a *specialité* of his own; his wife sat nearby talking to him quietly as he ate, her golden bracelets and earrings smoldering in the dim light.

"It is a beautiful night," Omar offered.

I nodded and looked up, past the tiles and white walls and parapets to the sky filled with the stars of summer.

"I will accompany you," Omar said. "Yes, yes, because it is difficult to find the way. The Semmarine market, which we usually walk through, is already locked for the night."

Up the steep stairs, in the shadows, the door swung inward, and in a moment we were out on the narrow, shabby street, which seemed narrower and shabbier than ever after our sojourn in the vast, luxurious, peaceful courtyard, with its bird trilling in the trees. A beggar, his bare knees showing through the rags of his trousers, crouched opposite the door of Si Abdullah the merchant.

"Oh, Mama, give him something," whispered Davy, and I passed a coin to my son, who placed it into the twisted and supplicating hand.

Bob and Omar were ahead, and Davy ran to catch up. The girls held onto my hands as we wound back along a new and complicated route, along zankas and alleys so narrow we could only walk single file unless we wanted to catch our clothes on the protruding ends of stones and bricks from houses long since abandoned or destroyed.

We circled the Semmarine, which, as Omar had said, was locked; heavy iron bars secured the doors of the largest emporiums. A single garbage man with a whiskery broom was sweeping out the refuse of the day's business transactions, scraps of silk, ends of string, bits of straw and dung from the donkey carts. Near the big pottery suq at the entrance to the spice market, a policeman sat talking to two boys.

"They watch the shops," explained Omar. "They sleep here."

"Wouldn't be too comfy," said Davy, and I agreed, thinking what a hard bed to be allotted one, among the brown glazed-pottery domes of the tajeen pots, the multicolored plates and odd-sized drums from Safi. I thought suddenly of *our* tajeen *specialité*, covered with cinnamon and sugar, which had been served in one of those clay pots. What, I wondered vaguely, would Omar's father be saying about the evening? I was not worried, I found; it had been a pleasant evening, with pleasant people, in the warmth of their family.

Djemaa el Fna was dark and almost deserted, except for a few food stalls with their own pressure lamps. We said good-by to Omar, shaking hands and murmuring thanks, and then we walked together through nearly empty streets toward our own home on Rue Trésor.

We passed along Bab Agnaou, where the boys slept in the darkened doorways, curled up on the sills of the closed shops.

"Boys of the street," Abdul Lateef would have called them.

"Vagabonds," Aisha would have said. "Riffraff!"

"People from no place," Kenza would have derided. "People with no family."

Indeed, I thought, they are probably all three, living without benefit of the advantages offered in the home we had just visited, without the more circumscribed haven of Aisha's two rooms and small court, or even of Kenza's house, barricaded into two rooms to save money. These vagabond boys sleeping in the doorways were more like the man of the bloody face I had seen beneath the cart near the police station, long ago, seeking privacy for his wounds; everyone was searching for a place that was separate, as removed as possible from the anonymous terrors of loneliness and homelessness and poverty.

Feeling grateful suddenly for our temporary haven, I mused sentimentally, but my reverie was cut short when I looked up, while Bob opened the door of our house to find Kenza staring balefully down, checking to see how long we'd stayed out at our exciting dinner party with the rich merchant and his sherifa wife! Her shutter stuck and she was forced to lean all the way out across the sill to get it closed tightly. There she stood, glaring. I smiled to myself, all the sentimental haze dispelled in the baleful glance of our jealous and miserly landlady. What would she have to say to me—and Aisha—tomorrow?

"That was fun," said Davy, when we stood inside our own silent court, where the goldfish moved and darted in the blue-and-yellow-tiled pond.

"Nice people," said Laura Ann.

"Yes," said Bob. "We're lucky. Abdul Aziz said that middle-class Moroccans never invited French people or any foreigners into their homes."

"Why not?" Laila asked.

"So the French couldn't touch their souls," Bob replied.

The children were silent. "Then why did they invite us?" Laura Ann asked.

"Why do you think?" Bob turned the question back.

Laura Ann shook her head.

"David?"

David looked embarrassed for a moment. "Well," he offered slowly, "I guess maybe they decided we weren't so bad. But, Baba, remember when those guys threw stones at us that time? Boy, I thought I'd never stand it here."

"I'd almost forgotten that, Davy."

"I hadn't," Laila said.

Her brother laughed and jerked her blond hair, and Laila pulled away from him angrily.

"See, they got used to us the same way Laila got used to people pulling her hair," David said. "Took a long time, but then it was okay."

"I will *never* get used to people pulling my hair," said Laila.

"Well," said Bob, "it's always easier to ignore people and say you dislike them than to try to get to know them, I guess."

"Oh, Baba," said Laura Ann, "you always make things so complicated."

Chapter 21

Bslama

Omar had come to see us twice since our lovely evening at his house, bringing greetings from Malika and his mother. Si Abdullah, he said, had expressed approval at the "good behavior of Bob's woman and children." I told the children that they had been praised. Laura Ann laughed. "You remember when we went to the wedding, Mama, and we didn't really know quite what to do?"

"Yes," I answered, "but we didn't need to. Hajja Kenza led us around by the nose."

When I thought of Kenza now, I felt only sadness. What had triggered the change in her personality that had become so marked in the past year? It was hard to say, and hard to assess what role, if any, I had played in the process. When I tried to discuss it with Aisha, she would simply shake her head. There seemed nothing more to say.

August had come, and next week we were going to return to America. Aisha and I had gone together to the city labor office twice, and filled out forms for work permits. I wanted to finish this task, at least, for Aisha, before we departed. It didn't seem possible that in a week we would have left Rue Trésor behind forever.

Aisha and I sorted and packed.

"Here're the pants Laura Ann was wearing when she fell from the roof, may God protect her," she said.

"Yes."

"Remember, Elizabetha, you wanted to have a karama then?"

"I remember."

"You didn't know much."

"No."

The clothes went into piles, one pile to go with us, one pile to go in the trunks to be shipped, a pile to be given away.

"You know, Elizabetha, we have not gone to Sidi Bel Abbas yet. You *must* find time to do that before you leave."

"Yes, Aisha. Tomorrow? The day after tomorrow?"

"Day after tomorrow. Because tomorrow we have to finish with the work permit."

"All right."

"And this is the dress Laura Ann wore to Rabia's wedding. She's grown a lot this year, Laura Ann!"

"Yes, she has. But Laila can wear it next year." The dress went into the trunk, a wool dress from France bought when we arrived in Marrakech.

"Kenza seems in a better mood since you gave her the electric coffee pot."

"Yes, I noticed. I heard her this morning, scolding the old man for banging the pieces of wood down when he threw them to Mbarak."

Aisha laughed. "Maybe she sold it in the suq for a good price," she said. "It was nearly new."

"Aisha!"

"Well, money always makes her feel good. Oh, yes," she added, "and Lalla Fadna sends you a message. She came yesterday, but you were away."

I was annoyed with myself. Too much business, too many visitors, too much last-minute shopping. Was I unconsciously pulling away, gently disentangling myself from the fragile ties I had established on Rue Trésor?

The door knocker banged. Aisha looked impatient. "If that's Youssef again . . ."

But it was not Youssef. "*Lebas, Madame! Lebas!*"

"Come in, Lalla Fadna! Come in!" I went quickly across the court to greet her.

"Madame, God be praised! He has saved us!"

I took the two hands she held out to me; her eyes, sunken and faded, were all that I could see between her black veil and the olive-drab hood of the djellaba carefully folded over her forehead, but those eyes seemed to sparkle, actually sparkle with joy.

"Thank God! What's happened?"

A babble of words emerged, which I could not put into a coherent pattern, especially since they were spoken through the silken thickness of the veil.

Aisha laughed, a happy sort of laugh. "Pull down your veil, Lalla Fadna, how can we understand what you're saying?"

"Oh! Oh! Yes, I'm sorry!" She pulled down the veil to show her wrinkled old face, more creased than ever with smiles.

"It's my son! It's Hamid! He's been paroled!"

"That's wonderful, Lalla Fadna! Thank God!"

Aisha smiled. "Tell her what happened."

"Well . . ." His mother had asked her lawyer to write a letter to the governor, asking for Hamid's parole, for "a man with two children and a wife to support, a man who had been tempted beyond human endurance" by the bad influence of the hotel, which no one in the neighborhood wanted, but there it was, "a monument to greed, money, and evil, as opposed to family, honor, and good." Lalla Fadna had pleaded with the governor to stand on the side of "family, honor, and good" and parole her son.

"Oh, the lawyer writes a beautiful Arabic, beautiful," she went on, "and the dear captain, the poor man, he said fine, that he would agree to the parole if Hamid would improve his behavior and be good to his wife and children."

"*Enshallah*, he'll do that," said Aisha. "He'd better," she added with spirit, "or he'll be back in jail."

"Oh, Aisha, don't say things like that, don't say it . . ." Lalla Fadna cried.

"All right, all right," Aisha put her arm around the old woman. "I was just talking."

"And thank you, thank you both for offering to sign my petition to the government," said Lalla Fadna, cheering up again.

"Not at all," I answered.

She wrung my hands again, smiling and smiling, and turned to go. No, she couldn't stay to tea, she had so many things to do. "It's good to have neighbors who understand the problems that children bring you, and who'll help," she said, and smiled once more. "Rue Trésor has always been that kind of neighborhood," she added, ambling to the door and clicking it open.

"Lalla Fadna!" shouted Aisha.

"Ah?" The old woman turned back.

"Pull up your veil!" said Aisha, laughing. "What will the neighbors think?"

"Ah, you're right, you're right. I'm so happy I don't know what I'm doing. Thank you, thank you. *Bslama!*" And she was gone.

"That's wonderful! I'm so glad for her!"

"Yes," Aisha admitted, "but will it last? He's not much good. But let's hope when he does something like that again, he doesn't do it on *this* street. We need our sleep!"

I had promised the girls that they could have their hands hennaed before we left, and Fatima Henna had agreed to do it. Laura Ann went to the suq to buy the henna herself and helped Aisha prepare the gooey green paste. I had told Aisha we could go to Sidi Bel Abbas (as the shuwafa had directed me so long ago) as soon as the girls had settled down to the henna ritual.

Why had I put off this pilgrimage again and again? There had been good reasons certainly: Aisha had been ill; I had been ill; we had had many visitors; there had been the folklore festival; the end of school party at the Lycée; saying a sad good-by to our close and dear friends the Harrises; entertaining, for the last time, the children's teachers from the Lycée; being entertained in return; receiving visits from Omar and his brother, from Abdul Aziz and his wife Zainab; from Lateefa and Zahia; there had been packing, arranging. Yes, there had been reasons, but was there also something I wanted to avoid?

Perhaps I had meant it to be this way, for if we had gone earlier, what would have happened? Would I have been drawn into the cycle of moussems more closely, given myself to the *derdaba* or ritual dance in spite of myself? Or could I have withstood making that final commitment? I was not sure.

I sat in the anteroom off the big wedding courtyard, watching Fatima Henna draw the henna paste in intricate patterns across Laura Ann's palm, covering my oldest daughter's hands with the ancient signs and symbols of Marrakech. Fatima Henna had started at noon; it was now nearly four, and it looked as though she could not possibly finish both girls before evening. I should leave for the shrine now.

"Mama, look, didn't I mix the henna right? Fatima Henna says so." Laura Ann was very proud of herself. Fatima Henna caught this and smiled approvingly.

Laila was less patient. "How long do I have to sit here, Mama? I want to go to the movies. Couldn't she do my hands tomorrow?"

Fatima Henna shrugged when asked for this favor. The low-cut blue cotton dress showed off her full bosom to advantage; it was a new dress, I thought, and very becoming.

"I'd rather finish both of them now," she said.

"Yes, all right."

"You know my family wanted to leave for El Jadida for the week's holiday at the ocean today," she explained.

I nodded.

"But they agreed to wait till tomorrow so I can go to the *haffla* of the zaweeya tonight."

"Oh."

"It's to be a big erss, Elizabetha, and I've been waiting and looking forward to it for a long time."

"Yes, I understand, Fatima Henna. Of course. It's Moulay Ibrahim, isn't it?"

She looked up from Laura Ann's palm, the stick of henna raised, her somewhat heavy features lifted in a momentary interest.

"Ah, yes, Elizabetha, I forgot. You went to Moulay Ibrahim, didn't you?"

I nodded.

She looked down at her work again, skillfully drawing on Laura Ann's thumb an elongated square and a series of five tiny lines, a kind of shortened symbol for the sign of the hand of Fatima, the good-luck charm to be found on every door and in every house in the city.

"Well, Elizabetha, too bad you're going home to America," she said. "You'd probably like the haffla if you liked the moussem. But you know, you can't just go for the experience. You have to give yourself to the saint, all of yourself."

"Yes," I said meekly, knowing only too well that I had not been willing to do that.

"Mama, Mama," Laila pulled on my arm. "I told you I wanted to go to the movies. What did Fatima Henna say?"

Laura Ann's friend from upstairs exchanged a word with her, and Laila's objections were voiced to Fatima Henna.

"Ya, Laila, you can go to the movies any time. When can you have henna?"

I repeated this to Laila and she subsided, a bit petulantly, I thought. "Maybe you'd like to come with Aisha and me to light a candle for yourself in the shrine?"

"No, Mama, no, no, no," she shook her head until her hair flew about her face. "I will just stay here and wait, I guess."

Laila would not be sorry to leave Marrakech. She could hardly wait. But yesterday she had gone with her father and Bob Hamilton to say good-by to Abdul Aziz and his beautiful wife Zainab.

"We had a nice time," she had reported. "Zainab brought us some Cokes, and she sent you this pretty key ring. And Mama," she had added, "something really funny happened. Mr. Hamilton didn't realize he was supposed to take his shoes off before he went into one of those rug rooms."

"What did Abdul Aziz say?"

"He didn't say anything," Laila reported. "Is that what tact means?"

I had nodded. She'd learned a great deal this year, in spite of herself. And why should she come with me to Sidi Bel Abbas now if she didn't want to? She was anxious that I light the candle, however, and had asked me about it many times.

I told the girls I was leaving, for Aisha was waiting for me in the courtyard of Fatima Henna's house.

"It's so hot," I said to Aisha. "Do I need my djellaba?"

"No."

"You're sure?"

She nodded her head vigorously. We set out, Aisha still wearing her old brown djellaba, I, in my yellow summer dress and sandals, obviously a Westerner.

We made good time along Rue Bab Agnaou, for it was not yet sunset, and many people were still asleep. In Djemaa el Fna the square was nearly empty. The man who walked on glass had set up his teetery combinations of green, jagged shards, but so far had not gathered any bystanders. In the spice market, it seemed much cooler and very fragrant, but still almost empty and we walked quickly through the carved gate of the Semmarine, past the flaming silks and golden brass, the piles of embroidered and sequined slippers. Omar's younger brother raised his hand in salute as we passed the djellaba shop. We kept on walking, through the dyers' bazaar where the wild loops of multicolored wool hung, dripping, in front of empty stalls, past the Essaouira marquetry tables, the wooden painted chests, to a small candle shop.

Aisha headed for this candle shop as though she had known all along exactly where she was going. There were many other candle shops, tiny counters before narrow stalls, but she approached an old man behind the counter, his sparse beard cupped in his hand, resting. He greeted Aisha warmly, like an old friend, and began to bring out candles—pink, white, green, long candles, short candles, fat, stubby candles—but Aisha was not satisfied. She wanted one particular candle and finally found it, in some hidden recess beneath the counter, a long, green candle with gold thread wrapped around it in a thin spiral from top to bottom.

I reached in my purse, but Aisha put her rough hand over mine.

"I have paid. It's from me." And she told the old man in no uncertain terms to wrap it up in rough pink paper. He did so, and we went on into Darb Saboon, and through the lumber market, where a small boy in a worn-out green gym suit like Davy's was balancing, rather precariously, two long, heavy planks on his shoulders. We walked carefully around him so as not to be hit in the head if the lumber should suddenly shift.

"There's Glaoui's husband," Aisha said briskly, but she did not stop or speak to the man in shirt sleeves, leather apron, and skullcap, who sat in the ironmonger's shop with his head bent over a piece of metal, molten metal that he was flattening with a heavy hammer. We passed by before the man raised his head, so I never saw his face, the face of the man who lived across the street from us the whole year.

"He's not a bad man," Aisha allowed grudgingly, and I decided not to mention the still delicate subject of Glaoui herself.

We passed through a brick yard, through the brass suq where the great trays were hung up like enormous shining amulets on all the inside and outside walls of the shops, through the area where television sets were being auctioned.

The doors of Medersa Ben Youssef were left behind, and Aisha and I were still walking, more slowly now, through other narrow suqs to Bab Taghzout. Here houses, new houses of traditional pattern, had been grouped around the square, which was in reality the neighborhood shopping center; vegetable and fruit markets stood open on our right, and on our left a cinema advertised "Hassaneen ka Devra" (a story of forbidden love between a Muslim and a Hindu), special matinee prices in force at this moment!

"Where is Sidi Bel Abbas?" I asked.

"Oh, it's there, not far." Aisha thrust her hand out in a general direction where the tip of a minaret and bits of the traditional green roof tiles could be seen in the distance.

I stood beside Aisha, waiting, while she argued with a peddler, a man sitting on the ground with dates, in clumps of six, arranged on a white cloth before him. I drew nearer and saw that a whole group of such peddlers sat there, men displaying orange paprika; powdered, dusky-green henna; yellow cumin; little bundles of *fuwa*, the dark red roots tied together with fiber. Aisha bought some cumin. We began to walk again.

We passed another row of peddlers, offering plastic dinnerware in orange and green; spotted melons past their prime, and more henna. We walked on and on in the heat. How much farther is it, I wanted to ask, but Aisha did not seem inclined to conversation. She forged ahead so quickly I had a hard time keeping up with her.

Finally we reached a long passageway of carved stone, a small street really, with niches cut in the sides to shelter the sellers of candles and spices and charms and fruit, supplies for the summer visitors to the shrine. In one of the niches an old woman sat. Like the rest of the peddlers she had a cloth spread out before her, but hers was totally empty. She rubbed one long hennaed fingernail against the other and stared vacantly into space. I watched her, and was startled to see Aisha, thrifty Aisha, put a small coin down onto the empty cloth. The woman did not move nor seem to notice.

At the end of the stone-carved passageway, the shrine was visible, green roofs rising one after the other, in gables and broad expanses, the minaret of the mosque pointing upward, upward. We reached the court before the shrine, a big open courtyard where many clean and respectable-looking beggars sat or stood; one pushed himself along in a wheelchair. He had no legs, only leather patches covering the stumps of the knees.

The sun was setting. The pale golden sky over the green-tiled roofs of Sidi Bel Abbas was slowly suffusing with pink. The beggars moved together and grouped themselves into a semicircle; it was time for evening prayers.

Here we were at the entrance to the shrine of the patron saint of Marrakech, one of the seven. I found myself suddenly and unaccountably nervous. Was Aisha gathering her strength to take me, the unfaithful infidel, into the last, most sacred shrine? Did I want to go in?

In the middle of the courtyard Aisha stopped.

"I'll go in and light the candle and say a prayer for your daughter Laila. You wait here."

I looked at Aisha. I was startled, but found I was not terribly surprised. I was not to go into the shrine at all. I didn't have to make any final decision. Aisha had made it for me. Hadn't I known, when she told me it was not necessary for me to wear my djellaba? She nodded at me, ducking her head in a quick motion, and turned, the candle in its rough pink paper held upright in her hand. She walked the length of the courtyard, removed her shoes, entered a narrow door set in the wall of the shrine, and disappeared.

"Allah! There is no God but Allah, and Mohammed is His Prophet!"

I stood in the outer courtyard of the ancient shrine, watching the believers, the beggars. They had prostrated themselves on the uneven flagstones, and the beggar without legs, sitting in his wheelchair, bent over as far as he could.

"Allah, the most merciful, the most compassionate, hear our prayer!"

Birds wheeled and raced and cried shrilly as they dipped up and down over the courtyard, above my head, then disappeared beyond the green-tiled roofs, where now, at sunset, somewhere inside, Aisha was saying a prayer for my daughter's well-being, before the tomb of the patron saint of Marrakech. Would her prayer be answered, I wondered anxiously? Surely, I thought, since she is a good woman and a faithful, pious Muslim. She believes. Moulay Mustapha had explained long ago, "The prayers of the faithful are answered through the good offices of the saints and mediators, Sidi Bel Abbas, Sidi Ghezwani, Allala Arkiya, Allala Fatima, Moulay Ibrahim, Mul el Ksour." That is what Aisha understands and believes, too.

The sun had set. The beggars had finished their prayers and were dusting their knees and arranging their clothes before settling back into their accustomed positions before the shrine. A curious, grinding noise jolted me out of my reverie. The beggar in the wheelchair was moving cautiously toward me. He was eyeing me curiously. What was I doing here? I stared back at him, a strange figure with his leather-patched legs, his bald head, almost as strange as me, a lone

Western lady in a yellow dress and sandals, standing unveiled and uncovered in the middle of the courtyard of the sacred shrine of Sidi Bel Abbas.

Creak, creak. The sky above the pale brick and the green-tiled roofs and the thrusting minaret was dusky red. The beggar came closer. Why had Aisha left me here alone? Yet I knew she was right. What else could she have done? For a brief time, here in Marrakech, I had tried to understand. Aisha had tried to help me understand, and perhaps I had learned something, a little about the beliefs and values that deeply affected the women I had come to know on Rue Trésor: Fatima Henna and Lateefa and Zahia and Rakosh and Lalla Fadna, and, yes, even Kenza. I was privileged to participate even a little, I saw now, and I thanked Aisha in my heart.

The wheelchair edged and creaked. The bald beggar wiped his hands on the leather patches that covered the stumps of his legs. What *was* I doing here? Why was Aisha taking so long inside? I took a few steps backward, toward the edge of the courtyard.

Aisha's willingness to make this last pilgrimage with me, her insistence on buying the slender green candle wrapped with gold thread, I took as an indication, I hoped, that she did not bear me ill will for my errors, but allowed for my human weaknesses and pride, as she had always allowed for her old friend, Kenza, now sinking into neurosis and avarice. What would become of Aisha and Kenza? And me? We would disappear, Aisha knew that, but Sidi Bel Abbas would remain.

The beggar was so close to me now that I could see clearly the sparse black hairs on his chin. I moved backward again, realizing suddenly what an incongruous figure I was in this setting, far more incongruous than the beggar, bald, broken, and patched as he was—for the beggar had a place in the shrine, he belonged here, this was his territory. I was a stranger, and alone. Where was Aisha? Why didn't she come?

At last she emerged from the narrow door where she had disappeared, and put on her shoes, a small, slight woman in a shabby brown djellaba, veiled to the eyes in black. She stared at the beggar, and he hesitated, then pushed the wheel of his chair, backward, into the courtyard of the shrine.

"I said a long prayer," she explained.

She took my hand and we went back together, for the last time, the way we had come, through the labyrinth of the medina, struggling against the sunset crowds that filled the narrow alleys, thronged through the Semmarine, pushed past the fragrant baskets in the spice market, nearly jostling the beggars' chorus.

In Djemaa el Fna the evening's entertainment was in full swing. The man balanced precariously on the points of broken green glass stepped down and demonstrated the miracle of his uncut feet to the disbelievers. "Allah!" cried the audience, clapping in appreciation. The acrobats leaped high. I could see the children in their red and green satin costumes far above the crowd, as they executed the final step in their human pyramid. "Allah!" cried the audience in awe. The pigeon man, too, was reaching the climax of his evening performance, calling to his birds, jingling the dozens of silver and brass and plastic amulets that decorated his long hashish pipe. But what exactly was he saying to the birds? I would never know. My education had just begun, and I was already leaving.

At the other end of the fixed assemblage of golden beer cans, oranges, and multicolored paper flowers, the blind assistant sat, answering each verse of the pigeon man's chants. "Allah!" he cried, and another pigeon fluttered its wings, in obedience to its master's command, and flew up, up, across the square toward the minaret of the Koutoubia. The snake charmer ran past us, a snake coiled daringly around his arm, his gap-toothed smile wide.

"Ha, *wahid dirham*, ya Marrakshi!" he urged, and I recoiled, then dropped a last coin into his dark hand, quickly, before the snake reared on his wrist. Was I afraid? No, I said to myself.

Aisha gave a short laugh. "They always know who lives here and who'll give them cash," she said.

We were forced to stop at the curb, by the Café des Glaciers, while the yellow-and-brown taxis, the black horse-drawn carriages, and dozens of motorcycles and bicycles roared and clopped and clattered past. The African boy selling cowrie shells sewn onto felt whispered in my ear in heavy, strangely accented Oxford English, "If you don't know the way, Madame, there is no other, you see."

What was he talking about? What did he mean?

I turned quickly, but he was gone.

"Tell me what he said," Aisha prompted, her hand on my arm.

I translated, and she nodded in a satisfied way. "I'm glad we went to Sidi Bel Abbas, Elizabetha."

"Yes, Aisha. Thank you for taking me."

Past the rush, the glare of headlights, the blaring of horns, we branched off into Riad el Zeitoon, a faster route home through the medina at this time of night. I had to feed my family. And Aisha had to feed her family. We wound through the narrow darb leading off Riad el Zeitoon, past the high walls of the houses. An occasional door stood ajar, a shutter was propped open to get the evening breeze, and from a rooftop someone called to us. We looked up, and Aisha shouted back a greeting. We continued on, walking quickly now, past the public water tap, the tuberculosis clinic, the school where Moulay Mustapha's pupils, too, cried "Allah!" every morning. The scribe's office was open, but the day-care center was closed for the summer. We passed the tile shop at the entrance to Rue Trésor, the street of the old post office. We passed Lalla Fadna's house, the Hôtel du Sud, Fatima Henna's house, Rakosh's house, our house, and continued on to the bakery to buy bread for supper from Moussa. Kenza's window was open, the geranium propped on the sill. Naima waved, but Kenza was nowhere to be seen. Laura Ann and Laila stood by the bakery, displaying their newly hennaed hands to admiring Youssef, Khadija, and Shadeeya, while David bought bubble gum.

"B.J.," called Bob from the upstairs window of our house, "where've you been?"

"Allah go with you," murmured Aisha.

"And with you."

"Bslama, Elizabetha."

"Bslama, Aisha."

Our furniture had been sold, the trunks had been carted away. We were to leave before noon, and the ritual of good-bys had gone on all morning. Now it was noon, and we stood in the courtyard waiting for Laura Ann to find one last missing item. The house was empty. Only the goldfish were left, a last, unplanned gift to Hajja Kenza.

"Will Hajja Kenza feed the fish, Baba?" David asked.

"She may, she may," said Bob. "Who knows what Hajja Kenza will do? Come on, Laura Ann, let's go! What are you looking for?"

"My silver bracelet! The one with my name on it in Arabic!"

"Well, hurry up. We can't wait all day. We want to leave."

"Yes, I want to get home," said Laila.

"It's here! I found it!" Laura Ann ran down the tiled steps from the balcony.

"Oh, I'll miss Aisha," she said. "Won't you, Mama?"

I nodded.

We stepped outside, shutting the heavy door behind us for the last time, the door with the silver hand of Fatima upon it, symbol of protection against the Evil Eye. Rue Trésor was deserted. The doors and windows were closed tightly, for it was siesta time.

At the bakery, Moussa snored peacefully, leaning back against the nearly empty shelves. Soon the sun would set and our friends would stir in their houses. Youssef, Shadeeya, and Ali would come out of the sibha to play hopscotch in the lengthening shadows on the street. Hajja Kenza would unlatch her shutter, push her white geranium to one side, and lean far over the sill.

"Ya Moussa!" she would holler. "A good fat loaf for me! And take something off the price. It's left over!"

Aisha, Lateefa, Zahia, Fatima Henna, Lalla Fadna, and Rachida would open up the windows and doors of their houses. They would pull on their djellabas and fasten veils over their faces before coming out to buy bread for the meal of this summer evening.

In our house, the goldfish would be there, darting about in the cool water of their blue-and-yellow-tiled basin. But we would have gone, down Rue Bab Agnaou, past the Koutoubia, Djemaa el Fna, Boulevard Mohammed Cinq, the ancient city walls, gone forever from Marrakech and the house on Rue Trésor.

GLOSSARY

aradda	the official inviter to weddings
baghreer	a kind of pancake
balak	take care, watch out
baraka	grace, blessing
baraka- *llahufik*	thank you; literally, blessings on you
besla	onions
bint	daughter, girl
bslama	good-bye; literally, peace go with you
burnoose	man's hooded cape
caftan	woman's dress
couscous	steamed semolina, North African dish served with vegetables and meat as a main course
darb	street, as in covered street or neighborhood
derdaba	religious dance
dirham	Moroccan coin; equal to about twenty-five cents
djellaba	men's and women's outer garment, hooded, with sleeves
enshallah	if God wills it
erss	meeting or dance party of members of a zaweeya or religious lodge
Fassi	native of Fez
fatiha	first verse from the Koran, also a prayer
fernatchi	man or boy in charge of stoking fires, as in the public bath
fki	male religious functionary, wise man
fuwa	roots used to flavor food and to color wool
ghaseel	a kind of hair conditioner, used as shampoo
hafla	party
haik	length of material used as a traditional all-enveloping garment
haj	the pilgrimage to Mecca, one of the five pillars or requirements of all Muslims
el hamdillaa	thanks be to God
hammam	bath
harateen	generic word for dark-skinned persons, former slaves

henna	a common plant; leaves are dried, powdered and used as a russet dye for hair and for decoration of hands and feet
Iid	religious holiday or feast
inta (m) *intii* (f)	you
karama	a ceremony of thanksgiving
khalifa	local administrative official
khizzu	carrots
kohl/	antimony, used as eyeliner
kooreeshaat	special sweets given to children on the feast of Ashura
ksar, ksour	village surrounded by walls, also a walled place
kuttab	Koranic school
Lalla	polite address for a woman; literally, "lady"
lebas	how are you?
lufa	bath brush made from a dried gourd
luisa	lemon verbena
Mabrook	Congratulations; a common compliment: literally "you are blessed"
Alf Mabrook	"you are a thousand times blessed"
mahram	coverlet ritually placed over the head
Marrakshi	a native of Marrakech
mateeyalum	curers of illness
matishah	tomatoes
mechouar	open plain or exhibition ground
medina	literally, city; in Morocco, the traditional area of the city
meskeen *mesakeen*	poor, the poor
Moulay	honorary title given to a descendant of the Prophet or of a saint
moussem	religious festival
msemmen	fried pancakes; literally, "the buttered ones"
mul	master; e.g. Mul el Ksour means literally, master of the palaces
muqaddam (m) *muqaddama* (f)	keeper of the shrine or mosque; an honorary position; literally, servant of the mosque or shrine
murabit	tomb of the saint, also the saint (French form is *marabout*)
na'ama	the good which is given by God to people on earth, e.g., water, land

naga	group which announces the coming of a moussem or religious festival and collects contributions for it
Nasrani	literally, Christian, in Morocco means a Frenchman
niyya	good intention
qadi	Muslim judge concerned with shari'a law, the canon law of Islam, rather than civil law
qubba	a shrine or tomb
Ramadan	month of religious fasting
raybi	a flavored yogurt drink
riyal	a small coin, worth about $1.25
saba'at rijal	literally, the seven men, title of the seven patron saints of Marrakech, the mystical seven who guard the city
sahr (m)	
sahra (f)	maker of magic
seeds	tombs of sidis or saints (also called murabits)
shargi	hot dry wind from the desert
sharia	street
shaykh (m)	a tribal chief
shaykha (f)	female musician or dancer
sherif (m)	
sherifa (f)	
shorfa (pl)	descendants of the Prophet Mohammed
shi baraka	a thing full of grace or blessing
shu'ur	magic
shuwaf (m)	
shuwafa (f)	fortuneteller
sibha	narrow, covered passageway
Sidi	honorary title for a saint or descendant of a saint
suq	market
sura	
suraat (pl)	verse, verses of the Koran
suweeka	little market
tajeen	Moroccan stew of meat and spices
talab (m)	
talaba (f)	
talabat (pl)	religious student, scholar
tariqa	literally, way; term for an individual religious mystical sect
tzaghreet	ululation; sound made by women particularly to express joy or sorrow

yom el baraka	day of grace; greeting, i.e., "truly this is the day of grace"
zanka	a narrow street or alley
zaweeya	community of religious, also the lodge which is the headquarters of the religious brotherhood or sisterhood
ziyara	pilgrimage
zween (m)	
zweena (f)	good, beautiful